T0338287

CORPORATE
BOARDS

Managers of Risk, Sources of Risk

Edited by Robert W. Kolb and Donald Schwartz

CORPORATE
BOARDS

Managers of Risk, Sources of Risk

A John Wiley & Sons, Ltd., Publication

Blackwell Publishing was acquired by John Wiley & Sons in February 2007. Blackwell's publishing program has been merged with Wiley's global Scientific, Technical, and Medical business to form Wiley-Blackwell.

Registered Office
John Wiley & Sons Ltd, The Atrium, Southern Gate, Chichester, West Sussex, PO19 8SQ, United Kingdom

Editorial Offices
350 Main Street, Malden, MA 02148-5020, USA
9600 Garsington Road, Oxford, OX4 2DQ, UK
The Atrium, Southern Gate, Chichester, West Sussex, PO19 8SQ, UK

For details of our global editorial offices, for customer services, and for information about how to apply for permission to reuse the copyright material in this book please see our website at www. wiley.com/wiley-blackwell.

Library of Congress Cataloging-in-Publication Data

Corporate boards : managers of risk, sources of risk / edited by Robert W. Kolb and Donald Schwartz.
    p.   cm. – (Loyola University series on risk)
  Includes bibliographical references and index.
  ISBN 978-1-4051-8585-1 (hbk. : alk. paper)
  1. Boards of directors. 2. Corporate governance. 3. Risk management. I. Kolb, Robert W., 1949– II. Schwartz, Donald E., 1930–
  HD2745.C623 2010
  685.15'5–dc22
                                                        2009015165

A catalogue record for this book is available from the British Library.

Set in Times 10.5/12pt by SPi Publisher Services, Pondicherry, India
Printed and bound in Singapore by Fabulous Printers Pte Ltd

001   2010

Contents

Notes on Contributors

Mohammad J. Abdolmohammadi earned his doctoral degree from Indiana University in 1982. He is currently the John E. Rhodes Professor of Accountancy at Bentley College. Having an interest primarily in behavioral auditing, ethics, and corporate governance research, Professor Abdolmohammadi has published regularly in many journals, including, among others, *Accounting and Business Research*, *Accounting Horizons*, *The Accounting Review*, *Advances in Accounting*, *Auditing: a Journal of Practice and Theory*, *Behavioral Research in Accounting*, *Contemporary Accounting Research*, the *International Journal of Accounting*, the *International Journal of Auditing*, *Issues in Accounting Education*, the *Journal of Business Ethics*, *Organizational Behavior and Human Decision Processes*, *Research on Accounting Ethics*, *Research in Accounting Regulation*, and *Research on Professional Responsibility and Ethics in Accounting (RPREA)*.

Steve H. Barr is Professor and Head of the Department of Management, Innovation and Entrepreneurship at the College of Management in NC State University. He received his PhD at the University of Iowa and served on the faculty at Iowa and Oklahoma State before joining the faculty of NC State in 1995. He has published numerous articles in the areas of individual decision-making processes and methods, group decisions and processes, and feedback and appraisal systems. His works have appeared in such journals as *Academy of Management Journal, Journal of Applied Psychology, Psychological Bulletin, Management Science, Decision Sciences, Personnel Psychology, Decision Support Systems, Journal of Engineering Technology Management, Journal of High Technology Management Research,* and *Entrepreneurship Theory and Practice.*

John R. Boatright is the Raymond C. Baumhart, S.J., Professor of Business Ethics in the Graduate School of Business at Loyola University Chicago. He has served as the Executive Director of the Society for Business Ethics, and is a past president of the Society. The author of the books *Ethics and the Conduct of Business* and *Ethics in Finance*, he received his PhD in philosophy from the University of Chicago.

Claire E. Crutchley is an Associate Professor at Auburn University where she teaches corporate finance. Crutchley has published numerous research articles in the field of corporate finance and corporate governance. She is also interested in the field of sustainability and business which she incorporates into the classroom and research. Crutchley is active in finance professional societies and will be the VP of Programs for the Eastern Finance Association in 2009. Crutchley earned her PhD in Finance at Virginia Tech.

Reza Dibadj is a Professor of Law at the University of San Francisco where he received the 2008 "Distinguished Professor Award." His recent work has been primarily in the corporate and securities area, though he also writes about antitrust, regulation and administrative law, and social welfare theory. He has published numerous academic articles and newspaper op-ed pieces. His recent book, *Rescuing Regulation*, has been released in both hardcover and paperback editions. Dibadj is a graduate of Harvard Law School, Harvard Business School, and Harvard College.

Shujun Ding received his PhD from the Haskayne School of Business, University of Calgary, Canada. He is currently an assistant professor at the School of Administrative Studies, York University. His recent work focuses on corporate governance in emerging markets, and behavioral aspects of decision making.

Donna J. Fletcher is the director of the Risk Management Program and the Wilder Associate Professor of Finance at Bentley College. She obtained her Doctorate in Business and Economics from Lehigh University in 1991, following her work as an auditor and CPA for Peat Marwick Mitchell & Co., and as an accountant and tax associate for Goldman Sachs & Co. Professor Fletcher's research and teaching interests focus on derivatives, international finance, investments, capital markets and corporate governance and compliance. She has articles published or forthcoming in, among others, the *Journal of Fixed Income*, the *Journal of Financial Engineering*, the *Journal of International Money and Finance*, the *North American Journal of Economics and Finance*, the *Project Management Journal*, the *Review of Economics and Statistics*, and the *Sloan Management Review*.

Chunxin Jia received his PhD from Peking University, China. He is currently an associate professor of finance in Guanghua School of Management at Peking University. His research interest includes banking, financial development, corporate governance, IPO, and empirical asset pricing. He has published in the *Journal of Banking and Finance* and many leading academic journals in China.

Michael A.M. Keehner is an Adjunct Professor of Finance and Economics at Columbia Business School, teaching courses in entrepreneurial finance and financial services, and is a Faculty Leader in corporate governance at the Sanford C. Bernstein & Co. Center for Leadership and Ethics. As a financial services executive and investment banker for more than 30 years, Keehner has executed major operating responsibilities in financial services globally and advised corporate leaders on complex strategic, financial and business issues. He holds an SB in Physics from MIT and an MBA with High Distinction from the Harvard Business School, where he was a Baker Scholar and a Loeb Rhoades Fellow. Keehner has served on the boards of many listed and private companies, both in the United States and Europe.

Denise Kleinrichert, PhD, Philosophy, has focused her research and teaching in the areas of business ethics, corporate social responsibility and sustainable business practices. She is Assistant Professor, Management/Ethics at San Francisco State University, where she teaches business in society and managerial ethics. She is a faculty member of the Sustainable Business Group and a co-organizer of SFSU's annual Business Ethics Week. Kleinrichert has authored academic articles on corporate social responsibility, business ethics education, charismatic leadership, economic chivalry, and corporate transparency. She previously taught at the University of South Florida, where she attained her PhD and two Masters degrees, subsequent to her corporate positions in human resources and risk management. Kleinrichert's undergraduate work at Indiana University in economics initiated her interests in labor and work issues.

David R. Koenig is the founding partner of Ductilibility, LLC, a private research network and advisory firm serving boards, Chief Risk Officers and other senior executives. David is the past Chair, Board of Directors of the Professional Risk Managers' International Association (PRMIA). He served as the Executive Director of PRMIA and the President of the PRMIA Institute until September of 2007. Prior to his role with PRMIA, Mr Koenig was the Head of Market and Institutional Credit Risk Management for US Bancorp Piper Jaffray. In his career of more than 20 years, he has built/developed three risk management programs and successfully managed more than $50 billion in nominal exposures. He was awarded the 2008

PRMIA Higher Standard Award for individual contributions to the global risk profession and was inducted by his peers as a charter member of the international Risk Who's Who honor society. David is a member of the UK-based Institute of Directors as well as the Professional Risk Managers' International Association. He serves on the Editorial Boards of the *Journal of Risk Management in Financial Institutions* and the *International Journal of Services Sciences*. Mr Koenig has an MA in Economics from Northwestern University and a BA in both Mathematics and Economics from Miami University where he was a member of the Pi Mu Epsilon mathematics honor society.

Robert W. Kolb (PhDs from the University of North Carolina at Chapel Hill in philosophy and finance) has taught at the University of Florida, Emory University, the University of Miami, the University of Colorado, and Loyola University Chicago, where he currently serves as Professor of Finance and holds the Frank W. Considine Chair of Applied Ethics. Kolb is the author or co-author of more than 50 research articles and 25 finance texts on topics, including financial derivatives, investments, corporate finance, and financial institutions. Kolb recently edited the *Encyclopedia of Business, Society, and Ethics*. Kolb also founded Kolb Publishing, Inc., which published finance and economics university texts and was acquired by Blackwell Publishing, now part of John Wiley & Sons, Inc.

William J. Lekse is past President/Founder of Black Diamond Company and past President of Blue Danube, Inc. Blue Danube, Inc was a major private holding company noted for its achievements in the communication, construction, manufacturing, mining, and transportation industries. Dr Lekse has conducted business in all regions of the globe. He received his research training from the University of Pittsburgh and Carnegie-Mellon University, graduating with a dual major in strategic management and management information systems. Dr Lekse has published in practitioner and academic journals and presented at international conferences in the areas of technology entrepreneurship, strategic management, and corporate governance. Professor Lekse is on the faculty of University of Michigan Dearborn and engaged in research projects in the US, France, Germany, and China.

Yuanshun Li is an Assistant Professor of Finance at Ted Rogers School of Business Management, Ryerson University. He is also a PhD Candidate in Finance at the Haskayne School of Business, University of Calgary. His research interest includes corporate finance, corporate governance, real options and game theory, and mergers and acquisition.

Barry M. Mitnick (PhD, University of Pennsylvania, political science) is Professor of Business Administration and of Public and International

Affairs, University of Pittsburgh. He serves in the leadership stream of the Social Issues in Management Division of the Academy of Management (PDW Chair, Program Chair, Division Chair), is associate editor of *Business & Society*, and has been Treasurer of the International Association for Business and Society, from which he received the Best Article Award in 2002. He was one of the two independent originators of the theory of agency in 1973, and is responsible for the institutional theory of agency. His research areas also include government regulation, corporate political activity, corporate governance, the assignment of credibility (the theory of testaments), and (with John Mahon) reputation.

Tom Nohel earned a PhD in finance from the University of Minnesota and has taught at the University of Minnesota, Rensselaer Polytechnic Institute, Cornell University, the University of Michigan, the Indian School of Business, and Loyola University Chicago where he serves as associate professor of finance. Nohel was also a visiting Economist at the Federal Reserve Bank in Minneapolis. Nohel has published numerous articles in leading academic journals including the *Journal of Banking and Finance*, the *Journal of Corporate Finance*, and the *Journal of Financial Economics*. His research has focused on corporate finance and corporate governance, and more recently on asset management.

Michael Potts is Professor of Philosophy at Methodist University in Fayetteville, North Carolina, and has taught there since 1994. He received his PhD in Philosophy from The University of Georgia in 1992. He is the co-editor of *Beyond Brain Death: The Case Against Brain-Based Criteria for Human Death* (2000), and has authored 11 scholarly articles, nine chapters in scholarly books, six encyclopedia articles, six letters to medical journals. He has also given more than 25 presentations at scholarly conferences.

Sridhar Ramamoorti, ACA, CPA, CITP, CIA, CFE, CFSA, CRP, CGAP, CGFM, CICA, FCPA, is a partner in the National Corporate Governance Group of Grant Thornton LLP. He leads the firm's thought leadership efforts on governance and accountability. His background includes serving as: Sarbanes–Oxley Advisor for Ernst & Young, principal in the Professional Standards Group of Arthur Andersen (key liaison for Andersen–MIT $10 million collaboration), and University of Illinois accountancy faculty. He earned the MAcc. and PhD from The Ohio State University, and has published extensively (some of his work has been translated into Chinese, French, Spanish, and Japanese). Dr Ramamoorti was chairman of the Academy for Government Accountability (2005–2008), and a Board Trustee of the Institute of Internal Auditors' (IIA) Research Foundation (2002–2008).

Donald Schwartz is Professor of Finance at Loyola University Chicago where he directs the Center for Integrated Risk Management and Corporate Governance and the MS in Finance program. Don holds a PhD from Purdue University. Prior to coming to Loyola, Don was a senior executive with Chase Manhattan Banking Corporation and two subsidiaries of Cargill Incorporated. Don has worked extensively with corporations and governments to design and execute market and financial risk programs.

Anita Silvers is Professor of Philosophy and Chair of the San Francisco State University Philosophy Department. She has published eight books and more than 150 articles on ethics, bioethics, political and social philosophy, law, public policy, aesthetics, disability studies, and education. Her current book project is on justice through trust and the dynamic between partial compliance and ideal justice theories. She has served on the boards of a number of nonprofits and government agencies, including the American Philosophical Association and the National Endowment for the Humanities.

Steve Swidler is the J. Stanley Mackin Professor of Finance at Auburn University. Previously, Swidler taught at the University of Texas at Arlington, Southern Methodist University, the University of Wisconsin-Milwaukee and Rice University. He has also held visiting positions at Victoria University (New Zealand), the Oslo School of Business (Norway), Tilburg University (the Netherlands), and the University of Vaasa (Finland). Swidler has published over 50 academic papers, including articles in the *Journal of Finance*, the *Journal of Money, Credit and Banking* and the *Journal of Banking and Finance*. In addition to his academic experience, Swidler has worked at the Office of the Comptroller of the Currency and at Lexecon, Inc. Swidler obtained his undergraduate degree from Oberlin College and PhD in Economics from Brown University.

Jay C. Thibodeau, CPA is the Edward F. Gibbons Research Professor at Bentley College and an associate professor of Accountancy. He received his BS degree from the University of Connecticut in December 1987 and his PhD from the University of Connecticut in August 1996. He joined the faculty at Bentley College in September of 1996. He currently serves as the Chair of the National Education Committee for the American Accounting Association's Auditing Section. Professor Thibodeau has recently published the second edition of a book entitled *Auditing after Sarbanes–Oxley: Illustrative Cases.* He has also been published in *Accounting Horizons, Auditing: A Journal of Practice & Theory, Issues in Accounting Education, Commercial Lending Review, Advances in Accounting Education, Asian-Pacific Journal of Accounting, Practical Accountant, Journal of Financial Education,* and *Managerial Auditing.*

Shann Turnbull (MBA Harvard) as chairman and/or CEO reorganized some of the 12 publicly traded Australian corporations that he and six others controlled through their private equity group from 1967 to 1974. He founded a number of enterprises, three of which became publicly traded. In 1975 he co-authored the first educational qualification in the world for company directors and wrote *Democratising the Wealth of Nations*. His books and many writings on reforming the theory and practice of capitalism are posted at http://ssrn.com/author=26239 including his PhD thesis. The thesis provided a basis to explain in subsequent papers why firms exist in their many forms and how to design the governance architecture of organizations to further their mission. He has lectured at a number of universities.

Manuel A. Utset is the Charles W. Ehrhardt Professor at Florida State University College of Law. He is a leading scholar on the application of behavioral law and economics to issues in corporate law, with recent emphasis on the implications of self-control problems on managerial misconduct and incomplete corporate contracting. He has taught and written on corporate governance and venture capital finance, and is a fellow of the International Institute for Corporate Governance. Before joining Florida State, he taught at the Boston University and University of Utah law schools.

Duane Windsor is the Lynette S. Autrey Professor of Management in the Jesse H. Jones Graduate School of Management at Rice University, where he has been on the faculty since 1977. He is editor, since January 2007, of the quarterly journal *Business & Society* sponsored by the International Association for Business and Society (IABS). He has served as president of IABS and as division chair of the Social Issues in Management (SIM) Division of the Academy of Management. He is the author or co-author of several books in addition to numerous research papers. His recent research concerns corporate social responsibility and stakeholder management. He holds a PhD from Harvard University and graduated from Rice University with a BA.

Zhenyu Wu is an Associate Professor of Finance in the Edwards School of Business at the University of Saskatchewan, Canada. He received his PhD degree from the University of Calgary, and his research focuses mainly on the applications of agency theory, corporate governance, and entrepreneurial finance. His articles appear in *Journal of Business Venturing, Journal of Small Business Management, Journal of Applied Finance, Annals of Finance*, and some other academic journals.

Greg Young is an Associate Professor in the College of Management of North Carolina State University where his teaching, research, and consulting focuses on the interaction of business ethics with the dynamics of competitive strategy. His work has been published in prestigious journals, including the *Strategic Management Journal*, the *Journal of Management*, *Organization Science*, the *Competitive Intelligence Review*, the *Journal of Business Research*, and the *Journal of Management Inquiry*. Dr Young is active in the Academy of Management, and from 2000 through 2002 he was on the editorial board of the *Academy of Management Review*. He is a member of the Society for Business Ethics, and is on the Editorial Board of the *Encyclopedia of Business Ethics and Society*, published in 2007.

Mengxin Zhao (PhD from the University of Pittsburgh) has taught at Bentley College and is currently with the University of Alberta. Mengxin Zhao's main research focus is in the area of corporate governance, mergers and acquisitions, corporate valuation and international corporate finance. She has published articles in the *Journal of Finance*, the *Journal of Corporate Finance*, the *Financial Management Journal* and the *Journal of Comparative Economics*. She has also presented her research at various institutions and conferences worldwide. In the past, she was a visiting scholar at the Chinese University of Hong Kong, Beijing University Shenzhen Business School, and the Development Bank of Japan. She also holds the qualification of Chartered Financial Analyst (CFA).

Preface

In April 2008 a group of scholars from the United States and from around the world gathered at Loyola University Chicago to present their research and exchange ideas on the topic of "Corporate Boards: Managers of Risk, Sources of Risk." The participants presented papers that were provocative and that stimulated a lively intellectual exchange. The papers that were presented and a portion of that discussion form the content of this volume.

This symposium was sponsored by the Center for Integrated Risk Management and Corporate Governance at the Loyola University Chicago's business school. Funding for the conference and monograph was provided by the university and the business school. In addition, much of the work of the Center, including this conference, has been made possible through the generosity of the Chicago Mercantile Exchange Trust.

This is the first volume in a contemplated series of monographs to be produced as a collaborative venture between Loyola University Chicago and John Wiley & Sons, Inc., under the general editorial supervision of George Lobell at John Wiley & Sons, Inc. and by Robert W. Kolb at Loyola University Chicago.

Robert W. Kolb
Donald Schwartz

Introduction

Robert W. Kolb and Donald Schwartz

Along with senior management, corporate boards have primary responsibility for managing the risk of the firm. In the contemporary corporation,
this duty has come more to the fore with boards and board committees
receiving regular and frequent reports on the risk position of the firm.
Although the information presented to boards can be extremely summarized and condensed, the board's responsibility for the overall management
of firm risk is now well-established.

Perhaps less apparent than the board's responsibility for managing risk
is the board as a source of risk for the firm. In the first few years of the early
twenty-first century a number of unfortunate events have served to give full
notice of the risk that board members can impose on the firms they serve.
Rather than managing risk, some boards and some board members behave
in a manner that imperils the firm.

Some of this behavior is so far beyond the pale that it is clearly criminal.
For example, Jeffrey Skilling of Enron, Dennis Kozlowski of Tyco, Bernie
Ebbers of WorldCom, and John and Timothy Rigas of Adelphia presently
languish in prison. These "stars" of some of the most notorious corporate
scandals all served as board members and high-level executives of their
respective firms. All misappropriated funds for their personal benefit in
one way or another; all imposed huge costs on their firms.

In the case of Enron, the criminal activities of Kenneth Lay (convicted
and now deceased), Skilling, and others were primarily responsible for the
bankruptcy and ultimate dissolution the firm. Dennis Kozlowski's behavior
destroyed firm value that can be conservatively reckoned in the hundreds of
millions of dollars. Having been convicted of misappropriating $400
million, his destruction of firm value may even have exceeded $1 billion.
The behavior of the Rigas "team" of father, John, and son, Timothy, led to
the dissolution of the firm that the father had founded. WorldCom has

followed a tortured path of bankruptcy, emergence from bankruptcy, consolidation, merger, and reorganization that has left behind a tale of unfulfilled financial obligations and shareholder loss in a financial melodrama of Byzantine complexity. These examples are, of course, rightly infamous and well-known, but they represent the extremes of harm that board members can cause the firms they are supposed to serve.

Even when board members behave in a manner that does not lead to prison terms, they can engage in conduct that is extremely harmful to their firms without being actually criminal. Patricia Dunn, whose business career led her from a position of temporary secretary at Wells Fargo to being chairman of the board at Hewlett-Packard, provides just such an example of "almost-criminal" board behavior. Concerned about leaks of company information that she believed originated from other board members at HP, Dunn instituted a policy of spying on her fellow board members to learn the source of the leaks. In doing so, she brought the concept of "pretexting" – the act of inventing a scenario to induce a target to release personal information – to public attention. Her behavior was "almost criminal" as she was indicted on four felonies, but these charges were ultimately dismissed. Nonetheless, her behavior not only led to her resignation as chairman of HP's board, but caused the corporation's market value to fall by hundreds of millions of dollars.

The history of Richard Grasso, former chairman and CEO of the New York Stock Exchange (NYSE), reveals a tale of personal and board conduct that caused serious reputational loss and unknown financial damage to the exchange. The dynamic Grasso rose from an $85 per week exchange clerk to become widely largely regarded as a highly effective executive and even a heroic leader of the exchange in the aftermath of the attacks of September 11, 2001. (Perhaps, however, the fact that he met with members of the Colombian rebel group, the FARC, in 1999 and urged them to visit the exchange to learn of the glories of capitalism should have been a warning signal.[1]) The controversy involving Grasso was never criminal, but as he prepared to retire from his glorious career at the NYSE in 2003, his retirement package came to light. The total value of his retirement package was $140 million. This retirement benefit would not have raised particular attention had Grasso been a CEO of an ordinary corporation similar to the NYSE in magnitude and importance, but the Grasso package had two special features. First, many thought of the NYSE as a regulatory entity and believed that the head of such an organization should have been paid like a regulatory bureaucrat. (At the time, the NYSE was organized as a not-for-profit entity.) Second, the retirement package had been approved by the compensation committee of the NYSE's board of directors, and Grasso had appointed many of those members.

In 2004, New York's attorney general, Eliot Spitzer, sued Grasso, demanding repayment to the NYSE of most of the $140 million. In the ensuing public uproar, newspapers were full of allegations that Grasso had controlled, misled, and duped his board, and he was asked to resign. But, of course, the board was composed largely of the barons of Wall Street, who had their own claims of being financial titans. (It would, in fact, be hard to find a board composed of members with a greater claim to business savvy and financial acumen. One can only wonder how these financial wizards liked being portrayed as the dupes of this working class former-clerk from Queens.) After initial adverse judgments, Grasso eventually triumphed in court in 2008 when the New York State Court of Appeals dismissed all claims and Andrew Cuomo, the current attorney general of New York, stated that he had no intention of pursuing the case. It is impossible to assess fully the reputational and financial damage that the NYSE suffered from the entire Grasso affair, but the injury was certainly very substantial, and was inflicted by the CEO, Grasso, as well as the board that determined his compensation.

While the kinds of notorious board behavior and public drama of the Enrons, WorldComs, Adelphias, Tycos, HPs, and NYSEs of this world garner much media attention, most risk-related board behavior surely escapes public notice. Certainly, when firm management and board oversight proceed in good order, the media and public take no particular notice. It is the case that most board risk management failures also escape public attention. In terms of actual financial losses and opportunity losses the unremarked management failures cost more in aggregate every year than the total financial effect of all of the spectacular board failures chronicled in this brief introduction.

In the financial industry, the subprime crisis that originated in 2007, continues in the present, and threatens the indefinite future, is largely a failure of risk management. Much of the board behavior or inactivity that allowed these billions of dollars of losses to occur is starting to come to public notice, but the board conduct at most firms will never garner any spectacular media play or public attention. Already a growth industry, the importance of risk management has been greatly emphasized by the financial meltdown engendered by the subprime crisis. The magnitude of losses and public outrage will almost certainly lead to legislation providing federal regulators with a greater role in the risk management of public firms, at least in the form of heightened regulation and greater strictures on firm activity.

The future is very likely to see a greater emphasis on risk management with an increasing risk management responsibility for corporate boards. Given the current structure of corporate governance, with boards meeting relatively infrequently and board members devoting relatively few hours per year to their duties, one must wonder whether corporate boards are really a match for the task of risk management as it has evolved in the recent past and as it is likely to develop in the future. The widespread use of "risk dashboards" – visual summaries of various dimensions of firm risk, often presented on a single page – at board meetings merely emphasizes the 40,000-foot overview of board oversight.[2] Given the complexity of risk and the huge financial implications of risk management, one can only wonder over the adequacy of this kind of extremely superficial risk oversight.

Even when board committees commit considerable time and thought to oversight in a particular areas of risk management, the outcomes can often be perverse. As a single example, consider the design of executive compensation, particularly the use of executive stock options designed to align the CEO's incentives with the desires of shareholders. In short, theory asserts that CEO stock options should provide strong incentives for risk-averse CEOs to undertake risky projects that will enhance firm value and will also lead to large financial rewards for successful CEOs. However, there can be little doubt that some CEO stock option packages have led to extremely perverse consequences, including earnings manipulation and mis-statements, taking excessive risk, failing to take sufficient risk, outsourcing services that should have been developed internally, altering dividend policy in a sub-optimal manner, choosing inefficient financing methods, altering capital structure, generating excessive stock repurchases, and so on.[3]

Beyond the design of CEO compensation packages, the firm faces many risks of greater magnitude with no particular board committee dedicated to their specific management or oversight. Thus, the lack of board oversight or insufficient board attention to a variety of serious risks may lead boards to sub-optimal risk management performance that can be extremely costly. As we have seen earlier in this introduction, in extreme cases board members may behave in a way to impose great risk and even ultimate destruction on the firms they are supposed to guide. However, it is highly likely that less extreme sub-optimal board performance is actually a much more significant source of financial loss.

In one way or another, all of the papers and discussion recorded in this volume attack the problems of risk management by corporate boards. The papers in this volume are organized into five parts. The first provides an interesting factual basis regarding board participation in risk management, while the articles in the second part address the question of whether or not board management of risk is even conceptually possible or practically feasible. Part III considers the interaction between the structure of corporate boards and the conduct of risk management. Part IV addresses the management of particular risks by corporate boards, while Part V considers the ethical dimension of risk management by boards of directors. Together, the articles in this volume attempt to give a fresh, yet comprehensive overview, of the corporate board as both managers of risk and as sources of risk for the firm.

Notes

1 See http://www.colombiasupport.net/199906/nysefarc.html.
2 For two fairly typical examples of risk dashboards, see: http://www.sas.com/industry/energy/dashboard.pdf and http://www.profitmetrics.com/managerisk.htm.
3 For a discussion and analysis of executive stock options, including the perverse incentives they can generate, see Robert W. Kolb, *Employee Stock Options: Financial, Social, and Ethical Issues*, forthcoming from John Wiley & Sons, Inc.

Part I
A Factual Basis

In their contribution, "The Relationship Between Boards of Directors and their Risk Management Organizations," Michael A.M. Keehner and David R. Koenig provide a fascinating current look into the actual practices of boards and the risk management organizations in their firms. Based on a survey of leading firms, Keehner and Koenig assess the extent to which boards are full participants in the risk management process. For example, a surprising number of boards do not engage in a regular review of the firm's risk management policy – although the majority do. Further, as is shown by the results of the Keehner–Koenig survey, a significant minority of chief risk officers question whether their boards are sufficiently skilled to understand their firms' risk management organization and its reports.

Further, in a majority of firms, the risk management organization either does not report to the board or reports to the board only indirectly. Only in a minority of firms is there a board member charged with being familiar with the firm's risk management organization. These insights, along with many others provided by the survey, give a sobering view of whether corporate boards are sufficiently prepared for the risk management responsibilities that contemporary corporate governance is forcing upon them.

1

The Relationship Between Boards of Directors and their Risk Management Organizations

Are Standards of Best Practice Emerging?

Michael A.M. Keehner and David R. Koenig

Executive Summary

Over the past decade risk management has evolved from a technical discipline focused on specific exposures to an expectation of shareholders, regulators and others affected by the performance of governance at publicly held companies. Various entities, some more effectively than others, have put into place frameworks to define best-practice governance. Further, risk management practices have developed organically at firms, which, albeit to varying degrees, are compatible with these publicly available governance frameworks.

Boards play an important role, not just in the satisfaction of their fiduciary duties, but as the ultimate authority influence in a company's hierarchy. If there is an expectation that employees are engaged in best-practice governance and risk management, to be achieved, it must be modeled from the top.

At an assembly of large company chief risk officers in late 2007, the extent to which top-level practices differ was strongly in evidence. As a follow-up to that meeting a survey of large institutions around the world was conducted, primarily targeting chief risk officers and company directors. Survey results confirm the anecdotal findings of our roundtable gathering and provide further evidence that a definition of applied best practices of risk management within a governance structure does not yet exist. However, there are patterns emerging in the position of risk management relative to the board, which committees have responsibility for oversight of the risk management organization and the extent to which risk management is used either as an audit and control function or a function for strategic advantage.

Sixty-five firms, across many industries and most among the largest in their industry, participated in our survey. Several companies provided follow-up interviews that provided further background information. Additional data were gathered from public SEC filings.

The full survey report provides substantial detail on the following key findings:

- There is substantial change occurring, bringing about a more robust incorporation of risk management within the governance structure of many organizations.
- There are a wide variety of current approaches to the implementation of risk management within the enterprise governance framework – even between participants in the same industry.
- Meaningfully different approaches to risk/governance implementation exist at the board committee and executive level, the chains of reporting within the executive suite and in patterns of communications to governance structures.
- The audit committee is the most frequent choice for board oversight of risk management, but risk committees are emerging as an important board-level committee.
- Organizational objectives in incorporating risk management within governance structures differ even between participants in the same industry, but they are almost always multifold.
- Most users of risk management as an element of governance agree that loss avoidance and control objectives are to be served, while a smaller number, but still a majority of respondents, identify an objective of securing a competitive advantage through use of this function.

- Some organizations employ ongoing efforts for the promulgation and improvement of governance and risk management practices within their board and employee populations, while a very substantial body of others do not have such capabilities in place.
- The effective communication of risk policies to employees is the most significant task found lacking, leading to possible overconfidence that employees fully understand the intent of such policies.

Interviewees provided examples of specific governance best practices that could be adopted across different industries.

The importance of identifying best practices has become increasingly evident in recent months. For example, CtW Investment Group, a firm that organizes labor union members having more than $1.5 trillion in pension money into a voice for corporate accountability, sent letters to members of the board of directors of Wachovia Corp. asking for an explanation of how their board had carried out its duty of care related to the acquisition of a mortgage company and additional mortgage exposure just prior to the subprime crisis and threatening to oppose their re-election as directors if satisfactory answers were not given.[1] Shareholders have sued Freddie Mac regarding its risk management practices.[2] Several CEOs and chief risk officers (CROs), including those from some of the largest financial institutions in the world (including UBS,[3] Merrill Lynch,[4] and Citigroup[5]), have been held accountable for their companies' losses in the subprime crisis, indicating that a growing personal liability may be developing in tandem with the search for best practices.

Our study seeks to provide a point-in-time benchmark for boards and senior risk executives as the internal debate continues regarding the appropriate relationship between risk management and governance structure and the objectives for deploying risk management within publicly held companies.

Background

In October of 2007, at a roundtable held in New York City, around twenty CROs of major US and international financial organizations and the authors discussed, among other things, the interactions between companies' risk management organizations (RMO) and their respective boards of directors.

The roundtable underscored three important conclusions:

- That there was considerable interest among the CROs in how best to facilitate the interaction between the board and the RMO.
- There were a wide variety of philosophies and practices present within the group and there was little consistency in current implementation.
- Many organizations were in the process of examining or had recently examined this interaction.

Since it appeared that the state of affairs was in a period of flux and/or evolution, and to better understand in practice how the alignment of risk management and governance has been established to address the director's fiduciary responsibilities and the enterprise's corporate objectives, the authors decided to conduct a broader study in order to see what insights, trends and notable practices that effort might yield. In this study, we explore the current state of affairs in the implementation of risk management within a representative sample of corporate governance structures in order to determine:

- Which of several possible corporate objectives for deploying risk management are being addressed by the enterprises.
- Whether there are any discernable trends in risk/governance implementation.
- Whether there are any notable best practice innovations that might be worthy of a broader exposure to the governance and risk management communities.

The basis of the analysis contained in this paper is an empirical survey of the CROs and board directors of large companies, as well as a survey of SEC filings, conducted during January and February of 2008.

Survey Respondent Profile

Sixty-five firms, most of them among the very largest in their industry, responded to our survey requesting information about the relationship between their boards of directors and the risk management organization at their firm, as well as the positioning of risk management in the organizational framework.

Table 1.1 My company is:

	Response (%)	Response count
Among the largest in our industry	60.0	39
In the largest 25% of firms in our industry, but not among the very largest	16.9	11
Average size for our industry	10.8	7
Smaller than average size for our industry	12.3	8

Table 1.1 shows that 76.9 percent of responses come from companies that are among the largest 25 percent in their industry.

The survey responses were received primarily from CROs, as is shown In Table 1.2.

Table 1.2 My role is:

	Response (%)	Response count
CEO	1.5	1
CRO/Head of risk management	72.3	47
Head of audit	0.0	0
Chief Financial Officer	1.5	1
Chief Operating Officer	3.1	2
Chief Investment Officer	4.6	3
Board member	7.7	5
Other	16.9	11

Those identifying themselves via the "Other" option include staff in the following positions: enterprise risk management leader, group credit risk director, chief compliance officer, regional head of risk management, head of risk analytics, enterprise risk manager, global risk head, non-executive chairman and head of credit policy.

Table 1.3 shows that the survey respondents represented a large number of industries.

Table 1.3 My company works in the following industry or industries:

	Response (%)	Response count
Aerospace & Defense	2.0	1
Agriculture, Food & Beverage	2.0	1
Alternative Investments	8.0	4
Banking	40.0	20

(Cont'd)

Table 1.3 (*Cont'd*)

	Response (%)	*Response count*
Chemicals	6.0	3
Computer	2.0	1
Diversified Financial Services	14.0	7
Energy	6.0	3
Environment	6.0	3
Government	6.0	3
Healthcare	4.0	2
Industrial Goods & Equipment	6.0	3
Insurance	14.0	7
Manufacturing	4.0	2
Mining & Mineral	2.0	1
Services	2.0	1
Software/IT	2.0	1
Telecommunications & Online Services	4.0	2
Traditional Asset Management	8.0	4
Transportation	2.0	1
Utilities	8.0	4
Other	12.0	6

Notes: Survey invitees were selected because each had evidence of an existing risk management organization. This selection decision necessarily introduces a bias toward acceptance of risk management on the part of responding companies. Except where specifically cited, the rest of this report contains analysis and results that are based upon the data of those respondents, indicating that they are either among the largest in their industry (39 responses) or among the top 25 percent in their industry (11 responses), a total of 50 responses. We note also that there is a concentration of respondents within financial services. Where survey response results for non-financial companies illustrate striking differences from those of financial service firms, they are highlighted in the report that follows.

A Brief History of Convergence

The subjects of risk management and governance are popular topics. In corporate circles, the practice of the formal identification and management of risks has been accelerating since the mid-1990s, when a series of corporate mishaps focused attention on the potential value of having an organizational function identify and attempt to characterize the nature of risks which an enterprise might undertake and/or encounter. The premise of this movement was that managers and boards of directors, as owner-surrogates, might be better prepared to make intelligent choices between competing investments on one hand, and forms or degrees of risk on the other. Such analysis was believed to foster the selection of appropriate combinations of risk and return, avoiding – or at least mitigating – the potential occurrence of others' missteps.

Similarly, since the 1980s considerable attention has been paid to the subject of corporate governance. This has led to a growing clarity on the distinctions, conflicts and tensions between corporate managers and board of directors as owner-surrogates. Another leg of the owner–manager–director triangle, the responsibilities of directors to shareholder constituents, has also received considerable attention and clarification in both legal studies and countless court cases.[6]

On a broad plane, the inevitable confluence of these developments is obvious. The actual intersection of governance and risk management, however, is not so easy to isolate; nor is the optimal mechanism by which to accomplish it necessarily clear.

Directors' Duties Drive Interest in Risk Management

The general expectation of responsible behavior on the part of boards of directors and managers by shareholders and regulators is usually expressed as corporate governance. Corporate governance is defined by the OECD as:

> The system by which business corporations are directed and controlled. The corporate governance structure specifies the distribution of rights and responsibilities among different participants in the corporation such as the Board manager shareholders and other stakeholders and spells out the rules and procedures for making decisions and corporate affairs. By doing this it also provides the structure through which the company objectives are set and the means of attaining those objectives and monitoring performance (OECD, 2004; available at http://www.oecd.org/dataoecd/32/18/31557724.pdf).

Over the past twenty years, the practice of risk management has developed from a technical discipline, focused primarily on specific areas of exposure, to an expectation held by investors, regulators and stakeholders that risk management will be a core element of the way in which a business is run.

Businesses exist to take risks for the benefit of their shareholders. As a result of their their geographic dispersion, disintermediation and varying interests, shareholders are relatively powerless to affect the way in which a company is managed. However, under our legal systems and traditions, their proxy can be found in the board of directors. Directors are elected by shareholders and are given certain powers, including the abilities to hire, fire, and evaluate management and to set corporate strategy. Legally, they are the ultimate decision makers within the corporation, bearing a fiduciary duty to protect and serve the interests of the shareholders.

Directors' fiduciary responsibilities include both a Duty of Care and a Duty of Loyalty to their shareholders.[7] These are often expressed in terms of a duty to act in the best interests of the corporation, rather than their own personal interests, and to be diligent, thoughtful, and professional in their oversight of the corporation. One manifestation of these duties is to set standards for corporate and employee behavior and another is to establish systems and controls through which to monitor and manage the corporation's opportunities, risks and operations.

Arguments for the Implementation of Risk Management

From the point of view of the corporate directors, the promise of isolating and managing risk, and in particular the promise of global enterprise solutions, makes it inevitable that companies should avail themselves of the technology of risk management – and for a whole variety of reasons. These range from the very pragmatic to the extremely esoteric. They also imply a variety of governance structures which might be deployed to effect the practice of risk management in any given corporate framework, depending upon the mix of objectives sought.

Certainly a body of financial thinking based upon theories of capital structure, efficient markets, and portfolio management does provide some reasons for effecting risk management within a framework of corporate governance. On the financial side, the usual reasons for implementing risk management include:[8]

- Reducing the costs of financial distress and bankruptcy.
- Developing financial plans and funding investment programs.
- Stabilizing cash dividends.

Clearly, each one of these issues is in the realm of a board-level consideration. And the recognition of financial agency theory contributes further governance-related reasons to manage risk within a governance framework; mindful of the fact that risk diversification options are starkly different for shareholders and managers:[9]

* Better aligning the interests of managers and shareholders.
* Designing appropriate compensation programs.

On yet another level, a director's fiduciary responsibilities provide more reasons to consider risk management as it bears on improving the execution of their duties to be informed and to make decisions that are loyal to the interests of their shareholder constituency.[10] Certainly the hazard of failing to avail oneself of a source of potentially relevant decisional information from a rapidly developing management technology alone raises considerations of risk management implementation. There are also parallel considerations that stem from board duties to ensure that compliance standards are met, and systems and controls are implemented and effective which may make a risk management infrastructure attractive.[11] And last but not least, there is the completely pragmatic consideration that a failure to implement risk management might impact a corporation's value in the eyes of various stakeholders and marketplaces.

Thus a board that is seeking to make use of the risk management tool might select from an array of objectives: some will have a bear on strategic matters, others will add capabilities relating to enhanced corporate discovery and fact-finding, while still others are focused more on the areas of added compliance and verification. The foregoing all implies that a variety of competing rationales will lie behind the actual design of a risk management organization, which are presumably reflected in the choices which boards have made in implementing their own unique approaches to risk management.

Existing Frameworks: A Bifurcation of Risk Management Choices – Compliance or Value Creation?

Emerging frameworks for best practice corporate governance and risk management include several structures designed by various organizations that are involved in the risk management of corporations and financial systems. Among the most widely recognized are the COSO/Treadway Commission standards[12] which have been developed primarily by the accounting and internal audit profession; Sarbanes–Oxley, a legislative and regulatory response to the corporate fraud cases of the late 1990s; and newer work in the area of governance risk and compliance (GRC), as evidenced by the OCEG framework.[13]

But perhaps the most widely known current approach to wide-ranging risk management is identified by the term enterprise risk management (ERM). Unsurprisingly, ERM means different things to different groups, ranging from very limited applications in IT – where ERM is designed primarily as a control to ensure the stability of an IT infrastructure – to much broader applications as defined by the actuarial and financial professions encompassing every aspect of risk that a corporation faces. A broader vision of enterprise risk management, as established by authors such as James Lam,[14] is focused on the value which might be added through the adoption of a holistic approach to risk management. In turn, this vision has come to dominate discussions of governance, risk and whether or not value is driven by risk management as a practice.

Lam and others position enterprise risk management and corporate governance as being fully integrated into the normal process of business decision making. Similarly, the governance and risk management principles as defined by the ANZ-4360 standard[15] and implemented in the Australian and New Zealand markets put governance in a flexible format that provides strategic services to various industries and organizations. Frameworks such as COSO, however, tend to put enterprise risk management and governance into a more rigid and compliance-focused focus. This bifurcation between risk management as a control capability (audit, for example) and risk management as a strategic utility at the executive and policy levels may have profound implications for the ability of risk management organizations and governance structures to create shareholder value, since the need for risk-related information is accentuated in the carrying out the functional duties of executive and directors and also by statutory demands.

Ultimately, the question for any board of directors returns to the purpose of a risk management organization within the company. Is its primary intention to be supportive, or even an enhancement of the firm's ability to pursue its strategic objectives? Is it intended to be more of a defensive tool? Or is it viewed and positioned to focus more on regulator compliance? Can an RMO be both control-oriented and strategically focused?

Substantial Change is Occurring in Risk Management and Governance Schemes

It is clear that the general state of board and risk management organization relationships is currently in flux as organizations achieve a better understanding of their needs and move to adapt risk management to contemporary demands. In our survey respondents were asked about significant changes in risk management and governance practices over the course of the past two years.

Below is a sample of some of the most significant responses:

- Our risk committee is now looking at risk management with more granularity.
- The board is applying a risk/return measure more consistently across the institution.
- Basel II is a big priority for the firm and has garnered more attention.
- The board has increased the level of detail and oversight.
- The board originally didn't have the finance committee overseeing risk policies.
- The amount of information sent to the audit committee has decreased somewhat.
- Better transparency at the Risk Committee on risk of the company – now in a better position to make their own judgment on the risk of the company with this transparency.
- Report design and content has been changed in order to make them more meaningful for the board.
- The board has added new members that were quite knowledgeable about risk management.
- The combined audit and finance committees now meet together when they used to be independent (two times each year) – the agenda for these meetings is set by the board and the chairs of both committees.
- More direct reporting from the CRO to the board.
- We've created a new board-level risk committee.
- Our chief risk officer's position was created two years ago.

Benchmarking Results

In our survey design and the analysis of the data, there are three core lines of inquiry related to the governance purpose and deployment of a risk management organization and emerging applied best practices. These are:

1. Are large companies exercising risk management as an element of governance?

2. How is risk management implemented within the enterprise governance framework?
3. Are there ongoing efforts for the promulgation and improvement of governance and risk management practices?

In the following sections, we have identified the survey data which bear on the answers to these and important subsidiary questions. Together, these answers provide an important guide to the present state of the art in the implementation and use of risk management within existing governance structures.

Question 1 Are large companies exercising risk management as an element of governance?

Three survey questions shed light on this issue:

A. Are effective policies in place?   The first is the question of whether the enterprise has a risk management policy, and whether or not that policy is understood within the organization. In our survey 90 percent of respondents report that their company has a formal risk management policy (see Table 1.4).

Table 1.4

DOES YOUR COMPANY HAVE A RISK MANAGEMENT POLICY?		Response (%)	Response Count
Yes		90.0	45
No		10.0	5

We must emphasize, however, that the existence of a risk policy is not necessarily the same as having a risk policy that is understood throughout the organization. This is particularly the case since the majority of respondents were CROs who often have direct responsibility for such promulgation. In fact, psychological literature suggests that any expectations that risk management and conduct policies are well understood is likely to be overstated by management.[16] (More on this subject is discussed in the Appendix at the end of this paper.)

A.1. Is the policy promulgated from the highest levels in the corporation?
The board tends to play an important role in the oversight of the risk management policy, with just 7 percent of those with a risk management

policy indicating that their board does not review it. This positions the risk management policy at the top of the corporate hierarchy. It is therefore represented to employees as an important document in the process of effective governance of the company.

At the board level, one would assume that there existed a broad level of understanding about the policy, its origins and its intent. Yet while 76 percent of respondents feel that their board has sufficient skill to understand their risk management organization, policies and reports, one in nine feels that they do not.

Table 1.5

	Strongly Agree	Agree	Neutral	Disagree	Strongly Disagree	Response Count
The board regularly reviews the risk management policy	40.0% (18)	44.4% (20)	8.9% (4)	6.7% (3)	0.0% (0)	45
The board, as a whole, is sufficiently skilled to understand our RMO and its reports	31.1% (14)	44.4% (20)	13.3% (6)	11.1% (5)	0.0% (0)	45

One generally accepted tenet of governance is the provision of sufficient competencies in critical areas of the corporation, including the board. At the board level, this means that members must be able to understand the business and the environment within which the enterprise operates and also that the board should be composed in a manner such that sufficient independence and expertise exist to offer a competent evaluation of the business structure and environment in which the corporation operates and to formulate appropriate responses. Certainly, the risks the firm is facing as reported by a risk management organization form a significant part of that business environment awareness; and by that measure, the fact that nearly 25 percent of respondents question whether there is a sufficient competency on their respective boards is worthy of note.

A.2. Are risk policies understood throughout the enterprise? Most respondents feel that their risk management policies are understood, but only 27 percent feel strongly that their policies are well understood throughout the organization.

Table 1.6

	Strongly Agree	Agree	Neutral	Disagree	Strongly Disagree	Response Count
Our risk management policy is well understood throughout the organization	26.7% (12)	53.3% (24)	11.1% (5)	8.9% (4)	0.0% (0)	45

We wish again to emphasize that typically there is an overconfidence on the part of managers that policies formulated and issued from executive levels are well understood.

B. Has the risk management responsibility been clearly assigned? If so, how? The second question concerns whether or not the enterprise has formalized the responsibility for risk management. While there are in principle many forms such assignment might take, the vast majority of these reporting companies have established a single point of risk management within the management hierarchy. More than 82 percent of those who responded to our survey indicate that their firm does have a chief risk officer (CRO) or other head of risk management for the entire organization.

Table 1.7

DOES YOUR COMPANY HAVE AN ENTERPRISE-WIDE CRO?		Response (%)	Response Count
Yes		82.0	41
No		18.0	9

Of those indicating that they did not have a chief risk officer, the responses came from the following industries:

Insurance (2)	Financial Services (2)
Banking (1)	Alternative Investments (1)
Computer (1)	Software/IT (1)
Chemicals (1)	

It is interesting to note that all of these responses came from firms identified as being among the very largest in their respective industries. At those firms with no CRO, responsibility for risk management resided with the:

CEO (2)	CFO (2)
COO (1)	CIO (1)
CIO/CFO jointly(1)	"Various people" (1)
Investment Committee (1)	

C. What organizational objectives are being pursued through the management of risks? Our results show that firms are indeed pursuing risk management as a strategic objective (to achieve competitive advantage), for loss avoidance and as a control. Further, compliance with regulations is a strong driver of risk management's purpose at more than one-third of the firms in our survey. Only a very small number of firms report having risk management exist primarily to serve their internal audit needs. Note, however, that these responses are primarily from CROs, and that the recitation of corporate objectives reported here may or may not be fully representative of the views of the boards of directors who established the risk management function and its objectives.

Table 1.8

	Strongly Agree	Agree	Neutral	Disagree	Strongly Disagree	Response Count
The primary purpose of our RMO is for competitive advantage	23.9% (11)	32.6% (15)	23.9% (11)	15.2% (7)	4.3% (2)	46
The primary purpose of our RMO is for regulatory compliance	8.7% (4)	26.1% (12)	28.3% (13)	28.3% (13)	8.7% (4)	46

(Cont'd)

Table 1.8   (*Cont'd*)

	Strongly Agree	Agree	Neutral	Disagree	Strongly Disagree	Response Count
The primary purpose of our RMO is for loss avoidance	15.2% (7)	54.3% (25)	19.6% (9)	4.3% (2)	6.5% (3)	46
The primary purpose of our RMO is for control	21.7% (10)	43.5% (20)	23.9% (11)	8.7% (4)	2.2% (1)	46
The primary purpose of our RMO is for internal audit	0.0% (0)	13.0% (6)	23.9% (11)	43.5% (20)	19.6% (9)	46

It is interesting to note that as is reported through this survey, in respect of their risk management organizations the domains of objective pursuit are not exclusive with these boards of directors. In other words, firms that feel that they may be pursuing risk management primarily for a strategic purpose often note that they also pursue it for control purposes; and, conversely, those who see the function as primarily supporting information and/or control purposes in some cases also identify it as having some strategic role.

These responses are detailed further in the following paragraphs. Where respondents indicated that they either "agree" or "strongly agree" with a statement this was taken as an affirmation of an objective they held for their risk management unit, whereas the responses "strongly disagree" or "disagree" were taken as indicative of an objective they did not hold for the risk management unit.

Of those respondents who indicated by "strongly agreeing" or "agreeing" that the primary purpose of their risk management organization was for competitive advantage, a majority also indicated it had the additional primary purpose of loss avoidance and control.

Table 1.9

	Strongly Agree	Agree	Neutral	Disagree	Strongly Disagree	Response Count
The primary purpose of our RMO is for competitive advantage	42.3% (11)	57.7% (15)	0.0% (0)	0.0% (0)	0.0% (0)	26
The primary purpose of our RMO is for loss avoidance	19.2% (5)	50.0% (13)	15.4% (4)	7.7% (2)	7.7% (2)	26
The primary purpose of our RMO is for control	23.1% (6)	42.3% (11)	23.1% (6)	7.7% (2)	3.8% (1)	26
The primary purpose of our RMO is for regulatory compliance	11.5% (3)	23.1% (6)	30.8% (8)	23.1% (6)	11.5% (3)	26
The primary purpose of our RMO is for internal audit	0.0% (0)	15.4% (4)	30.8% (8)	30.8% (8)	23.1% (6)	26

Among those respondents who indicated that the primary purpose of their risk management organization was for control, more than 80 percent said that it had an additional primary objective of loss avoidance, which is not a surprising pattern. However, a majority of the same respondents said that risk management was also aimed at achieving competitive advantage.

Table 1.10

	Strongly Agree	Agree	Neutral	Disagree	Strongly Disagree	Response Count
The primary purpose of our RMO is for control	33.3% (10)	66.7% (20)	0.0% (0)	0.0% (0)	0.0% (0)	30
The primary purpose of our RMO is for loss avoidance	23.3% (7)	60.0% (18)	13.3% (4)	0.0% (0)	3.3% (1)	30
The primary purpose of our RMO is for competitive advantage	26.7% (8)	30.0% (9)	20.0% (6)	16.7% (5)	6.7% (2)	30
The primary purpose of our RMO is for regulatory compliance	6.7% (2)	33.3% (10)	30.0% (9)	23.3% (7)	6.7% (2)	30
The primary purpose of our RMO is for internal audit	0.0% (0)	16.7% (5)	36.7% (11)	33.3% (10)	13.3% (4)	30

From the data, it would seem that firms believe a solid foundation of loss avoidance and control is necessary in order to be able to pursue risk management for competitive advantage.

And, finally, regulatory compliance was identified as a primary driver of risk management organizations by 16 of the 46 respondents to this question; but again, it was generally not to the exclusion of the pursuit of additional objectives of competitive advantage, control or loss avoidance.

Table 1.11

	Strongly Agree	Agree	Neutral	Disagree	Strongly Disagree	Response Count
The primary purpose of our RMO is for regulatory compliance	25.0% (4)	75.0% (12)	0.0% (0)	0.0% (0)	0.0% (0)	16
The primary purpose of our RMO is for loss avoidance	12.5% (2)	68.8% (11)	18.8% (3)	0.0% (0)	0.0% (0)	16
The primary purpose of our RMO is for control	18.8% (3)	56.3% (9)	25.0% (4)	0.0% (0)	0.0% (0)	16
The primary purpose of our RMO is for competitive advantage	18.8% (3)	37.5% (6)	25.0% (4)	12.5% (2)	6.3% (1)	16
The primary purpose of our RMO is for internal audit	0.0% (0)	25.0% (4)	25.0% (4)	50.0% (8)	0.0% (0)	16

Comments from Respondents in Respect of Organizational Risk Management Objectives

"The ownership and management of risk falls to the business and business leaders. Our RMO facilitates the program that helps them identify, define, assess, and if necessary mitigate, control, and improve the risk management capabilities within the business. The control environment is reviewed via our Internal Audit plan and SOX requirements; however, the RMO assesses this aspect of risk when determining what mitigation efforts are needed."

"The primary purpose of our RMO is to ensure there are no surprise losses, and to ensure that we are properly compensated for the risks we take."

"The primary purpose is to drive economic growth and preserve long-term capital."

C.1. Is risk management an exercise in due diligence? Another relevant question in this study of the interaction and objectives of the board of directors and the RMO is to what degree the risk management organization is perceived to be an extension of the board's duties to be diligent and well informed on the condition of the corporation (their "due diligence" obligations). In our survey, 50 percent of respondents agreed that their risk management is a due diligence process for the board. However, more than 20 percent disagreed with this assessment.

Table 1.12

	Strongly Agree	Agree	Neutral	Disagree	Strongly Disagree	Response Count
Risk management is a due diligence process for our board	8.7% (4)	41.3% (19)	28.3% (13)	15.2% (7)	6.5% (3)	46

Finally, as a further indication that these corporations were quite diverse in their overall views of the purpose of their risk management organizations, more than one in three did not regard risk management as being a managerial/administrative responsibility in their organization, with a roughly equal number saying that it was such a responsibility. We also offer the possibility that these statements are open to diverse interpretations, but we note the responses as a point of possible interest to readers.

Table 1.13

	Strongly Agree	Agree	Neutral	Disagree	Strongly Disagree	Response Count
Risk management is a managerial/administrative responsibility	10.9% (5)	26.1% (12)	28.3% (13)	21.7% (10)	13.0% (6)	46

Question 2 How is risk management implemented within the enterprise governance framework?

Here we examine responses which bear on how these large companies have chosen to position risk management within the governance structures used to manage their enterprises. The authority influence of the risk management organization is highly dependent upon its placement within the firm's hierarchy.

A. Is there a direct involvement with risk management on the part of the board of directors? A.1. Is there a direct reporting relationship to the board of directors? The growing significance of risk management to the governance structures at these companies is further evidenced by data showing that among large companies more than 78 percent report, either directly or indirectly, to the board of directors.

The strongest governance connection, a direct board reporting relationship, is evident in 37 percent of the respondents, while 41 percent have some intermediary in the management structure interposed between the RMO and the board of directors. The remainder, comprising only 22.4 percent of these companies, have no relationship to the board.

Table 1.14

DOES YOUR RISK MANAGEMENT ORGANIZATION REPORT TO THE BOARD?		Response (%)	Response Count
Does not report to the board		22.4	11
Reports to the board directly		36.7	18
Reports indirectly		40.8	20

In this sample, the most common route for indirect reporting is through the CFO (9), although for nearly as many, the CRO reporting route is through the CEO/president/general manager (7). Other routes found were through the investment committee (1), the chief counsel (1), the audit committee (1) and the executive committee (1).

Another generally accepted tenet of governance is the preservation of open and uninterpreted communications channels for important auditing and control functions so as to insure the flow of independent facts and judgments to governance authorities. In recent times independent board reporting relationships for internal audit groups have been the most conspicuous form of this communications protection on the part of directors. Those taking part in this survey provide us with one assessment of whether the risk management organization also has an independent route to the board of directors. As shown above, of the large firms, only 37 percent of the risk management organizations report directly to the board. However, through our interviews and also through our own anecdotal experience, we believe this to be a substantial growth from the norm of five to ten years ago, with a particular acceleration in independent board reporting for risk management happening over the past few years. In some instances we encountered other forms of organizations taking steps to insure that risk management communications channels to the board would not be interfered with by management fiat.

A.2. Is there a single individual accountable for risk management on the board of directors? Another measure of governance seriousness of purpose concerning risk management matters is whether or not there is a single board-level individual with responsibility for being familiar with the risk management organization of their firm. We note that only 31 percent of firms report that such clear accountability is in place, even among those firms selected for our study, which we assume are likely to be more advanced in their approaches.

Table 1.15

IS THERE A SINGLE INDIVIDUAL ON THE BOARD WITH RESPONSIBILITY FOR BEING FAMILIAR WITH THE RISK MANAGEMENT ORGANIZATION OF THE FIRM?		Response (%)	Response Count
Yes		31.3	15
No		68.8	33

B. What is the governance committee structure being used at the board of directors level to manage these enterprises and to effect governance broadly? Over time, organizations have evolved a set of board committees they have considered necessary to exercise their governance responsibilities. Some of these are mandated by various regulators and supervisory agencies while others have come into being through choice. Overall, within the population of committees which these large enterprises currently use to exercise governance broadly, an audit committee can be found at nearly 90 percent of respondent firms, while a risk committee exists at just 26 percent:

Table 1.16

Range of Committees Present in Respondents' Boards

Audit	86.0%
Executive	56.0%
Nominating	40.0%
Governance	40.0%
Management	38.0%
Risk	26.0%
Finance	14.0%
Compensation	6.0%
Credit	4.0%

B.1. Which board committee has been assigned the primary oversight responsibility for risk management? Presumably these organizations have made a choice in selecting the most appropriate board committee to exercise the risk management oversight functions after some consideration of issues, including functional similarities, the available talent, and the anticipated volume of effort. In some cases, they have selected an existing committee to assume this responsibility, and others have formed (often recently) a new committee to oversee the risk function. The following table indicates where this responsibility has been vested.

Table 1.17

Board Committee Having Primary Oversight Responsibility for Risk Management

Audit	31%
Risk	17%
Management/Executive	13%
Finance	4%
Governance	4%
Risk Policy Capital	4%
Credit	4%
BoD	4%

There was some consistency among respondents as to where the risk management organization reported to the board of directors. More survey respondents firms place oversight of the risk management organization with the audit committee than with any other board committee. Eight respondents (about 17 percent of these companies) indicate the existence of a board-level risk committee or risk management committee that has the ultimate oversight responsibility for risk management.

The executive (or management) committee of the board is the third most common reporting location and is particularly evident among the smaller respondents in this sample of large and very large companies. One or another of these three board committee location choices was made by more than a majority of the survey group.

Beyond the foregoing, it is difficult to discern much consistency in the choices made by these respective companies. If anything, the assignments probably reflect a combination of assessments of company-specific issues, board member talents and some reflection of an uncertainty about where this assignment might ultimately reside most effectively. The minority not choosing one of the three committees above vest the responsibility for risk management oversight in a variety of different board committees. In some instances, the risk management assignment is added to a pre-existing standing committee which was deemed appropriate for this new responsibility for company-specific reasons, while still others represent an expanded former committee with a new name. Some companies have adopted a dual reporting scheme and others assign the duty to the board as a whole; both probably reflecting the widespread applicability of RMO information and considerations. Finally, some companies have delegated the responsibility for risk oversight to the CEO or chairman alone in their capacity as a board member. In general, this dispersion can probably be seen as evidence that the board of directors' interface with the risk management organization has yet to be settled into a widely acceptable pattern, and the relationship evolution will continue as functional demands, potential regulations, new studies and best practices become evident.

Table 1.18

Board Committee Responsible for Risk Management in Large Companies	Financials	Non-Financials	Total Sample
Executive (Management) Committee	6		6
Audit Committee	12	3	15

Risk Committee	8	8
Audit and Risk Management Committee	1	1
Risk and Finance Committee	1	1
Risk Management & Compliance	1	1
Risk Policy Capital Committee	2	2
Finance Committee	2	2
Credit (Credit Risk) Committee	1 1	2
Governance (and Nominating) Committee	2	2
Board of Directors as a Whole	2	2
Chairman/CEO	2	2
Dual Reporting Schemes:		
Audit + Finance Committee(s)	1	1
Risk + Audit Committee(s)	1	1
Finance, Credit + Board as a Whole	1	1
Audit + Investment and Capital Committee(s)	1	1
Total Responses	41 7	48

It is worth noting that the multiplicity of objectives cited as reasons for deploying risk management within a governance structure are also reflected in these committee choices. In particular, the divergence between audit-like risk functionality and strategic risk management functionality (mentioned in an earlier paragraph) is probably very influential in some of the choices companies have made between audit (and similar) committees as the appropriate venue for risk; and other choices, like newly-formed risk committees and executive committees, which may be more appropriate for strategic or operational committee work. This dichotomy of functionality was best highlighted by one respondent who made the distinction that their audit committee deals with "what has happened," while their risk committee deals with "what could happen."

B.2. How frequently does this primary board committee meet to exercise its oversight? There is a large amount of variability in the frequency of meetings held by the board committee with responsibility for risk oversight. Quarterly meetings are most typical, but more frequent meeting cycles are also used by many of these respondents. Of those answering "Other," most reported meeting between six and 10 times per year, while 22.7 percent report that they meet on a monthly basis.

Table 1.19

HOW MANY TIMES A YEAR DOES THE BOARD COMMITTEE HAVING RISK MANAGEMENT ORGANIZATION OVERSIGHT RESPONSIBILITY MEET?		Response (%)	Response Count
Monthly		22.7	10
Quarterly		59.1	26
Twice each year		11.4	5
Annually		2.3	1
Only as needed		4.5	2
Other			9

When these committees meet, in more than 80 percent of the cases, the chief risk officer or person responsible for risk management organization attends:

Table 1.20

DOES THE CRO OR THE PERSON RESPONSIBLE FOR RISK MANAGEMENT ALWAYS ATTEND MEETINGS OF THIS COMMITTEE?		Response (%)	Response Count
Yes		81.6	40
No		18.4	9

Of the 18 percent who say that the CRO does not attend, nearly 90 percent indicated that someone else in senior management attends who is responsible for risk management. Typically this was the CEO, the CFO or the Chief Counsel.

C. Do other board committees take an interest in risk management activities even where there is another committee primarily responsible for the risk management function?   The response to this question was somewhat surprising as many board committees do take an active interest in risk management results, even where there is a primary committee with board-level oversight responsibility present. This may be a function of the relative novelty of the assignment of risk management oversight duties within the board structure, overlaps in committee charter definitions, an acknowledgment of the pervasive nature and perceived relevance of risk management data or one of many other factors which are generally outside the scope of this study. Nevertheless, the degree of overlapping interest and reporting requirements is surprising, since the head of risk management will typically meet with a number of committees, as Table 1.21 indicates.

Table 1.21

WITH WHICH OTHER BOARD COMMITTEES (OTHER THAN THE PRIMARILY RESPONSIBLE COMMITTEE) DOES THE CRO OR HEAD OF RISK MEET (AND HOW OFTEN)?		
	Yes	No
Audit Committee	83.7% (36)	16.3% (7)
Executive Committee	55.6% (15)	44.4% (12)
Management Committee	50.0% (11)	50.0% (11)
Governance Committee	26.3% (5)	73.7% (14)
Nominating Committee	6.3% (1)	93.8% (15)

Table 1.22

HOW FREQUENTLY?	Monthly	Quarterly	Twice each year	Annually	Only as needed
Audit Committee	8.6% (3)	42.9% (15)	25.7% (9)	11.4% (4)	11.4% (4)
Executive Committee	50.0% (8)	18.8% (3)	0.0% (0)	12.5% (2)	18.8% (3)
Management Committee	54.5% (6)	36.4% (4)	9.1% (1)	0.0% (0)	0.0% (0)
Governance Committee	20.0% (1)	40.0% (2)	20.0% (1)	0.0% (0)	20.0% (1)
Nominating Committee	0.0% (0)	100% (1)	0.0% (0)	0.0% (0)	0.0% (0)

D. How are risk management reports circulated within the governance organization? Much like the results reported above, several board committees receive regular reports from the risk management organization in addition to the committee with primary responsibility:

Table 1.23

WHICH BOARD MEMBERS RECEIVE REGULAR REPORTS FROM THE RISK MANAGEMENT ORGANIZATION?		
	Yes	No
Board Audit Committee Members	90.9% (20)	9.1% (2)
Board Risk Management Committee Members	88.9% (16)	11.1% (2)
All Board Members	86.2% (25)	13.8% (4)
Board Governance Committee Members	71.4% (5)	28.6% (2)
Board Executive Committee Members	66.7% (8)	33.3% (4)
Board Management Committee Members	57.1% (4)	42.9% (3)
Board Nominating Committee Members	40.0% (2)	60.0% (3)

The frequency of these reports varies widely:

Table 1.24

HOW OFTEN ARE THESE REPORTS DELIVERED?							
	Daily	Weekly	Monthly	Quarterly	Twice each year	Annually	Response count
Board Audit Committee Members	0.0% (0)	0.0% (0)	10.5% (2)	73.7% (14)	10.5% (2)	5.3% (1)	19
Board Risk Management Committee Members	0.0% (0)	0.0% (0)	40.0% (6)	60.0% (9)	0.0% (0)	0.0% (0)	15

All Board Members	4.2% (1)	0.0% (0)	41.7% (10)	45.8% (11)	0.0% (0)	8.3% (2)	24
Board Governance Committee Members	0.0% (0)	0.0% (0)	66.7% (2)	33.3% (1)	0.0% (0)	0.0% (0)	3
Board Executive Committee Members	0.0% (0)	12.5% (1)	50.0% (4)	25.0% (2)	0.0% (0)	12.5% (1)	8
Board Management Committee Members	0.0% (0)	33.3% (1)	66.7% (2)	0.0% (0)	0.0% (0)	0.0% (0)	3
Board Nominating Committee Members	0.0% (0)	0.0% (0)	0.0% (0)	100.0% (1)	0.0% (0)	0.0% (0)	1

We also asked whether the risk management organization communicates with the entire board of directors. More than three-quarters reported that the RMO gives regular briefings to the entire board, but a full 24 percent have no such direct communication with the entire board of directors.

Questions that Board Members Ask of Risk Managers

We asked our interviewees if the board members asked any particular questions that seemed to stand out for their importance or effectiveness in terms of the oversight of the risk function. Their responses highlighted several areas of focus:

- "How do we know that everything is under control?"
- "How do current headlines or risks influence the risk to our business plan?"
- They know that mistakes in business strategy will be the end of our company and they focus on this aspect of risk.

- They are now focused more on liquidity and funding than in the past and ask good questions on this.
- They challenge the quality of the risk management function's radar report.
- They challenge the RMO metrics and quantitative methods and assumptions.
- They vary the amount of time they spend, and points on which they go into greater detail – they don't ask for great detail every time, but the RMO must be prepared in case they do.
- The board regularly asks two questions about the value of the RMO: First, "Are we driving value?" Second, "Are we a reporting function only?"

Question 3   What is the level of ongoing promulgation and improvement of governance and risk management practices?

The third area addressed in this study of governance and risk management was to focus on what these organizations are doing to increase the comprehension and proficiencies in risk management at the board level and otherwise throughout the enterprise.

A. To what extent is there formal risk management education at the board level?   In respect of the formal risk management education of board members, a majority of respondents have engaged in such, but a substantial minority (37 percent) have not held any formal educational programs for their board:

Table 1.25

HAS YOUR RISK MANAGEMENT ORGANIZATION HELD AN EDUCATIONAL SESSION FOR BOARD MEMBERS?	Response (%)	Response Count
Yes	63.0	29
No	37.0	17

One member of multiple boards made an important distinction in respect of how well supported the board is in the area of risk management. They noted that board risk committees do not commonly have outside expert advisors available in the area of risk management to counsel committee members, while other board committees (such as compensation, audit) do regularly avail themselves of such outside experts as a part of their deliberations. This is, among other things, probably a reflection of the scarcity of independent professionals with sufficient risk industry experience, education and/or seniority, to meet this potential need.

How Boards are Increasing Their Proficiency

These notes come from comments made by our interviewees:

- Often the board will arrange for practitioners from the firm to come to a meeting to discuss their specific product or their work.
- Working with the communications group on how they can transmit more risk management knowledge to employees.
- Each May is dedicated to an education-only session, with the agenda set by the audit and finance committees.
- New board members get a rigorous one-day or two half-day seminars that are packed with information.
- Quarterly, the risk team will focus on one specific risk issue and study it in great detail.
- They actively seek out board members from other companies, across different industries, and ask them about how they manage risk.

B. To what extent is there formal risk management education at the employee level? Another common indicator of governance activity is whether or not the firm provides ongoing education and training to all employees on the role of governance in the corporation. In respect of the specific area of risk management, just 13 percent of respondents "strongly agreed" that their regular training program for new employees included a focus on the risk management policy. An equal percentage "strongly agreed" that their employees are regularly updated about awareness of the risk management policy. Overall, only slightly more than half of the respondents "agreed" or "strongly agreed" that such a training program existed, which suggests there remains a significant gap in this element of good governance. (Note that this survey did not ask whether there was an ongoing training initiative for risk management employees alone, or whether other broad governance training programs existed. But we would assume that the risk management policy would be included in any such broad governance training and would thus have been noted by respondents.)

Our aforementioned concern that an awareness of risk policy may not be as high as believed is underscored further by noting that only slightly over half of the respondents indicate that they have a regular training program about risk management policies for new employees, even for these large – and presumably risk-sensitive – firms.

Table 1.26

	Strongly Agree	Agree	Neutral	Disagree	Strongly Disagree	Response Count
We have a regular training program for new employees that includes a focus on the risk management policy	13.3% (6)	37.8% (17)	13.3% (6)	28.9% (13)	6.7% (3)	45

Further, while a majority of the same firms say that they regularly update employees about the risk management policy, fully 21 percent – or more than 1 in 5 – indicate that their firm does not regularly update employees on risk policies.

Table 1.27

	Strongly Agree	Agree	Neutral	Disagree	Strongly Disagree	Response Count
We regularly update our employees' awareness of the risk management policy	13.6% (6)	40.9% (18)	25.0% (11)	18.2% (8)	2.3% (1)	44

C. To what extent does your company use external validation and bench-marking of governance processes?   A further inquiry into respondents' practices in implementing risk management is the use of outside reference sources to measure and critique the risk management systems employed by the subject organization. Such a practice can provide a benchmarking of the effort and awareness of ongoing developments in the broader risk management industry.

In fact, we found that fewer than half of all respondents report using external consultants to provide them with benchmarking data.

Table 1.28

DO YOU USE AN OUTSIDE CONSULTANT TO BENCHMARK YOUR RISK MANAGEMENT ORGANIZATION PRACTICES AND INFRASTRUCTURE?	Response (%)	Response Count
Yes	45.7	21
No	54.3	25

Of those who do engage in external benchmarking via consultants, typically this was carried out every two years or so, with many commenting that benchmarking is done "as needed."

Table 1.29

HOW OFTEN DO YOU USE AN EXTERNAL SOURCE FOR SUCH BENCHMARKING?	Response (%)	Response Count
Twice each year	0.0	0
Annually	33.3	4
Biannually (every two years)	66.7	8

Assessing the Firm's Risk Culture and Risk Awareness

One of our interviewees detailed a program that his firm has developed to assess the extent to which a risk-aware culture had permeated the firm. It is creatively based on a behavioral model that described a pro-active risk culture in which people felt confident to report all mistakes or "bad news" to managers, who would then receive it affirmingly.

The core behaviors of this model are prevention, detection, recovery, and continuous improvement, which we note are highly aligned with the new work from OCEG in their Red Book 2.0 (see http://www. oceg.org/view/foundation). Together with key context influencers of role clarity, training, accountability and an encouraging environment, they define the status of the firm's risk culture.

This firm uses their annual employee survey, which they report has an 84 percent participation rate, to ask 10 Risk Culture Index questions (spread throughout the survey) that focus on risk management behaviors.

The results from the survey are used to calculate a Risk Culture Score for all teams and business units within the company where there are more than 15 employees. The results are transparent to all managers and the performance assessment and annual bonus of each manager is partly dependent upon the risk culture score that their group achieves.

This company began their surveys in 2003 and has now rolled them out globally.

Of those firms who do not use consultants, most rely on industry reports and studies to provide them with guidance as an alternative source for information, with more than half relying on regulators to provide this service.

Table 1.30

PLEASE IDENTIFY ANY OF THE SOURCES BELOW THAT YOU USE FOR EXTERNAL BENCHMARKING:		Response (%)	Response Count
Industry reports and studies		89.2	33
Internal Audit		32.4	12
Regulators		54.1	20
Internal innovation and reporting		43.2	16

Rating Agencies are Helping Some Firms

From one respondent: "We actually use various external sources including membership in the CRO Forum, Standard & Poor's ERM rating, external consultants [and] membership of [various industry] bodies to monitor the performance of our Risk Function."

The emergence of rating agency standards for ERM was also mentioned by another respondent.

In 2005, Standard & Poor's began to include ERM in their rating evaluations for financial institutions and insurance companies. It has made an evaluation on two key types of information: the degree to which a firm has comprehensive mastery of the risks that it faces, and the extent to which the firm's management optimizes revenue for the risk it is willing and able to take. In some cases, S&P asserts that its confidence in management's ability to control risk taking allows them to conclude that a firm could absorb an apparently high level of potential risk exposure, and still qualify for high ratings. Conversely, firms with relatively low prima facie risk exposure, but with a weak ability to control risk, might receive lower ratings. S&P announced a plan to expand ERM ratings to the non-financial sector in 2008.

How Do the "Smaller" Companies Compare to the Larger Companies?

Fifteen of the responses received were from firms that indicated they were not in the top 25 percent of firms in their industry. The substantial majority of the firms in this category (80 percent) report involvement in banking. We compare their responses on a several significant survey findings to those of the large firms:

- 43 percent (vs. 31 percent for the larger organizations) have a single board member responsible for being familiar with the risk management organization.
- 60 percent (vs. 37 percent) of these companies have an RMO that reports directly to the board.
- 93 percent (vs. 82 percent) have a chief risk officer or enterprise-wide risk officer.
- 87 percent (vs. 90 percent) have a risk policy.

- 77 percent (vs. 80 percent) agree that risk policy is well understood.
- 80 percent (vs. 76 percent) have a regular or other briefing for the entire board of directors.
- 92 percent (vs. 76 percent) believe their board is sufficiently skilled to understand the risk management organization and its reports.

It is interesting to note that on many of the study measures of risk management and governance organizational integration, the those firms in the survey sample that were either average in size or smaller than average appear to be more advanced than the larger firms in terms of the implementation of risk management within the governance structure. This may be a reflection of the complexity faced by the larger firms, or the fact that smaller companies have the ability to focus on organizational needs and to execute their plans more effectively. This is also probably a reflection of the sample bias. As noted, the firms invited to be participants in the survey were ones known to have risk management already in existence, and we believe it is not appropriate to extrapolate our findings to conclude that smaller firms are better than larger firms at risk management.

Conclusion

Our survey responses and one-on-one interviews make it clear that the large companies who participated in our survey, many of them global leaders in their field, have rapidly advanced the effectiveness of the interaction between the board of directors and the risk management organizations over the past few years.

As various public and private bodies continue to develop and recommend interesting and innovative practices around the issue of governance it will be the actual implementations that determine what the standard will be in terms of shareholder expectations. The impact and importance of actual implementations may even extend to regulators as well if Basel II – Pillar I and Pillar III practices are emulated.

We found in the survey data that risk management is placed very high in the executive hierarchy of responding organizations. Most have risk policies in place and have RMOs who report, either directly or indirectly, to the board. There may be more confidence than is warranted that risk policies are understood throughout the firm since the education programs around such policies for new and existing employees appear to leave room for improvement.

Firms are pursuing risk management and governance for the purposes of competitive advantage, control, loss avoidance, and regulatory compliance. Often the same firm will be pursuing several such goals simultaneously.

There are multiple models for the assignment of board committee risk oversight. The most popular choice is a company's audit committee, but dedicated risk committees or executive (or management) committees are also popular. However, there are many other variations, including some dual assignments for this very important governance decision. A growing minority of firms have a single board member with responsibility for being familiar with the risk management organization of the firm. This is a highly challenging accountability, given that sufficiently skilled outside resources to support committee or individual oversight of the risk management organization are relatively scarce.

Most firms represented in our survey have held educational sessions for their boards, but a substantial percentage has not. Less than half of our respondents reported the use of outside consultants to help them to benchmark their internal practices. Rather, much reliance is placed upon a review of industry publications and studies, input from regulators and an emerging use of rating agency ERM reviews.

In the survey we identified several gaps between the current practices and those considered to be good principles of corporate governance. We especially note the need for further development of risk education and risk awareness at both board level and across the corporation in order to achieve the successful implementation of risk management with the overall governance structure. It can be concluded that further study of the means for effective communication of the corporate risk appetite, risk policy, and risk data/ reporting expectations is warranted to ensure that firms are creating the kind of effective culture that their boards are increasingly seeking to foster.

Appendix

In this section we provide a little more background on two matters of importance to the effectiveness of board oversight and its relationship to the risk management organization.

The Influence of Authority and the Responsibility of the Board[17]

Within the world of organizational behavior, it is critical to have an understanding of how authority figures and authority structures influence corporate behavior. Research shows that of all modes of influence, authority is the one that chiefly distinguishes how people behave inside an organization from how they might behave as individuals outside of an organization. Employees, who are subject to the hierarchy, accept that those higher up the authority structure give commands and directions that are thought to specify what actions they should take to fulfill the plans of the organization. These directions, or policies, are often communicated in an incomplete manner.

Typically, middle level managers or line employees within a company will not know which of the choices that are available to them best maximize the organization's objectives. For example, should a company increase its rate of production and accept the likely increase in production errors that come with that change, or is it more important to meet the customers' expectations of quality? If the order to increase production comes from higher up the hierarchy, it will be assumed that it is based on expertise and knowledge. Most employees will treat authority within an organization as being legitimate, expert and a requirement of a complex structure that relies on a coordination of tasks.

The most critical breakdown in the effective implementation of top-level objectives and policies is the belief by superiors that their subordinates have sufficient knowledge and sufficient understanding of the intent of the orders they receive. Often this means that the higher-ups will not even be contemplating the possibility that their instructions have not been understood fully.

Within most firms risk management policies, corporate codes of conduct, and corporate procedures are already in place. However, these companies may well fall into the same trap. Just because these policies exist and have been established by the board or other top-level entities within the corporate hierarchy, does not mean they are understood fully. There is ample evidence in psychological literature that overconfidence that these policies are well understood is the norm.

If there is incomplete communication, a board may have an unwarranted belief that its governance structure is effective. Further, if those lower down the hierarchy think that the board's failure to fully communicate their intent, or to effectively educate on their intent is a sign of their attitude toward such policies, the policies will have little effect and may, in fact, lead to behavior that runs counter to the intent of the policy.

Adherence to Commonly Found Governance Principles

In the preceding pages, we referenced several "common" governance principles. We draw the readers' attention to the PRMIA Governance Principles.[18] In 2004, an esteemed Blue Ribbon Advisory panel of the Professional Risk Managers' International Association (PRMIA) reviewed a number of existing best practice governance documents with the intent of identifying common principles that could be found in most, if not all. The objective of their exercise was to establish a minimum set of principles which should rightly be expected to be adhered to at all public companies.

From this study came the seven key PRMIA Governance Principles:

- Principle One: Sufficiency of Key Competencies
- Principle Two: Sufficiency of Resources and Process
- Principle Three: Independence of Key Parties
- Principle Four: Clear Accountability
- Principle Five: Ongoing Education and Discernment
- Principle Six: Disclosure and Transparency
- Principle Seven: External Validation

PRMIA uses these principles to develop applications to the board as well as to the organization as a whole. Some highlights from this include:

Boards and Audit Committees Must:

- Be effectively aware of the business structure and environment in which the corporation operates (sufficiency of key competencies, sufficiency of resources and process, ongoing education and discernment)

- Be composed in a manner such that sufficient independence and expertise exist to competently evaluate the business structure and environment in which the corporation operates (independence of key parties, sufficiency of key competencies, disclosure and transparency)

- Clearly articulate the corporate risk appetite to senior management (clear accountability, disclosure and transparency, ongoing education and discernment)

- Thoroughly review compensation plans of potentially "highly compensated positions" for consistency with corporate risk appetite, competitive market conditions and fiduciary responsibility to shareholders (independence of key parties, disclosure and transparency, ongoing education and discernment)

- Have a single member formally given responsibility for understanding and reporting the effectiveness of the corporation's risk management infrastructure (sufficiency of key competencies, sufficiency of resources and process, clear accountability, disclosure and transparency)

- Continually review the application of standards of corporate governance to the risk management infrastructure, financial accounting and reporting infrastructure and the organization as a whole (clear accountability, ongoing education and discernment, external validation)

- Be fully accountable to shareholders through equitable voting rights (sufficiency of resources and process, clear accountability)

The Risk Management Infrastructure Must:

- Be independently staffed and report to an executive committee (operating committee) level employee who is not a business unit leader (Independence of key parties, clear accountability)

- Be of sufficient funding, intellectual and technological capacity to adequately understand and communicate the risks presented by the business structure and environment (Sufficiency of key competencies, sufficiency of resources and process, disclosure and transparency)

- To the extent possible, avoid silos of control and oversight (sufficiency of resources and process, clear accountability)
- Have a budget that is established by a subset of the executive committee or board, excluding the influence of individual business-unit leaders (independence of key parties, sufficiency of resources and process)
- Provide a clear escalation policy for the employees of the organization as a whole to escalate matters of concern without the threat of inappropriately adverse impact (independence of key parties, sufficiency of resources and process)
- Actively provide ongoing professional development for risk management staff and require them to be committed to standards of best practice, conduct and ethics in their work (sufficiency of key competencies, sufficiency of resources and process, ongoing education and discernment)
- Provide general corporate governance training for employees of the organization as a whole (sufficiency of resources and process, ongoing education and discernment)

Financial Accounting and Reporting Infrastructure Must:

- Accurately represent the corporation's current and known financial condition in a timely manner (disclosure and transparency)
- Only use off-balance sheet transactions which have a legitimate economic, tax, risk transfer or risk mitigating purpose (clear accountability, disclosure and transparency)
- Provide a detailed description of the risk management infrastructure in the corporation's annual report to shareholders (disclosure and transparency, ongoing education and discernment)
- Provide an auditable annual statement of compliance with the board's publicly stated standards of corporate governance to the board and audit committee (disclosure and transparency, ongoing education and discernment, external validation)

The Organization as a Whole Must:

- Provide ongoing education and training to all employees on the role of risk management and corporate governance in the corporation (ongoing education and discernment)

- Provide an environment in which an escalation policy can be effective (disclosure and transparency)

- Commit itself to actual enforcement of corporate governance polices (clear accountability) Commit itself to full compliance with local laws, regulations and customs, to the extent that such customs do not conflict with local laws and regulations (ongoing education and discernment)

- Publish an external auditor's opinion that the corporation is in compliance with the board's publicly stated standards of corporate governance (disclosure and transparency, external validation)

Notes

1   See http://www.ctwinvestmentgroup.com/index.php?id=58.
2   See http://www.washingtonpost.com/wp-dyn/content/article/2007/11/21/ AR2007112102335.html.
3   See http://www.businessweek.com/magazine/content/08_09/b4073030425608. htm?chan=top+news_top+news+index_businessweek+exclusives.
4   See http://www.bloomberg.com/apps/news?pid=20601087&sid=anPpji_PBsF8 &refer=home.
5   See http://www.reuters.com/article/bondsNews/idUSWNAS277720071116.
6   Many discussions of a director's obligations, duties and challenges are available. For example, see John L. Colley 2003. *Corporate Governance*. New YorK: McGraw-Hill Professional.
7   These duties are actually based upon laws of the state where the corporation is chartered; however there are many approximate statements of the duties in the US generally. See, for example, American Law Institute. 1992. *Principles of Corporate Governance: Analysis and Recommendations*.
8   Financial reasons for managers to manage risk have been described by various authors' literature since the 1980s. A textbook discussion is found in Mark Grinblatt and Sheridan Teitman. 2001. *Financial Markets and Corporate Strategy*. Boston: Irwin/McGraw Hill.
9   Agency theory and the need to monitor the alignment of shareholder/manager interests have been described by many authors. See, for example, E. Fama and

M. Jensen. 1983. Separation of ownership and control. *Journal of Law and Economics*, 26 (June): 301–25.

10 Directors' duties are widely described. See, for example, Dennis J. Block, Nancy E. Barton, Stephen A. Radin. 1998. *The Business Judgment Rule: Fiduciary Duties of Corporate Directors*, 5th edn. New York: Aspen Law & Business.

11 These board obligations for sound controls have been discussed more in relation to implementing accounting and audit functions than risk management, per se. However, the arguments are generally applicable. See, for example, J. Cohen, G. Krishnamoorthy and A. Wright. 2002. Corporate governance and the audit process. *Contemporary Accounting Research*, 19(4) (Winter): 573.

12 See http://www.coso.org/.

13 See http://www.oceg.org/Default.aspx.

14 James Lam. 2003. *Enterprise Risk Management: From Incentives to Controls*. Hoboken, NJ: Wiley.

15 See http://www.riskmanagement.com.au/.

16 See John Darley, David Messick and Tom Tyler. 2001. *Social Influences on Ethical Behavior in Organizations*. Mahwah, NJ: Lawrence Erlbaum Associates Publications.

17 This is a summary of some key points made by John Darley in his essay "The Dynamics of Authority Influence in Organizations and the Unintended Action Consequences." In John Darley, David Messick and Tom Tyler. 2001. *Social Influences on Ethical Behavior in Organizations*. Mahwah, NJ: Lawrence Erlbaum Associates Publications.

18 See http://www.prmia.org/pdf/PRMIA_Governance_Principles.PDF.

Part II

Is Risk Management by Corporate Boards Even Possible?

In "Risk Management, Chaos Theory, and the Corporate Board of Directors," Michael Potts argues that corporations are chaotic systems and raises the question of whether risk management is even possible within such a system. Is the presumption of risk management merely an example of hubris in the face of a complexity that overwhelms human ingenuity and its accompanying presumption of mastery? Even within chaotic systems, Potts argues, periods of relative stability do allow for some planning and control. Potts uses an analogy between weather systems and corporations to make his point on the limitations of risk management. Essentially, Potts argues, the chaotic nature of weather systems imposes limits on the time horizon over which weather predictions can have any hope of accuracy. In a similar vein, the chaotic nature of corporate organizations limits the time horizon and degree of control in risk management.

In "Anti-Social Norms, Risky Behavior," Reza Dibadj questions whether we have a satisfactory framework within which we can understand the behavior of corporate boards. In Dibadj's view, agency theory remains too attached to the assumptions of neoclassical economics and the focus on maximizing agents. Dibadj's central claim may well be that "Boards cannot be simply conceptualized as facilitating a series of efficient contracts." Rather, asserts Dibadj, it is more accurate to think of corporate boards as social creatures that evolve norms that can be dangerous, and, in his view, this gives a significant role for law and regulation. In sum, given the nature of boards as he sees it, Dibadj urges for greater shareholder rights, a de-emphasis on the business judgment rule, and the giving of greater power to state laws.

Manuel A. Utset develops a model of the relationship between managers and board members in his paper, "Time-Inconsistent Boards and the Risk of Repeated Misconduct." Utset argues that managers develop the ability to control boards, thereby achieving their own entrenchment to a greater degree than is generally understood. The key to his analysis is the idea of time-inconsistency, the observation that preferences and their ordering persist over time and that individuals possess the self-control to act on those preferences in the short and long run. As Utset puts it: "In other words, people routinely make short-term decisions to yield to the transient lure of immediate gratification, notwithstanding their long-term preference to be patient." This leads to excessive consumption of short-term benefits and to the deferral of actions that incur immediate costs for greater future gains. One of the mechanisms by which managers can gain ascendancy and control over board members is by imposing short-term costs on board decisions that the manager wishes to avoid. According to Utset, this is particularly hazardous when this time-inconsistency leads boards to procrastinate in complying with various legal requirements or in making managerial changes.

Sridhar Ramamoorti discusses the general issues raised by the papers and provides detailed comments on each contribution.

2

Risk Management, Chaos Theory, and the Corporate Board of Directors[1]

Michael Potts

Introduction

Robert Solomon points out that in recent years the role of a corporate board of directors has "come under increased scrutiny" (Solomon and Martin, 2004: 134). In particular, there is an increasing emphasis on the function of corporate boards in overseeing risk management, particularly in response to the Enron disaster. Although in the past corporate board members were able to deny responsibility for such disasters, today they are expected to take greater responsibility for the operation of the company, instead of leaving it wholly up to the management they hire.

Yet how much control and responsibility can the corporate board have in risk management? There is a body of management theory influenced by chaos theory (many current studies refer to the broader "complexity theory"). On the surface, it seems that chaos theory poses a threat to the very idea of risk management and *a fortiori* to the corporate board playing a role in risk management. Chaos theory emphasizes "sensitive dependence on initial conditions;" that is, an infinitesimal change in a chaotic system can lead to massive changes. This makes predicting the exact future state of a chaotic system impossible. If corporations, as I shall argue, are chaotic systems, and if the future course of a corporation cannot be accurately predicted due to sensitive dependence on initial conditions, what is the use of risk management? And if risk management is of no use, then the corporate board should waste no time on it.

This picture of chaos theory and risk management, however, is inaccurate. Despite sensitive dependence on initial conditions, there are periods of self-organization and stability produced in chaotic systems. Within these windows of stability, short-term predictions are possible, although such prediction will be limited in accuracy. I will argue that risk management is possible in a chaotic framework. The key word for management in general as well as risk management in a chaotic world is "flexibility," which involves, I shall argue, a less hierarchical management structure with decentralization of authority. But this must be combined with accurate information sharing throughout the organization, from the board of directors down to the lowliest employee. There should be openness to new ideas at all levels as well as to the possibility that there may be multiple acceptable solutions to problems, willingness to change plans on the spot in response to contingencies, and a toleration of conflict within the corporation. These steps will allow a corporation to adapt to the multiple rapid changes in the current global economy as well as function to minimize risk.

Even in such a decentralized framework, the corporate board has a role to play in risk management. I shall list the characteristics of a corporate board that manages risks well, and suggests that up-to-date information about all facets of the corporation facilitates information-sharing among managers and other employees. This will help a board to anticipate short-term future events that may affect the company during periods of equilibrium, and will also make it easier to hire a CEO who will work for such innovations.

The first section of the paper will discuss risk management in general and current discussions of the role of the corporate board in risk management. The second section will discuss chaos theory and its application to risk management. The final section will outline characteristics of a board that help it to manage risk in a chaotic world.

Risk Management and the Corporate Board

Risk is an unavoidable part of life, including business life. David Garland notes that "Risk always exists in the context of uncertainty" (Garland, 2003: 52). In a world in which the memory of the past is sometimes flawed and our knowledge of the present is incomplete, it is no surprise that predicting the future is an uncertain task, involving, at best, probabilistic inferences. Because the future carries with it risks as well as opportunities, it is important for corporations to minimize risk as much as possible. It is impossible to eliminate risk entirely.

Risks to corporate health may be internal or external. Internal risks include, for example, overestimating demand for a product, or poor quality control leading to the manufacture of a flawed product. External risks include, for example, a crisis in the Middle East that disrupts oil supplies and the economy as a whole or unexpected competition from an entrepreneurial rival.

Much contemporary risk management has taken a utilitarian approach to risk. It is, as Tim Lewens states, "largely based on a quantitative methodology [that measures the severity of a risk] as the probability-weighed severity of the negative outcome the risk refers to. ... In other words, risk is defined as the product of probability and severity" (Lewens, 2007: 27). The standard utilitarian paradigm of risk management assumed that "actual" risks could be "objectively measured" (Garland, 2003: 55). Any qualitative differences between types of risk are ignored in favor of quantitative measurement; "risk is risk." If this were true, then it should be possible to give a near-exact numerical value of the probability and severity of particular risks to a company. The company could then choose the best courses of action based on a reasonably accurate prediction of both short- and long-term risks.

Despite the increased sophistication of utilitarian risk management under the influence of decision theory and game theory, the notion of a purely objective measurement of risk has come under attack. As Garland notes, rather than "risk" being in some purely objective world independent of particular forms of life, "risk assessments depend for their validity upon a prior system of categorization and metrics, which are in turn, grounded in specific conventions, and forms of life" (Garland, 2003: 56). In addition, as Martin Peterson points out, it is problematic to assume "that all risks and benefits have to be compared on a common scale" (Peterson, 2007: 70). He prefers a "multi-attribute approach," in which "each risk and benefit is measured in the unit deemed most suitable for that attribute" (Peterson, 2007: 70). For example, the measure of investment risk may be a monetary amount, but the measure of automobile safety may be the number of accidents and fatalities and injuries from those accidents.

Of course, the multi-attribute approach raises its own problems of measurement, for "the outcome of the decision process sometimes depends on which attribute is chosen" (Peterson, 2007: 74). Another problem with at least long-term prediction of risk, the findings of chaos theory, will be discussed in the next section of this paper.

The increasing emphasis on the role of the board of directors in corporate governance has been extended to risk management. In the United Kingdom, the Turnbull Report "requires embedded risk management to be a critical and integral part of managing the business" (Shimell, 2002a: 7), including both financial and non-financial risks. The Combined Code of the London Stock Exchange, which came into effect in 1999, required directors to:

- review the effectiveness of all internal controls, financial and non-financial;
- include a corporate governance compliance report in their annual report and accounts;

- ensure that performance-related remuneration formed a significant proportion of the executive's compensation package;
- incorporate challenging criteria in incentive schemes;
- name non-executive directors in their annual report;
- ensure that the remuneration committee and the majority of the audit committee were independent non-executive directors. (Shimell, 2002a: 6–7)

Pamela Shimell emphasizes the role of each employee in the company, from the board on down, to understand the risk management system; the system should be "enterprise-wide" (Shimell, 2002b: 103). She believes that if each employee participates in an "integrated" risk management strategy, which "should leave nothing to chance," the company will have "a universe of risk model which 'captures' all significant risks and identifies, analyzes, prioritizes, and manages those risks" (Shimell, 2002b: 103).

What is the level of responsibility of the board of directors in risk management? On the one hand, there is an increasing emphasis on the board of directors taking responsibility for and being actively involved in the process of risk management. On the other hand, as Peter Morgan points out, the new economy is less hierarchical than the old, with teamwork across the entire organization emphasized (Morgan, 2002: 62). The board of directors must play a leadership role in this model of risk management, but their role also includes a greater responsibility to communicate with the CEO, other executives, and "ordinary" employees as part of a corporate-wide risk management approach.

But chaos theory seems to make it impossible to predict risks accurately and the very prospect of risk management questionable. If risk management were problematic, then the corporate board as well as other company employees should opt out of a useless enterprise. The next section of the paper will discuss chaos theory and its application to risk management and show how risk management can survive in a world of chaos.

Chaos Theory and Risk Management

Chaos theory

Lately most discussion of chaos theory has been subsumed under the broader category of complexity theory, but in this paper I shall use the term "chaos theory." Chaos theory is really a group of theories dealing with certain kinds of deterministic behavior that paradoxically yield results that appear to be random (Lorenz, 1993: 4). Examples of such behavior are easy to find: the atmosphere is a chaotic system, as are waves in bodies of water and the human heartbeat. Long-term predictability is impossible in chaotic systems, since the randomness generated by chaos "is fundamental. Gathering more information does not make it go away" (Crutchfield et al., 1986: 46).

Chaotic systems are a subset of dynamical systems that "vary deterministically as time progresses" (Lorenz, 1993: 8) The futures of some dynamical systems (such as the future behavior of a swinging pendulum) are predictable, given knowledge of their initial conditions (such as the size and mass of the pendulum and speed of its motion) with a high degree of accuracy. Chaotic systems, on the other hand, are unpredictable due to their being "*sensitively dependent on initial conditions*" (Lorenz, 1993: 8; italics his). Henri Poincaré described this phenomenon in 1903:

> ... it may happen that small differences in the initial conditions produce very great ones in the final phenomena. A small error in the former will produce an enormous error in the latter. Prediction becomes impossible, and we have the fortuitous phenomenon. (Poincaré, cited in Crutchfield et al.: 48).

Systems do not have to be complex to exhibit chaotic behavior; even simple systems, such as drops from a water faucet, can become chaotic. It is possible in a slow drip to accurately predict when the next drop of water will fall, since they fall in a periodically regular pattern. But if the dripping reaches a critical stage, the pattern becomes irregular, and it will not be possible to predict exactly when the next drop will fall.

The notion of "sensitive dependence on initial conditions" has been popularized as "the butterfly effect" (Gleick, 1987: 20). The idea is that a butterfly flapping its wings in Brazil, for example, might cause a hurricane to develop off the coast of Africa. Seemingly minuscule changes in initial conditions can have massive effects on later stages of chaotic systems. It was Edward Lorenz who noticed this about the weather in 1961 – when he computed the same initial weather conditions into a computer, the results varied considerably (Gleick, 1987: 16–17). One reason for the variance is that the atmosphere is a chaotic system – no matter how much data about initial atmospheric conditions are fed into a computer, some initial conditions will be left out. It is, therefore, impossible in principle to accurately predict the weather beyond a relatively short period of time, and even then forecasters will sometimes be wrong. Such problems with prediction are found in all chaotic systems; as Crutchfield and his colleagues note:

> ... no exact solution, no short cut to tell the future, can exist. After a brief time interval the uncertainty specified by the initial measurement covers the

entire attractor [the "attractor" is the end point of the system's behavior] and all predictive power is lost: there is simply no causal connection between past and future. (Crutchfield et al., 1986: 53)

Now if chaos were only about unpredictability, its only use to a task such as weather forecasting would be to show that it is a futile effort beyond a short period of time. But "chaos" is not pure randomness; it only *seems* random. The equations of chaos are deterministic differential equations. What appears to be random is due to our intrinsic finitude – our inability to measure initial conditions in chaotic systems with enough accuracy to predict long-term results.[2]

There are "ordered patterns" in chaos theory; chaos theory has been characterized "as a search for *order*" (Kellert, 1993: 112; emphasis his). As Toby J. Tetenbaum puts it, "chaos describes a complex, unpredictable, and orderly disorder in which patters of behavior unfold in *irregular but similar* forms" (Tetenbaum, 1998: 24). She uses snowflakes in her example; although no two snowflakes are identical, each one is similar to another.[3]

Stable patterns arise in chaotic systems through "bifurcations," which produce both novelty and order. We have seen that small changes in chaotic systems can cause large-scale changes "in the system's behavior: from steady to almost periodic, or from steady, periodic, or almost periodic to chaotic" (Lorenz, 1993: 69). In such alternation, "chaos can change abruptly to more complicated chaos, and ... each of these changes can proceed in the opposite direction" (Lorenz, 1993: 69). The important point is that new order can arise from a bifurcation in a chaotic system. Periods of seemingly random behavior may be followed by periods of relative stability. In population dynamics, periods of relative stability in a population of a particular organism in an ecosystem are followed by periods of chaotic decreases or increases in population. Stock markets provide another example; periods of relative stability in the market are followed by periods of rapid change (such as the 1929 crash), after which a new equilibrium emerges.[4]

Since bifurcations can naturally occur in chaotic systems in response to very small changes, but lead to emergent properties and forms of order not found in earlier stages of the system, such systems are said to be "self-organizing" (Daneke, 1997: 253–4). Such self-organization is found in weather systems, in living organisms, and in biological evolution, but is also found in business. For example, no one person is responsible for the development of Silicon Valley or for the world economy, but such systems "emerged" over time (Tetenbaum, 1998: 25).

Nevertheless, although it is clear that long-term predictions are not possible in chaotic systems, there is still room for prediction at a more limited level. Weather forecasters, for example, can predict the weather with a high degree of accuracy for about a week in the future. Short-term prediction is possible in systems functioning "at the edge of chaos," because bifurcations occur in bounded patterns. Since the number of initial conditions is magnified, the larger the system, short-term predictions are not possible "on a global or comprehensive basis" but are possible on "an incremental or local basis" (Cartwright, 1991: 54). Computer modeling of such patterns, as takes place in modeling of atmospheric conditions, with accurate, up-to-the-minute data and a sufficient amount of data, can result in good short-term predictions of future behavior (Chorafas, 1994: 31–6).

Even though short-term predictions in chaotic systems will not be completely accurate and long-term prediction is impossible, chaos theory "accepts and recommends the idea of being aware of, having knowledge about, and anticipating the future" (Djavanshir & Khorramshahgol, 2006: 19). "Anticipating the future" involves being aware of the range of trajectories the future could take – and that range is limited. Although we may not be able to know the precise path the future will take, we can have a general idea, just as weather forecasters formulate their forecasts from a range of computer models (Cartwright, 1991: 53).

How chaos theory fits into risk management

Traditional risk management involves careful planning for future short-term and long-term contingencies. It is based on the assumption that we can, using mathematical models, predict the future with a high degree of accuracy. Chaos theory shows that this assumption is false. As Tony Burlando notes, "It is this preoccupation with predictability that has made the traditional sciences nearly worthless for risk management applications" (Burlando, 1994: 60).

An examination of business through time, whether such examination involves the history of a particular corporation or of the economy of the United States, reveals that business is a chaotic system. It is not, as A. Coskun Samli suggests in his application of chaos theory to marketing, "disorderly disorder" (Samli, 2007: 34). "Disorderly disorder" would be pure chaos, and pure chaos would be unknowable as well as unmanageable. Although markets do go through periods of relative stability and change; they are dynamic, but not in a totally disorderly way. There is a finite range of future possibilities, and prediction of short-term market trends may be possible – the more local the prediction the better.

The dynamics of a large corporation involve a number of variables: the financial health of the company, the relations between the employees, between the lower-level employees and management, and between upper management and the board of directors. Supply and demand for the company's goods and/or services can undergo rapid changes, and the company must make good decisions in response to such changes. External risks – trends in the global economy, wars or the threat of wars – can also threaten the health of a company and can come unexpectedly. Given the number of these variables and sensitive dependence on initial conditions, there is no way that long-term risk management can work under the old paradigm of predictability. However, risk management can be useful for a company if it takes account of the findings of chaos theory.

If there is any theme that resonates throughout the literature on business and chaos theory, this is the theme of "flexibility" or "adaptability" (Chorafas, 1994: 66; De Meyer, Loch, & Pich, 2002: 61; Daneke, 1997: 254; Djavanshir & Khorramshahgol, 2006: 20; Heyward & Preston, 1998: 180). The company should have a policy of flexibility in a world that is constantly changing. The same flexibility should be characteristic of risk management. Rather than being bound by plans that may not reflect the current condition of the company, companies should adapt "to the changing environment and its evolving rules" (Chorafas, 1994: 66). If a company sticks to "blueprints of results" rather than to a "capacity for adaptation" (Cartwright, 1991: 54), it may find itself reeling from risks it either did not consider as possibilities or underestimated. Sears, for example, assumed that customer loyalty to its brand name would remain even with new competition from K-Mart and Wal-Mart. The slowness of Sears' management to adapt to a rapidly changing market let to major profit losses in the 1980s (Beam, 1990: 11–12; Samli, 2007: xxii).

Adapting to a chaotic business world requires adequate information. As G. Reza Djavanshir and Reza Khorramshahgol note, "to create order out of chaos, information and knowledge sharing become critical factors: therefore, to ensure knowledge and information sharing and to promote the free flow of information, we must have effective information sharing knowledge management systems within organizations" (Djavanshir & Khorramshahgol, 2006: 21). Corporations should promote an open environment in which knowledge of what is going on in the company is shared with the entire workforce. Continuous learning, then, becomes a key part of dealing with chaos. As Toby Tetenbaum states, "Knowledge and information-sharing go hand-in-glove. The traditional practice of hoarding knowledge in order to enhance one's personal power is not only unacceptable in the new order; it will backfire" (Tetenbaum, 1998: 27). One can note the obvious fact that if Enron executives had shared their knowledge of what was really going on in the company outside their inner circle, disaster might have been averted. A positive example of knowledge sharing is Hewlett-Packard, who issues "an award called 'Not Invented Here.' It is an honor bestowed on a division that implements the most ideas from other divisions in the company" (Tentenbaum, 1998: 27).

The learning process is connected to the need for flexibility, since a company can only adapt to changing conditions if it has adequate knowledge of these conditions. The information gained by knowledge-sharing can be "seen as activating a process by which strategy can emerge across an organization" (Heyward & Preston, 1998: 179). Knowledge-sharing can aid in risk management by making a diverse workforce with different skills aware of any risks or potential risks the company might face.

But discussing risk (and other company issues) must also allow for a diversity of ideas. Today's business environment requires "innovation and creativity" and this should include "an environment that supports experimentation, risk-taking, and failure, and views trial-and-error as a viable process" (Tetenbaum, 1998: 27). Given sensitive dependence on rapidly changing initial conditions, such risk-taking is, paradoxically, the best way for a company to manage risk. Tetenbaum suggests that:

> To achieve a high level of creative thought, it is necessary to bring together diverse groups of people: people with different levels of expertise (including representatives of non-business disciplines), employees at all levels of the organization (representing a variety of ages, experiences, and backgrounds), people outside of the organization (customers, suppliers), and, above all, people representing a broad spectrum of ideas. (Tetenbaum, 1998: 28)

But for such a group to succeed, there must be "a high tolerance for conflict" (Tetenbaum, 1998: 28). Tetenbaum gives as an example 3M, which has "new recruits take a course with their supervisors on risk-taking in which they are explicitly taught to be willing to defy their supervisors," and such conflict stimulates innovation (Tetenbaum, 1998: 28). But a tolerance for conflict also aids in risk management, since employees will often point out problems or potential risks to the company only in an atmosphere of openness.

Information sharing across the company and openness to conflict require a less hierarchical management model. Although a corporation must have a hierarchical structure and a chain of command, management should be flexible and open, willing to receive input – and criticism – from employees in the company. Overly rigid, dictatorial managerial control of information and policy will not make for a successful company, since top managers may miss important risks that may be identified through a more relational approach to management in which each employee plays a role in risk management and in helping develop future company policy.

An important contribution of chaos theory to risk management arises from the fact that order can be found in chaos. The range of outcomes of a chaotic system can be predicted, albeit with some "fuzziness" (Burlando, 1994: 60). Managers, including those involved in risk management, can "identify a number of probable pathways" a chaotic system may take (Hayward and Preston, 1999: 175). The shorter the future prediction time, the more narrow the range of pathways will become and the more accurate the prediction of future risks and opportunities.

The more a person understands the relational dynamics through which changes occur in a company, the better the person will be at managing risks. Much of what goes on in an organization is driven by qualitative relationships between systems, subsystems – and people. One element of being able to predict short-term risk is understanding, as Ruth Anderson and her colleagues note, "the interdependencies and interactions among the elements that create the whole system" (Anderson et al., 2007: 673). Anderson et al. were researching problems in a nursing home, problems which led to tensions between regulators and nursing home management. These problems related to individual staff members misinterpreting patients' activities, such as crying and failure to eat, as temper tantrums rather than symptoms of depression. It was by understanding the narrative of human relationships in the nursing home that a solution to a global company problem was found (Anderson et al., 2007: 673–4). If such problems could be anticipated in advance, the relationship between regulators and management could be improved.

Risk management, then, should focus at the local level and on the short-term future, where potential problems can be identified that could later cause harm to the company. In some cases, qualitative analysis, involving a task as simple as talking with people and writing down a narrative of their interactions, may identify unexpected risks or help to manage problems that are already present.

Because chaotic systems are "self-organizing," and tend to settle down into a period of equilibrium after a period of turbulence, some writers have suggested creating intentional turbulence in a company to generate innovation. Samli suggests that creating intentional "disruptive innovations" is the best route to a company's "survival and success in the *short run*" (Samli, 2007: 74; see also Hayward & Preston, 1999: 179; Tetenbaum, 1998: 30). Cartwright suggests that "it may be easier to plan for a chaotic system by deliberately 'over-shooting' or 'under-shooting' the goal, or even by a sequence of such steps, than by going straight towards it. Planning for chaotic systems may be more successful when it is viewed as a succession of judicious 'nudges' rather than as a step-by-step recipe" (Cartwright, 1991: 54).[5] Thus the best way to avoid risk of catastrophic loss may be to "stir things up" in the company – but any such efforts should be based on the model of open sharing of knowledge so that the company makes wise decisions.

Risk Management, Chaos Theory, and the Corporate Board of Directors

The corporate board of directors must set an example of leadership in risk management. Board members have a responsibility to all stakeholders to be more than placeholders around a table and to do their part for the health of the corporation. Risk management in light of chaos theory still leaves a number of risk management tasks that can be performed by the board of directors. The list of six tasks is not necessarily exhaustive, but is a starting point for discussion on how the board can practically act in the process of risk management.

Set an example

Setting an example for the corporation would be an important task no matter what theory of risk management with which the company is operating. This implies good ethics, a commitment to do the work necessary to help with risk management, and the courage to take responsibility when things go wrong.

Gain knowledge

Board members must be as knowledgeable as possible about how the company operates, and this involves more than reading over and signing off on the financial and other reports. They should visit the various units of the company and talk not only to upper managers, but to employees at all levels. They should be familiar with both key internal relationships between people and units in the company and also with relationships that fan outside the company, such as those with customers, suppliers, and regulatory agencies. They should be aware of current market conditions, safety concerns about their products, and reactions to the quality (or lack thereof) of their products. The information they receive should be as current as possible given rapid shifts in the economy and sensitive dependence on initial, sometimes seemingly minuscule, conditions. If potential or actual risks are found, they should be aware of them and monitor management's reactions to such risks.

Set a climate of flexibility

Because flexibility is so important in managing chaos, the board must leave room for it. Board members should be open to a diversity of ideas, and this begins with the board itself. Board members should allow for conflict in their meetings – constructive conflict which leads to a good resolution. Whether the issue is hiring a new CEO or dealing with a threat to the market of the company's products, creative tension can help the board to find a workable solution.

Such openness should also extend to relations between the board and management. Managers should be encouraged to come up with new ideas and disagree with the board when they disagree with the direction the board is taking. While effective teamwork is important, effective teamwork often involves conflict – thus, it is wrong to interpret "team player" as "yes man."

Anticipate risks

Although accurate quantitative prediction is not possible in a chaotic world, it is possible to anticipate a range of risks that could affect the company. The board should have a sound enough overview of what is going on in the company to anticipate risks and take action to deal with those risks. If members of the board of Sears had anticipated the risk from K-Mart (and, later, Target and Wal-Mart), they may have been able to be proactive in hiring reform-minded managers who would move the company forward, perhaps by lowering prices (which is what the company eventually did anyway). Although short-term predictions would be better left to particular units of the company, the board should be aware of such predictions to better anticipate trends. Contingency management should be a part of the board's responsibility.

Hire innovators

The board should consider hiring managers who have a history of innovation and creative thinking, managers willing to tolerate conflicting ideas and come up with new solutions. The board could consider hiring managers that they know have different ideas for product development. But such managers should also be committed to working together – conflict is necessary in order to find the best solution to problems.

Make risk management company-wide

Finally, no one person or group of people in the company is responsible for risk management. The board should communicate to its managers and make it clear that every employee has responsibility for risk management. According to chaos theory, global problems can begin locally; thus, there is a need for employees at even the smallest factories and offices in the company to be aware of what is going on locally and to communicate potential risks. Management should be willing to listen to such employee concerns and act on them if they are legitimate. The more aware all employees are regarding risk management, and the more they are practically involved, the better prepared the company is to anticipate and deal with risks as they occur.

Notes

1   I appreciate the help Steven Magnusen, my student worker at Methodist University, gave me in research for this paper. I would also like to thank my colleague, Michael Colonnese, for proofreading and critiquing the paper.
2   Chaos theory does not tell us that the world is *metaphysically* indeterministic or unpredictable. The world may well be indeterministic; one route to argue for indeterminism would be an appeal to the indeterminism of quantum mechanics. But chaos theory does mean that determinism in the sense of *epistemological predictability* is no longer a viable option. Chaotic systems are, from a human point of view, unpredictable beyond constrained limits. For a detailed discussion of different senses of determinism and chaos theory, see Kellert, 1993: 49–76.
3   Such "self-similarity" is also characteristic of "fractals," particularly associated with the work of the mathematician Benoit Mandlebrot. A "fractal" is a set with a "fractional dimension" (Lorenz, 1993: 169). An example in nature of a fractal is a coastline. Computer-generated coastlines based on mathematical models reveal more eddies no matter how much the coastline is magnified. Although the particular pattern of eddies is different with each degree of magnification, "the degree of roughness or irregularity looks the same" (Gleick, 1987: 95). The patterns of change in chaotic systems have similar "irregularly regular" patterns.
4   Philosophers of science will notice a similarity to Thomas Kuhn's picture of the development of science in *The Structure of Scientific Revolutions* (Kuhn,

1970). Kuhn argues that in periods of "normal science," scientists working within a "paradigm" will attempt to solve problems within that paradigm. But anomalies build up until a crisis is reached. At some point, unpredictable in principle, a scientific revolution occurs, in which the old paradigm is replaced with a new paradigm. Scientific revolutions are similar to bifurcations in chaos theory.

5   Aristotle said something similar about ethics in his *Nicomachean Ethics*. He notes that for people prone to extreme behavior in morality, they must "drag [themselves] off in the contrary direction." He also notes that it is difficult to find the exact mean in ethics; often we must take "the lesser of evils" (Aristotle, 1999: p. 29 [II, 9, 1108b34–1109b7]). In managing a company it may be necessary to go to extremes in order to choose either one of a range of possible goods or the "lesser of evils."

References

Anderson, R.A., B.F. Crabtree, D.J. Steele, and R.R. McDaniel. 2007. Case study research: the view from complexity science. *Qualitative Health Research*, 15(5) (May): 669–85.

Aristotle. 1999. *Nicomachean Ethics*. Translated by Terence Irwin. 2nd edition. Indianapolis: Hackett Publishing Company.

Beam, H.H. 1990. Strategic discontinuities: when being good may not be good enough – strategic business planning. *Business Horizons*, July–August: 10–14.

Burlando, T. 1994. Chaos theory and risk management. *Risk Management*, 41(4) (April): 54–61.

Cartwright, T.J. 1991. Planning and chaos theory. *Journal of the American Planning Association*, 57(1) (Winter): 44–57.

Chorafas, D.M. 1994. *Chaos Theory in Financial Markets: Applying Fractals, Fuzzy Logic, Genetic Algorithms, Swarm Simulation & the Monte Carlo Method to Manage Market Chaos and Volatility*. Chicago and Cambridge: Probus Publishing Company.

Crutchfield, J.P., J.D. Farmer, N.H. Packard, and R.S. Shaw. 1986. Chaos. *Scientific American*, 255(6) (December): 46–57.

Daneke, G.A. 1997. From metaphor to method: nonlinear dynamics and practical management. *The International Journal of Organizational Analysis*, 5(3) (July): 249–66.

De Meyer, A., C.H. Loch, and M.T. Pich. 2002. Managing project uncertainty: from variation to chaos. *MIT Sloan Management Review*, 43(2) (Winter): 60–7.

Djavanshir, G.R. and R. Khorramshahgol. 2006. Applications of chaos theory for mitigating risks in telecommunication systems planning in global competitive market. *Journal of Global Competitiveness*, 14(1) (July): 15–24.

Garland, D. 2003. The rise of risk. In R.V. Ericson and A. Doyles (eds), *Risk and Morality*. Toronto: University of Toronto Press.

Gleick, J. 1987. *Chaos: Making a New Science*. New York: Viking.

Hayward, T. and J. Preston. 1999. Chaos theory, economics, and information: the implications for strategic decision-making. *Journal of Information Science*, 25(3) 173–82.

Kellert, S.H. 1993. *In the Wake of Chaos*. Chicago: University of Chicago Press.

Kuhn, T. 1970. *The Structure of Scientific Revolutions*. Chicago: University of Chicago Press.

Lewens, T. 2007. Introduction: risk and philosophy. In T. Lewens (ed.), *Risk: Philosophical Perspectives*. London and New York: Routledge.

Lorenz, E. 1993. *The Essence of Chaos*. Seattle: University of Washington Press.

Morgan, P. 2002. New economy risks. In T. Lewens (ed.), *Risk: Philosophical Perspectives*. London and New York: Routledge.

Peterson, M. 2007. Multi-attribute risk analysis. In T. Lewens (ed.), *Risk: Philosophical Perspectives*. London and New York: Routledge.

Samli, A.C. 2007. *Chaotic Markets: Thriving in a World of Unpredictability*. Westport, CT and London: Praeger.

Shimell, P. 2002a. What is risk? In P. Shimell (ed.), *The Universe of Risk: How Top Business Leaders Control Risk and Achieve Success*. London: Financial Times/Prentice-Hall.

Shimell, P. 2002a. The risk model. In P. Shimell (ed.), *The Universe of Risk: How Top Business Leaders Control Risk and Achieve Success*. London: Financial Times/Prentice-Hall.

Solomon, R. and C. Martin. 2004. *Above the Bottom Line: An Introduction to Business Ethics*. Belmont, CA: Thomson-Wadsworth.

Tetenbaum, T.J. 1998. Shifting paradigms: from Newton to chaos. *Organizational Dynamics*, 26(4) (Spring): 21–32.

3

Anti-Social Norms, Risky Behavior

Reza Dibadj[1]

Introduction

To understand how boards can serve as both managers and creators of risk, a prerequisite would be to have a satisfactory framework within which to conceptualize board behavior. Unfortunately, such a basic structure is lacking. This chapter explores this curious anomaly and proposes that the intersection of boards and risk can only be understood through a counter-intuitive application of sociological norms. Only once existing misconceptions are set aside can reform follow.

The argument is structured in three parts. Part I explores the limitations of conventional models: neoclassical economics, industrial organization (IO), and institutional economics. It also explores why the behavioral project – whether expressed through behavioral economics or organizational behavior (OB) – is incomplete. Based on the notion of "organizational behavioral economics," Part II then proposes a structure within with to understand board behavior using the concept of norms. Finally, Part III presents suggestions for reform, with an emphasis on enhancements to corporate and criminal law.

Part I: Limitations of Conventional Models

Conventional economic models – whether neoclassical economics, IO, or even institutional economics – have provided unsatisfactory frameworks with which to model boards. For its part, the behavioral project – whether behavior economics or OB – is still incomplete.

Mainstream concepts

Traditional microeconomics has done a lousy job modeling how boards of directors manage risk. To the neoclassical economist, the board is simply a highly stylized "black box" – inputs go in one end, outputs come out the other, and profits are magically maximized in the process.[2] As Harold Demsetz points out, "[t]he chief mission of neoclassical economics is to understand how the price system coordinates the use of resources, not to understand the inner workings of real firms."[3]

IO, which necessarily pays more attention to organization, offers only very limited improvement. The two most significant insights in the IO tradition have been recognition that profit maximization is a fanciful representation of actual board behavior, and the introduction of game-theoretic tools – each contribution, however, is incomplete. First, while moving beyond a single-minded belief in profit maximization is an important analytical refinement, it merely replaces one simplistic utility function with another; namely, profits with sales. Second, traditional game theory, which has its roots in John Nash's celebrated paper,[4] remains wedded to Nash's idealization of the bargaining problem where he assumes that the players "are highly rational, that each can accurately compare his desires for various things, that they are equal in bargaining skill, and that each has full knowledge of the tastes and preferences of the other."[5] Unfortunately, modeling the behavior of boards of directors may not be as simple as assuming rational actors to derive the Nash equilibrium.[6] Put starkly, economists can push the theory of the firm only so far by remaining focused on the orthodox notion of microanalytic equilibria drawn from assumptions of individual rationality.[7]

For its part, the emerging field of institutional economics does squarely attempt to develop an understanding of the firm that goes well beyond the economic orthodoxy. The field has its roots in Ronald Coase's famous and fundamental insight that firms and markets are different: since markets settle via prices, the "main reason why it is profitable to establish a firm would seem to be that there is a cost of using the price mechanism."[8] In other words, "the distinguishing mark of the firm is the supersession of the price mechanism."[9]

Crucially, contract becomes to Coase's "entrepreneur-co-ordinator"[10] what the price mechanism is to the market: each becomes a method of organizing economic relations. Contracting, in turn, involves transaction costs which include "the costs of identifying the parties with whom one has to bargain, the costs of getting together with them, the costs of the bargaining process itself, and the costs of enforcing any bargain reached."[11]

According to this line of thinking, the study of the firm thus becomes a study of transaction costs. Thus, as Coase himself suggests, "in the absence of transaction costs, there is no economic basis for the existence of the firm"[12] – indeed, the "limit to the size of the firm is set where its costs of organizing a transaction become equal to the cost of carrying it out through the market."[13]

A specific type of transaction cost purportedly provides insight into board behavior: agency cost. In a nutshell, the term captures "the inevitable conflicts of interest that occur when individuals engage in cooperative behavior."[14] More concretely, as Michael Jensen and William Meckling articulate in their celebrated article, *Theory of the Firm*:

> We define an agency relationship as a contract under which one or more persons (the principal(s)) engage another person (the agent) to perform some service on their behalf which involves delegating some decision making authority to the agent. *If both parties to the relationship are utility maximizers there is good reason to believe that the agent will not always act in the best interests of the principal.*[15]

What concerns Jensen and Meckling is how to minimize the welfare loss, or agency costs,[16] inherent in the agency relationship. While agency costs are ubiquitous,[17] their approach has a special appeal in the context of the modern public corporation, where the separation of ownership and control – between a large group of dispersed shareholders and a small group of inside directors and managers – remains the central problem of corporate governance.[18]

But how to minimize agency costs? Agency theorists have suggested a number of putative constraints to protect shareholder-principals.[19] These include aligning shareholder interests to managers' compensation, the use of debt and outside ownership as a disciplining tool, the threat of takeovers, and competitive labor markets.[20] Most importantly for our purposes, however, agency theorists argue that a board – in particular its outside directors – also serves as a mechanism to discipline self-serving agents.[21] This seductive idea has crossed over from the economics literature to the legal literature on corporate governance. Note, for instance, how one prominent legal scholar defends boards of directors:

> During the 1980s and 1990s, several trends coalesced to encourage more active and effective board oversight. Much director compensation is now paid in stock, for example, which helps align director and shareholder interests. ... modern boards of directors are typically smaller than their antecedents, meet more often, are more independent from management, own more stock, and have better access to information.[22]

Yet despite such optimistic pronouncements, a slew of recurring scandals amply demonstrate that independent directors have, at best, had mixed success in making boards provide better oversight of risk.

Why has the independent director – after all, a central constraint in the world of the agency theorist – been unable to rein in loose agents? One perceptive analysis of this puzzle is provided in Gerald Frug's humorous explanation of the unrealistic expectations traditional corporate governance place on what an outside director might actually be able to accomplish:

> Into the chaos of the world of the expertise model, they [theorists who legitimize bureaucracy] insert a figure truly worthy of comic-book adventure stories: Super-Expert. … In corporate law … he could assume a position within the bureaucracy itself by becoming a so-called "independent" or "outside" director of the company. In such a role, he would be responsible for monitoring the activities of the pseudo-experts – the "inside" directors and the corporate executives – either on issues within his special area of expertise or on matters considered particularly suspect. … To bring a truly outside perspective to bear on corporate transactions, an outside director would have to be fully insulated from the vision of the world that renders inside directors' self-approval of their own activities suspect. To possess this kind of objectivity, Super-Expert might have to come from Krypton.[23]

Frug derives a crucial conclusion: "[o]nly in our imagination can a super-hero be sufficiently outside the world to remain unprejudiced by contacts with it yet still be able to intervene effectively in the world to prevent might from making right."[24] No wonder that the board of directors rarely serves as a forceful check on the often risky activities of senior management.

While scholars continue to refine and apply agency theory,[25] its empirical results leave much to be desired. Part of the answer may lie in the fact that for all its admirable focus on trying to understand the internal workings of firms, agency theory remains wedded, at its core, to the simplifying, nonfalsifiable assumptions of neoclassical economics. After all, its fundamental contention is that the "behavior of organizations is the *equilibrium* behavior of a complex contractual system made up of *maximizing agents* with diverse and conflicting objectives."[26] Developing a better approach to firm behavior requires questioning this central assumption. Boards cannot be simply conceptualized as facilitating a series of efficient contracts.

Behavioral project

The untidy nature of contracting among firm players – who might not necessarily espouse rationality or efficiency – is precisely what limits the usefulness of institutional economics. Any realistic inquiry into the behavior of the firm must thus necessarily venture beyond rational agents contracting with each other.

An emerging group of scholars in behavioral law and economics has begun using methods and data from the social sciences – notably cognitive psychology – to challenge the assumptions of neoclassical microeconomics. Two of the field's pioneers, Amos Tversky and Daniel Kahneman summarize well the fundamental methodology: "people rely on a limited number of heuristic principles [rules of thumb] which reduce the complex tasks of assessing probabilities and predicting values to simpler judgmental operations"[27] – "[t]hese heuristics are highly economical and usually effective, but they lead to systematic and predictable errors."[28] In the landscape of behavioral economics, "people exhibit bounded rationality, bounded self-interest, and bounded willpower."[29] An approach seeking to understand cognitive biases and limitations stands in striking contrast to the neoclassical "Chicago School" of law and economics where rational actors go about their business magically maximizing their utility.[30]

Behavioral economists have studied two psychological traits that have particular relevance in the context of boards of directors as both managers and sources of risk: overconfidence and the self-serving bias. Perhaps the psychological reality of overconfidence is simplest to conceptualize. As Donald Langevoort summarizes:

> One of the most robust findings in the literature on individual decisionmaking is that of the systematic tendency of people to overrate their own abilities, contributions, and talents. This egocentric bias readily takes the form of excessive optimism and overconfidence, coupled with an inflated sense of ability to control events and risks.[31]

This feature has been well-studied in the context of individuals.[32] Langevoort is the rare scholar, however, who notes the special importance of overconfidence in the context of organizational behavior:

> High levels of self-esteem and self-efficacy are associated with aggressiveness, perseverance, and optimal risk-taking. *These biases may be particularly adaptive in business settings, where decisiveness and aggressiveness are considered indicators of a successful manager.* Certainly, overconfidence at times leads to disaster and severe career failure. Those who fail too visibly are often weeded out. However, there is little evidence that successful managers learn humility very well.[33]

Overconfidence can help explain a variety of business behaviors. Take, for instance, William Bratton's observation on the reasons behind the

Enron fiasco, which applies equally well to any of a number of corporate scandals:

> The firm [Enron] collapsed for the most mundane of reasons – its managers suffered the behavioral biases of successful entrepreneurs. They overemphasized the upside and lacked patience. They pursued heroic short-term growth numbers that their business plan could not deliver. That pursuit of immediate shareholder value caused them to become risk-prone, engaging in levered speculation, earnings manipulation, and concealment of critical information.[34]

Closely related to the overconfidence bias is the "self-serving" bias, "the term used to describe the observation that actors often interpret information in ways that serve their interests or preconceived notions."[35] This bias, in turn, can help explain board behaviors that would seem puzzling under the rational actor model.

Exacerbating individual cognitive biases is the simple fact that boards typically involve people working together as a group. As Robert Shiller notes, "[p]eople who interact with each other regularly tend to think and behave similarly."[36] A phenomenon, typically labeled "groupthink" or "herding,"[37] emerges, where "groupthink causes members of a group to unconsciously generate shared illusions of superiority that hinder critical reflection and reality testing."[38] The mechanism that underlies this phenomenon is a desire by members of the group to be judged favorably by their superiors and peers,[39] leading to facile consensus at the expense of constructive dissent.[40]

Perhaps the herding bias sheds additional light on why, much to the chagrin of agency theorists, boards of directors are not as effective as they might be in reducing agency costs. After all, the boards of many large corporations are composed of "like-minded people, insulated from others"[41] – in such an environment, groupthink may exacerbate already overconfident beliefs that all will go well: hindering challenge of, for instance, dubious accounting policies or unrealistic profit targets. Careful risk management too often becomes a secondary consideration.

To be sure, then, an understanding of individual biases such as overconfidence, combined with the phenomenon of groupthink, can help shed light on why boards may be flawed managers of risk. Unfortunately, however, behavioral economics does not provide further insight than pointing to these behavior biases. This shortfall, however, is to be expected given that behavioral economists focus on individuals, not institutions such as boards, as their unit of analysis. As one scholar succinctly notes, "[t]o date, organizational economics has not been a leading area for applications of behavioral economics."[42] Taking the step from "behavioral economics" to true "organizational behavioral economics" requires greater emphasis on organizational structures, or what goes on in the interstitial spaces among individuals within the firm.

Fortunately, organizational behavior (OB), a vibrant area of research in business schools, tries to get beyond mechanistic reporting relationships to understand power, influence, and culture – all essential to understanding how boards manage risk. As Robert Gibbons emphasizes:

> Organizational sociologists have long emphasized the distinction between formal and informal aspects of organizational structure. Formal aspects include official job descriptions and reporting relationships, as well as formal contracts. Informal aspects include norms and mutual understandings, as well as networks of non-reporting relationships among individuals. Roughly speaking, the formal structure is the organization chart, whereas *the informal structure is the way things really work.*[43]

In contrast to behavioral economics' focus on psychology, OB introduces a sociological component. Take, for instance, the striking similarity between OB's concern with informal power relations and Mark Granovetter's sociological argument that "the behavior of institutions to be analyzed are so constrained by ongoing social relations that to construe them as independent is a grievous misunderstanding"[44] OB then, much like behavioral economics, presents a step forward.

While squarely focused on understanding what makes organizations such as boards actually tick, OB is unfortunately too often based on anecdotal case studies rather than falsifiable theories. Sadly, economics has done a poor job modeling the insights of OB. The neoclassical "black box" theory simply isn't interested. IO has not done much better. Institutional economics – while occasionally making reference to the realities of organizational life[45] – continues to view organizational arrangements as an efficient contractual response to transaction costs. There is a huge gap in conventional approaches.

Part II: Toward Norms

Each of the approaches so far helps fill in one part of the puzzle of firm behavior. The institutionalists have encouraged looking inside the "black box" of neoclassical fame, but remain wedded to pseudo-scientific notions of "efficiency" and "maximization." Behavioral economics, for its part, counsel us to look beyond such nonfalsifiable rationalizations, but do not tell us how to aggregate individual psychological foibles. OB wisely counsels us to look at power, influence, and culture, but does not seem to offer a structured framework.

The central challenge to understanding the intersection of boards and risk, then, becomes developing "organizational behavioral economics" by blending the economic framework of behavioral law and economics with the institutional focus of organizational behavior. Put slightly differently, going from behavioral economics to organizational behavioral economics necessarily requires some sort of aggregation theory: how can a theory of the firm be derived from the strengths and foibles of individual actors? We need some way of going from the individual heuristics of the behavioralists to the insightful anecdotes about how boards actually behave – how they manage risk and become sources of risk.

Adapting and reapplying the concept of social norms may be the key to developing an aggregation theory, and, in doing so, reconceptualizing how we think about boards. Appreciating the centrality of norms to organizational life will necessarily require an interdisciplinary approach – integrating insights not only from law and economics, but also from psychology, sociology, and even anthropology.

Norms are typically conceptualized as positive: "informal social regularities that individuals feel obligated to follow because of an internalized sense of duty, because of a fear or external non-legal sanctions, or both."[46] To use norms fruitfully to understand how boards deal with risk, however, requires moving away from the conventional notion that they necessarily represent positive social phenomena such as trust and fairness. Put bluntly, it is important to recognize that norms can also be negative.

Richard McAdams' esteem theory of norms is particularly illuminating if applied to an analysis of board behavior. McAdams argues that "the initial force behind norm creation is the desire individuals have for *respect* or *prestige*, that is, for the relative *esteem* of others."[47] To boot, "[o]n average, the smaller the group, the more intensely esteem is valued."[48] Furthermore, "the relative advantages that small, close-knit groups enjoy in enforcing norms make it possible for them to enforce norms that run contrary to the norms of society."[49] This last point is crucial to a new understanding of norms, since it implies that groups can develop norms that are counter to those society would cherish.[50] McAdams is thus able to provide elegant theoretical underpinnings to the counterintuitive view that norms can reduce welfare.[51]

To add insult to injury, groups can develop self-reinforcing mechanisms that keep in place dangerous norms:

> Once the norm becomes harmful, why do individuals not recognize as much and scale down the norm? Here, the problem is strategic. Once the norm

exists, there is a price to norm criticism. For strong norms, secondary enforcement norms will typically require punishing anyone who challenges the primary norm. Thus, esteem competition can make very costly any individual behavior designed to "brake" the escalation of norm enforcement. Inefficiently high norm activity levels may therefore be an equilibrium.[52]

The bottom line is simple and disturbing: norms are useful in analyzing boards and, once powerful and destructive norms are embedded, they can lead to disaster. While the recurring instances of poor risk management are poorly explained using conventional economics, they are rather easily explained by viewing poor risk management as a manifestation of anti-social norms.

Understanding how boards work requires learning from sociologists who recognize that "both order *and* disorder, honesty *and* malfeasance have more to do with structures of such relations than they do with organizational form."[53] Many of the distasteful activities we have witnessed boards allow – fudging accounting statements, lying to employees and prosecutors, flaunting conflict of interest rules, and the like – are puzzling to more conventional interpretations of board behavior precisely because these activities cannot be explained through the lens of rational actors going about maximizing utility.

But seen through a norms-based lens, a clearer picture emerges. Boards, like any tightly-knit group, develop norms. Board members often come from similar social backgrounds. Some even enjoy interlocking directorships. They are looking to enhance their social and financial status, to be judged favorably by their peers or by management. In such an environment, a norm of facile consensus emerges at the expense of constructive dissent. Behavioral biases – overconfidence, the self-serving bias, and herding – only fuel the dysfunctionality.

Board members are, in the sociologist's parlance, "embedded" in a network of social relations which exerts pressure on them to take risks a rational actor might view as stupid, even suicidal. As Mark Granovetter insightfully notes, "[m]anagers who evade audits and fight over transfer pricing are acting nonrationally in some strict economic sense, in terms of a firm's profit maximization; *but when their position and ambitions in intrafirm networks and political coalitions are analyzed, the behavior is easily interpreted.*"[54] Similarly, other commentators have noted the importance of "thinking about organizations in terms of structural pressure to engage in unlawful behavior"[55] or shown how "economic condition was more or less irrelevant to the question of law-breaking."[56]

In the realm of corporate governance, even the discourse of agency theorists has gone from not understanding "why boards of directors are so easily, and unprofitably, influenced by implicit political pressures"[57] to a more nuanced realization:

> Board culture is an important component of board failure. The great emphasis on politeness and courtesy at the expense of truth and frankness in boardrooms is both a symptom and cause of failure in the control system. CEOs have the same insecurities and defense mechanisms as other human beings; few will accept, much less seek, the monitoring and criticism of an active and attentive board.[58]

Boards cannot be modeled as rational actors engaged in maximizing behavior, but rather as a series of messy interactions between social creatures vying for esteem – and hence, power, influence, and all the other perquisites of the "good life." Hardly a satisfactory recipe for managing risk.

Part III: Proposals for Reform

If there is merit in the argument that boards are social creatures that evolve often dangerous norms, then public law has an important role to play. Government must serve as a countervailing force to the dangerous norms that boards perpetrate. The overarching thrust of reform should be to encourage positive norms, and, perhaps more importantly, discourage negative norms.[59] I suggest reform of corporate law and criminal sanctions as a starting point for discussion.

Corporate law, which putatively regulates corporate governance, is to a large extent based on the "firm as contract" mantra. This, of course, brings with it all the fallacies of the contractarian ideology[60] – assuming, for example, that parties to the corporate contract are rational actors[61] with equal bargaining power.[62] In large part based on these faulty assumptions, state corporate law currently represents little more than specialized contract law and does little, if anything, to manage risk: enabling statutes around which parties can putatively contract, and fiduciary duties that are little more than rhetorical flourish circumvented by clever procedural maneuvers. Layer upon this the usual indemnification clause and insurance, and directors have virtually unlimited discretion to take risks. Put simply, the law serves as a very weak check on their power. Scandals, of course, erupt with troubling frequency. Conveniently, rather than re-examine why basic state corporate law is empty, layer upon layer of complex federal legislation and regulation is added in large part to manage risk – Sarbanes–Oxley is but the most recent example.

Fortunately, there is a far more effective and less confusing approach: give teeth to state corporate law. Current corporate law couches fiduciary duties in vague terms. Yet, as Donald Langevoort argues, "[w]hat does seem likely is that highly indeterminate legal standards – such as those based on 'reasonableness' or 'good faith' – will have a less direct impact on firm behavior than we would like to think. The managerial bias is to perceive the firm's actions as both reasonable and in good faith."[63] Further, the business judgment rule gives managers almost unlimited protection. As one commentator notes, "[t]he purported duty of managers to maximize shareholder wealth can be almost meaningless because the business judgment rule gives corporate managers enormous discretion in deciding how to try to generate profits."[64] The upshot is a group of insulated directors and managers who enjoy extraordinary legal leeway.[65] In such a permissive legal environment, it is perhaps no surprise that some would be overly aggressive risk takers – not only poor managers of risk, but actually sources of risk.[66]

Beyond eminently reasonable proposals to give shareholders greater say in corporate elections,[67] one way out of this mess is to give fiduciary duties much greater teeth[68] while de-emphasizing the business judgment rule. There are a multitude of reasons that support this perspective, provided one is willing to move beyond the facile assumptions of a contractual, inherently private vision of what a board does.

Reformers need to focus on the pernicious aspects of board culture and design laws to change behavior. A few illustrative examples should hopefully drive the point home. If directors are overconfident and tend to dismiss early warnings of trouble for the firm,[69] then corporate law should impose a fiduciary duty to warn of impending trouble such as bankruptcy.[70] To begin remedying vast and increasing income inequality within the corporate hierarchy, the board might have a fiduciary duty to its employees.[71] If the corporate ethos does not take conflicts of interest seriously, then the law needs to restrict events like related-party transactions.[72] If informational cascades prevent bad news from reaching the top of the corporate food chain, then we need to relax the scienter requirements for fraud liability.[73] Each time, the pattern is the same: focus on the organizational behavioral problem, then design countervailing public policy.

Lest these sound like impractical proposals, it is important to remember that making fiduciary duties meaningful while de-emphasizing the business judgment rule is nothing but a simple and intuitive reform: making "standards of review" congruent with "standards of conduct." This is really only tantamount to asking courts to hold board members to manage risk with a reasonable level of care and loyalty – the way judges generally hold citizens in society. This would not only accord with the vast body of doctrine outside corporate law, but would also make judicial review simpler and more meaningful at the same time. It is time to begin asking why state corporate law has been conspicuously absent in the wake of board scandals; put bluntly, it would be difficult to argue that the perpetrators in the recent corporate scandals were either careful or loyal.

Beyond traditional doctrinal reform, instituting mechanisms to prevent dangerous herding is also an area ripe for exploration. Cass Sunstein's observation, made in the context of the public sphere, applies with equal force to private firms: "cohesive groups of like-minded people whose members are connected by close social ties often suppress dissent and reach inferior decisions, whereas heterogeneous groups, building identification through focus on a common task rather than through other social ties, tend to produce the best outcomes."[74] Corporate law must understand this tendency, and encourage diversity in corporate discourse,[75] especially at the board level. For example, it should develop mechanisms to ensure that at least one board member at each meeting actively encourages alternative viewpoints.[76] Board diversity also needs to be increased,[77] perhaps even to include employees' representatives.[78] Other possibilities commentators have proposed are also worth discussing, including separating the role of chairman and CEO, and even fostering a class of professional directors without the usual thick web of social ties. Corporate law's attempt to improve the board's risk management thus needs to be twofold: a relentless focus on creating legal safeguards, and at the same time and encouragement of the selection of decision makers who are less insular.

Beyond corporate law, legal reform must also address how boards envision the risk of criminal punishment. A complementary possibility is to reframe criminal sanctions to increase their deterrent effect. One might, for instance, adopt ideas developed in the context of street crime to white collar crime. As one scholar has shown, an "order-maintenance" strategy – one in which law enforcement places an emphasis on visible responses to criminal activity[79] – is both cheaper and more effective "than simply 'raising the price' of serious crimes through either investments in law enforcement or longer terms of imprisonment."[80] The underlying reason for this rather puzzling anomaly, one which contradicts basic tenets of neoclassical economics, is that order-maintenance conveys a message about the social unacceptability of criminality:

> The level of crime, this account suggests, turns not just on the price of crime but also on the direction of social influence. A strategy of low-certainty/high-severity can create social meanings that point social influence toward criminality. This is so because of what a low probability of conviction does to the norms of law-breakers and what severe punishments express to law abiders.[81]

Today, the law by and large tries to deter corporate malfeasance with a low-certainty/high-severity punishment regime. Perhaps it is little surprise that this strategy has had, at best, mixed success.

To the extent we can pay attention to the norms that underlie criminal activity in the organizational context, then criminal law should move to a high-certainty/low-severity regime whose "beneficial effects ... on the direction of social influence might well compensate for what appears to be a greater-than-optimal investment in certainty of conviction."[82] The intersection of criminal and business law should be driven by an understanding of how boards create and react to social meaning.

Conclusion

Traditional microeconomics has been ineffectual in modeling how boards of directors manage risk. The "firm as contract" mantra of the institutional economists, though elegant, is left wanting. The behavioralists, true to their psychological lens, are focused on individuals. OB scholars attack the right issues, but lack a satisfying framework.

This essay has argued that there is an overarching need for "organizational behavioral economics," a discipline that unfortunately has yet to emerge. In particular, one way out of the confusion is to conceptualize the firm as a series of relationships that promote norms. Specifically, to understand the intersection of boards and risk, the board needs to be reconceptualized as an entity that evolves norms within a social construct, some positive but many destructive. Making boards better managers of risk desperately cries for revamping the legal framework. Corporate and criminal law would be two good places to begin.

Notes

1 I thank Professors Robert W. Kolb and Donald Schwartz of the Center for Integrated Risk Management and Corporate Governance, Loyola University Chicago Graduate School of Business, for the opportunity to present this article in Chicago, Illinois on April 17, 2008. This work builds upon previous efforts, including Dibadj (2006), Dibadj (2005a), and Dibadj (2005b).
2 See, e.g., Jensen & Meckling (1976: 306).
3 Demsetz (1983: 377).
4 Nash (1950).

5 Nash (1950: 155).
6 Cf. Ellickson (1991: 159: "Because game theorists make use of the rational-actor model, they assume that players want to maximize their individual pay-offs.").
7 See also Leibenstein (1979: 477: "The question of how individuals in multi-person firms influence firm decisions seems like such a natural question to ask that it is amazing that it is not part of the formal agenda of economists as a profession. ... Part of the reason for this lies in the maximizing and optimizing biases of conventional micro theory.").
8 Coase (1937: 390).
9 Coase (1937: 389).
10 Coase (1937: 389).
11 Polinksy (1989: 12). See also Dahlman (1979: 148: transaction costs include "search and information costs, bargaining and decision costs, policing and enforcement costs").
12 Coase (1988: 14).
13 Coase (1988: 7).
14 Jensen (1993: 870).
15 Jensen & Meckling (1976: 308; emphasis added).
16 Jensen and Meckling define agency costs "as the sum of: (1) the monitoring expenditures by the principal, (2) the bonding expenditures by the agent, and (3) the residual loss" (Jensen & Meckling, 1976: 308).
17 Jensen & Meckling (1976: 309: "agency costs arise in any situation involving cooperative effort").
18 Indeed, this divergence is central to Berle and Means' seminal text on corporate organization. See Berle & Means (1932).
19 Cf. Baldwin (1964: 253: "under appropriate external and organizational restraints, the activities of a managerial group can be directed towards an organizational goal of profits without undue conflict.").
20 See generally, Jensen & Meckling (1976).
21 See, e.g., Fama & Jensen (1983: 314: "Given that the board is to be composed of experts, it is natural that its most influential members are internal managers since they have valuable specific information about the organization's activities. It is also natural that when the internal decision control system works well, the outside members of the board are nominated by internal managers.").
22 Bainbridge (2002: 9).
23 Frug (1984: 1328–9).
24 Frug (1984: 1331).
25 See, e.g., Triantis (2004: 1108–9: "The internal capital markets explanation of organizational boundaries is a financial agency theory, and like other theories of this type, it is based on a premise that competition in external markets promotes the emergence of efficient financing and governance arrangements. ... Thus, the market for corporate control and the market for managers may be two continuing checks on such midstream misbehavior.").

26   Jensen (1983: 327). See also Jensen & Meckling, "Theory of the Firm" (1976: 307: "We retain the notion of maximizing behavior on the part of all individuals in the analysis to follow.").

27   Tversky & Kahneman (1974: 1124).

28   Tversky & Kahneman (1974: 1131). See also Korobkin & Ulen (2000: 1069: "actors often fail to maximize their expected utility, but instead make suboptimal choices among competing options given a set of preferences and use a range of heuristics – rules of thumb – rather than complex cost–benefit analysis").

29   Jolls et al. (1998: 1471).

30   See, e.g., Harris (2003: 665: "Chicago School law and economics scholars claimed to be interested not only in legal rules but also in how legal incentives affect individuals' behavior. However, their research did not focus on studying the behavior of individuals, and the behavior of societies and basic social structures and trends was entirely beyond the scope of their research agenda.").

31   Langevoort (1997: 139).

32   See, e.g., Griffin & Tversky (1992: 432: "The significance of overconfidence to the conduct of human affairs can hardly be overstated.").

33   Langevoort (1997: 153–4) (emphasis added).

34   Bratton (2002: 1283).

35   Korobkin & Ulen (2000: 1093).

36   Shiller (1995: 181).

37   See also Cooter (2000: 8: "People are notoriously susceptible to group pressures, which are variously described as conformity, herd effects, or social solidarity.").

38   O'Connor (2003: 1238–9). O'Connor draws on the pioneering work of Irving Janis.

39   See, e.g., Sunstein (2000: 88: "The first explanation of group polarization – social comparison – begins with the claim that people want to be perceived favorably by other group members and also to perceive themselves favorably.").

40   See, e.g., Sunstein (2000: 92: "social ties among deliberating group members tend to suppress dissent and in that way lead to inferior decisions.").

41   Sunstein (2000: 105).

42   Gibbons (2003: 16).

43   Gibbons (2000: 35) (emphasis added).

44   Granovetter (1985: 482). Granovetter concludes that "power relations cannot be neglected" (1985: 502).

45   See, e.g., Coase (1988: 62: "A workman does not move from Department Y to Department X because the price in X has risen enough relative to the price in Y to make the move worthwhile for him. He moves from Y to X because he is ordered to do so."); Williamson (1967: 134–5: "We, therefore, borrow from the bureaucracy literature the proposition that control loss occurs between successive hierarchical levels (and that this tends to be cumulative) and introduce it into a theory of the firm").

46 McAdams (1997: 340). See also Cooter (2000: 1580: "a norm can be defined as an obligation backed by a nonlegal sanction. Sanctions such as criticizing, blaming, refusing to deal or shunning are nonlegal insofar as the people who impose them are not state officials.").
47 McAdams (1997: 342). See also McAdams (1997: 357: "A crucial feature of esteem seeking is that individuals care how they are evaluated in comparison to others."). Note the striking similarity to the herding phenomenon explored in the context of behavioral economics.
48 McAdams (1997: 389).
49 McAdams (1997: 390).
50 McAdams (1997: 397: "By whatever normative criteria one uses, some group and societal norms are desirable and some are not. Sometimes norms are the cure; sometimes the disease.").
51 McAdams (1997: 342–3: "Though norms can be socially productive or unproductive, the esteem theory identifies new situations in which norms reduce social welfare.").
52 McAdams (1997: 420).
53 Granovetter (1985: 502–3). See also Granovetter (1985: 491: "I have argued that social relations, rather than institutional arrangements or generalized morality, are mainly responsible for the production of trust in economic life.").
54 Granovetter (1985: 506; emphasis added).
55 Vaughan (1982: 1387). See also Vaughan (1982: 1391: "Organizational processes, then, create an internal moral and intellectual world in which the individual identifies with the organization and the organization's goals. The survival of one becomes linked to the survival of the other, and a normative environment evolves that, given difficulty in attaining organizational goals, encourages illegal behavior to attain those goals.").
56 Lane (1953: 154).
57 Baker et al. (1988: 611).
58 Jensen (1993: 863). See also Jensen (1993: 867: "there are strong tendencies for boards to evolve a culture and social norms that reflect optimal behavior under prosperity, and these norms make it extremely difficult for the board to respond early to failure in its top management team").
59 Cf. McAdams (1997: 347: "Norms matter to legal analysis because (1) sometimes norms control individual behavior to the exclusion of law, (2) sometimes norms and law together influence behavior, and (3) sometimes norms and law influence each other.").
60 See, e.g., Greenfield (2002: 583–4: "The dominant contemporary view of corporate law is contractarian, meaning that corporate constituencies are assumed to be best able to determine their mutual rights and obligations by way of voluntary arrangement.").
61 See, e.g., Greenfield (2002: 584, which notes how traditional corporate law "depends fundamentally on the notion that the participants in the corporate contract are economically rational actors").

62   See, e.g., Kostant (2002: 679–80: "The neoclassical theorists exaggerate the importance of private contracting and market forces in corporate law, and largely ignore the importance of the disparity of bargaining power among corporate constituents caused by pre-existing entitlements and wealth.").

63   Langevoort (1997: 169).

64   Kostant (2002: 677).

65   Cf. Bebchuk (2003: 31: "The weakness of shareholders vis-à-vis boards of directors in publicly traded companies is often viewed as an inevitable corollary of the modern corporation's widely dispersed ownership. But this weakness is partly due to legal rules that insulate management from shareholder intervention. Changing these rules would reduce the extent to which boards can stray from shareholder interests and would much improve corporate governance.").

66   See also Kostant (2002: 671: "Currently, the unchecked power of inside senior managers is the greatest obstacle to corporations behaving in a socially responsible manner, obeying the laws, and treating their constituents fairly.").

67   See, e.g., Bebchuck (2003).

68   See also Orts (1998: 317, which notes how the law should "reinvigorate fiduciary duties (along with the procedural means to enforce them)").

69   See, e.g., Dickerson (2003: 4: "the unwillingness of directors to admit defeat is consistent with a well-established behavioral trait: the overconfidence bias").

70   See id. Dickerson (2003: 54: "Specifying that directors have a fiduciary duty to the firm to file timely a bankruptcy petition will help combat the behavioral biases that prevent directors from filing early bankruptcy petitions and will also help clarify the current uncertainty directors face when considering the scope of their fiduciary duties post-insolvency.").

71   See, e.g., Greenfield (2002: 639).

72   For a discussion of how the law allows these conflicts of interest, see Emshwiller (2003: A1: "In the wake of Enron and other corporate scandals, these types of [related party] transactions – generally defined as business deals involving an outside director, senior executive, significant shareholder or a relative of one of those people – are attracting attention from government officials and business and labor leaders. ... [R]elated-party transactions remain legal and deeply entwined in the corporate culture.").

73   See, e.g., Langevoort (1997: 158: "If we are seriously interested in deterring corporate deception, then fraud liability should not turn on conscious awareness by the specific senior executives responsible for corporate communications of their misstatements or omissions. ... [T]he law would want to create incentives (if not direct requirements) to force the 'debiasing' of corporate inference. Within the scienter-based regime of Rule 10b-5, the first step toward achieving this end would be to develop a definition of corporate scienter that focuses on the attribution of knowledge to the firm. Such emphasis would echo a comparable doctrinal development in the law of insider trading, within which

liability turns on simple possession of information rather than identifying a specific misuse of its by natural persons within the organization.").

74 Sunstein (2000: 109).

75 See also Sunstein (2000: 114: "Of course, any argument pool will be limited. No one has time to listen to every point of view. But an understanding of group polarization helps show that heterogeneous groups are often a far better source of good judgments, simply because more arguments will be made available.").

76 Cf. O'Connor, supra note 38, at 1304 ("boards should assign a different director at each meeting to serve as a formal devil's advocate"); Sunstein, supra note 41, at 115 ("What is necessary is not to allow every view to be heard, but to ensure that no single view is so widely heard, and reinforced, that people are unable to engage in critical evaluation of the reasonable competitors.").

77 See, e.g., O'Connor (2003: 1304).

78 See, e.g., Greenfield (2002: 643).

79 See, e.g., Kahan (1997: 371).

80 Kahan (1997: 373).

81 Kahan (1997: 378).

82 Kahan (1997: 382).

References

Bainbridge, S.M. 2002. Why a board? Group decisionmaking in corporate governance. *Vanderbilt Law Review*, 55: 1–55.

Baker, G.P et al. 1988. Compensation and incentives: practice vs. theory. *Journal of Finance*, 43: 593–616.

Baldwin, W.L. 1964. The motives of managers, environmental restraints, and the theory of managerial enterprise. *Quarterly Journal of Economics*, 78: 238–56.

Bebchuk, L.A. 2003. Making directors accountable. *Harvard Magazine*, Nov.–Dec.: 29–31.

Berle, A.A. and G.C. Means. 1932. *The Modern Corporation and Private Property*. London: Macmillan.

Bratton, W.W. 2002. Enron and the Dark Side of Shareholder Value. *Tulane Law Review* 76, 1275–361.

Coase, R.H. 1988. *The Firm, The Market and the Law*. Chicago: University of Chicago Press.

Coase, R.H. 1937. The nature of the firm. *Economica*, 4: 386–405.

Cooter, Robert D. 2000. Three effects of social norms on law: expression, deterrence, and internalization. *Oregon Law Review*, 79: 1–22.

Cooter, R. 2000. Do Good Laws Make Good Citizens? An Economic Analysis of Internalized Norms. *Virginia Law Review*, 86: 1577–601.

Dahlman, C.J. 1979. The problem of externality. *Journal of Law and Economics*, 22: 141–62.

Demsetz, H. 1983. The structure of ownership and the theory of the firm. *Journal of Law and Economics*, 26: 375–90.

Dibadj, R.R. 2006. *Rescuing Regulation*. Albany, NY: State University of New York Press.

Dibadj, R. 2005a. Delayering corporate law. *Hofstra Law Review*, 34: 469–533.

Dibadj, R. 2005b. Reconceiving the firm. *Cardozo Law Review*, 26: 1459–534.

Dickerson, A. M. 2003. A behavioral approach to analyzing corporate failures. *Wake Forest Law Review*, 38: 1–54.

Ellickson, R.C. 1991. *Order Without Law*. Cambridge, MA: Harvard University Press.

Emshwiller, J.R. 2003. Many companies report transactions with top officers. *Wall Street Journal*. Dec. 29: A1.

Fama, E.F. and M.C. Jensen. 1983. Separation of ownership and control. *Journal of Law and Economics*, 26: 301–25.

Frug, G.E. 1984. The ideology of bureaucracy in American law. *Harvard Law Review*, 97: 1276–388.

Gibbons, R. 2000. Why organizations are such a mess (and what an economist might do about it). Unpublished manuscript. Available at atom.univ-paris1.fr/documents/Org_mess.pdf.

Gibbons, R. 2003. How organizations behave: toward implications for economics and economic policy. Unpublished Manuscript. Available at http://www.bos.frb.org/economic/conf/conf48/papers/gibbons.pdf.

Granovetter, M. 1985. Economic action and social structure: the problem of embeddedness. *American Journal of Sociology*, 91: 481–510.

Greenfield, K. 2002. Using behavioral economics to show the power and efficiency of corporate law as a regulatory tool. *U.C. Davis Law Review*, 35: 581–644.

Griffin, D. and A. Tversky. 1992. The weighing of evidence and the determinants of confidence. *Cognitive Psychology*, 24: 411–35.

Harris, R. 2003. The uses of history in law and economics. *Theoretical Inquiries in Law*, 4: 659–96.

Jensen, M.C. 1993. The modern industrial revolution, exit, and the failure of internal control systems. *Journal of Finance*, 48: 831–80.

Jensen, M.C. 1983. Organization Theory and Methodology, *Accounting Review*, 58, 319–39.

Jensen, M.C. and W.H. Meckling. 1976. Theory of the firm: managerial behavior, agency costs and ownership structure. *Journal of Financial Economics*, 3: 305–60.

Jolls, C. et al. 1998. A behavioral approach to law and economics. *Stanford Law Review*, 50: 1471–550.

Kahan, D.M. 1997. Social influence, social meaning, and deterrence. *Virginia Law Review*, 83: 349–95.

Korobkin, R.B. and T.S. Ulen. 2000. Law and behavioral science: removing the rationalist assumption from law and economics. *California Law Review*, 88: 1051–144.

Kostant, P.C. 2002. Team production and the progressive corporate law agenda. *U.C. Davis Law Review*, 35: 667–704.

Lane, R.E. 1953. Why business men violate the law. *Journal of Criminal Law, Criminology & Police Science*, 44: 151–65.

Langevoort, D.C. 1997. Organized illusions: a behavioral theory of why corporations mislead stock market investors (and cause other social harms). *University of Pennsylvania Law Review*, 146: 101–72.

Leibenstein, H. 1979. A branch of economics is missing: micro-micro theory. *Journal of Economic Literature*, 17: 477–502.

McAdams, R.H. 1997. The origin, development, and regulation of norms. *Michigan Law Review*, 96: 338–433.

Nash, J.F., Jr. 1950. The bargaining problem. *Econometrica*, 18: 155–62.

O'Connor, M.A. 2003. The Enron board: the perils of Groupthink. *University of Cincinnati Law Review*, 71: 1233–320.

Orts, E.W. 1998. Shirking and sharking: a legal theory of the firm. *Yale Law and Policy Review*, 16: 265–329.

Polinsky, A.M. 1989. *An Introduction to Law and Economics*, 2nd edn. Boston, MA: Little, Brown.

Shiller, R.J. 1995. Conversation, information, and herd behavior. *American Economic Review*, 85: 181–5.

Sunstein, C.R. 2000. Deliberative trouble? Why groups go to extremes. *Yale Law Journal*, 110: 71–119.

Triantis, G.G. 2004. Organizations as internal capital markets: the legal boundaries of firms, collateral, and trusts in commercial and charitable enterprises. *Harvard Law Review*, 117: 1102–62.

Tversky, A. and D. Kahneman. 1974. Judgment under uncertainty: heuristics and biases. *Science*, 185: 1124–31.

Vaughan, D. 1982. Toward understanding unlawful organizational behavior. *Michigan Law Review*, 80: 1377–402.

Williamson, O.E. 1967. Hierarchical control and optimum firm size. *Journal of Political Economy*, 75: 123–38.

4

Time-Inconsistent Boards and the Risk of Repeated Misconduct

Manuel A. Utset

Introduction

In their 1932 book, *The Modern Corporation and Private Property*,[1] Adolf Berle and Gardiner Means argued that large public corporations are controlled by managers rather than shareholders. This "separation of ownership and control" is in part a product of corporate law, which requires that shareholders delegate managerial tasks to a board of directors, which in turn delegates the day-to-day running of the corporations to corporate officers.[2] It is also a product of the collective action problems associated with shareholder voting in public corporations,[3] something that makes it highly unlikely that shareholders will be actively involved in monitoring and disciplining managers.[4] Until fairly recently, economists and legal scholars paid little attention to the board of directors as an independent organ of corporate governance. In the last few years, a number of commentators have argued that not only do boards play a role in corporate governance, but that they are in fact the defining or most important institution in corporations.[5] These claims of board primacy are not wholly persuasive, and may provide shareholders with a false sense of security. After all, boards do not meet regularly enough to be directly involved in the day-to-day management of the company; moreover, in order to make informed decisions, independent directors will have to rely on the information which managers provide them.[6]

This paper develops a simple model of the relationship between managers and board members that shows that managers will be able to control boards of directors, and thus entrench themselves, to a much greater extent than predicted by current law and economics models. The model relaxes the standard rational choice assumption that corporate actors have time-consistent preferences and thus have no self-control problems; it thus accounts for the growing empirical literature in economics finding that people become increasingly impatient the closer that they get to immediate payoffs. In other words, people routinely make short-term decisions to yield to the transient lure of immediate gratification, notwithstanding their long-term preference to be patient.[7] These hyperbolic or time-inconsistent actors exhibit self-control problems, as they "would 'like' to behave in one manner, but instead 'choose' to behave in another."[8] Time-inconsistent preferences can lead individuals to override their long-term preferences and overconsume goods that provide them with immediate benefits; it can also lead them to procrastinate taking actions that require them to incur immediate costs – e.g., exerting effort or acquiring information necessary to make a decision.

I show that a manager can control the board by imposing relatively small immediate costs on time-inconsistent board members; in other words, imposing costs that are lower than those that standard economic theory predicts would be effective. Suppose that board members have determined that the expected benefits of firing a manager are $100 and the expected costs $75, and thus have formed an intention to fire her. If one assumes that board members have time-consistent preferences, the manager can avoid getting fired only if she can increase the expected costs to board members by at least $25.[9] I show, however, that if board members have time-inconsistent preferences and the additional costs imposed by the manager are immediate in nature, then they only have to be sufficiently great to cause board members to procrastinate following through with their long-term preference to fire the manager. It follows that the ability of managers to entrench themselves will be greater than usually assumed. The model also predicts that if board members receive an immediate benefit from engaging in misconduct – e.g., engaging in illegal activities or violating their fiduciary duties – they will engage in greater amounts of misconduct than predicted by standard law and economics models.

1. Intertemporal Governance Risks: Time-Inconsistent Misconduct

Corporations are embedded within a temporal frame. They are artificial entities, brought into existence by the filing of a certificate of incorporation and persisting until they are dissolved, merged, or terminated by the state. Intertemporal issues come into play whenever the consequences of decisions – in the form of costs and benefits – are experienced at different points in time, as well as in situations in which the order in which events occur affects the overall outcome.[10] Most corporate decisions – including the decisions of managers, board members, and gatekeepers of whether to violate the law or engage in self-dealing transactions – are intertemporal in nature. Therefore any corporate governance model needs to consider the extent to which the intertemporal nature of these decisions affects the ultimate choices made by corporate actors.

Managers have the ability to engage in opportunistic behavior[11] because corporate contracts are substantially incomplete.[12] This incompleteness leaves open the possibility that one or more corporate actors will have sufficient organizational power[13] to engage in costly strategic behavior.[14] Additionally, the complexity of modern corporations, financial statements, and disclosure documents, gives managers leeway to act opportunistically in crafting disclosures and timing their release. The ability of managers to impose agency costs[15] on shareholders is constrained to a certain extent by corporate fiduciary duties. The duty of care requires, at the very least, that managers not be grossly negligent in making corporate decisions.[16] The duty of loyalty imposes a stricter duty than the duty of care: managers cannot engage in self-dealing transactions, unless they can show that the transactions are "intrinsically fair" to shareholders.[17] Additionally, Federal securities laws require managers to take a number of affirmative actions on behalf of their corporations – e.g., prepare and file periodic and annual reports with the SEC.[18] The Federal securities laws also impose a number of requirements on gatekeepers.[19]

A simple model of managerial decision making

This section assumes that a shareholder hires a manager to act as the sole corporate officer and board member. The manager will undertake a series of actions which can either benefit or harm the shareholder. I will say that a manager engages in "misconduct" whenever she takes an action to benefit herself at the expense of the shareholder. Managerial misconduct can lead to legal sanctions as well as informal ones, such as the loss of reputation.[20] I will assume, without loss of generality, that the misconduct involves illegal activity that triggers formal legal sanctions. Under standard economic theory, the optimal expected sanctions for misconduct will be set equal to the expected harm,[21] and a manager will engage in misconduct only if her expected benefits exceed the expected costs.[22]

Intertemporal decisions are usually modeled using an intertemporal utility function that sums up the instantaneous utility (the payoffs) in each relevant time period, as discounted to account for an actor's time preference. A rational corporate actor will choose her behavior to maximize her discounted intertemporal utility. Suppose that the manager has the ability to engage in misconduct in multiple periods. A rational manager will engage in misconduct in the current period only if, given her beliefs of how she plans to act in the future, the action maximizes her current *and* future well-being.[23] This means that when the manager is deciding whether or not to engage in misconduct she will try to predict how her preferences may change over time.

Time-inconsistent corporate actors   In the standard law and economics model the rational corporate actors have time-consistent preferences: the preference of their long-run *and* short-run selves will always coincide. The principal challenge to the time-consistency assumption of neoclassical economic theory originated in a series of experiments finding that people value immediate gratification and therefore exhibit declining, instead of constant, discount rates.[24] In an early study, the economist Richard Thaler told subjects to imagine that they had won a lottery and could choose to either receive the money immediately or leave it in the bank earning interest.[25] When asked how much interest they would require to make them indifferent between receiving $15 either immediately or in three, 12, and 36 months, the required median returns were $30, $60, and $100, respectively, which translates into continuously compounded discount rates of 277 percent, 139 percent, and 63 percent, for the three-, 12-, and 36-month delays. As can be seen, the implicit discount rate declined as the delay in receiving the money increased.[26]

Some of the strongest evidence that people have time-inconsistent preferences comes from the fact that people routinely adopt commitment devices.[27] Commitment devices are mechanisms that restrict a person's future ability to yield to the pull of immediate gratification.[28] Such devices are costly to implement, and even if they were available at zero cost, people are reluctant to restrict their ability to act freely unless they believe that pre-commitment was otherwise worthwhile.[29] This means that in a world wholly inhabited by time-consistent actors, commitment devices would not exist.[30]

Economists model intertemporal decisions of time-inconsistent actors using a quasi-hyperbolic discount function[31] with the following characteristics:

- Payoffs in the current period – i.e., at t = 0 – are given full weight.
- Payoffs in periods t = 1, 2, 3…, T, are discounted using two discount factors:

- ○ The same long-term discount factor, δ, used in exponential discounting, were the instantaneous utilities in period 1, 2, 3,..., T, are discounted by $\delta, \delta^2, \delta^3, ..., \delta^T$.
- ○ A short-term discount factor, β, which is set to less than or equal to 1, and captures a decision-maker's preference for immediate gratification.
- Payoffs are captured by the instantaneous utility, ui, received in each period and are discounted in the following manner:
  - ○ $u_0, \beta\delta u_1, \beta\delta^2 u_2, \beta\delta^3 u_3, ..., \beta\delta^T u_T$.

From a long-term perspective, when all costs and benefits are delayed, the quasi-hyperbolic and exponential models are identical. That is, in period 0, both the exponential and hyperbolic actor would discount their delayed instantaneous utility in periods 1 through T using an exponential function: $\delta u_1, \delta^2 u_2, \delta^3 u_3, ..., \delta^T u_T$, where the discount factor, δ, which is set to less than 1, captures their long-run impatience. Both types of actors will have a long-term preference to act in a manner that maximizes the sum of these δ-discounted instantaneous utilities.

The difference between the two approaches only arises when an actor has the prospect of grabbing an immediate benefit (or incurring an immediate cost). From the perspective of period 1, the exponential actor will give full weight to the instantaneous utility in that period while discounting those in periods 2 through T using the same exponential function as before: $u_1, \delta u_2, \delta^2 u_3, \delta^3 u_4, ..., \delta^{T-1} u_T$. As can be seen, from both a long-term and short-term perspective, she will compare her instantaneous utility in periods 1 and 2, by discounting the latter by δ. More generally, under the exponential function, a person will always discount payoffs between *any* two adjacent periods by her discount factor δ. This ensures that she will have time-consistent preferences, given that she will always reach the same conclusion vis-à-vis the relative value of payoffs, regardless of the time-period in which she makes that assessment.[32]

The short-term discount factor, β, introduced into the quasi-hyperbolic function is set to less than 1 and thus acts as a multiplier that is inert when all payoffs are in the future but magnifies immediate costs and benefits. This short-term multiplier captures a hyperbolic actor's preference for immediate gratification. In period 0, exponential and hyperbolic actors discount their delayed period-1 instantaneous utility using their long-term discount factor – they value it as δu_1. From the short-term perspective of period 1, an exponential actor values the immediate payoff at its face value (as u_1); however, a hyperbolic actor's preference for immediate gratification leads her to give it greater weight, a shift in preferences captured by the multiplier. In other words, the hyperbolic actor values the immediate payoff as u_i/β. For example, a person with a β of 0.5 gives 50 percent greater weight to a reward when it is immediate in nature than she did from a long-term perspective, while someone with a β of 0.7 gives 30 percent added weight.

It is this discrepancy between the manner in which a hyperbolic discounter compares adjacent payoffs when they are both delayed and when one of them can be received immediately that creates the potential for time-inconsistent behavior.[33] Suppose that in period 0, a hyperbolic discounter with a $\beta = 0.5$ and $\delta = 1$, compares payoffs of \$100 and \$120 in periods 10 and 11. Since both payoffs are delayed, the person's short-term factor does not come into play. She will therefore choose to wait for the larger payoff in period 11. However, when period 10 arrives she will reverse her original decision, since she now gives added weight to the \$100, valuing it at \$100/0.5 = \$200, which exceeds the \$120 that she would receive in period 11.

Time-inconsistent misconduct   From a long-term perspective, both a time-consistent and a time-inconsistent corporate actor will have a preference to engage in future misconduct if and only if the benefits are greater than the expected sanctions. The time-consistent actors in standard law and economics models do not, by definition, give added weight to the prospect of immediate payoffs, and, as a result, they never override their long-term preferences merely because they have become more impatient. However, even a relatively small preference for immediate gratification and overoptimism about their future willpower can lead time-inconsistent corporate actors to repeatedly override their long-term preference to abstain from non-worthwhile misconduct – i.e., misconduct that from a long-term perspective has negative expected returns. This is because of the following important characteristic of misconduct: there will usually be a temporal gap between the time that a corporate actor engages in misconduct and the time when it is discovered and she is sanctioned. In other words, the benefits from misconduct will usually be immediate in nature, but any disutility from formal or informal sanctions will be delayed.[34]

Both time-consistent and hyperbolic corporate actors will consider misconduct to be long run worthwhile only if:

(1) (delayed benefits) – (delayed expected sanctions) > 0.[35]

Because time-consistent actors have a short-term factor of $\beta = 1$, all other things being equal, they will conclude that engaging in misconduct is short-run worthwhile if and only if it was long-run worthwhile.

On the other hand, hyperbolic corporate actors will conclude that misconduct is short-run worthwhile whenever:

(2) (immediate benefits)$/\beta$ – (delayed expected sanctions) > 0.

Therefore, they will engage in *time-inconsistent misconduct* whenever the following holds:

(3) (immediate benefits)$/\beta$ – (delayed expected sanctions) > 0 ≥ (delayed benefits) – (delayed expected sanctions).

In short, time-inconsistent corporate actors, who from a long-term perspective have concluded that engaging in misconduct is not economically worthwhile, may nonetheless repeatedly override their detached, long-term intentions. As a result, the prospect of grabbing immediate rewards can lead hyperbolic corporate actors to consciously "overconsume" misconduct in the same manner that they may be tempted to do so in other areas of her life – e.g., food, cigarettes, leisure, and income that they had wanted to save for retirement. This can lead them to engage in repeated time-inconsistent misconduct, a phenomenon that is foreclosed by the standard assumptions of neoclassical theory, but one with important implications for questions of corporate governance. Finally, all other things being equal, the optimal sanctions under standard economic models will under-deter time-inconsistent corporate actors. This is because the optimal sanctions are set equal to the expected harm, with the thought that people should undertake an action only if the benefits that they receive exceed the harm they produced.[36] However, since hyperbolic corporate actors give added weight to immediate benefits they will violate the law even when the benefits that they receive (as valued from a long-term perspective) are less than the expected harm.

"Nibbling opportunism" and procrastination   The immediate benefits from misconduct can be of two types. First, a corporate actor may take a prohibited action that provides her with an immediate reward, such as embezzling funds, discharging pollutants into a stream, or making a false disclosure in a securities filing. We can call this sort of time-inconsistent misconduct "nibbling opportunism" since it is analogous to the behavior of actors with a long-term preference not to smoke or overeat, but who repeatedly succumb to temptation. Secondly, a number of legal rules require corporate actors to take an action by a specific date – for example, filing tax returns, making corporate disclosures, and complying with environmental

regulations. However, complying with legal rules often requires actors to exert effort and, in most cases, incur other immediate costs. A corporate actor who has a long-term preference to take a required action at the appropriate time will have an incentive to delay following through in each period in which these immediate costs, as magnified by the short-term multiplier, are greater than the incremental delayed sanction of waiting one more period.[37] Each time that she "procrastinates" in this manner, she engages in time-inconsistent misconduct. For example, assume that an environmental regulation requires compliance by a specified deadline and triggers expected sanctions of $100 for each one-day delay. If the immediate cost of taking the required action is $60, a hyperbolic actor with a short-term factor of 0.5 will choose to procrastinate i.e., $60/0.5 = $120 > $100.

Welfare losses   There are two principal types of social costs associated with time-inconsistent misconduct by corporate actors. First, aggregate social welfare is reduced each time that a corporate actor engages in misconduct that from a long-term perspective provides her with a benefit that is less than the harm that she produces. Even if each act of time-inconsistent misconduct produces a relatively small welfare loss, the aggregate loss produced by all time-inconsistent corporate actors can be large.[38] The second type of social cost is counter-intuitive but no less real than the first: hyperbolic corporate actors harm themselves each time that they override their considered long-term preferences to abstain from misconduct. In other words, time-inconsistent misconduct is a type of rationality "mistake." A hyperbolic actor's welfare losses will increase as her preference for immediate gratification, as captured by the short-term multiplier, increases; moreover, the maximum welfare loss from *one* act of time-inconsistent misconduct cannot exceed her *immediacy premium*, which is equivalent to the benefits, as perceived from a short-term perspective, minus the non-distorted benefits from a long-term perspective – (benefits)/β – (benefits). However, as we will see in the next section, repeated time-inconsistent misconduct can lead to large aggregate welfare losses.

Awareness, commitment, and repeated time-inconsistent misconduct
Since time-inconsistent misconduct can lead hyperbolic corporate actors to suffer welfare losses, those who are sufficiently aware of their self-control problems will adopt commitment devices to prevent their future selves from yielding to the pull of immediate rewards. One of the insidious aspects of repeated self-control problems is that, even when individuals are yielding in the current period, they are often overly optimistic about their future willpower. It is these incorrect beliefs about how they expect to behave in the future that can lead actors to continually forego adopting commitment

devices and thus succumb to repeated time-inconsistent misconduct.[39] One can generally distinguish between three levels of awareness.

Naïve hyperbolic actors always believe that even though they are engaged in time-inconsistent misconduct in the current period, they will definitely behave in a time-consistent manner in the following period. Because of this false optimism, naïve actors will see no value in adopting commitment devices and little harm in indulging in the current period – it is the same phenomenon as taking an extra slice of cake believing that the diet will definitely start tomorrow. For these two reasons, naïve corporate actors are the most likely to engage in repeated time-inconsistent misconduct and incur large aggregate welfare losses.

At the other end of the awareness spectrum are sophisticated hyperbolic actors – those who know that they have self-control problems and correctly predict the magnitude of the short-term discount factor that they will use in future periods. A sophisticated corporate actor who has available cost-effective commitment devices will not engage in repeated time-inconsistent misconduct. However, the empirical evidence shows that, even when people know that they have self-control problems, they still often fail to correctly predict the magnitude of their future temptations – i.e., they are partially naïve.[40] A partially naïve actor may adopt commitment devices, but those devices may not be sufficiently high-powered to foreclose all non-worthwhile misconduct. Importantly, even relatively small prediction errors can lead a partially naïve corporate actor to act in the same manner as a naïve one and, therefore, to incur large aggregate welfare losses.

An example: repeated managerial misconduct

Suppose that there are two identical managers, one with time-consistent preferences and the second with time-inconsistent preferences and a short-term discount factor of 0.7, which means that she gives 30 percent extra weight to immediate benefits and costs. They each will have the opportunity to embezzle $1,000 each day for a year; however, each time that they do so they will trigger expected sanctions of $1,250. From a long-term perspective, embezzling funds is not worthwhile, so both managers will adopt a long-term plan or intention to abstain from misconduct throughout the 365-day period. Although misconduct is not long-run worthwhile, what ultimately matters is the managers' behavior when they are faced with an immediate opportunity to take the $1,000.

The time-consistent manager will always reach the same long-term and short-term decision and thus (barring new information) will always keep to her planned course of action. This means that she will abstain from stealing the funds all 365 days and therefore will not trigger any sanctions. A time-inconsistent manager, on the other hand, is one who, by definition, may reverse her long-term intentions, given that when she makes short-term decisions, she will magnify any immediate benefit or cost using her short-term multiplier. The hyperbolic manager in this example has a short-term factor of 0.7, which is sufficiently great so that she will always conclude that embezzling the $1,000 is short-run worthwhile – i.e., $1,000/0.7 = $1,429 > $1,250.

A naïve hyperbolic manager will embezzle all 365 days – each day believing incorrectly that it will be the last time – and will incur an aggregate welfare loss of $91,250.[41] On the other hand, a sophisticated manager will correctly predict her future self-control problems and thus will see the benefit of adopting a commitment device to prevent her "future selves" from engaging in non-worthwhile misconduct. Finally, even a relatively small misprediction about her future willpower can lead a partially naïve manager down the path of repeated misconduct. For example, a partially naïve manager who mistakenly believes that her short-term discount factor is 0.8 (or higher) instead of 0.7 will end up embezzling funds all 365 days and will incur a welfare loss equal to that of a naïve manager. The manager believes incorrectly that her future selves will conclude that misconduct is not short-run worthwhile, given that $1000/0.8 = $1,250, which equals the expected sanction. As a result, she will see no value in adopting a commitment device.

2. Hyperbolic Boards and Managerial Power

This section develops various implications of the time-inconsistent misconduct model introduced in Section 1. First, I show that rational managers who want to entrench themselves and otherwise maximize the amount of discretion that they have in managing the company can do so by taking advantage of the time-inconsistent preferences of board members. Secondly, I show that, in order to reduce the sub-optimal behavior due to the time-inconsistent preferences of corporate actors, it is necessary to directly target the short-term preferences of these actors. Finally, I argue that certain provisions of the Sarbanes–Oxley Act have just that effect.

How managers can control hyperbolic boards

The boards of directors of public corporations are entrusted with making major corporate decisions and monitoring managers to whom they delegate the day-to-day managerial decisions. Certain corporate decisions cannot be delegated to managers; moreover, even decisions that can be delegated require board oversight.[42] Suppose that a corporation has a single project that has been approved by the board of directors and will be implemented by a manager. Each period, the manager receives information regarding the state of the project and decides whether or not to disclose that information to the board. The board has the ability to directly inquire about the state of the project, but doing so requires effort and may create a number of other immediate costs, such as the disutility from having to confront the manager – i.e., second-guessing her decision not to disclose information to the board. The board has the power to terminate the project in any period and thereby end the manager's employment. Further suppose that in period 0, the board has adopted the following governance rule: if in any period the manager discloses that the discounted present value of the project is negative, the board members will terminate the project and fire the manager; in other words, in period 0, the board determines that the expected costs to themselves of continuing such a negative present value project are greater than the expected benefits. For the moment, I will assume that this long-term preference of board members is identical to that of shareholders. This is the best possible scenario of board governance.

Suppose that there are two identical boards, one with members with time-consistent preferences and the other with time-inconsistent members, and that in period 1, the manager discloses that the project has a negative present value. The time-consistent board members, by definition, will terminate the project and dismiss the manager. On the other hand, the time-inconsistent board will do so only if the incremental expected costs that they will bear in period 2, if they were to decide to continue the project, are greater than the immediate costs of terminating the project immediately; where the immediate costs will be magnified by the board member's immediacy premium. As a result, to the extent that these immediate costs and the immediacy premium are sufficiently great, the hyperbolic board members will have an incentive to procrastinate terminating the project. How many periods they ultimately end up procrastinating will depend on their awareness of the magnitude of their immediacy premium and the availability of commitment devices. Since the shareholders do not bear this immediate cost of terminating the project, the hyperbolic board's procrastination will create a "short-term agency cost" of a type that is foreclosed by standard agency theory analyses.

A rational manager who is aware of the time-inconsistent preferences of the board members can take advantage of it by increasing the immediate costs that the board would have to incur to terminate the project. For example, she may decide not to disclose negative information so that the board is forced to bear the immediate effort and confrontation costs of affirmatively seeking it out. Now suppose that board members and managers have been engaging in joint misconduct and that one board member decides to exit that collusive group – i.e., blow the whistle. One implication of the time-inconsistent misconduct model is that the punishment needed to prevent that board member from exiting, if immediate enough, will be *lower* than those predicted by standard collusion models. In other words, the punishment only has to be high enough to foster procrastination, not necessarily to make the costs of exit greater than the benefits from continuing in the joint misconduct.

More generally, if one allows for time-inconsistent preferences, board members may fail to undertake their monitoring/disciplining responsibilities either because: (1) the expected costs to board members of engaging in those activities exceed the expected benefits (the standard explanation); or (2) notwithstanding the board members' baseline preferences to monitor and discipline managers, the immediate costs of doing so are always sufficiently high to lead them to repeatedly procrastinate following through. Moreover, since managers control the production and dissemination of information within the corporation and have available a number of mechanisms to penalize board members who decide to defect from the status quo, they will be able to entrench themselves to a far greater extent than predicted by standard theories that assume that board members have perfect self-control.[43]

A number of recent studies have found that time-inconsistent preferences can lead individuals to procrastinate making analogous exit decisions. One study measured the effort expended by unemployed workers searching for new jobs.[44] Because search costs are immediate in nature, and the benefits – finding and starting a new job – are delayed until future periods, one would expect that individuals who give greater weight to immediate gratification will exhibit lower levels of search intensity and remain unemployed longer. Using various proxies of short-term impatience, the authors found that those with a higher level of impatience did, in fact, search less.[45] A second study looked at employees deciding whether to stay in their current jobs and seek promotions, a process that requires more time and patience (but potentially much higher rewards), or to switch jobs in order to receive a more immediate increase in salary.[46] Again, using standard proxies for short-term impatience, the study found that those with higher levels of impatience were more likely to switch jobs. Finally, researchers studied single women with children and their decisions on whether to work or participate in welfare programs.[47] The authors fitted the evidence to a model that allowed for time-inconsistent preferences and concluded that the data regarding the women's decisions to delay exiting welfare programs were best explained as reflecting time-inconsistent behavior; in particular, that the women procrastinated finding jobs because of immediate costs.

As we have seen, the time-inconsistent preferences of board members allow managers to control the board far more effectively than standard theory predicts; it follows that the same holds true for time-inconsistent shareholders. Suppose that a public corporation has two shareholders who have a short-term discount factor, β, of 0.5 and can each incur an immediate cost of $100 to organize a voting coalition to replace the board. Furthermore assume that replacing the board will give them each an expected benefit of $150 in the following period. By definition, these shareholders will not have a collective action problem and will have a long-term preference to replace the board. Nonetheless, from a short-term perspective they give added weight to the immediate cost of forming the voting coalition – perceiving it as $200 – and thus will have an incentive to procrastinate. A manager or board that is aware of this will find it in their interest to increase the immediate costs borne by shareholders who want to increase their involvement in governing the corporation. Finally, similar arguments would apply in the relationship between managers and gatekeepers such as auditors and lawyers.

Reducing the risk of repeated time-inconsistent misconduct

In choosing between governance devices to properly monitor and discipline managers the board of directors and regulators would want to compare the direct and indirect costs of alternative mechanisms and choose the one that produces the desired behavior at the lowest cost. The most effective way of reducing the risk of repeated time-inconsistent misconduct is to target the short-term preferences of hyperbolic managers, board members, and gatekeepers by either increasing the delayed expected sanctions or decreasing the immediate benefits from misconduct. In other words, if we assume that corporate actors do not have long-term impatience, a time-consistent actor would perceive a $1 increase in expected sanctions in the same manner as a $1 decrease in immediate benefits and would be equally deterred by either method. However, because hyperbolic actors give added weight to immediate benefits of misconduct, all other things being equal, reducing benefits by $1 will increase deterrence by a greater amount than increasing sanctions by the same amount. Since a hyperbolic corporate actor has a short-term discount factor $\beta < 1$, it will always be the case that: (benefits) – $1/\beta >$ (expected sanctions) + $1.

Recall that the hyperbolic manager in the example in Section 1 had a short-term incentive to repeatedly embezzle the $1,000 notwithstanding the delayed sanctions of $1,250, because her short-term discount factor of 0.7 led her to conclude that misconduct was short-run worthwhile – i.e., $1,000/0.7 = $1,429 > $1,250. In order for a regulator to properly deter the hyperbolic manager it can either: (1) increase the delayed expected sanctions by at least $179 (to $1,429); or (2) decrease the immediate benefits from embezzlement from $1,000 to at least $875 (given that $875/0.7 = $1,250); one way to accomplish this is by making sure that the manager does not have immediate access to more than $875.

More generally, one can reduce the immediate benefits from misconduct by adopting mechanisms that effectively: (1) reduce a corporate actor's access to a portion (or all) of the benefits; or (2) delay their receipt, so that they are no longer received immediately. For example, financial institutions, casinos, and other industries in which employees handle large amounts of cash adopt internal controls to limit access to those funds to a small group of well-monitored employees; these controls are sometimes required by regulators or are part of internal auditing controls under accounting rules. One of the commonly given rationales for segregation controls is to remove the "temptation to steal" that comes from easy access, a type of temptation that only afflicts time-inconsistent individuals.

The Sarbanes–Oxley Act: Reducing the risk of hyperbolic boards and managers

Managers who otherwise have a long-term preference to abstain violating the securities laws may nonetheless repeatedly do so if complying with the law would lead them to incur immediate costs – e.g., disclosures of negative results have an immediate negative effect on the manager's reputation (and pride). Deadlines are an important type of commitment device to address procrastination problems.[48] The primary goal of Sections 403 and 409 of the Sarbanes–Oxley Act[49] is to make it more difficult for managers with long-term preferences to delay making negative disclosures from being able to do so; however, it is also possible to characterize these two sections as valuable commitment devices for managers who have long-term preferences to make timely disclosures, but face repeated temptations to procrastinate following through.

The certification requirements under Sections 302 and 906 of the Act[50] help reduce the costs of identifying and prosecuting misbehaving managers and thus increase the expected costs of misconduct. Additionally, they help deter time-inconsistent misconduct by targeting the short-term preferences of managers who may be tempted to repeatedly procrastinate addressing problems that they are aware of, but whose resolution would require them to incur immediate costs (even if merely the exertion of effort). Certification makes salient the costs associated with each one-period delay in addressing the problem and with each act of nibbling opportunism.

Sarbanes–Oxley includes a number of provisions that help reduce the incentive of gatekeepers to engage in this type of procrastination. It does so through a series of provisions that: (1) reduce the immediate costs to gate-keepers of monitoring and challenging managers; and (2) increase the magnitude and saliency of the delayed sanctions faced by gatekeepers. Section 301 require companies to use wholly independent audit committees, which has the effect of reducing the ability of managers to increase the immediate costs to board members of challenging financial statements prepared by managers.[51] Section 303 makes it illegal for managers to try to pressure auditors to adopt favorable accounting interpretations; it therefore helps reduce the immediate costs to auditors of challenging managers.[52] Finally, Section 307 imposes new disclosure requirements on corporate lawyers. A lawyer is now required to "report evidence of a material violation of securities law or breach of fiduciary duty" to the chief legal counsel or chief executive officer, and if those officers fail to remedy the problem the lawyer has to take that information "up the ladder" to the audit committee and board of directors.[53] In effect, Section 307 helps reduce the immediate costs to lawyers of confronting managers who are acting illegally, and of withdrawing their representation of a corporate client. It also increases costs to lawyers who procrastinate taking information "up the ladder" or following through once they become aware that their original disclosure did not lead to the required change in corporate policy. This in turn has the effect of increasing the costs to board members who may otherwise prefer to delay disciplining managers.

Finally, one way of increasing the immediate costs of misconduct is by using gatekeeper schemes in which gatekeepers not only engage in their usual monitoring activities vis-à-vis managers, but also police each other. The highly criticized Section 404 of the Act adopts this type of cross-monitoring procedure. It requires managers to make representations regarding the company's internal control procedures and auditors to "attest to, and report on, the assessment made by the management of the issuer."[54] Managers and accounting firms, in turn, hire lawyers to help prepare these attestations. It may well be that critics are correct that Section 404 imposes high compliance costs. However, the rule also increases the immediate costs to managers and auditors of engaging in certain types of illegal activity and, thus, helps deter time-inconsistent misconduct by managers and auditors.

3. Conclusion

This paper developed a simple model of corporate governance based on the concept of time-inconsistent misconduct. The model relaxes the standard rational choice assumption that corporate actors have time-consistent preferences and thus have no self-control problems; it thereby directly accounts for the behavioral economics literature findings that people routinely exhibit a preference for immediate gratification that can lead them to act in a dynamically inconsistent manner. I argued that time-inconsistent preferences can lead corporate actors to overconsume misconduct in the same manner that they overconsume other goods that provide them with immediate utility. Moreover, time-inconsistency can lead actors to repeatedly procrastinate taking actions required by law, to the extent that they need to incur immediate costs to comply with the legal requirements. I then showed that managers can exploit the time-inconsistent preferences of board members to entrench themselves to a much greater degree than predicted by standard economic models.

Notes

1   Adolf A. Berle, Jr. and Gardiner C. Means. 1932. *The Modern Corporation and Private Property*. New York: Macmillan.
2   See, e.g., DEL. CODE ANN. tit. 8, Section 141(a) (1991) ("The business and affairs of every corporation organized under this chapter shall be managed by or under the direction of a board of directors …").
3   For example, a shareholder who owns 5 percent of the stock of a corporation that she believes is being mismanaged can spend her own money to wage a proxy fight to replace the board of directors. While she bears the whole cost of waging the proxy fight, she only receives a 5 percent share of any increase in value of the corporation brought about by the change in the composition of the board. More importantly, however, the other shareholders will receive 95 percent of the gain, even though they did not contribute to the proxy fight. The gain in corporate value is a collective good to be shared pro rata by all of the shareholders. As a result, no shareholder has an incentive to incur any expenses to carry out the proxy fight (unless its pro rata share of the collective good exceeds its cost of waging the proxy battle). Instead it makes sense to wait and take a free ride on the actions of other shareholders; the end result is that no shareholder takes any action. See generally Mancur Olson, Jr. 1965. *The Logic of Collective Action: Public Goods and the Theory of Groups*. Cambridge, MA: Harvard University Press.

4   The concentration of equity holdings in the hands of institutional investors have, at least in theory, made it easier for shareholders to make use of the voting mechanism to discipline managers. See, e.g., Bernard S. Black. 1990. Shareholder passivity reexamined. 89 *Michigan. Law Review*, 520. But see Manuel A. Utset 1990. Disciplining managers: shareholder cooperation in the shadow of shareholder competition. 44 *Emory Law Journal*, 71 (arguing that problem will subsist even when there is a relatively small group of institutional investors owning a majority of the shares, given that sharing information in order to form voting coalitions can put shareholders at a disadvantage when competing with each other in the capital markets).

5   One theory is that the board acts as a mediating hierarch that helps reduce the team production problems within a corporation; a second theory – that of board primacy – posits that what makes corporations distinctive is the fact that boards can act freely, without having to account for the wishes or preferences of shareholders. See Margaret M. Blair and Lynn A. Stout. 1999. A team production theory of corporate law. 85 *Virginia Law Review*, 247. See also Stephen M. Bainbridge. 2003. Director primacy: the means and ends of corporate governance. 97 *Northwestern. University Law Review*, 547.

6   See *Smith* v. *Van Gorkom*, 488 A.2d 858 (Del. 1985) (under corporate law, boards can rely on the information that they receive from managers, but this reliance has to be reasonable under the circumstances).

7   See Christopher Harris and David Laibson. 2003. Hyperbolic discounting and consumption. In Mathias Dewatripont et al. (eds), *1 Advances in Economics and Econometrics: Theory and Applications*, Eighth World Congress. Cambridge: Cambridge University Press, p. 258 (summarizing empirical literature on hyperbolic discounting and time-inconsistent preferences).

8   Ted O'Donoghue and Matthew Rabin. 2000. The economics of immediate gratification. 13 *Journal of Behavioral Decision Making*, 233.

9   Assuming that the board will keep the manager if they are indifferent. Moreover, the manager only needs to have a majority of the board side with her.

10 Intertemporal decisions are those that have deferred consequences; they involve the general problem of how to choose between outcomes that are distributed over time. See George Loewenstein and Richard H. Thaler. 1989. Anomalies: inter-temporal choice. *Journal of Economic Perspectives*, 181 (defining intertemporal choices as "decisions in which the timing of costs and benefits are spread out over time").

11 See Williamson. 1998. Opportunistic behaviour, in *2 The New Palgrave Dictionary of Economics & the Law*, 703–10 (Peter Newman ed.) (stating that "[o]pportunism is a type of self-interest seeking and may be contrasted both with stewardship (unself-interest seeking) and with simple self-interest seeking (look to your interests but keep all of your promises)").

12 No contract of any length or complexity is ever complete: the transaction costs of identifying all possible contingencies, bargaining over the obligations of parties to account for those contingencies, and writing contracts that correctly specify the parties' understanding will in most cases exceed the benefits. See

Alan Schwartz. 1998. Incomplete contracting, in *2 The New Palgrave Dictionary of Economics & the Law*, 277 (Peter Newman ed.). See Frank H. Easterbrook and Daniel R. Fischel. 1991. *The Economic Structure of Corporation Law*, 34 (arguing that corporate law provides a set of "off-the-rack" default rules that help shareholders and other corporate constituencies economize on the transaction costs of bargaining over their own governance rules).

13   Generally, ownership of a venture's tangible assets is a principal source of ex post bargaining power within a firm since it allows the owner the ability to exclude others from using the firm's physical assets needed for production. See Oliver Hart. 1995. *Firms, Contracts, & Financial Structures*, 30 (stating "the owner of an asset has residual control rights over the asset: the right to decide all usages of the asset in any way not inconsistent with a prior contract, custom or law") (emphasis in original).

14   See Luigi Zingales. 1998. Corporate governance. In Peter Newman (ed.) *1 The New Palgrave Dictionary of Economics & the Law*. Basingstoke: Palgrave, pp. 498–9 (arguing that in a world of complete corporate contracts, there would be no need for the ex post governance provided by the board of directors and other corporate governance mechanisms, since all potential future conflicts would be anticipated and resolved ex ante); Oliver E. Williamson. 1985. *The Economic Institutions of Capitalism*. New York: Free Press, pp. 30–1 (arguing that if parties have unbounded rationality, they can reach a comprehensive bargain ex ante and if parties are not opportunistic they can reach self-enforcing agreements).

15   See Michael C. Jensen and William H. Meckling. 1976. Theory of the firm: managerial behavior, agency costs, & ownership structure, 3 *Journal of Financial Economics*, 305 (developing agency theory of the firm).

16   See, e.g., *Smith* v. *Van Gorkom*, 488 A.2d 858 (Del. 1985).

17   A self-dealing transaction is one in which a manager has a conflict of interest because she appears on both sides of the transaction, raising the prospect that she will act in a manner that hurts shareholders. See, e.g., *Litwin* v. *Allen*, 25 N.Y.S.2d 667 (Sup. Ct. 1940); *Globe Woolen Co.* v. *Utica Gas & Elec. Co.* 121 N.E. 378 (N.Y. 1918); *Marciano* v. *Nakash*, 535 A.2d 400 (Del.1987).

18   See Thomas L. Hazen. 2005. 2 *Treatise on the Law of Securities Regulation* Sections 9.1–9.6 (2005) (discussing reporting requirements under the Securities Exchange Act of 1934).

19   For a discussion of gatekeepers see John C. Coffee, Jr. 2002. Understanding Enron: "It's all about the gatekeepers, Stupid." 57 *Business Law*, 1403; Reinier H. Kraakman. 1986. Gatekeepers: the anatomy of a third-party enforcement strategy. 2 *Journal of Law Economics & Organization*, 53, 60.

20   Eugene F. Fama. 1980. Agency problems and the theory of the firm. 88 *Journal of Political Economy*, 288 (discussing role of market for managers in reducing agency costs); Dan M. Kahan. 1996. What do alternative sanctions mean? 63 University of Chicago Law Review, 591, 637–47 (discussing the

role of shaming in deterring criminal behavior and effecting other potential goals of punishment).

21 Gary S. Becker. 1968. Crime and punishment: an economic approach. 76 *Journal of Political Economy*, 169, 191–5 (setting forth theory of optimal criminal sanctions).

22 See A. Mitchell Polinsky and Steven Shavell. 2000. The economic theory of public enforcement of law. 38 *Journal of Economic Literature*, 45, 47 (suggesting that a person will violate the law if and only if the expected utility from doing so, taking into account the expected benefits and sanctions, exceeds the utility that she would get from obeying the law).

23 See Ted O'Donoghue and Matthew Rabin. 2001. Choice and procrastination. 116 *Quarterly Journal of Economics*, 121, 128 (setting up a general model where people act with reasonable beliefs about future actions and choose current actions to maximize preferences in light of those beliefs).

24 See George Ainslie. 1992. *Picoeconomics: The Strategic Interaction of Successive Motivational States Within the Person*. New York: Cambridge University Press, pp. 63–80 (describing evidence of declining discount rates and using hyperbolas to model them); George Loewenstein and Drazen Prelec. 1992. Anomalies in intertemporal choice: evidence and an interpretation. 107 *Quarterly Journal of Economics*, 573, 579–81 (setting forth hyperbolic discount function).

25 See Richard H. Thaler. 1991. Some empirical evidence on dynamic inconsistency. *Quasi Rational Economics*. New York, Russel Sage, pp. 127, 128–9.

26 Ibid., 129–30.

27 See Ted O'Donoghue and Matthew Rabin. 1999. Doing it now or later, 89 *American Economic Review*, 103, 105 (1999) (noting that economists use commitment devices as evidence – "smoking guns" – of time-inconsistent preferences); David Laibson. 1998. Life-cycle consumption and hyperbolic discount functions. 42 *European Economic Review*, 861, 868 (discussing commitment devices to deal with procrastination in saving for retirement, including channeling funds to illiquid assets such as defined benefit pensions, 401(k)'s, social security contributions, and home equity); T.C. Schelling. 1978. Egonomics, or the art of self-management, 68 *American Economic Review*, 290, 290 (discussing externally imposed self-control devices such as creating an inaccessible savings account and overstating dependents for tax purposes in order to reduce tax liability in April); Klaus Wertenbroch. 1998. Consumption self-control by rationing purchase quantities of virtue and vice, 17 *Marketing Science*, 317, 318 (describing the strategic self-imposition of constraints in the context of purchasing cigarettes).

28 More generally, a commitment device is a type of externally imposed self-regulation mechanism adopted to overcome self-control problems when relying on internal sources of self-regulation is not sufficient. See Roy F. Baumeister et al. 1994. *Losing Control: How and Why People Fail at Self-Regulation* San Diego, CA: Academic Press, pp. 6–7 (describing the ability among human beings "to exert control over one's own inner states, processes,

and responses" and defining self-regulation as "any effort by a human being to alter its own responses" so as to override the push to act in ways that diverge from what they really want).

29 Once we introduce the potential of uncertainty regarding future payoffs, an intertemporal decision maker may find it valuable to have an option to reverse her original decision. See Avinash K. Dixit and Robert S. Pindyck. 1994. *Investment Under Certainty*. Princeton: Princeton University Press, pp. 6–9 (discussing valuation of projects requiring irreversible investments, where waiting to make until a decision maker has acquired greater information may create an embedded option); Daniel T. Gilbert and Jane E.J. Ebert. 2002. Decisions and revisions: the affective forecasting of changeable outcomes. 82 *Journal of Personality & Social Psychology*, 503, 510–11 (finding that, although the individuals who were given the choice to change their minds about which photography prints to keep liked their choices less than those individuals who had no ability to change, individuals still preferred having the option to change).

30 See Dan Ariely and Klaus Wertenbrook. Procrastination, deadlines, and performance: self-control by precommitment. 13 *Psychological Science*, 219, 223 ("A rational decision maker with time-consistent preferences would not impose constraints on his or her choices.").

31 This quasi-hyperbolic function captures the basic empirical fact that individuals give greater weight to immediate payoffs, without adding too much complexity to models. See David Laibson. 1997. Golden eggs and hyperbolic discounting. 112 *Quarterly Journal of Economics*, 443, 449–51 (1997) (setting forth quasi-hyperbolic function). For an early treatment on time-inconsistent preferences, see R.H. Strotz. 1955–56. Myopia and inconsistency in dynamic utility maximization. 23 *Review of Economic Studies*, 165, 165 (introducing intertemporal planning problem in which individuals choose consumption plans to maximize intertemporal utility, but have incentive to diverge from their chosen plans once they have to be carried out in future).

32 See O'Donoghue & Rabin, Doing it, at 106 (stating that under constant discounting, "[a] person's relative preference for well-being at an earlier date over a later date is the same no matter when she is asked").

33 See O'Donoghue & Rabin, Doing it, at 103 (stating that time-inconsistent preferences are due to a "tendency to grab immediate rewards and to avoid immediate costs in a way that our 'long-run selves' do not appreciate"); David Laibson. 2003. Decision-making, intertemporal, in *1 Encyclopedia of Cognitive Science*. London: Nature Publishing Group, pp. 915, 918 (Lynn Nadel ed.) (stating that time-inconsistency is due to the fact that projects may appear worthwhile from a distance, "but as the moment for sacrifice approaches the project becomes increasingly unappealing").

34 A corporate actor may bear an immediate disutility in shame or anxiety if she is caught in the act.

35 Because the only difference between exponential and hyperbolic actors is in how they discount immediate payoffs, in what follows we will assume, with

no loss of generality, that there is no long-term discounting, or, equivalently that actors have a long-term discount factor, δ, that is equal to 1. This allows us to isolate the role played by an actor's present-biased preferences in the decision to engage in repeated misconduct.

36 Suppose that an offense produces a harm, h, and the probability of detection is p. The sanction, s, is discounted by p—$p * s$—and if we set $p * s = h$, and the optimal sanction is reached by multiplying the harm by the probability multiplier 1/p. Therefore, the optimal sanction is h/p.

37 See George A. Akerlof. 1991 Procrastination and obedience. 81 *American Economic Review*, 1, 1 (declaring that individuals procrastinate "when present costs are unduly salient in comparison with future costs, leading individuals to postpone tasks until tomorrow without foreseeing that when tomorrow comes, the required action will be delayed yet again").

38 The harm to society is analogous to the one created by actors who commit crimes when: (1) the benefits they receive are lower than the harm to society; but (2) those benefits are higher than the maximum fines that they will be able to pay due to wealth constraints. See A. Mitchell Polinsky and Steven Shavell. 1979. The optimal tradeoff between the probability and magnitude of fines. 69 *American Economic Review*, 880, 884–5.

39 See O'Donoghue & Rabin, supra, note 27, at 108 (describing the difference between time-consistent and hyperbolic individuals as the fact that the latter have incorrect beliefs of how they expect to behave in future periods).

40 See Dan Ariely & Klaus Wertenbrook. Procrastination, deadlines, and performance: self-control by precommitment. 13 *Psychological Sciences*, 219, 222–3 (detailing a study finding that a group of students with external deadlines performed better than a second group who underappreciated the full extent of their propensity to procrastinate and, thus, adopted sub-optimal deadlines); Stefano DellaVigna and Ulrike Malmendier. 2006. Paying not to go to the gym. 96 *American Economic Review*, 694, 716–17 (finding that people are overoptimistic about how much they will use a gym membership and then procrastinate in canceling the membership).

41 The manager's decision to embezzle all 365 days exposes her to expected sanctions of $456,250, and because her aggregate benefits equaled only $365,000, she incurs a net penalty of $91,250.

42 See *In re Caremark International Inc. Derivative Litigation*, 698 A.2d 959 (Del. Ch. 1996) (discussing the board's ongoing duty to monitor managers).

43 Note that penalizing board members may require managers to incur immediate costs that may lead them to procrastinate; however, if the immediate benefits to them are sufficiently great then they will still have a short-term preference to follow through with the planned penalty.

44 See Stefano DellaVigna and M. Daniele Paserman. 2005. Job search and impatience. 23 *Journal of Labor Economics*, 527, 569 (2005).

45 See id. at 565 (finding that higher levels of impatience led to lower search intensity and that the level of impatience was negatively correlated with the exit rate from unemployment). The proxies used to measure impatience are

similar to those used in other studies. Individuals are deemed to have higher levels of impatience if they smoke, consume a lot of alcohol, fail to use contraceptives, or do not have life insurance or bank accounts. See id. at 547–51 (discussing variables and other studies using similar proxies to measure impatience).

46 See Francesco Drago. 2005. *Career Consequences of Hyperbolic Time Preferences 1–3* (IZA Discussion Paper No. 2113). Available at http://ssrn.com/abstract=706281.

47 See Hanming Fang and Dan Silverman. 2006. Time-inconsistency and welfare program participation: evidence from the NLSY 1, February (unpublished manuscript, on file with *The Houston Law Review*).

48 See Ariely & Wertenbroch, supra, note 40, at 220–3.

49 See Sarbanes–Oxley Act of 2002, Pub. L. No. 107–204, Section 403, 116 Stat. 745, 789 (codified at 15 USC Section 7262) (amending Section 16 of the 1934 Act to require accelerated filing of Section 16 reports triggered by transactions in shares by managers and board members); Section 409 (removing flexibility in timing of disclosures by mandating "real-time issuer disclosures" in various contexts).

50 See Section 302 of the Sarbanes–Oxley Act of 2002 (general certification requirement); and § 906 (certification for filings that include financial reports; criminal sanctions).

51 Sarbanes–Oxley Act of 2002 Section 301.

52 Sarbanes–Oxley Act of 2002 Section 303.

53 Sarbanes–Oxley Act of 2002 Section 307, 15 USC Section 7245 (2000 & Supp. II 2002).

54 Section 404 of the Sarbanes–Oxley Act of 2002 (addressing management assessment of internal controls).

5

Discussion

Sridhar Ramamoorti

Three very interesting papers, with distinct perspectives, were presented at this session. The first two papers take a somewhat pessimistic approach, suggesting that corporate boards are *fundamentally incapable* (Potts: "chaos theory seems to make the ability to accurately predict risks impossible and the very prospect of risk management questionable") or *predictably ineffective* (Utset: "time-inconsistent preferences of board members can be a major obstacle in the board's ability to properly monitor and discipline managers"). Given the board's oversight mandate with respect to executive management, the first two papers collectively point to a fatal flaw, indeed a "governance chasm" presaging systemic governance and risk management failures. However, as if to present a countervailing argument, Professor Dibadj, while acknowledging the corporate board's formidable task in overseeing the management of risk, nevertheless remains hopeful that corporate governance solutions do exist or can be devised through legal and regulatory reform. Specifically, drawing upon insights provided by the literature in organizational behavioral economics, he exhorts us to vigorously pursue such governance-oriented risk management structures, processes, and practices, including contemplating changes to state laws on corporate governance. In these discussant remarks, I will offer my critique on each of these contributions, and, with some reservations, espouse the approach taken by Professor Dibadj. Along the way, I will also lay out my own ideas about crafting a responsive research agenda to deal with the governance dilemma.

Discussant Prefatory Remarks and Questions
for Panelists/Presenters

All three of the papers presented in this session assumed that the term "risk" referred unambiguously to "downside risk." However, as the 2004 Enterprise Risk Management (ERM) Integrated Framework from the Committee of Sponsoring Organizations of the Treadway Commission (COSO) emphasizes, organizations exist to exploit opportunities (also called "upside risk") while managing "downside risk." Thus, risk and opportunity are two sides of the same coin. It would have been helpful to see corporate boards contributing to "value creation" and "value innovation"[1] rather than just "value preservation" activities by adopting a defensive posture and thinking only about downside risk. After all, missed opportunities could prove to be catastrophic too!

Similarly, it is important to recognize that it is meaningless to speak of corporate governance without reference to corporate performance. As reported in the *Financial Times*, a UK-based financial analyst, when told about a company's investment in corporate compliance infrastructure as a means of enhancing corporate governance, responded sharply: "I guess it is time for me to short the stock! After all, where's the alpha[2] in merely improved or beefed up corporate governance?" Unfortunately, all three papers focused on the board's role in constraining executive management's risk-taking role, but not helping them in making calculated gambles in a dynamic and uncertain environment.[3] Moreover, the litigious environment as well as regulatory "second guessing" of reasonable management responses to risk can have a dramatic effect on risk-taking propensity. When otherwise reasonable judgments, ex ante, are evaluated as being poor in hindsight and punished, the business environment would suffer from a dearth of entrepreneurs willing to take risks – the very basis of wealth creation in capitalist systems. Certainly, ends should not be allowed to justify the means (e.g., interpreting "whatever it takes" to mean the commission of fraud, if necessary). Nevertheless, the reward system in capital markets should place a premium on organizations that take on prudent risks with expectation of commensurate returns and generally operate with ethics and integrity. Perhaps the presenters should have devoted some attention to the process of making decision makers accountable in a fair and reasonable way (rather than accept the status quo of quick settlements of frivolous lawsuits that might possibly end up in a wild jury verdict against the defendant). To be fair to the presenters, most researchers do not question that effective corporate governance and good corporate performance are probably joined at the hip (i.e., highly correlated), but we have precious little empirical evidence for "good corporate governance" at companies that are otherwise performing poorly. As *Zimmerman's Law of Complaints* informs us: Nobody notices when things go right.

With this backdrop, I offer the following conjecture: "It seems to me that corporate governance in good times differs dramatically from corporate governance in crisis mode (i.e., when a financially distressed company or a well-performing company in a troubled industry confronts a risky future)." Here are a set of three questions for each of the panelists:

- How does this "corporate governance/performance conjecture" affect your contribution? For instance, how do we distinguish "good judgments leading to bad outcomes" and "bad judgments leading to good outcomes"? Indeed, what is the role of luck in risk management decisions and governance?
- How do accounting, law, economics, and the behavioral sciences (e.g., psychology, sociology and anthropology) interact when studying the complex topic of corporate governance? Do we already have a robust conceptual framework or are we still like the "six blind men and the elephant"? (Corporate governance being the "elephant in the room.")
- How can we promote more interdisciplinary research in corporate governance recognizing that applied professions such as accounting and finance (the gatekeepers of market integrity) must inevitably draw on reference disciplines such as economics and psychology?

Critical Reviews of Papers by Discussant

"Risk Management, Chaos Theory, and the Corporate Board of Directors" by Michael Potts

Professor Potts presents an interesting way to look at the "chaotic" global business environment using the lens of "chaos theory" (cf. Wheatley, 1994). However, using analogies is risky when the underlying structures of the phenomena modeled are not comparable and/or compatible. It is not clear to me that the modeling of non-linear dynamical systems in nature is directly relevant and applicable to business, noting in particular that Nobel Laureate Herbert Simon regarded business, medicine, and engineering as falling under the category of "the sciences of the artificial" (Simon, 1981). Human intentionality and design are important considerations in both the construction of markets and also organizational responses to risk (for instance, the Northern Trust Company chose not to participate in the sub-prime mortgage markets and hence, has been left largely unscathed by the recent subprime liquidity crisis). Also, consider that every large stock exchange, such as the New York Stock Exchange (NYSE) or the Japanese Nikkei, has trigger points or circuit breakers[4] that could shut down the markets entirely; similarly, the Federal Reserve and the Securities and Exchange Commission are engaged in discussions about enhancing the regulatory infrastructure in the US in light of the subprime crisis. Such interventions do not exist in nature, and so, we are merely left with an unfounded comparison of large-scale systems, transaction volumes, complexity, shifts in environment and risk patterns, etc. It should be noted that Sergei Brin and Larry Page's gambit with Google as the search engine for the world wide web is a stark reminder that disruptive change can serve up incredible opportunities too, for those well-prepared and well-informed about market needs. Most importantly, chaos theory cannot and should not be used as an argument that organizations are buffeted by change and are consequently quite helpless to do anything about it. In this context we should recall Peter Drucker's sage advice: "The best way to predict the future … is to create it!" It may not be possible to accurately predict when the next tsunami or earthquake will hit, but that is no excuse for not developing and simulating risk response plans through scenario analysis. In closing, it would have been insightful if Professor Potts had chosen to use chaos theory to look at corporate governance not only "in the worst of times" but also "in the best of times."

"Time-Inconsistent Boards and the Risk of Repeated Misconduct" by Manuel A. Utset

Professor Utset highlights intertemporal governance risks through illustrations of time-inconsistent misconduct (i.e., the tendency for people to "routinely make short-term decisions to yield to the transient lure of immediate gratification, notwithstanding their long- term preference to be patient"). If this is indeed the crux of the problem, then employing Harvard psychologist William James' description of "habit as the enormous flywheel of society" I would submit that we focus on human beings as creatures of habit. We know from experience that military "boot camp" training seems to cure most army personnel of "self-control problems or delusions." So, why not have such individuals with military backgrounds run corporations?[5] In reality, Professor Utset's characterization of "hyperbolic corporate actors"[6] can at best be regarded as a partial explanation of the governance gap he seeks to explain. The characterization of "rational economic actors" on which the quasi-hyperbolic function is modeled flouts basic behavioral assumptions and as such, has become increasingly suspect. Three decades of carefully documented experimental psychological research on heuristics and biases in human decision making shows that these so-called "rational economic actors" are quite fallible after all, and frequently adopt heuristics that lead to systematic and predictable errors (see Kahneman, Slovic & Tversky, 1982; Ariely, 2008).

Sometimes, it appears that both board and management (perhaps for reasons of collusion) exhibit consistently time-inconsistent behavior. For instance, consider the granting of "ethics waivers" (not once, but twice!) by the audit committee of Enron Corporation to its former CFO, Andrew Fastow. Such incidents certainly raise questions about the independence of the audit committee, and the ability of executive management to manipulate the board for their own purposes (in this case, to undertake "self-dealing" with prior authorization). Professor Utset may wish to explore this kind of (con)joint analysis of collusive behavior by boards and executive management. The question of what do when the overseers themselves are co-opted or compromised is a vexing one and the board's position in such circumstances can be somewhat likened to "the fox guarding the henhouse."

In the section on "nibbling opportunism" and procrastination, Professor Utset seems to regard the perpetration of fraud as being comparable to eating, drinking, and smoking. Do human beings have innate desires to willfully deceive others? Certainly, if fraudsters succeed in "ripping off" others with impunity and with little chance of being held accountable, it stands to reason that they would probably become increasingly brazen in their behavior. There is some evidence that fraud perpetrators are frequently repeat offenders and exhibit recidivist tendencies. If such individuals and their associated behaviors sound plausible, then we must take seriously psychiatrists such as Paul Babiak and Robert Hare who, in their recently published book, *Snakes in Suits*, talk of "industrial psychopaths" having infiltrated the business world (Babiak & Hare, 2007). However, this is estimated to be a fairly minuscule percentage of corporate actors (less than 1–2 percent).

The psychology of white collar crime, a complex topic in which I have taken a serious interest over the years, suggests that there are "bad apples" (e.g., rogue traders), "bad bushels" (after all, fraud is frequently a team sport and requires collusive behavior), and bad contexts/environment (a corrupt organizational culture, such as the Mafia). Corporate misconduct requires more than "cost–benefit analysis" as the explanatory variable. According to the conceptual framework of the "fraud triangle" it requires opportunity and access, some kind of pressure or motivation, and, most importantly, "rationalization" on the part of the offender (Cressey, 1973). This line of reasoning would demand a careful discussion of the "fraud triangle" conceptually formulating a means–motive–opportunity analysis (see resources from the Association of Certified Fraud Examiners at www. acfe.com), and also a discussion of the concept of "cognitive dissonance" (Festinger, 1957), "trust violators" and rationalization (Cressey, 1973). Further, there are many other reasons why fraud is committed: "catch-me-if-you-can game playing" (cf. Frank Abagnale, later the subject of a Hollywood movie), revenge fraud (where disgruntled employees who feel "overworked and underpaid" simply want to get even), actions done for the greater good of the company (die-hard loyalty), obeying one's superiors (the "good soldier" defense), vulnerable employees "used" because of their economic independence (e.g., Betty Vinson at WorldCom), etc.

"Anti-Social Norms, Risky Behavior" by Reza Dibadj

Overall, as noted in my prefatory comments, for me Professor Dibadj's approach to the Loyola University of Chicago Academic Conference theme of "Corporate Boards as Sources of Risk, Managers of Risk" was the most appealing for several reasons:

1 As a professor of law, his perspective is critically important when discussing corporate governance;
2 Many problems can be traced back to the inadequacy of economic models particularly the questionable assumptions they make about human behavior;[7] and
3 He addresses the inexorable need to espouse interdisciplinary research drawing from various disciplines to craft the most conceptually robust and practically relevant solutions.

Professor Dibadj begins by highlighting the limitations of conventional economic models, and expressing serious reservations about continuing in the same vein: "Put starkly, economists can push the theory of the firm only so far by remaining focused on the orthodox notion of microanalytic equilibrium drawn from assumptions of individual rationality." Questioning whether or not "boards can be conceptualized as facilitating a series of efficient contracts," Professor Dibadj then moves on to an extended discussion of the "behavioral project" (i.e., the adoption by scholars in behavioral law and economics of methods and data from social sciences such as cognitive psychology to challenge the assumptions of neoclassical economics). Although initially favorably disposed to the field of organizational behavior (OB) in his consideration of concepts such as "power, influence, and culture," he reluctantly concludes that OB does not offer a structured framework to carry on a meaningful analysis.

I particularly liked the following synthesizing paragraphs from the paper: "The central challenge to understanding the intersection of boards and risk, then, becomes developing 'organizational behavioral economics' by blending the economic framework of behavioral law and economics with the institutional focus of organizational behavior. Put slightly differently, going from behavioral economics to organizational behavioral economics necessarily requires some sort of aggregation theory: how can a theory of the firm be derived from the strengths and foibles of individual actors? ... Adapting and reapplying the concept of social norms may be the key to developing an aggregation theory, and in doing so, reconceptualizing how we think about boards. Appreciating the centrality of norms to organizational life will necessarily require an interdisciplinary approach – integrating insights not only from law and economics, but also from psychology, sociology, and even anthropology."

Professor Dibadj should be careful not to apply the conceptual scheme of "the behavioral project" too broadly and then to try to indicate that "organizational behavioral economics" (OBE) transcends the behavioral project, for it doesn't! The way the contribution is currently written this is a Churchillian "terminological inexactitude" and leads to some confusion. Similarly, he should avoid using the term "behavioralists" to refer to members of the now-discredited "stimulus–response" school of psychology called "behaviorism" (cf. Pavlov, Skinner) who have been superseded by today's cognitive psychologists who do not treat the brain as a "black box." Also, to the extent the concepts of "power, influence, culture, norms" are all to be baked into the enlightened school of "organizational behavioral economics" and to make the enterprise global in scope, it may be best to place it under the rubric of "economic anthropology."

Former New York Mayor Rudy Giuliani's strongly articulated view of the "social unacceptability of criminality" speaks powerfully to the culture issue, and is also consistent with the "broken windows theory"[8] in sociology and criminology. In addition, to utilize the power of social comparisons – a powerful vehicle for motivation – the further development of non-legal, non-monetary variables such as "shame" and "pride" in deterring white collar crime should be explored further. If these can be integrated with the literature on "social norms" and combined with Professor Dibadj's proposals for reform, especially of state law, we would be making significant advances in corporate governance theory and practice.

The views expressed herein are solely those of Dr Sridhar Ramamoorti and should not be attributed to his firm, Grant Thornton LLP. Dr Ramamoorti would like to thank Dr Robert Kolb and Dr Donald Schwartz from Loyola University of Chicago for inviting him to be a discussant at the opening session of the April 2008 Academic Conference. He also acknowledges the helpful feedback on an earlier version of these discussant remarks from Mr Jeffery Robinson, a Loyola University alumnus and Chicago-based partner of Grant Thornton LLP.

Notes

1   Kim and Mauborgne (2005) make a useful distinction distinguish between value creation and value innovation: "*Value creation* as a concept of strategy is too broad, because no boundary condition specifies how value should be created. A company could create value, for example, simply by lowering costs by 2 percent. … Although you can create value by simply doing similar things in an improved way, you cannot create *value innovation* without stopping old things, doing new things, or doing similar things in a fundamentally new way" (emphases in italics added).

2   "Alpha" refers to the abnormal rate of return on a security or portfolio in excess of what would be predicted by an equilibrium model like the Capital Asset Pricing Model (CAPM). Thus, an alpha of 1.0 means the fund outperformed the market by 1.0 percent. A positive alpha is the extra return awarded to the investor for taking additional risk rather than accepting the market return.

3   In this regard, it is instructive to remember the National Association of Corporate Directors' (NACD) 2006 "Director of the Year" and Methode Electronics Chairman of the Board Warren Batts' helpful acronym "NIFO = noses in, fingers out." NIFO underscores how important it is for boards not to cramp executive management's strategy, flexibility, and style, and to avoid micromanaging. Such "breathing down the management's neck" can produce ultra-conservative, risk-averse behavior with attendant undesirable consequences, such as missing market opportunities by being slow to respond.

4   In January 2008, the New York Stock Exchange set its criteria for trading halts in the event of a steep market drop, making only slight changes for the first quarter from the fourth, according to data on the NYSE web site. For the first quarter, circuit breakers will kick in if there is a drop of 1,350 points, or 10 percent, in the Dow Jones Industrial Average (DJIA). There will be a one-hour halt in trading if the drop happens before 2 p.m., a 30-minute halt if the decline occurs between 2 p.m. and 2.30 p.m., and no halt after 2.30 p.m., according to the NYSE. If the Dow drops 2,700 points or 20 percent, there will be a two-hour halt if it happens before 1 p.m., a one-hour halt if the slide occurs between 1 p.m. and 2 p.m. and the market will halt for the rest of the day if the slide happens after 2 p.m. A plunge of 4,000 points or 30 percent – no matter what

time it occurs – would result in the market being closed for the day. The previous trigger was slightly higher at 4,050 points. Normal trading hours on the NYSE are 9:30 a.m. to 4 p.m.

5 Interestingly, there are countries, such as Israel, South Korea, and Turkey, that make the "military draft" mandatory for every young man of a certain age, with few exceptions. Perhaps these countries have recognized only too well the value of such a military boot camp training in helping men lead a disciplined life, even in their subsequent civilian roles. Of course, because women are typically not part of such armed forces conscription, we do not have any way of knowing whether such rigorous training would produce similar effects.

6 Utset describes a "hyperbolic corporate actor" as follows: "Intertemporal decisions are usually modeled using an intertemporal utility function that sums up the instantaneous utility (the payoffs) in each relevant time period as discounted to account for an actor's time preference. A rational corporate actor will choose her behavior to maximize her discounted intertemporal utility. Time-inconsistent behavior can be modeled using a quasi-hyperbolic discount function that draws a sharp distinction between immediate and delayed gratification …[people give greater value to the same exact payoff when they can receive it immediately than when it is delayed by *any* amount of time] …The quasi-hyperbolic function introduces a short-term discount factor, β, which is set to less than 1, that acts as a multiplier that is inert when all payoffs are in the future but magnifies immediate costs and benefits. This short-term multiplier captures a hyperbolic actor's preference for immediate gratification" (italics in original).

7 See the comment by Leibenstein (1979) noted by Professor Dibadj: "The question of how individuals in multiperson firms influence firm decisions seems like such a natural question to ask that it is amazing that it is not part of the formal agenda of economics as a profession. … Part of the reason for this lies in the maximizing and optimizing biases of conventional micro-theory." Indeed, economists are known to make "rational actor" self-interest maximization assumptions to deal with averages and aggregates, as well as concerns about mathematical tractability. Hence, we must turn to (social) psychologists to understand individual differences among personalities, and group dynamics such as "social pressure and conformity," "groupthink biases," "escalation of commitment," "power, influence and perception," "social comparisons," and even "cultural taboos."

8 "Broken windows theory" states that it is easier to deal effectively with a small problem before it snowballs into a big problem. Wilson and Kelling (1982) provide the following rationale: "Consider a building with a few broken *windows*. If the windows are not repaired, the tendency is for *vandals* to break a few more windows. Eventually, they may even break into the building, and if it's unoccupied, perhaps become *squatters* or light fires inside …" The theory thus makes two major claims based on the intuition of "nipping it in the bud": the more petty crime and low-level anti-social behavior is deterred, the higher the likelihood that major crime will, as a result, be prevented. Application of

"broken windows theory" in preventing or deterring white collar crime shows promise because most financial frauds start small (Young, 2002).

References

Ariely, D. 2008. *Predictably Irrational: The Hidden Forces That Shape Our Decisions*. New York, NY: HarperCollins.

Babiak, P. and R.D. Hare. 2007. *Snakes in Suits: When Psychopaths Go To Work*. New York, NY: HarperCollins.

COSO. 2004. *Enterprise Risk Management – Integrated Framework*. Committee of Sponsoring Organizations of the Treadway Commission (COSO).

Cressey, D. 1973. *Other People's Money: A Study in the Social Psychology of Embezzlement*. Montclair, NJ: Patterson Smith.

Dibadj, R. 2008. Anti-social norms, risky behavior. Paper presented at the Loyola University of Chicago Academic Conference themed "Corporate Boards: Sources of Risk, Managers of Risk" from April 16–17, 2008.

Festinger, L. 1957. *A Theory of Cognitive Dissonance*. Stanford, CA: Stanford University Press.

Kahneman, D., P. Slovic and A. Tversky (eds). 1982. *Judgment Under Uncertainty: Heuristics and Biases*. Cambridge, MA: Cambridge University Press.

Kim, W.C. and R. Mauborgne. 2005. *Blue Ocean Strategy: How to Create Uncontested Market Space and Make the Competition Irrelevant*. Boston, MA: Harvard Business School Press.

Leibenstein, H. 1979. A branch of economics is missing: micro-micro theory. *Journal of Economic Literature, 17*: 477. (Quoted in Dibadj (2008) paper presented at Loyola University Conference.)

Potts, M. 2008. Risk management, chaos theory, and the corporate board of directors. Paper presented at the Loyola University of Chicago Academic Conference themed "Corporate Boards: Sources of Risk, Managers of Risk," April 16–17, 2008.

Simon, H.A. 1981. *The Sciences of the Artificial*. Cambridge, MA: MIT Press.

Utset, M. 2008. Time-inconsistent boards and the risk of repeated misconduct. Paper presented at the Loyola University of Chicago Academic Conference themed "Corporate Boards: Sources of Risk, Managers of Risk," April 16–17, 2008.

Wheatley, M.J. 1994. *Leadership and the New Science: Learning about Organization from an Orderly Universe*. San Francisco, CA: Berrett-Koehler Publishers, Inc.

Wilson, J.Q. and G.L. Kelling. 1982. Broken windows: the police and neighborhood safety. *Atlantic Monthly*.

Young, M. 2002. *Accounting Irregularities and Financial Fraud: A Corporate Governance Guide*. New York: Aspen Law and Business.

Part III
Board Structure and the Management of Risk

In "Theories of Governance and Corporate Moral Vulnerability," Greg Young and Steve H. Barr explore the hazards of operating subsidiaries in countries with corrupt regimes. In Young and Barr's conceptualization, a firm has a portfolio of moral hazard risks that it is compelled to manage. The size and scope of that portfolio is an important element of corporate governance that firms can choose to expand or contract. Focusing on pharmaceutical firms, Young and Barr develop and empirically test two hypotheses regarding the relationship between corporate governance and management's appetite to expand their portfolio of moral hazards. Firms with boards that are more exposed to shareholder power choose smaller portfolios of moral hazard risks. Perhaps counter-intuitively, Young and Barr find that corporate profits decrease as the portfolio of moral hazards increases.

In his essay, "Mitigating the Exposure of Corporate Boards to Risk and Unethical Conflicts,"Shann Turnbull questions the extremely widespread practice of single-board governance of firms. In Turnbull's analysis, corporations with single boards fail to govern effectively because the single board has excessive power and becomes a source of risk to the firm. Further, such single boards lack processes to secure information about firm operations that are independent of managers. Turnbull urges that corporate charters be revised to implement a multi-board structure that effectively separates governance powers from the powers of business management. In support of his idea, Turnbull points to instances of multi-board structures that he believes work rather well.

"Supervisory Board and Financial Risk-Taking Behaviors in Chinese-Listed Companies," by Zhenyu Wu, Yuanshun Li, Shujun Ding, and Chunxin Jia, dovetails with and extends the idea of Turnbull's essay on multi-board structures. Wu, Li, Ding and Jia point out that Chinese companies very frequently have two boards – one analogous to the board of directors common in the United States and a second board that functions like the supervisory board in the German system of corporate governance. In fact, by law, all publicly listed Chinese firms must have a dual-board governance mechanism. The authors focus on the characteristics of supervisory boards, with an emphasis on their monitoring functions. The empirical results of Wu, Li, Ding, and Jia contrast with those of other studies of supervisory boards that have found that supervisory boards play only a minimal role in corporate governance. In the current study, the authors find that meeting frequency of supervisory boards plays a significant role in controlling the financial risk taking of Chinese firms.

David Koenig provides a discussion of these papers, along with many suggestions for future improvements.

6

Theories of Governance and Corporate Moral Vulnerability

Greg Young and Steve H. Barr

Abstract

Our research focuses on the moral hazards presented by positioning corporate subsidiaries in countries with known magnitudes of corruption. We introduce the construct of corporate moral vulnerability to capture the notion of a portfolio of moral hazard risks. Using a sample drawn from publicly traded pharmaceutical companies, we test two hypotheses that address the relationship between corporate governance and management's appetite for moral hazard risks in the corporate portfolio. We find that when the board of directors is more accountable to shareholders' democratic power, the company portfolio has a lower magnitude of corporate moral vulnerability. Interestingly, while the level of corporate profit decreases as the magnitude of corporate moral vulnerability increases, the productivity of the corporation's human resources increases. These results provide preliminary evidence of the validity of the corporate moral vulnerability construct. Accordingly, we discuss a future research stream to advance our understanding of managing the risks and strategic implications of the corporation's portfolio of moral vulnerability.

The paper is organized as follows: the next section develops the construct of corporate moral vulnerability and builds on agency and stewardship theories of corporate governance to hypothesize management's appetite for moral hazard risks in the corporate portfolio. Our method section describes the operationalization of the constructs into measures and the sample we constructed to test our hypothesis in the US pharmaceutical industry. Our results section notes the empirical support we found for our hypothesis. Our discussion section, while noting the limitations of this study, presents results of our post-hoc analysis that offer preliminary empirical evidence for the validity of the corporate moral vulnerability construct. Our discussion concludes by suggesting an agenda for further research on corporate moral vulnerability that we believe has the potential to add new understanding of important issues in risk management, relational strategic resources for competitive advantage, leadership, and reputational capital.

Introduction

From the stakeholders' perspective, moral hazards exist whenever their performance is determined by the reliability and trustworthiness of an *alter* who has volitional decision-making power and whose behavior is not controlled by the stakeholder. For example, the financial objectives of shareholders may be functions of the (*more, less*) trustworthy behavior of their management-agents (corporate *alters*) who position corporate assets in (*more, less*) corrupt industries and countries, and select (*more, less*) honest suppliers, customers, and governments with whom to enter into transactions. In this situation, many people consider corruption and bribery to be two of the most important moral hazards confronting business today.

Our research focuses on the moral hazards presented by positioning corporate assets and activities in countries with known magnitudes of corruption and bribery, and we empirically test two hypotheses (developed below) that address the relationship between corporate governance and management's appetite for such positions of corporate moral vulnerability. In our framework, corporate moral vulnerability is an outcome of corporate governance mechanisms influencing management's decisions to accept or reject options to enter foreign countries, and each option presents management with a knowable amount of moral vulnerability. We argue that management has a measurable appetite for corporate moral vulnerability – in other words, they are aware of the moral hazard risks from the perception of stakeholders, and they are willing to tolerate an observable magnitude of these risks in their corporate portfolio of strategic positions.

An important function of corporate governance is to control and discipline management by establishing mechanisms to mitigate moral hazard risks. Such mechanisms include monitoring and control systems to identify and recover from any corporate behavior that acts out the moral hazard, and reward structures that allocate consequences to give incentives to avoid and preempt such behavior.

Corporate governance research often applies agency theory to study the efficacy of various mechanisms available to protect stockholders from the moral hazard of management behavior. This theory adopts a narrow perspective on managerial volition by arguing that managers, if left uncontrolled, are likely to pursue their own self-interest even to the point of dishonesty and absence of moral constraint on their behavior. An important alternative to agency theory is stewardship theory, which applies a more trusting view of managerial volition. Stewardship theory argues that managers voluntarily make decisions for their organizations' best interest.

While both owners and managers are interested in the pursuit of profitable opportunities, they differ in their preference, or appetite, for variability in returns (Eisenhardt, 1989). Managers have their entire attention, reputation, and careers focused on the fortunes of their employer – all their eggs in one corporate basket – and so are not likely to easily tolerate large downturns in performance to earn premium compensatory returns. Conversely, shareholders can diversify their risk across a portfolio of holdings and so are more likely than managers to tolerate a larger downside to achieve premium returns for higher risk.

Corporate managers – the agents of owners – who are exposed to opportunities for corruption may decide to pursue them. Reasons may include denial of opportunities for their competitors, conformance with local practices, and achievement of benefits greater than the perceived negative consequences (Aragandoña, 2005: 259). Thus, a moral hazard risk arises for the corporate principals from their agents' exposure to corrupt macroeconomic environments. In this context, a strategic decision that allocates corporate resources to investment in a foreign country with a known level of corruption is a type of corporate moral hazard.

One of the most significant forms for management deployment of corporate assets is in the accumulation of business units, or portfolios, that can respond efficiently to profit-making opportunities. For multinational corporations (MNCs) that position business units in foreign countries, the macroeconomic and institutional environment of host countries are important factors for the generation of shareholder wealth. Alternative locations offer both a variety of business opportunities and a variety of local institutions, customs, and practices. Moreover, the subsidiary's ability to successfully capture local business opportunities may depend on its responsiveness to local practices and institutional context (Kostova and Roth, 2002: 215). The MNC subsidiary is immersed in the local context, geographically remote from yet still a unit of the parent corporation. Thus, the local management of each subsidiary, while still active agents for shareholders, are influenced both by the requirements of the host country as well as by the governance of its parent corporation (Kostova and Roth, 2002: 216).

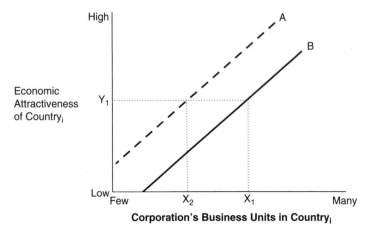

NOTES:
X1 = Corporate units in country$_i$ with no host-country-corruption; **zero cost from moral hazard risk**.
X2 = Corporate units in country$_i$ with host-country corruption; **corporate vulnerability to moral hazard risk**
     imposes costs to control potential business misbehavior and consequences.
X1–X2 = *Corporate scope in country$_i$ subject to **managerial appetite for moral hazard risk**.*

Figure 6.1   Corporate moral vulnerability – A portfolio of moral hazard risks:
Example of subsidiaries exposed to host-country corruption

We illustrate our research question with the example of corruption,
which we define as the act or consequence of giving or receiving consideration (a thing of value) in order to receive a benefit in a manner that violates duties of legal compliance or moral responsibility. Business
participation in corrupt transactions has both direct and indirect financial
costs. Over time, the financial costs of corrupt conduct may absorb substantial amounts that limit the resources available for other strategic and
operational investments. When corporate management positions subsidiary
units in a country in response to the economic attractiveness there, it takes
on the moral hazards of exposure, or vulnerability, to the level of corruption in that host country. We argue that the scope, or number, of corporate
units management will position in a country is a function both of the economic opportunity and the managerial appetite to bear the moral hazard
risk in the corporate portfolio. We illustrate this argument in Figure 6.1.
The figure shows in Line B the expected number of business units for a
given level of host-country economic attractiveness without any moral
hazard risk from corruption, and the expected number with the risks of corruption in Line A. We propose that the distance between these two lines can
be bridged by management's appetite, or tolerance, for exposing the corporation to the moral hazard risks of operating in a corrupt country. Below we
develop hypotheses that relate agency and stewardship theories of corporate governance to the appetite for moral risks in the corporate portfolio.

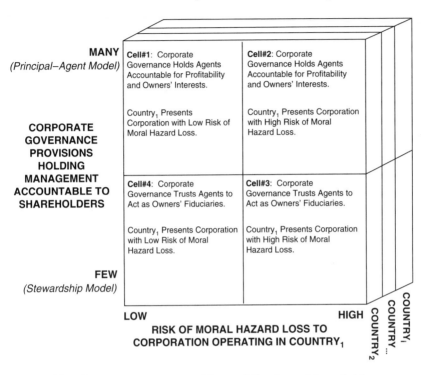

Figure 6.2   Corporate governance and its portfolio of moral hazard risks

Business decisions on how to behave in corrupt environments should be made at the highest corporate level (Aragandoña, 2005: 260). Approaches to manage the risks of operating in corrupt macroenvironments may include avoidance (such as not locating corrupt assets in corrupt countries), or controlling the risks by taking action to prevent corrupt behavior in its own activities. We propose here that corporate governance provisions holding management accountable to shareholders are a form of controlling the appetite for such moral hazard risks as participation in corrupt activities.

An important function of corporate governance is to control and discipline management by establishing mechanisms to mitigate moral hazard risks. Such mechanisms include monitoring and control systems to identify and recover from any corporate behavior that acts out the moral hazard, and reward structures that allocate consequences to give incentives to avoid and preempt such behavior.

We introduce the construct of corporate moral vulnerability to reflect the portfolio of moral hazard risks embedded in the operations of the corporation. In our example, illustrated in Figure 6.2, the corporation may operate in more than one country, and each country has its own institutional practices with differing degrees of corruption. Thus, the portfolio of the corporate business units has embedded in it an aggregate amount of vulnerability to moral hazard risks.

We argue here, however, that these reasons are less compelling in the presence of internal safeguards against such behavior. Further, we hold that shareholders' financial interests are better served when the corporation refrains from participating in corruption.

Based on our illustration of the moral hazard posed by operating in corrupt macroeconomic environments, we propose that the principal–agency model of corporate governance that holds management accountable to shareholder interests will lead to less of a management appetite for moral hazard risks in the corporate portfolio. Stated as a hypothesis:

> **H1**. As the number of corporate governance provisions that hold management accountable to shareholders increases, the magnitude of moral hazard risks in the corporate portfolio decreases.

Aragandoña (2005: 258) lists several risks corruption poses to corporate wealth creation, including the absence of effective accounting controls, the erosion of incentives to invest in resource-based advantages, the loss of social capital and important strategic relationships, and lost visibility into the corporation's true prospects. In addition to the above, businesses convicted of corrupt practices may face substantial judicial fines, constraints on operations, and legal fees. Bribery and corruption also add to business costs. For example, corruption may limit competition, force selection of vendors with substandard performance, require payment of above-market prices, and may continue over long periods of time (Wells, 2003). Thus, we hypothesize:

> **H2**. Corporate profit decreases as the magnitude of moral hazard risks in the corporate portfolio increases.

Method

Our research question addresses the relationships among corporate governance provisions, risk management in the principal–agent relationship, and the corporation's exposure, or vulnerability, to moral hazard risks in its portfolio of foreign subsidiaries. Our sample observation is at the level of the corporation, and we have one observation per corporation for hypotheses testing. Our sample and measures are described below.

We collected data on 83 publicly traded US firms in the pharmaceutical industry (SIC = 2834) that are listed in the LexisNexis Academic database of business information. The LexisNexis Academic database includes company financial information from government sources, market research, industry reports, and actual SEC filings. We composed our sample from just one industry to avoid confounding interpretation with multiple contexts and industry-specific characteristics.

The pharmaceutical industry, with $630.7 billion in global sales over the 12 months through June 2007 (Saftlas & Diller, 2007: 12), has a complex production and distribution process that is heavily regulated throughout the world. The prospect of substantial rewards from evading ethical practice and regulatory regimes makes the industry prone to corruption (Transparency International, 2006: 76). Nevertheless, the pharmaceutical industry is perceived to have a moderate level of corruption compared to other business sectors (Transparency International, 2002), so we expect to find good variability in our measures.

In June 20004, for example, Schering-Plough agreed to pay a fine in the US because over the course of several years the manager of its Polish subsidiary, unknown to its corporate headquarters in New Jersey, made illegal payments to a Polish government official in order to influence hospital purchases of pharmaceutical products in its favor (Transparency International, 2006: 78). In Central America, one government purchased unusually large and unnecessary quantities of antibiotics because bureaucrats there received "fees" for their orders (Transparency International, 2006: 82). An individual firm may make a rational decision to pay bribes in order to cut through "red-tape" delays of government (Kaufmann and Wei, 2000). When the Chinese government recently cracked down on corruption in the country's health care industry, for example, it had an adverse affect on pharmaceutical businesses operating there (Saftlas & Diller, 2007: 13).

Corporate governance measures of managerial accountability to shareholders

We draw on the RiskMetrics Governance Database, formerly known as the IRRC Takeover Defense database, to construct four measures of corporate governance. Our approach follows that of Gompers et al. (2003), but since our research focuses on managerial *accountability* to shareholders while those authors focus on *protection* from shareholders we reverse score the RiskMetrics Governance data. Higher values in our data indicate that corporate governance provisions hold management more accountable to shareholders. Below we describe our four measures of corporate governance, and we refer the interested reader to Gompers et al. (2003: Appendix A) for detailed information about each of the governance provisions that compose our measures.

Our first corporate governance measure is Board Timeliness, which is the count of four separate provisions that, if present, would block shareholders power to call for the board of directors to meet. Board Timeliness in our research is the reverse of the Gompers et al. "Delay" Governance Provision. Thus, higher values on Board Timeliness indicate more accountability to shareholders because they are less hindered in their power to easily and speedily call board meetings.

Our second measure is C-Management Compensation & Protection. This counts five separate provisions that, if present, would shield management from negative "pocketbook" consequences of shareholder dissatisfaction. The reverse of the Gompers et al. "Protection" Governance Provision, higher values on this measure in our research mean that management has fewer personal financial immunities such as attractive compensation packages, contracts, golden parachutes, severance packages, indemnification and liability protection.

The third corporate governance measure is Shareholder Voting, composed of six separate provisions that, if present, would block shareholders from democratically exercising power over the Board of Directors. The reverse of the Gompers et al. "Voting" Governance Provision, higher values on this measure in our research mean shareholders have more voice in corporate governance and decision making.

The fourth is Other Protections, composed of six separate provisions that, if present, would protect management from the negative consequences of hostile takeovers. The reverse of the Gompers et al. "Other" Governance Provision, higher values on this measure in our research mean managers are more accountable to provide shareholders with full corporate full financial value.

Corporate moral vulnerability

This measure is the average country-level corruption a corporation is exposed to in the environment of all its foreign subsidiaries. We use World Bank Corruption Indices (Kaufmann, 2004) of a country's corruption/ethical standards reported by respondents in the country's enterprise sector, and reverse score the World Bank data so that in our research higher values indicate higher levels of corruption. We use the World Bank corruption indices for corporate illegal corruption (including bribery for procurement and banking), public sector ethics (including government favoritism in procurement), and judicial effectiveness (including judicial bribery and property protection).

For each parent corporation, we create a measure of its exposure to corruption in the environment of each of its foreign subsidiaries by multiplying the number of its subsidiaries in a country by the country-level corruption index we calculated from the World Bank data discussed above. We count the subsidiaries owned at least 50.1 percent by the parent and record their location as listed in the LexisNexis Corporate Affiliations database of subsidiaries. The LexisNexis database contains approximately 6,000 US public parent companies and 40,000 subsidiaries, and we find that 56 of the 83 pharmaceutical firms listed in the LexisNexis Academic database have foreign subsidiaries listed in the LexisNexis Corporate Affiliations database. We then calculate *corporate moral vulnerability*, an index number that is the corporation's sum of exposures across all countries in which its subsidiaries are located, divided by the number of its foreign subsidiaries. Stated algebraically, the parent's Corporate Moral Vulnerability is

$$= \left(\sum_{i=1..i} (S_i * C_i) \right) \Big/ T$$

where:

$i = i$th Host Country for the focal corporation's subsidiaries.

S = Count of Corporation's Subsidiaries located in Host Country$_i$.

C = Host Country$_i$ Corruption Index *(reverse scored World Bank index)*.

T = Total Number of Corporation's Foreign Subsidiaries in all countries.

In order not to drop observations of domestic only parents, we create a difference score that anchors the above calculation on the World Bank's Corruption Index for the United States. In this way, the parent's Moral Vulnerability exposure is zero when it is equal to the World Bank's Corruption Index for the United States; it is a positive number when the parent's subsidiaries expose it to more corruption than that of the United States; and negative when the parent's subsidiaries expose it to corruption that is on average less than that found in the United States.[1]

Because the separate corruption indices for corporate illegal corruption, public sector ethics, and judicial effectiveness are all highly correlated with one another, we sum them into a single index number for each parent corporation. Higher values on this index reflect a corporation's overall exposure to foreign country-level institutions and business practices that are more corrupt than the United States, lower values indicate exposure to foreign country-level institutions and business practices that are less corrupt than the United States.

Corporate profitability measures

We used two measures of corporate profit from the Compustat North America database of publicly held companies: Earnings Before Interest and Taxes (EBIT), and Income Before Extraordinaries (IBC; *reported in US$ millions*), which represents the income of a company after all expenses, but before provisions for dividends and before extraordinary items and discontinued operations. For each parent corporation, we calculated the average EBIT and the average IBC using 2005 and 2006 performance results. We used these average measures to avoid unusual short-term events that may influence profit in a single year. To test the corporation's profitability we divided the profit measures by its number of employees in 2006 as reported in Compustat.

Controls   We controlled for the size of the corporation by including the number of its employees in 2006 as reported (*in thousands*) by Compustat.

We also controlled for the macroeconomic attractiveness of the corporation's portfolio of subsidiaries by using the 2006 Gross Domestic Product of each country (*reported in US$ millions*) in which its businesses are located. We constructed each portfolio's macroeconomic attractiveness with an approach that is similar to the construction of our corporate moral vulnerability measure. Specifically, the portfolio's macroeconomic attractiveness

$$= \left(\sum_{i=1..i} (S_i * C_i) \right) / T$$

where:
i = ith Host Country for the focal corporation's subsidiaries.
S = Count of Corporation's Subsidiaries located in Host Country$_i$.
C = Host Country$_i$ 2006 Gross Domestic Product (*reported by the World Bank in 2007*).
T = Total Number of Corporation's Foreign Subsidiaries in all countries.

So as not to drop observations of domestic only parents, we added the GDP of the United States to each portfolio's macroeconomic attractiveness. Finally, we did a log transform to reduce the scale of this measure relative to the other measures in our sample.

Sample for hypotheses testing   After accounting for missing data, our final sample consists of 70 observations, each a unique US publicly traded company in the pharmaceutical industry. Our sample includes 81 percent of the pharmaceutical companies listed in the Standard & Poor's Industry Survey (Saftlas & Diller, 2007).

Table 6.1 shows the descriptive statistics and correlations in the sample.

Table 6.2 shows the summary descriptives broken down according to the four quadrants displayed in Figure 6.2.

We test the hypotheses with linear regression. Table 6.3 shows Model#1 with Corporate Moral Vulnerability as the dependent variable and only the controls for Corporate Size and the Corporate Business Portfolio's Macroeconomic Attractiveness entered as independent variables. The results for Model#1 show that the *Corporate Size* control is positive and significantly related to Corporate Moral Vulnerability ($\beta = 0.38$; $p < .001$). The Corporate Portfolio of Macroeconomic Attractiveness is marginally significant and negatively related to Corporate Moral Vulnerability ($\beta = -0.17$; $p < .10$).

Importantly, our review of regression diagnostics such as variance inflation factors and graphic displays of predictor variables plotted against residuals (not reported here but available from the first author) shows no harmful multicollinearity in any of the models reported below.

Results

In Hypothesis#1 we predict that the *Corporate Moral Vulnerability* embedded in the portfolio of subsidiary business units will be less as the corporate governance provisions holding management accountable to shareholders increase. Model 2 in Table 6.3 shows that the Hypothesis is supported for the Shareholder Voting provision ($\beta = -0.21$; $p < .05$) but not for the other provisions. When the board of directors is more accountable to shareholders' democratic power, the magnitude of *Corporate Moral Vulnerability* is less. Further, the inclusion of corporate governance provisions in the model increases the explanatory power over the amount of variance explained by controls alone in Model 1.

In Hypothesis#2 we drew on the competitive inefficiencies of corrupt macroenvironments and the corporate costs of monitoring and controlling for moral hazard losses to predict that corporate profit will decrease as the magnitude of *Corporate Moral Vulnerability* increases. Model 2 in Table 6.4 shows that, after controlling for corporate size and macroeconomic attractiveness, the Hypothesis is marginally supported for an EBIT measure of profit ($\beta = -0.09$; $p < .10$).

Table 6.1 Descriptive statistics and correlations

Variables	Mean	Std. Dev.	1	2	3	4	5	6	7	8	9
1. Moral Vulnerability	10.88	33.92									
2. Profit (*$thousands*)	593.05	1901.63	0.27*								
3. Profitability (*income per employee*)	−100.75	304.54	0.31**	0.26*							
4. Corporate Size	8.94	20.33	0.38*	0.91***	0.24*						
5. Foreign Subsidiaries	11.09	23.83	0.35**	0.86****	0.25*	0.89***					
6. Corporate Portfolio's Macroeconomic Attractiveness	16.48	0.06	−0.17	0.01	−0.06	0.01	0.01				
7. Board Timeliness	1.57	1.07	−0.13	−0.10	−0.05	−0.12	−0.10	−0.04			
8. C-Management Compensation & Protection	4.02	0.91	−0.13	0.24*	−0.05	−0.34*	−0.30*	0.08	0.09		
9. Shareholder Voting	5.57	0.58	−0.29*	−0.10	−0.29*	−0.29*	−0.19	−0.09	0.18	0.12	
10. Other Protections	5.20	0.50	0.04	0.12	0.04	0.07	0.09	−0.17	0.34*	0.15	0.06

$n = 70$; *$p < .05$; **$p < .01$; ***$p < .001$; two-tail significance reported.

Table 6.2 Quadrant descriptives

CORPORATE GOVERNANCE PROVISIONS HOLDING MANAGEMENT ACCOUNTABLE TO SHAREHOLDERS

MANY (Principal–Agent Model)

N = 22	Means	Std. Dev.	N = 15	Means	Std. Dev.
Moral Vulnerability	-8.116	12.602	Moral Vulnerability	37.652	39.103
Income per Employee	-125.14	312.07	Income per Employee	-133.66	333.94
EBIT	112.707	248.764	EBIT	1286.158	3515.206
Corporate Size	1.691	2.312	Corporate Size	9.887	27.066
Foreign Subsidiaries	1.36	2.34	Foreign Subsidiaries	14.4	37.02
Macroeconomic Attractiveness	16.455	0.073	Macroeconomic Attractiveness	16.494	0.046
Board Timeliness	2.266	0.858	Board Timeliness	2.049	0.897
C-Management Compensation	4.308	0.613	C-Management Compensation	4.518	0.440
Shareholder Voting	5.864	0.351	Shareholder Voting	5.716	0.480
Other Protections	5.415	0.455	Other Protections	5.351	0.459

FEW (Stewardship Model)

N = 18	Means	Std. Dev.	N = 15	Means	Std. Dev.
Moral Vulnerability	-14.857	14.373	Moral Vulnerability	42.855	19.230
Income per Employee	-153.96	377.74	Income per Employee	31.78	41.10
EBIT	356.091	1191.951	EBIT	2530.902	4099.164
Corporate Size	1.447	2.207	Corporate Size	27.627	27.565
Foreign Subsidiaries	3.39	5.01	Foreign Subsidiaries	31.27	26.76
Macroeconomic Attractiveness	16.485	0.0706	Macroeconomic Attractiveness	16.484	0.0266
Board Timeliness	0.987	0.833	Board Timeliness	0.776	0.903
C-Management Compensation	3.771	0.988	C-Management Compensation	3.415	1.123
Shareholder Voting	5.581	0.488	Shareholder Voting	4.982	0.670
Other Protections	4.949	0.508	Other Protections	5.019	0.420

LOW   **CORPORATE PORTFOLIO OF MORAL HAZARD RISKS FROM BUSINESS UNITS IN COUNTRIES$_{1...k}$**   HIGH

Table 6.3 Results of regression analysis predicting corporate moral vulnerability

	Model 1		Model 2	
Variables	Beta	s.e.	Beta	s.e.
Board Timeliness			−0.06	3.82
C-Management Compensation & Protection			0.03	4.54
Shareholder Voting			−0.21*	6.84
Other Protections			0.01	8.41
controls				
Corporate Size	0.38***	0.19	0.32**	0.19
Corporate Business Portfolio's Macroeconomic Attractiveness	−0.17+	62.37	−0.19*	62.37
R^2	0.17**		0.22*	
adj. R^2	0.15		0.15	

$n = 70$; $^+p < .10$; $^*p < .05$; $^{**}p < .01$; $^{***}p < .001$;
one-tail significance; standardized Beta; intercept not reported

Table 6.4 Results of regression analysis predicting corporate profit[a]

	Model 1		Model 2	
Variables	Beta	s.e.	Beta	s.e.
Corporate Moral Vulnerability			−0.09+	4.50
controls				
Corporate Size	0.91***	6.91	0.94***	7.41
Corporate Business Portfolio's Macroeconomic Attractiveness	0.00	2323.85	−0.01	2339.64
R^2	0.83***		0.82*	
adj. R^2	0.83		0.81	

$n = 70$; $^+p < .10$; $^*p < .05$; $^{**}p < .01$; $^{***}p < .001$;
one-tail significance; standardized Beta; intercept not reported
[a] Profit measure used is EBIT.

Discussion

The introduction of the *corporate moral vulnerability* construct is one of the major contributions of this research. We use it here to contrast a principal–agent model of corporate governance in which managers are held accountable to the interests of shareholders, with a stewardship model in which corporate provisions are not used to hold managers accountable to shareholders. Using a sample of 70 publicly traded pharmaceutical companies, we find that the corporate appetite for moral hazard risk is less as the provisions for voting for the board of directors tends toward the principal–agent model of corporate governance.

Interestingly, we find that the corporate appetite for moral vulnerability in its portfolio of foreign subsidiaries increases as the governance provisions for management compensation and liability protection tend more toward the stewardship model. At the same time, we observe that corporate provisions holding management accountable for protecting the value of the firm is associated with increase in foreign subsidiaries. Thus, we observe an incentive structure for management to seek moral hazard risks and achieve expedient profitability, even at the expense of longer-term income.

We suggest that the results reported below in Tables 6.5a and 6.5b offer preliminary evidence for the nomological validity of this construct. Table 6.5a reports on our ex post expectation that there should be some premium available for an appetite for moral hazard risk as there is for other forms of risk. In Table 6.5a we observe this risk–reward premium from *Corporate Moral Vulnerability* in the model predicting the magnitude of income per employee (*Profitability*), even after controlling for corporate size and the macroeconomic attractiveness of its portfolio of subsidiaries ($\beta = 0.25; p < .01$). Here we find agreement with prior literature that argues a corrupt environment can increase corporate overhead costs substantially while simultaneously providing mechanisms that remove regulatory barriers to the expedient productivity of assets on hand. As we see in Model#2 of Table 6.5a, *Corporate Moral Vulnerability* explains more variance in *Profitability* per employee than the control measures explain alone.

We see in Table 6.5b preliminary evidence for the external validity of the *corporate moral vulnerability* construct in the positive and significant relationship between it and the number of *foreign subsidiaries* a corporation has in its portfolio ($\beta = 0.30; p < .01$), even after accounting for controls and the influence of corporate governance provisions. The United States is one of the less corrupt countries according to the World Bank indices we apply in this research, thus we expect that a firm will be vulnerable to relatively higher levels of country-level corruption as it locates more subsidiaries throughout the world.

Despite encouraging preliminary evidence of theoretical and external validity, the research reported here has many limitations. It reports analyses of a single-industry sample, so the generalizability of results to other industries needs to be explored. As with any new construct, much work

Table 6.5a   Results of regression analysis of profitability[a]

Variables	Model 1 Beta	s.e.	Model 2 Beta	s.e.
Corporate Moral Vulnerability			0.25**	1.14
controls				
Corporate Size	0.25*	1.77	0.15	1.88
Corporate Business Portfolio's Macroeconomic Attractiveness	−0.67	595.51	−0.02	593.91
R^2	0.06		0.12*	
adj. R^2	0.04		0.07	

$n = 70$; $^+p < .10$; $^*p < .05$; $^{**}p < .01$; $^{***}p < .001$;
one-tail significance; standardized Beta; intercept not reported
[a] Profitability measure is income per employee (cash before extraordinaries).

Table 6.5b   Results of regression analysis

Variables	Profitability Beta	s.e.	Foreign Subsidiaries Beta	s.e.
Corporate Moral Vulnerability	0.25**	1.14	0.30**	0.08
Board Timeliness			−0.09	2.67
C-Management Compensation & Protection			−0.28**	2.99
Shareholder Voting			−0.05	4.85
Other Protections			0.17+	5.80
controls				
Corporate Size	0.15	1.88		
Corporate Business Portfolio's Macroeconomic Attractiveness	−0.02	593.91	0.11	45.63
R^2	0.12*		0.22*	
adj. R^2	0.07		0.15	

$n = 70$; $^+p < .10$; $^*p < .05$; $^{**}p < .01$; $^{***}p < .001$;
one-tail significance; standardized Beta; intercept not reported
[a] Profitability measure used is income per employee (before extraordinaries).

remains to be done to show its validity. For example, we use a single kind of moral hazard risk, exposure to country-level corruption, to measure this new construct. Future research needs to explore the convergent validity of *corporate moral vulnerability* with additional measures of moral hazard risk.

Nevertheless, the results reported here encourage us to invite more research applying the *corporate moral vulnerability* construct to risk management problems and corporate governance of the principal–agent relationship. Using the techniques in this research, for example, we can measure the *change in moral vulnerability* associated with the consequences of corporate strategic options. The formation, maintenance, and termination of strategic alliances are options that we expect will have measurable consequences for a firm's magnitude of *corporate moral vulnerability*. We may add to our understanding of alliance attractiveness and sustainability if we examine the impact of these options on the corporation's vulnerability to moral hazards and the influence of corporate governance on the allocation of risk.

Corporate moral vulnerability may also add to our understanding of the competitive dynamics of strategic rivalry and action. For example, risk management of the corporation's portfolio of moral hazards may influence the attractiveness of rivalrous action and response in multi-market competition. Strategy theories of competitive advantage grounded in relational or resource views of the firm also may benefit from considering *corporate moral vulnerability* as an important part of the context that moderates direct strategic relationships.

We suspect that there will be important differences in the distribution of moral vulnerability within the corporation. A corporation in which moral vulnerability is homogeneously distributed, for example, may call for broad corporate-wide risk management systems to monitor, control, and insure the entire corporation. For firms in which *moral vulnerability* is heterogeneously distributed, risk management practitioners may rank order business units within the corporation in order to focus their efforts where the risk of moral hazard losses are more concentrated.

In this research, we argue that the magnitude of moral hazards embedded in the corporation can be thought of as its portfolio of *corporate moral vulnerability*. We believe that scholarly effort would be well-spent in the development of this construct, the exploration of its role in risk management of moral hazards, and toward understanding its relationship with corporate performance.

Note

1   Our difference score measure of the parent corporation's exposure to corruption, anchored on the United States, is perfectly correlated with the measure calculated for only parent corporations with foreign subsidiaries.

References

Aragandoña, A. 2005. Corruption and companies: the use of facilitating payments. *Journal of Business Ethics*, 60: 251–64.

Eisenhardt, K.M. 1989. Agency theory: An assessment and review. *Academy of Management Review*, 14(1): 57.

Ellstrand, Alan E., Laszlo Tihanyi, and Johnathan L. Johnson. 2002. Board structure and international political risk. *Academy of Management Journal*, 45(4): 769–77.

Gompers, Paul A., Andrew Metrick, and Joy L. Ishii. 2003. Corporate governance and equity prices, *Quarterly Journal of Economics*, 118(1): 107–55.

Jensen, M. and W. Meckling. 1976. Theory of the firm: managerial behavior, agency costs, and ownership structure. *Journal of Financial Economics*, 3: 305–60.

Kaufmann, Daniel. 2004. Corruption, Governance and Security: Challenges for the Rich Countries and the World, chapter in the Global Competitiveness Report 2004/2005. www.worldbank.org/wbi/governance/pubs/gcr2004.html (accessed February 15, 2008).

Kaufmann, Daniel and Shiang-Jin Wei. Does "grease money" speed up the wheels of commerce? International Monetary Fund, Working Paper No. 00/64. www.worldbank.org/wbi/governance/pdf/grease.pdf (accessed February 14, 2008).

Kostova, Tatiana and Kendall Roth. 2002. Adoption of an organizational practice by subsidiaries of multinational corporations: institutional and relational effects. *Academy of Management Journal*, 45(1): 215–33.

Saftlas, Herman and Wendy Diller. 2007. Healthcare pharmaceuticals industry survey, November 27, Standard & Poor's Industry Surveys 175(48). McGraw-Hill Companies, NY; http://www.lib.ncsu.edu (accessed February 14, 2008).

Transparency International 2006. Corruption in the pharmaceutical sector, Part 5 of the *Global Corruption Report 2006*. London: Pluto Press. http://www.transparency.org/publications/gcr/download_gcr/download_gcr_2006; (accessed February 14, 2008).

Transparency International 2002. (May 14, 2002) Bribe Payers Index 2002 (May 14) http://www.transparency.org/policy_research/surveys_indices/bpi (accessed February 15, 2008).

Wells, Joseph T. 2003. Corruption: causes and cures. *Journal of Accountancy*, April: 49–52.

7

Mitigating the Exposure of Corporate Boards to Risk and Unethical Conflicts

Shann Turnbull

Abstract

Directors of corporations governed by a single board: (i) Have excessive and unethical powers to become "Sources of risk;" and (ii) Lack processes to systematically obtain information independently of management on the Strengths, Weaknesses, Opportunities and Threats (SWOT) of either their managers or the business to be "Managers of Risk." The removal and/or mediation of unethical conflicts can be achieved by amending corporate constitutions to separate governance powers from the power to manage business operations. Systematic independent information on the SWOT of managers and the business can be obtained by the corporate constitution introducing advisory councils appointed by those individuals on whom the business depends for its existence, such as its customers, suppliers and other stakeholders. In addition to mitigating the operating, reputational and financial risks of directors and the firm, evidence is provided to show how stakeholder councils have produced competitive advantages. The changes in corporate constitutions described protect the reputations and personal liabilities of directors by removing perceptions of unethical conduct and provide them with credible evidence that they can carry out their fiduciary duties with due care and diligence to monitor managers and manager business risks.

Introduction

This paper describes how a corporation governed by a single board exposes directors to: (i) conflicts of interests that create unethical relationships; and

(ii) naïve self-deluding acceptance of operating risks. Conflicts can be mediated by including in corporate constitutions the type of arrangements used by venture capitalists in shareholder agreements or by banks in loan agreements. The mitigation of both conflicts and operating risks can be achieved by introducing changes in corporate constitutions and/or by-laws along the lines found in some European firms.

Directors of publicly traded corporations (PTCs) in the US, the UK and other Anglophile countries have absolute power to manage their own conflicts of interests. This situation arises because corporate constitutions typically delegate to directors what Monks and Sykes (2002: 2) described as "at least six inappropriate powers giving rise to serious conflicts of interest". These "inappropriate powers" can be accepted in closely knit corporations when the individuals who delegate corporate powers as shareholders are the same individuals who obtain the powers as directors.

Many European corporations have constitutions where shareholders provide directors with the power to manage the business, but they withhold governance powers that can create serious conflicts of interest such as determining their own appointment, remuneration and control of the auditor. Conflicts can expose directors to unethical conduct, reputational risk and personal liabilities. The separation of governance power from the power to manage a business is widely practiced but little noticed or studied in Anglo countries.

Research into corporate boards and corporations is prolific and represents what Kuhn (1970: 24) referred to as "Normal Science". Kuhn described "Normal Science" as that which does not "call forth new sorts of phenomena: indeed those that will not fit the box are often not seen at all."

However, most Anglo-based PLCs are governed by more than one board, although this phenomenon often goes unnoticed. "Not seen at all" is the second board created by a controlling shareholder who carries out the governance powers that would otherwise be undertaken by directors of a corporation with diverse shareholders. Indeed, some controlling shareholders may also be responsible for making strategic decisions. The separation of strategic and operational decision making can be obscured when the owner is also the manager, as found in Microsoft and the News Corporation. A dominant shareholder represents a supervising control center or what is in effect a supervisory or "governance board". The ubiquity of dominant shareholders in PTCs globally has been reported by Porta, Lopez-de-Silanes, and Shleifer (1999), and in the US by Holderness (2007).

In referring to the two-tiered board structure created by a Leveraged Buy-Out Association (LBO), Jensen (1993: 869) states that they represent "a proven model of governance structure" while Shleifer and Vishny (1996: 45) found "that LBOs are efficient organizations."

To describe firms controlled by more than one board or control center I coined the phrase "compound board" (Turnbull, 2000c: 1). This is a phenomenon that is found widely, but rarely noticed. Compound boards can be created within a corporation as found in Europe and/or through dominant shareholders and/or stakeholders like financiers who obtain contractual control rights. An external compound board is created in a Japanese Keiretsu where supplier and customer firms appoint members of a Keiretsu council together with the dominant shareholder (Analytica, 1992: 130). The competitive advantages of such arrangements are discussed later in the paper.

Some European countries, such as France and Germany, require companies to have two or more boards (Analytica, 1992) and firms with three or more boards can be described as having "network governance." Jones, Hesterly, and Borgatti (1997) have described how network governance in the US is adopted through competitive pressures by firms operating in the more dynamic and/or complex industries such as electronics and bio-technology.

Network governance is also a characteristic of nontrivial sustainable worker owned firms (Turnbull, 2000c: 178). The ubiquity of network governance in stakeholder-controlled firms supports the conjecture that network governance is a condition for firms to become self-governing like democratic nation-states. This conjecture is supported by the findings of Persson, Roland, and Tabellini (1996) and also by the work of Diermeier and Myerson (1999).

The competitive advantages of network governed firms over hierarchical firms are illustrated by the success of Visa International Inc. (Hock, 1994) and Mondragón (Turnbull, 2000c: 199–224). Both of these firms posses hundreds of boards with each board possessing quite different responsibilities. In this way network governance introduces distributed intelligence with the decomposition of decision making to a degree that permits ordinary individuals to collectively manage an extraordinary variety of complex activities much more successfully than in centralized command and control hierarchical organizations (Turnbull, 2000c: 245).

As noted above, simple compound boards are commonly created by shareholder agreements with venture capitalists who invest in a private firm on the condition of obtaining control rights over such matters as the nature of expenditures, the appointment of directors, the CEO and the auditor. Simple compound boards can also be created by loan agreements when bankers obtain similar rights to determine how their funds are spent, approve changes in directors and the appointment of the auditor.

The widespread use of shareholder and loan agreements that limit the power of directors illustrates that such a division of power is acceptable to firms as a condition for accessing finance. The widespread acceptance also illustrates how a division of powers can be introduced without inhibiting firm performance. Indeed, the network firms cited above provide evidence of superior performance and competitiveness, as will be discussed later in the paper.

This paper limits its discussion to some general principles of introducing a separation of powers to eliminate, mitigate and/or manage director conflicts of interests and to enhance director access to feed forward and feedback information independently of management to reduce risks to them, the business and to enhance performance. We also give some indication of how compound boards can be designed and introduced not only to mitigate risk and unethical conflicts for directors, but also to improve firms' operating efficiency and competitiveness.

The next section considers the systemic problems of a unitary board in exposing directors to conflicts and how these can be removed and/or managed by separating the power of directors to manage the business from those required to govern the corporation. Then we describe how directors lack systemic processes for obtaining operating information independently of management in order to verify the information provided by management for evaluating the level of risk management either in the management or in the firm as a whole. This is followed by a discussion of how network governance mitigates risks and provides competitive advantages. the paper ends with some concluding remarks.

Director Conflicts: Their Elimination, Mitigation, and Management

This section identifies the inappropriate powers possessed by directors and how they can be removed or managed in an ethically acceptable manner.

Directors of a unitary board have power to both serve their own interests and support their position of the board, as set out in Table 7.1. While the exercise of some of these powers could be illegal as well as unethical, it may be impossible for shareholders, regulators or others to discover inappropriate actions until after the event. The ability for shareholders or regulators to take corrective action could become problematical, if not also costly. As a result directors obtain absolute power to manage their own conflicts of interests. This bears out the famous maxim of Lord Acton (1887) that "power tends to corrupt and absolute power tends to corrupt absolutely."

There are many ways in which corporate constitutions could be written to remove, limit and/or manage the inappropriate powers listed in Table 7.1.

Table 7.1   Corrupting powers of a unitary board

Directors have the power to:

A. *Obtain private benefits for themselves (and/or control groups who appoint them) by*:
- (a) Determining their own remuneration and payments to associates
- (b) Directing business to interests with which they are associated
- (c) Issuing shares or options at a discounted value to themselves and/or their associates
- (d) Selling assets of the firm to one or more directors or their associates at a discount
- (e) Acquiring assets from one or more directors or their associates at inflated values
- (f) Trading on favored terms with parties who provide directors with private benefits
- (g) Using firm resources and/or their status in other ways.

B. *Maintain their board positions and private benefits by*:
- (a) Reporting on their own performance and influencing "independent" advisers by:
  - (i) Selecting auditors and other "independent" advisers
  - (ii) Determining their fees
  - (iii) Controlling the process by which auditors are appointed by UK shareholders
  - (iv) Terminating the appointment of auditors and other "independent" advisers
  - (v) Paying additional fees for work which is not required to be "independent"
  - (vi) Determining the terms of reference on which "independent" advice is provided
- (b) Determining the level of profit reported to shareholders by:
  - (i) Selecting the basis for valuing or writing off trading and fixed assets
  - (ii) Determining the life of assets and so the cost of depreciation
  - (iii) Selecting the basis for recognizing revenues and costs in long term contracts
  - (iv) Selecting accounting policies within accepted accounting standards
  - (v) Selecting, controlling and paying "independent" valuers and determining the basis on which valuations are to be carried out
- (c) Not disclosing full pecuniary or nonpecuniary benefits – even if required to do so
- (d) Determining how any conflicts of interest are managed
- (e) Filling casual board vacancies with people who support their own positions

(Cont'd)

Table 7.1 (*Cont'd*)

(f) Nominating new directors who support them at shareholder meetings

(g) Controlling the nomination and election procedures and processes

(h) Controlling the conduct of shareholder meetings

(i) Appointing pension fund managers for the firm who also provide them proxies

(j) Voting uncommitted proxies to support their own election

(k) Not allowing the firm to compete with related parties who can vote for them.

Shareholder agreements with venture capitalists and loan documents with financiers typically specify veto powers over a number of the items listed in Table 7.1 as a way of protecting their interests. But when a company becomes publicly traded any such veto powers by venture capitalists are removed. The powers of financiers may not be made public and are unlikely to be as comprehensive as those introduced by a venture capitalist.

It can be argued that regulators and stock exchanges are being irresponsible in allowing corporations to have their shares publicly traded while providing directors with absolute power to serve their own interests before those of their investors. It is irresponsible because the role of regulators and stock exchange listing rules are to protect the interest of investors and other stakeholders against rogue directors.

Regulators have in effect legitimized directors obtaining unethical conflicts of interests. This has been further reinforced by so-called codes of corporate governance best practices also accepting the unethical structure of Anglo PTCs. As a result investors, governments, law makers and their regulators accept the unethical structure of Anglo corporations as the "natural order" of a capitalist system. The unethical relationships have become institutionalize into law by the Sarbanes–Oxley (SARBOX) legislation and codes of so-called "best practices" found around the world. However, some scholars, such as Romano (2004), describe SARBOX as "quack corporate governance."

In order to drive home the point of the present unethical structure of Anglo PTCs, consider how a court of law is structured as indicated in Figure 7.1. A fundamental requirement for justice is that the judge should be independent of the accused.

It would be unethical for any person accused of a crime to be able to select, hire and remunerate the judge as shown in Figure 7.2.

Judges in a court of law may excuse themselves from officiating when it is perceived that they could have a conflict of interest. But not only is the

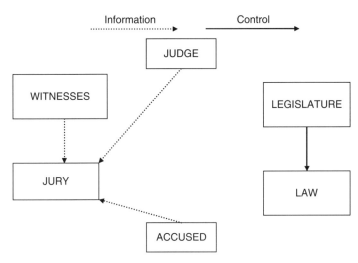

Figure 7.1   Ethical relationships in a law court. Judge, jury, and experts independent of accused

judge/auditor of Anglo PTCs employed by the directors/accused being judged – so are the so-called "Independent" experts. In addition, the directors being judged can employ the judge to undertake additional duties that in effect can act as a bribe.

The most insidious aspect of the Anglo system is to be found in the US where accounting rules to be used by auditors to judge directors can be influenced by CEOs (Monks, 2007). In this way, the rules used to judge the accounts prepared by US directors can be influenced by those being judged – as indicated in Figure 7.2. Such influence would be considered ethically unacceptable in a court of law that has no such influence. As shown in Figure 7.1 the nature of the law used to judge the accused is determined independently – by precedents and the legislature. In addition, the judge is also appointed and paid independently of the law makers in most countries. Another problem is that because the four largest audit firms in the world are US based, the business model and practices of US auditors are applied globally in jurisdictions where the practice and purpose of auditing can be quite different (Turnbull, 2005b).

Tax auditors are appointed by the government, rather than the taxpayer. The idea of the government appointing financial auditors for PTCs was raised by *The Economist* (2002) and in the US Congress in the aftermath of the Enron scandal. This idea had previously been considered by Hatherly

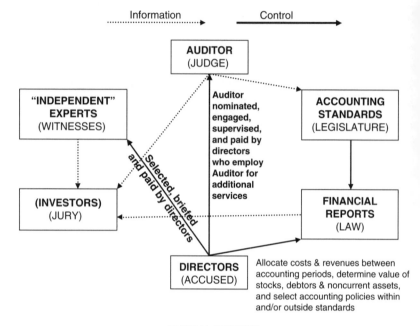

ETHICAL REMEDY:

DIVISION OF POWER BY SEPARATING THE GOVERNANCE
POWER OF DIRECTORS FROM THEIR EXECUTIVE POWERS

Figure 7.2   Unethical relationships created by a unitary board: Conflicts of
interests for directors, auditors, and experts

(1995), who also considered four other options. His conclusion was that
PTC auditors should be appointed by a committee of shareholders, as proposed in the model constitution attached to the English Companies Act of
1868 and as currently practiced in a number of European jurisdictions. In
2004 the National Association of Pension Funds made a recommendation
to the UK government that auditors be appointed by a committee of shareholders as reported by *AccountancyAge* (2004).

   The author adopted the approach of having a committee of investors
appointing and controlling the auditor in two ventures he established in
Australia. No change in the law was required. The arrangements were
embedded in the investment contracts of the first venture which was established on an unincorporated basis in order to allow tax benefits to be shared
by the investors (Turnbull, 2002b). In the second venture the arrangements
were established by changes to the corporate constitution in 1996 as
described in the Appendix to Turnbull (2000a: 152–5). The shareholder

committee was described as a "Corporate Senate" (Turnbull, 1993). In Figure 7.3 the Corporate Senate is also described as a "Governance Board", a name adopted in a minority report recommending the idea to the Australian Parliament (Murray, 1998).

The approach recommended by Senator Murray (1998) removed the power of directors to make decisions in those instances where a conflict was involved. The approach used by author (Turnbull, 1993, 2000a) did not remove any powers of the directors except to appoint and remunerate the auditor, chair the AGM and manage its voting processes. However, under this approach the Senate had the power to veto any activity in which a director had a conflict of interest – such as determining their remuneration or nomination. The veto could be overturned if the directors obtained approval of shareholders voting on the normal plutocratic basis of *one vote per share*. The three individuals on the Senate were elected on a democratic basis of *one vote per shareholder*, rather than one vote per share, in order to protect minority interests from being exploited by a dominant shareholder.

If a dominant shareholder did use its votes to overturn a Senate veto then the market price of the shares would become the final arbiter of the decision. However, the incentive for a dominant shareholder to exercise exploitive control over minority investors was reduced as a result of the directors being elected by cumulative voting (Bhagat & Brickley, 1984; Gordon, 1993). Cumulative voting, a form of preferential voting, allows minority shareholders to appoint directors and so provides them with the will to act against the majority. The Corporate Senate or Governance Board provided them with the means to act as a whistle blower *privately* and *independently* of any majority of directors or even a parent company. Similar arrangements have been proposed in the US by a legal scholar (Dallas, 1997).

European countries offer various ways of introducing checks and balances on the powers of directors. However, little research has been undertaken on their relative advantages and disadvantages. But the introduction of a separation of powers and/or a process to manage conflicting powers of directors is a fundamental requirement in minimizing directors as a source of risk for investors and other stakeholders.

The establishment of a shareholder committee to control the auditor is not a sufficient condition for the protection of investors. This was illustrated by the failure in 2003 of Parmalat that was incorporated in Italy (Melis, 2004, 2005). In the Parmalat case, the statutory shareholder audit committee was appointed on the basis of one vote per share as for the directors. In contrast to the Corporate Senate established by the author in Australia, the Italian practice allowed the dominant shareholder, who provided the CEO and controlled the directors, to also control the audit arrangements. As a result, there was no effective separation of power to provide checks and balances.

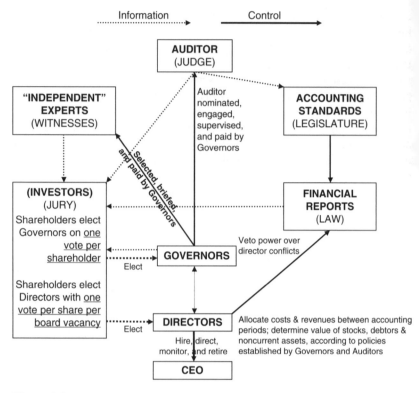

Figure 7.3 Ethical relationships created with a democratically elected governance board

Taken in isolation the separation of powers to remove and/or manage director conflicts does not provide a basis for directors to carry out their most fundamental function of directing and monitoring management with due care, diligence and vigilance. This is because of the communication limitations introduced by hierarchical organisations as considered in the next section.

Exposure of Directors to Operating Risks

This section considers the exposure of directors to operating risks from not being adequately informed of them by management and/or senior management not being adequately informed by subordinates. A second related source of risk is that directors can also be exposed to the risk of management obscuring their mismanagement and/or bad management. A third source of risk in complex firms and/or those operating in fast changing complex environments are the inability of hierarchies to detect and appropriately respond to new threats and opportunities. A fourth source of risk is the propensity of good people to accept and/or undertake bad and/or unethical actions as shown by Milgram (2004) and Bazerman, Loewenstein, and Moore (2002).

The exposure of directors to inadequate, incomplete, missing and/or misleading information is an inherent feature of hierarchies. Even with the most skilled managers with the highest integrity and motivation, communication can become distorted, garbled or missing when messages have to be passed through a number of levels. This problem is demonstrated by the party game of "Chinese Whispers." In this game a message is privately given to one person who must relay the message privately to another with the relay repeated another couple of times. The last person in the relay then makes public the message they received to compare it with starting message to reveal what was lost, misunderstood and/or inadvertently changed.

In a command and control hierarchy the problem of accurate communications is compounded. This is because messages down the hierarchy need to be interpreted according to local relevance and messages up the hierarchy need to be condensed to avoid information overload. In analysing hierarchies, Downs (1967) conservatively assumed that the biases of managers resulted in 10 percent of the true meaning of the information being lost each time it was relayed through each level. He also assumed that 5 percent of the true meaning is lost from errors in transmission. The loss of meaning and errors reduced the correct information by 15 percent per level. Correct information would only represent 85 percent of that which was condensed by 50 percent at each level. The cumulative compounding result in a hierarchy of five levels is shown in the "correct" and "missing" columns of Table 7.2. The table highlights the possibility that even the Chief Executive Officer (CEO) may not have the information required to regulate the organization as 96.7 percent of the information available to workers four levels below is either lost or wrong The table illustrates the point made by Jensen (1993: 864) that "Serious information problems limit the effectiveness of board members in the typical large corporation."

This problem is compounded even further in a hierarchy because it is not in the self-interest of any subordinate to report to superiors on any problems for which they could be perceived as being accountable. Unlike a party game, there is a serious incentive for not trying to communicate with complete accuracy. Indeed, there is an incentive to omit or filter bad

Table 7.2 Loss and distortion of information in hierarchies

Hierarchy (public or private sector)	Information upwards			Employees	
	Volume	Correct	Missing	With say a span of 5	
Legislature Minister/shareholder(s)	(50% lost/level)	(85% of lower level)	or wrong meaning	per level	accumulated total
Board of directors	3.1%	1.4%	98.6%		
Chief Executive Officer	6.3%	3.3%	96.7%	1	1
Senior management	12.5%	7.7%	92.3%	5	6
Middle management	25.0%	18.1%	81.9%	25	31
Team leaders	50.0%	42.5%	57.5%	125	156
Workers	100.0%	100.0%	0.0%	625	781

news, and to bias reports in a self-serving manner. As a fundamental role of a board is to monitor and evaluate both the business and its executives, directors who rely only on information provided by managers are being naïve and irresponsible in carrying out their fiduciary duties with due care and diligence. The incentive for managers and CEOs to provide self-serving information represents a second ubiquitous source of risk for directors.

A third source of risk inherent in hierarchical firms operating in complex activities and/or in rapidly changing environments is their ability to identify problems and opportunities and take constructive action on a timely basis. A fundamental law of the science of governance described as "Ashby's Law" states in effect that the control of many variables requires a requisite variety of regulators (Ashby, 1968: 212). A corollary of the law is that the capacity to control many variables is also dependent upon communication channels with an adequate "bandwidth" to communicate the variety of variables (Ashby, 1968: 211).

By their very nature command and control hierarchies possess limited communication channels and also lack the flexibility to act in a timely fashion to detect and react to internal shortcomings and/or external threats and opportunities. The defeat in Vietnam of the most powerful military force in the world illustrates the problem of a command and control hierarchy attempting to control the diversified dynamic complexity of an organization such as the Viet Cong. Company directors are likewise exposed to being ambushed by a variety of small nimble competitors, many of whom may be unknown. This insight explains why some business leaders preach the need to be continually paranoid about competition within and external to the firm to survive – a view famously articulated by the former US Secretary of Defense Donald Rumsfeld's discussion of "unknown unknowns" (Rumsfeld, 2002).

CEOs and directors involved in complex businesses and/or operating in dynamic environments are being dangerously naïve and self-deluding in attempting to manage risk without knowledge of Ashby's law of requisite variety. According to Ashby, the "[L]aw of requisite variety, like the law of Conversation of Energy absolutely prohibits any direct and simple magnification but it does not prohibit supplementation" (Ashby, 1968: 268). The time may come when courts and class action litigants will take action against CEOs and directors who have not established processes of "supplementation" to control risks.

Supplementation of regulation is achieved in social organizations through the establishment co-regulators. The law of requisite variety also means that there needs to be a requisite variety of co-regulators to control risks.

In a business situation, a common example of supplementation to indirectly regulate complexity is provided by the appointment of auditors. This example also illustrates how supplementation can fail when the co-regulator can be captured by those who are being regulated. On many occasions, Auditors have failed to detect imminent corporate collapses. The impossibility of auditor independence has been documented by a number of scholars (Bazerman, Loewenstein & Moore, 2002; Bazerman, Morgan & Loewenstein, 1997; Bush 2004; O'Connor 2004; Shapiro 2005; Turnbull 2000b).

The take home message for directors is that there is a risk in relying on audited information when the auditors are engaged by the people they judge rather than by the stakeholders they have been appointed to protect. The risk of auditors being misleading is supported by their ability to attest in their reports that they are "independent" when in the ordinary meaning of the word they are paid agents of the people they are judging (Turnbull, 2006). The propensity for auditors to provide the answers that directors require is an illustration of how good people can do bad things, as shown by the experiments undertaken by Milgram (2004) to explain the behaviour of good people in Nazi Germany. This is a fourth area of risk for directors, shareholders and other stakeholders.

In order for co-regulation to be effective in supplementing regulation, the co-regulators need to be serving those parties who the regulators are created to protect (Turnbull, 2007). The appointment of a shareholder committee, Senate or Governance Board to control the auditor meets this test. To protect CEOs and/or directors from the risk of them receiving incomplete, inadequate biased or wrong reports, it is necessary for additional and independent channels of communications to be established. The number of politically independent new channels of feedback and feed forward communications need to be sufficient to cover the variety of variables that affect the operations of the firm.

One reason for a requisite variety of communication channels is to provide sufficient bandwidth to report on those variables affecting the firm and also to establish control as required by the corollary of Ashby's Law. Another reason is Shannon's Law of communications which states that errors in communications can be reduced as much as desired from a requisite variety of channels to cross-check communications (Shannon & Weaver, 1949). Shannon's mathematically grounded law explains why CEOs, directors, and government regulators cannot reliably monitor the operations of a firm from a single source. Indeed, it could be said that CEOs, directors, and regulators are each being irresponsible in not establishing a requisite variety of communication channels to obtain information that can cross-check and challenge the hegemony of management views.[1]

Even journalists seek a number of sources to collaborate their reports. Therefore it is dangerously naïve for directors not to protect themselves and the business by systematically obtaining a number of independent sources to safeguard the integrity of the information by which they monitor and direct a corporation whether or not it is a PTC or government owned enterprise.

While auditors are supposed to provide an alternative view, they may be unwilling with their current conflicted relationships to publicly provide an opposing view – as has been witnessed in a number of recent corporate collapses. In any event the remit of auditors is narrowly limited to financial *results* rather than *risks* and so is able to omit reporting on nonfinancial operations and risks.

Practicing company directors can often be skeptical about the relevance of "The Science of Corporate Governance" (Turnbull, 2002c) to their risk exposure. They may claim that they can evaluate the integrity of management information by the character of the CEO, "the cut of his jib," accessing subordinates and other subjective and idiosyncratic processes. While all such processes can be of value, subjective and idiosyncratic processes do not represent a systemically creditability basis to responsibly protect the savings of millions of pensioners and perhaps also millions of stakeholders involved in the larger and more complex firms.

In particular, CEOs obtain their status because of their verbal and non-verbal communication and other skills. The assumption that nice guys are also good guys is not necessarily true – as is evidenced from a number of corporate collapses of firms managed by charming and charismatic CEOs. All directors need to ask themselves what objective and reliable systematic processes they have put in place to determine when their trust in management might be misplaced.

As one of the basic roles of directors is to carry out monitoring of the management and the business, directors cannot claim to carry out their fundamental fiduciary obligations if they have no such creditable processes to determine when their trust in management might be misplaced. Relying on auditors, outside analysts and/or subjective and idiosyncratic value judgements is simply not good enough. Directors need a highly visible objective and creditable systematic basis to demonstrate to their various constituencies and/or litigators and that they are protecting the interests of all stakeholders – including themselves – from being misled by management. Even if the CEO has the highest integrity he may not be fully informed. Just one rogue trader can destroy a company, as demonstrated by the failure of Barings Bank in 1995 (Allen, 1997).

Some of the security traders in the banks that were dealing with Barings were aware of the risk exposures that were being accepted. But as occurred in the case of the individuals that had early concerns about Enron and many other corporate collapses there was no socially safe simple facility for them to share their concerns. An early warning system is needed not just to avoid and correct problems but also to exploit opportunities.

The individuals who are best placed to provide feedback and feed forward information on the Strengths, Weaknesses, Opportunities and Threats (SWOT) to a business and of its executives are its employees, customers, suppliers, dealers, agents and various other stakeholders. The very variety of stakeholders that are involved with complex organizations provide the basis for establishing a requisite variety of communications and controls to reliably, systematically and comprehensively identify and manage the SWOT of the business and its managers. How this might be achieved is considered in the following section.

Introducing Network Governance to Manage Risks

This section considers how to design the governance architecture of corporations to reduce risk and increase their level of competitiveness.

The guiding design principles are based on the control and communication systems found in all forms of life to manage their survival in uncertain, unpredictable, and complex dynamic environments. The simplest forms of biota adopt control and communication strategies that economize the energy and material required to sustain their existence. This is why the strategies identified by the science of governance for managing complexity also provide competitive advantages to firms as they minimize transactions and so costs.

However, the competitive advantage of adopting network governance found in nature is not intuitively obvious. Likewise the change from "U-Form firms" to "M-Form firms" (Williamson, 1985: 279–83) was not intuitively obvious in simpler times.

The paradox of achieving simplification through complexity was noted by Hock (1994) who stated: "Nothing can be made simpler without it becoming more complex." Thus while network governance may make the organization more complex it simplifies the need for individuals to receive, store, process, and communicate data and its higher order derivatives of information, knowledge and wisdom, as indicated by Turnbull (2000c: 245). As stated by Hock (1998):

> *The fascinating thing is that the greater the capacity to receive, store, utilize, transform and transmit information, the more diverse and complex the entity.*
>
> This holds true throughout the history of the rising chain of life – from particle to neutrino, to nucleus, to atom, to amino acid, to protein, molecule, cell, organ and organism – from bacteria to bee, bat, bird and buffalo, right on through to baseball player.

Implicit with the introduction of network governance is the introduction of multiple boards and/or control centres. In this way network governance introduces distributed intelligence to allow the de-composition of decision-making labor. The need for a requisite variety of decision making follows the insights of both Von Neumann (1949) and the reasoning used by Williamson (1985: 279–83) to explain why large US firms in the beginning of the twentieth century changed from a unitary (U-form) architecture to a Multi-divisional (M-form). The specialization of decision making by adopting a divisional form reduced the problem of information overload by managers. Von Neumann showed that the accuracy of decision making can be improved as much as desired by introducing a requisite variety of decision makers.

It is through the amendment of corporate constitutions to engage with stakeholders that requisite variety of communications, regulation and decision making can be achieved that will secure the reduction of risks and will also provide competitive advantages. However, stakeholder engagement for PTCs needs to be designed primarily to protect the interests of both shareholders and directors. This is an overriding requirement to obtain sufficient votes from shareholders in order to amend the corporate constitution.

While the introduction of network governance could and should be unilaterally introduced by directors and the CEOs of firms in the private or government sector, it is unlikely that the full benefits would be achieved unless shareholder and/or regulators became involved. The full benefits of stakeholder engagement demand that their involvement is not at the grace and favor of the CEO and/or the directors. Without political independence from the directors and the CEO, the objective of obtaining the other side of the management story can be lost, subverted, and/or suppressed.

It is very much in the interest of both shareholders and stakeholders that directors hear the other side of the story reported by management. In addition, to obtain stories and intelligence that management might not know about or even be accessible to them – from market researchers, trade associations, and/or consultants. It is for this reason that corporate constitutions and/or by-laws need to provide stakeholders with the power to elect their own boards of advice to the CEO, the directors, and, when appropriate, also to the shareholders and so the public.

As no business can exist without employees, customers, and suppliers these will be described as "strategic stakeholders." Strategic stakeholders may also include sub-contractors to suppliers, agents, distributors and other, according to the particular business model being used. The nature of strategic stakeholders could change over time so by-laws, which can more easily be changed than the corporate constitution, might be used to provide some flexibility in defining those parties who meet the definition of strategic stakeholders.

In some cases provision may be needed to include nonstrategic but operationally important stakeholders who could provide competitive advantages such as specialist education or training, and trade, professional or industry associations. Examples of such arrangements are provided in some of the stakeholder-owned and -controlled firms that make up the Mondragón Corporación Cooperativa (MCC) in the Basque area of Spain. The examples referred to later involve a pig farm and a work experience cooperative.

It is important that each stakeholder constituency elects its own advisory council. One reason for this is to increase the range of politically independent feed back and feed forward information available. Another reason is that there can be competing interests between different stakeholder constituencies that will generate their own particular biases, distortions, and omissions and business intelligence that is different from other stakeholders as well as being different from management information.

Indeed, Pound (1992) has argued that competition for corporate influence and/or control within a corporation provides a much more efficient and effective mechanism to enhance performance than relying on competition for corporate control through the stock market. The variety of different and/or opposing viewpoints that the CEO and directors might obtain from

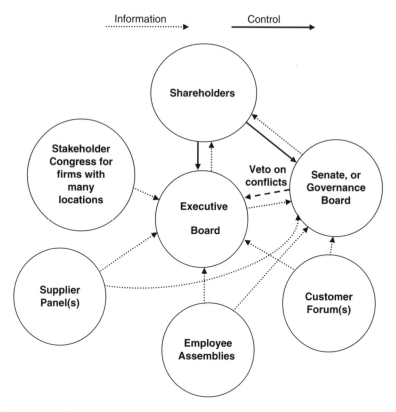

Figure 7.4   Network governance

different stakeholder constituencies demonstrates the degree to which directors would be irresponsible in confining their source of decision-making communications to only the viewpoints of their managers.

The need for formal meetings by directors with the various stakeholder boards is likely to vary from business to business. For instance, multi-national businesses might have a specific sub-councils for each region. An indicative and simplified architecture of the arrangements is presented in Figure 7.4.

It may well be the case that directors might want to meet with some councils more often than others, but it is envisaged that meetings would be held not more than four times a year. Management might desire more frequent engagement in order to achieve operating benefits as stakeholder councils provide a means of organizing the Just-In-Time delivery of goods, Total Quality Control of products, Six Sigma risk management and product innovations as described by Hippel (1996). These operating and competitive advantages are described in greater detail in Turnbull (1997, 2000a, 2000b, 2000c, 2002a, c).

Formal reporting by stakeholder councils, independently of management would be provided to the governance board on an annual basis. At the discretion of the Governance Board the contents of stakeholder reports would be shared with both shareholders and investors. This would remove the need for directors to make "triple bottom line" social and environmental reports, leading to a reduction in directors' reporting obligations and also their duties. There would be no need for social audits as the stakeholder reports would be independent of management (Turnbull, 1995, 2002a, 2005a).

There would be no fees paid to stakeholders to participate in the various stakeholder forums as they would be furthering their own interests in a much more direct and meaningful manner than volunteering their time, effort, and resources to participate in nonprofit protest groups. Such nonprofit activists could be included in appropriate stakeholder bodies. The spontaneous formation of firm-specific stakeholder action associations can be observed in a number of countries. In some countries such as Australia and Sweden there are nonprofit shareholder associations that act as public watchdogs and activists to protect investor interests in many companies. The existence of such bodies illustrates how individuals will commit their own resources to provide a "free ride" to provide greater benefits for others than they can obtain for themselves.

However, apathy is widespread and it may well be the case that only a minority of stakeholders will exercise their right to vote for a representative to further their particular interest – and that fewer still be willing to be nominated for election. However, the experience of Ralph Nader in setting up Citizen Utility Boards (CUBs) demonstrates the willingness of stakeholders to participate (Givens, 1991). Millions of customers of various regulated US utilities providing water, gas, or communication services were invited to donate funds to set up firm-specific consumer advocate units to lobby the regulator to resist price increases. While fewer than 5 percent of the consumers donated this was sufficient to finance professional watchdog units to negotiate efficiency improvements that resulted. in many instances, in a net benefit for those that provided a free ride for those who did not contribute funds.

There appears to be a substantial and growing body of concerned citizens who are willing to promote various causes on a voluntary basis that could be harnessed by corporations to improve their governance and competitiveness. Stakeholder councils provide a systemic process for directors to obtain information to evaluate the SWOT of both their executives and the business independently of management. In this way stakeholder councils can not only reduce the risk of directors and the business but also legitimize the role of directors as monitors of both management and the business in a credible and systematic manner. Appropriately designed network governance provides a basis for directors to demonstrate in a court of law that they were carrying out their fiduciary duties with due care, diligence and vigilance.

The outstanding efficacy of network governance has been demonstrated by the nested networks of network firms formed around the town of Mondragón in the Basque region of Spain. The operating and competitive advantages were reported by Thomas and Logan (1982: 126–7) who stated that:

> Various indicators have been used to explore the economic efficiency of the Mondragón group of cooperatives. During more than two decades a considerable number of cooperative factories have functioned at a level equal to or superior in efficiency to that of capitalist enterprises. The compatibility question in this case has been solved without doubt. Efficiency in terms of the use made of scarce resources has been higher in cooperatives; their growth record of sales, exports and employment, under both favourable and adverse economic conditions, has been superior to that of capitalist enterprises.

My study of Mondragón (Turnbull, 2000c: 199–225) identifies how the architecture of the vertically and laterally recursive networks follow the architecture found in the physical and biological spheres to create and manage complexity. Another feature is how the architecture of the nested component firms is also designed to bond strategic stakeholders to the business. One important consequence is that this feature also provides operating and strategic intelligence to the firm. For instance, the work experience cooperative has a third of its supervisory board appointed by its employees, a third by the parents of the children being educated and a third by the firms who are interested in hiring the students. Similarly, the supervisory board of the pig breeding business has representatives of the farmers who supply the piglets, firms that provide feed and other supplies, employees, and customers who purchase the product. Similar relationships are found in some Japanese firms.

The compound boards of Mondragón possess a separation of powers along the lines found in the US Constitution between the legislature, executive and judiciary. The supervisory board of a Mondragón firm would represent the legislature, making laws under which the executive board operates. The watchdog board, which provided the inspiration for a Corporate Senate, represents the judiciary that manages conflicts between the legislature and the executive and/or constituents. These components are contained in all MCC firms, as indicated in the bottom shaded rectangle of a "Primary cooperative" shown in Figure 7.5 (taken from Turnbull, 2000c: 207).

The operating advantages and competitive advantages introduced by the governance architecture of a compound board of a MCC firm can be indicated by a consideration of how the functions of a unitary Anglo board are taken over by the five components of a MCC compound board. The internal and external conformance and performance functions of an Anglo unitary board have been identified by Tricker (1994: 245 & 287) as shown in Figure 7.6.

A MCC compound board de-composes the five different types of decision-making labor indicated in the five segments of Figure 7.6 into five differently constituted control centers shown in the lower shaded area of Figure 7.5. The five components of a MCC compound board are shown in Figure 7.7. The components are the: Watchdog Board, Supervisory Board, Work Unit, Social Council and Executive Board. In addition to simplifying the role, duties and workload of the directors of a unitary board the MCC compound board introduces distributed intelligence, with enhancements in the variety of information sources, control centers and decision making to allow ordinary individuals to produce extraordinary results.

In addition, the MCC compound board facilitates the three elements of social capital identified by Evans (1996) and Woolcock (1988). The work groups develop "bonding social capital." The social councils develop "bridging social capital" and the bottom-up participation develops "linking social capital" (Evans, 1996; Woolcock, 1998). These links are replicated between groups of firms as shown in the upper shaded box in Figure 7.3.

The degree to which a MCC compound board distributes the roles, duties and functions of a unitary board widely among all employees is indicated in Table 7.3.

Table 7.3 illustrates how management roles, duties, and functions are merged into governance roles, duties, and functions. The ability of a compound board to decompose data processing to simplify the roles, duties, and functions of directors of a unitary board are indicated by the distribution across the five components of a MCC compound board by the "X" symbol in the bottom four rows.

The MCC has compound boards both internal and external to the firm as indicated in the higher shaded rectangle in Figure 7.5 that represents "Relationship Associations or Groups" of primary cooperatives. An external compound board is also found in Japanese Keiretsu as shown in Figure 7.8.

The Keiretsu Council consists of the CEOs of supplier and customer firms with representatives of the major shareholder, who is typically a bank

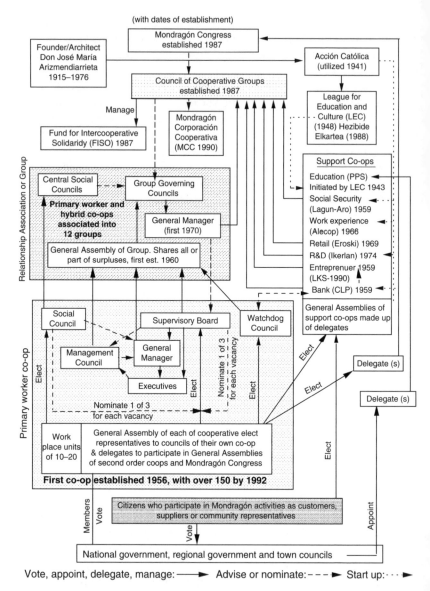

Figure 7.5 MCC system with dates of establishing components (Turnbull, 2000: 207).

Sources: CLP, 1992; MCC, 1992; Mollner, 1991; Morrison, 1991; Whyte and Whyte, 1988

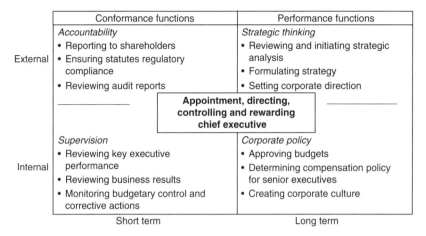

Figure 7.6   Functions and activities of a unitary board

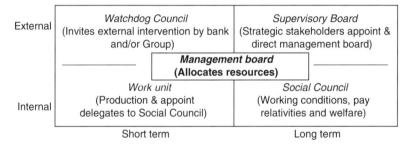

Figure 7.7   Functions and activities of the Mondragón compound board.
Source: Whyte and Whyte, 1988

or trading house. As a result, the CEO of the producer company and the most influential shareholder obtains business intelligence from sources external to the firm that are both independent of management and knowledgeable. Their trading relationship not only makes them knowledgeable but also provides them with the incentive to provide feedback and feed forward intelligence on how to improve operations.

The resulting competitive advantage for Japanese firms was noted by Porter (1992: 13) who stated:

The US system may come closer to optimising short-term returns. However, the Japanese and German systems appear to come closer to optimising

Table 7.3 Mondragón compound board compared with unitary board
Degrees of decomposition of data processing by individuals is indicated by allocations of "X"

Board type ⇒	Mondragón compound board					Anglo
Control centres[1]	Watchdog Council	Supervisory board	Management board	Social Council	Work group	Unitary board
Individuals:	3	5–8	4–6	~5–25	~10–20	~4–12
Function[2]	Governance processes	Appoint management board	Organize operations	Worker welfare	Production, Elect Social Council	Manage
Activities	Efficacy & integrity of processes	Integrate strategic stakeholders	Efficient allocation of resources	Establish working conditions	Job organization & evaluation	Direct & control
Internal[2]	X		X	X	X	XXXX
External[2]	X	X				XX
Short term[2]	X		X		X	XXX
Long term[2]		X		X		XX

Notes:

[1] Omits the General Assembly, which elects Watchdog Council, and Supervisory board.

[2] Descriptions follows typology of Tricker (1994: 244 & 287) as presented in Figure 7.5.

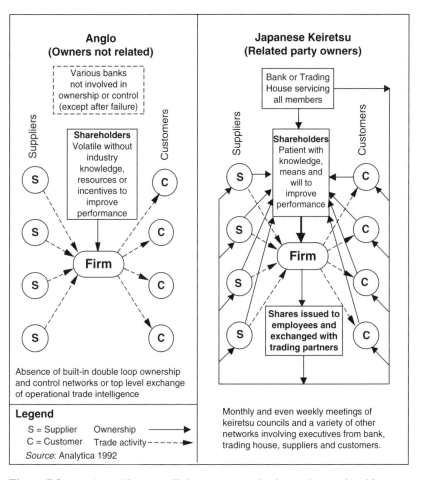

Figure 7.8   Anglo and Japanese Keiretsu communication and control architecture

long-term private and social returns. Their greater focus on long-term corporate position and an ownership structure and governance process that incorporate the interests of employees, suppliers, customers, and the local community allow the Japanese and German economies to better capture the social benefits that can be created by private investment.

Porter, a professor at the Harvard Business School, had been commissioned by a high-level US council on competitiveness to determine why US firms were not as competitive as those in Japan and Germany. To follow up his observation cited above, Porter (1992: 16) recommended that US firms "Encourage long-term employee ownership" and "Encourage board representation by significant customers, suppliers, financial advisors, employees, and community representatives."

This latter recommendation was rightly ignored as it would have introduced intolerable conflicts of interests. In common with other scholars, what Porter did not note was that in Europe and Japan stakeholder engagement was achieved through the existence of compound boards that removed, resolved and/or mediated the conflicts of interests between shareholders and other stakeholders. The recommendations of Porter illustrate how compounds boards that do "not fit the box are not seen at all" (Kuhn, 1970: 24).

The existence and role of compound boards in Europe would also seem to have been overlooked by Williamson (1975: 140) who stated "Imitation of the M-Form innovation was at first rather slow" and that "prior to 1968, most European companies administered their domestic operations through U-Form or holding company internally structures." The need for M-form corporations was lower in Europe because their compound boards already provided some of the advantages that were also produced in M-firms, such as decomposing in decision-making labor and reducing the level of information overload.

Concluding Remarks

The introduction of network governance provides a superior method for directors to identify and manage risk, and improve operating efficiencies and competitive advantages. Democratic processes are introduced to organizations governed on a plutocratic basis by shareholders or on an autocratic basis by governments. Governance boards and stakeholder councils are elected on a one person, one vote basis to counter the one vote per share voting by shareholders that concentrates power in the hands of the wealthy. Citizen participation in the governance of firms becomes open to all of those affected. In this way citizens can participate in the governance of business to protect and/or further their own interests for the mutual benefits of all concerned.

Network governance provides a process for breaking down the exploitive power of hierarchies that can be poorly accountable and so operate in an insensitive and unresponsive manner. Network governance offers a compelling facility for directors and shareholders to reduce their risks as well as enhancing performance of the firms while simultaneously enhancing ethics, accountability, and democracy.

In summary, the advantages of network governance are to:

- Decompose decision-making labor, as found in M-form firms;
- Reduce information overload, as is also achieved in M-form firms;
- Increase the variety of feed forward and feed back information independently of management to facilitate the direction and control of firms;
- Legitimize the role of nonexecutive directors by providing them with information independent of management to carry out their duties to monitor management and business;
- Enrich the available intelligence for specialized and operational decision making;
- Introduce a division of power to remove/avoid conflicts of interest and provide processes for creditably managing any remaining conflicts;
- Introduce checks and balances on executive power to provide interdependency and inclusiveness in decision making and participation to merge management in governance;
- Improve error identification and correction;

The conclusions of this paper for corporations governed by a single board are that directors:

- Are both "Sources of risk" and "Managers of risk" because they respectively:
  - Have excessive and unconscionable unethical powers, and
  - Lack processes to access a requisite variety of competing sources of information so that they can carry out their fiduciary duties to direct and control executives with due care, diligence and vigilance as required by law;
- Can reduce their role, duties, liabilities, and exposure to reputation risk by introducing appropriately designed forms of network governance.
- Can enhance the operational and competitive advantages of their firms by introducing network governance that also mitigates risks for the firm, its directors, employees, shareholders and other stakeholders.

There are compelling advantages and safeguards for shareholders to vote for the changes required in corporate constitutions in order to secure these benefits. This point is supported by the experience of the author in obtaining shareholder approval to establish a corporate senate and stakeholder councils in a start-up venture (Turnbull, 1993, 2000a).

One must also conclude from the insights presented by the science of governance that stock exchanges, regulators and governments are being irresponsible in allowing corporations to be publicly traded without requiring their corporate constitutions to introduce a division of power to allow those citizens the government wishes to protect to become active as co-regulators to protect themselves. Co-regulation created by network governance provides the means to reduce the intrusiveness of government, its inefficiencies and cost while enriching democracy with citizen participation.

Note

1   Refer to "Are Regulators and Stock Exchanges irresponsible?" Posted by Robert Jackson, Managing Editor, Harvard Law School Corporate Governance Blog, on Thursday November 8, 2007 at 12:45 pm. Available at http://blogs.law.harvard.edu/corpgov/2007/11/08/are-regulators-and-stock-exchanges-irresponsible.

References

AccountancyAge. 2004. NAPF urges Auditor shake-up, December 13. http://www.accountancyage.com/news/1138949.

Acton, Lord. 1887. Letter to Bishop Mandell Creighton, April 5 – Acton, *Essays on Freedom and Power*, ed. Gertrude Himmelfarb, pp. 335–6 (1972). Available at http://www.bartleby.com/73/1443.html.

Analytica. 1992. *Board Directors and Corporate Governance: Trends in the G7 Countries Over the Next Ten Years*. Oxford: Analytica Ltd.

Allen, W.T. 1997. Inherent tensions in the governance of US public corporations: the uses of ambiguity in fiduciary law. Paper presented to Max Planck Institute Conference on Comparative Corporate Governance, May. Available at http://papers.ssrn.com/sol3/papers.cfm?abstract_id=10565.

Ashby, W.R. 1968. *An Introduction to Cybernetics*. London: University Paperbacks.

Bazerman, M.H., G. Loewenstein, and D.A. Moore. 2002. Why good accountants do bad audits. *Harvard Business Review*, (November): 95–8.

Bazerman, M.H., K.P. Morgan and G.F. Loewenstein. 1997. The impossibility of auditor independence. *Sloan Management Review*, Summer Issue, 38(4): 89–94.

Bhagat, S. and J.A. Brickley. 1984. Cumulative voting: the value of minority shareholder voting rights. *Journal of Law & Economics*, 27 (October): 339–65.

Bush, T. 2004. Where economics meets the law: the US financial reporting system compared to that of other jurisdictions. Mind the GAAPs. Working Paper, Hermes Focus Asset Management Limited, London. Available at http://www.

hermes.co.uk/pdf/corporate_governance/commentary/Where_Economics_
Meets_The_Law_Final.pdf.

CLP. 1992. *Annual Report*, Caja Laboral Popular, Euskadiko Kusxa, Spain.

Dallas L.L. 1997. Proposals for reform of corporate boards of directors: The dual
board and board ombudsperson. *Washington and Lee Law Review*, 54:1:
92–146.

Diermeier, D. and R.B. Myerson. 1999. Bicameralism and its consequences for the
internal organisation of legislatures. *The American Economic Review*, 89(5):
1182–96.

Downs, A. 1967. *Inside Bureaucracy*. Boston, MA: Little Brown & Co.

Economist. 2002. Enron and auditing: the lessons from Enron, February 7.

Evans, P. 1996. Government action, social capital and development: reviewing the
evidence on synergy. *World Development*, 24(6): 1119–32.

Givens, B. 1991. *Citizens' Utility Boards: Because Utilities Bear Watching*, San
Diego, CA: Centre for Public Interest Law, University of San Diego School of
Law.

Gordon, J. 1993. What is relational investing and how cumulative voting can play
a role. Paper presented to Columbia University Law School's Centre for Law
and Economic Studies' Conference on 'Relationship investing: Possibilities,
patterns and problems', New York Hilton, May 6–7.

Hatherly, D.J. 1995. The case for the shareholder panel in the UK. *The European
Accounting Review*, 4(3): 535–53.

Hippel, E. von. 1986. Lead users: a source of novel product concepts. *Management
Science*, 32(7) (July): 791–805.

Hock, D.W. 1994. Institutions in the age of mindcrafting, Bionomics Annual
Conference, October 22, San Francisco, California, p. 5. Available at http://
www.cascadepolicy.org/dee_hock.htm.

Hock, D.W. 1998. An epidemic of institutional failure: Organizational Development
and the new millennium. Presented to Organization Development Network
Annual Conference New Orleans, Louisiana, 16 November. Available at
http://www.hackvan.com/pub/stig/etext/deehock–epidemic-of-institutional-
failure.html.

Holderness, C.G. 2007. Myth of diffuse ownership in the United States. *Financial
Review of Studies*, http://rfs.oxfordjournals.org/cgi/content/full/hhm069v1.

Jensen, M.C. 1993. The modern industrial revolution: exit and the failure of internal control systems. *The Journal of Finance*, 48(3) (July): 831–80.

Jones, C., W.S. Hesterly and S.T. Borgatti. 1997. A general theory of network governance: exchange conditions and social mechanisms. *Academy of Management
Review*, 22(4): 911–45. Available at http://www.analytictech.com/borgatti/
oppamr6z.htm.

Kuhn, T.S. 1970. *The Structure of Scientific Revolutions*, 2nd edn. Chicago; The
University of Chicago Press.

MCC. 1992. *Annual Report*. Mondragón, Spain: Mondragón Corporación
Cooperativa.

Melis, A. 2004. On the role of the board of statutory auditors in Italian listed companies. *Corporate Governance: An International Review*, 12(1) (January): 74–84.

Melis, A. 2005. Corporate governance failures: to what extent is Parmalat a particularly Italian case? *Corporate Governance: An International Review*, 13(4): 478–88. Available at http://ssrn.com/abstract=754287.

Milgram, S. 2004. *Obedience to Authority: An Experimental View*. New York: HarperCollins.

Mollner, T. 1991. *The Prophets of the Pyrenees: The Search for the Relationship Age*. Northampton, MA: Trustee Institute.

Morrison, R. 1991. *We Build the Road as We Travel*. Philadelphia: New Society Press.

Monks, R.A.G. 2007. *Corpocracy: How CEOs and the Business Roundtable Hijacked the World's Greatest Wealth Machine – And How to Get It Back*. New York: Wiley.

Monks, R.A.G. and A. Sykes. 2002. *Capitalism Without Owners Will Fail: A Policymaker's Guide to Reform*. New York: Centre for the Study of Financial Innovation (CSFI). Available at http://www.ragm.com/library/topics/MonksSykesCSFI.pdf.

Murray, A. 1998. *Minority Report, Report on the Company Law Review Bill, 1997*. Australian Parliamentary Joint Committee on Corporations and Securities, March. Available at http://www.aph.gov.au/senate/committee/corp_sec_ctte/companylaw/minreport.htm.

Neumann, J. von. 1947. *Theory of Games and Economic Behaviour*, New Haven, CT: Yale University Press.

O'Connor, S.M. 2004. Be careful what you wish for: how accountants and congress created the problem of auditor independence. *Boston College Law Review*, 45. Available at http://papers.ssrn.com/abstract_id=587502.

Persson, T., G. Roland and G. Tabellini. 1996. *Separation of Powers and Accountability: Towards a Formal Approach to Comparative Politics*, Innocenzo Gasparini Institute for Economic Research (IGIER), Working Paper, No. 100, Milan, July.

Porta, R.L, R.F. Lopez-de-Silanes, and A. Shleifer. 1999. Corporate ownership around the world. *Journal of Finance*, 54: 471–517.

Porter, M.E. 1992. *Capital Choices: Changing the Way America Invests in Industry*, A research report presented to the Council on Competitiveness and co-sponsored by The Harvard Business School.

Pound, J. 1992. Beyond takeovers: politics comes to corporate control. *Harvard Business Review*, March–April: 83–93.

Romano, R. 2004. The Sarbanes–Oxley Act and the making of quack corporate governance, ECGI – Finance Working Paper 52/2004. Available at http://papers.ssrn.com/abstract_id=596101.

Rumsfeld, R. 2002. News transcript, US Department of Defense, June 9, http://www.defenselink.mil/transcripts/transcript.aspx?transcriptid=3490. (Audio transcript at http://www.youtube.com/watch?v=IsV-r1-8Jo8.)

Shannon, C.E. and W. Weaver. 1949. *The Mathematical Theory of Communications*. Urbana, IL: The University of Illinois Press, pp. 1–94.

Shapiro, A. 2004. Who pays the auditor calls the tune?: Auditing regulation and clients' incentives, Legal Studies Research Paper Series, paper No. 04–014, Cornell Law School, forthcoming *Seton Hall Law Review*, 30, June, http://papers.ssrn.com/abstract_id=587972.

Shleifer, A. and R.W. Vishny. 1996. *A Survey of Corporate Governance*, National Bureau of Economic Research, Working paper 5554, Cambridge, MA.

Tricker, R.I. 1994. *International Corporate Governance*. Singapore: Simon & Schuster.

Thomas, H. and C. Logan. 1982. *Mondragón: An Economic Analysis*. London: George Unwin.

Turnbull, S. 1993. Improving corporate structure and ethics: a case for corporate "Senates". *Director's Monthly*, National Association of Company Directors, Washington, DC, May, 17(5): 1–4.

Turnbull, S. 1995. The need for stakeholder councils in social audits. *Social & Environmental Accounting*, The Centre for Social and Environmental Accounting Research, University of Dundee, 15(2) (September): 10–13. Available at http://papers.ssrn.com/paper.taf?ABSTRACT_ID=55769.

Turnbull, S. 1997. Stakeholder co-operation. *Journal of Co-operative Studies*, Society for Co-operative Studies, 29(3): 18–52 (no. 88), January, 1997. Available at http://ssrn.com/abstract=26238.

Turnbull, S. 2000a. Corporate charters with competitive advantages. *St. Johns Law Review*, St. Johns University, New York City, 74(44) (Winter): 101–59. Availabke at http://ssrn.com/abstract=10570.

Turnbull, S. 2000b. Stakeholder governance: a cybernetic and property rights analysis. In R. Tricker (ed.), *Corporate Governance: The History of Management Thought*. London: Ashgate Publishing, pp. 401–13.

Turnbull, S. 2000c. *The governance of firms controlled by more than one board: Theory development and examples*, PhD Dissertation, Macquarie University, Sydney, Graduate School of Management, http://ssrn.com/abstract=858244.

Turnbull, S. 2002a. A *New Way to Govern: Organisations and Society after Enron*, New Economics Foundation, Public Policy Pocket Book No. 6, London, http://ssrn.com/abstract_id=319867.

Turnbull, S. 2002b. Corporate watchdogs: past, present and future? Working Paper, February, http://ssrn.com/abstract=608244.

Turnbull, S. 2002c. The science of corporate governance. *Corporate Governance: An International Review*, 10(4) (October): 256–72. Available at http://ssrn.com/abstract_id=316939.

Turnbull, S. 2005a. Enhancing corporate operations and social accountability. Submission to the Australian Joint Parliamentary Committee on Corporations and Financial Services inquiry into Corporate Responsibility, November. Available at http://ssrn.com/abstract=800904.

Turnbull, S. 2005b. How US and UK auditing practices became muddled to muddle corporate governance principles. *The ICFAI Journal of Audit Practice*, 2(3) (July): 49–68. Available at http://ssrn.com/abstract=608241.

Turnbull, S. 2006. How can auditors lie about being independent? *Keeping Good Companies*, Chartered Secretaries Australia, 58(10) November: 582–3.

Turnbull, S. 2007. Streamlining regulation with self-enforcing co-regulation, submission to the Australian Treasury of February 14 in response to their 'Streamlining Prudential Regulation Project'. Available at http://papers.ssrn.com/abstract_id=979531.

Whyte, W.F. and K.K. Whyte. 1988. *Making Mondragón: The Growth and Dynamics of the Worker Co-operative Complex*. New York, NY: ILR Press.

Williamson, O.E. 1975. *Markets and Hierarchies: Analysis and Antitrust Implications*. New York: The Free Press.

Williamson, O.E. 1985. *The Economic Institutions of Capitalism*. New York: Free Press.

Woolcock, M. 1998. Social capital and economic development: toward a theoretical synthesis and policy framework. *Theory and Society*, 27(2): 151–208.

8

Supervisory Board and Financial Risk-Taking Behaviors in Chinese Listed Companies

Zhenyu Wu, Yuanshun Li, Shujun Ding,
and Chunxin Jia

Abstract

The dual-board corporate governance mechanism adopted by publicly listed companies in China combines the board of directors found in the American system and the supervisory board in the German system. Using agency theory, this study investigates the effects of the characteristics of the supervisory board, and in particular its monitoring functions, on the financial risk-taking decisions made by corporate boards. We find that the frequency with which a supervisory board meets can be divided into monitoring-driven and non-monitoring-driven components, and that its monitoring effects on financial risk-taking behaviors are non-linear.

Introduction

China is one of the world's fastest-growing economies, and has received considerable attention from both institutional and individual investors from around the world. The Chinese market has also been seen to be one of the most typical emerging markets in the global economy. With the in-depth transition from planned to market-oriented economy in China and the increasing popularity of global financial integration, an increasing number of issues are addressed extensively to help investors and policy makers know more about and get more benefits from the Chinese economy. Among these issues, the risk taken by corporate boards is one of the core concerns in emerging markets, and it is of interest and of both academic and practical importance.

Amended three times after its enactment in 1993, the Chinese Corporate Law requires public companies to have a dual-board corporate governance mechanism. This dual-board system consists of a board of directors, as required in the Anglo-American system, and a supervisory board, which is one of the two boards in the German system. In practice, both the American and the German governance systems have been shown to be successful in protecting shareholders' benefits, one of the primary objectives of corporate governance (Shleifer & Vishny, 1986, 1997). As claimed by the China Securities Regulatory Commission (CSRC), this governance mechanism with two monitoring organs, supervisory board and independent directors, is unique, and doing so helps protect minority shareholders' benefits.

In the corporate governance literature, the effects of the supervisory board in the German system have not been addressed extensively, and studies on those in the Chinese dual-board corporate governance mechanism are still at an early stage (e.g., Dahya, Karbhari, Xiao, & Yang, 2003; Bai, Liu, Lu, Song, & Zhang, 2004; Xi, 2006; Ding, Wu, Li, & Jia, 2008). Researchers have also realized that there is as yet little literature on the risk-taking behaviors determined by corporate boards. To help fill in this gap, we use the data from 2001 to 2006 to investigate the influence of the supervisory board in the unique Chinese corporate governance system on financial risk-taking behaviors in publicly listed Chinese companies. Contrary to the extant literature which concludes that supervisory boards in Chinese listed companies are dysfunctional (Xiao, Dahya, and Lin, 2004; Xi, 2006), our empirical results show that, while the supervisory board has no effect on financial risk-taking behaviors in companies that run well, it does help control financial leverage in companies which are in financial distress. In other words, there is a non-linear relationship between supervisory board activities and the financial risk-taking behavior in Chinese public companies.

We anticipate that the current study will make many contributions to the academic literature and also real-world practice. First, it adds to the corporate governance literature by addressing the effects of governance mechanisms on financial risk taken by corporate boards. As mentioned above, this issue has not been widely addressed, and the research contained herein serves as one of the exploratory studies in this field. Second, it sheds light on the effectiveness of the supervisory board in the Chinese dual-board corporate governance system, and the findings show that, contrary to what prior studies have concludes, the supervisory boards in Chinese publicly listed companies function well in helping control financial leverage in those companies that are in financial distress. Third, it provides important implications for policy makers in emerging markets, and helps foreign investors to have a better understanding of the Chinese market and therefore to make proper and rational investment decisions.

The paper is organized as follows: in the next section we discuss the background and the relevant literature for the study. Data and methodologies are then introduced, followed by an analysis of the empirical results. The paper ends with some concluding remarks.

Background and Literature

The economic reform which started in 1978 has attracted much attention from the world, and recent evidence has illustrated the increasingly important role played by the Chinese economy. A typical emerging market with a high growth potential, the Chinese market is becoming increasingly mature, with strengthened protection of investors' interests. One of the major contributions to this development has been made by the Chinese government's improvements of the country's legal environment. For instance, the Chinese Corporate Law has been revised three times in the past eight years to ensure its proper functioning (Ding et al., 2008).

In an attempt to provide better protection of minority shareholders' benefits, as advocated by the CSRC, two monitoring organs – a supervisory board and independent directors on the board of directors – are mandatory in the unique Chinese dual-board corporate governance mechanism. Whereas the corporate governance literature offers extensive investigation of the agency effects of independent directors (e.g., Cotter, Shivdasani, & Zenner, 1997; Ferris & Yan, 2007; Luan & Tang, 2007), it is rare to find similar examination of supervisory boards using agency theory. To some extent, several studies (e.g., Dahya et al., 2003; Xi, 2006) examining corporate governance in China have touched supervisory boards, and they conclude that the role of the supervisory board does not play an important role in the governance system. In another study, Firth, Fung and Rui (2007) examine the effects of supervisory boards, among other governance elements, on the quality of earnings using data up to 2003.

To the best of our knowledge, however, no study to date has systematically examined the unique monitoring effects of supervisory boards, in collaboration with independent directors in China, on the risk-taking behaviors of the board of directors and the management team. This is true not only in relation to the literature relating to the Chinese governance system, also in respect of the entire field of corporate governance (John, Litov, & Yeung, 2008). It is widely accepted that risk-taking behaviors are critical in the determination of shareholders' benefits. Corporate boards are responsible for making investment and financing decisions, but some components on the boards monitor these risk-taking behaviors to protect the benefits of shareholders – and in particular of minority shareholders. While investor's protection has been well addressed in recent years (e.g., La Porta, Lopez-de-Silanes, Shleifer, & Vishny, 1997, 1998, 2000; Shleifer & Wolfenzon, 2002; Castro, Clementi, & MacDonald, 2004), risk-taking issues in this field need further investigation (e.g., Durnev, Li, Morck, & Yeung, 2004; John et al., 2007).

In addition to conducting an exploratory study of the role played by the supervisory board, a special monitoring organ in Chinese corporate governance mechanism of determining financial-risk-taking behaviors of public companies, we also consider another issue about those companies with special treatment into consideration. According to the rules published by the stock exchanges, public companies that face a high level of risk of being delisted are still traded in the stock markets, but a special label "ST" is added to their stock names. These companies include those that are experiencing financial distress. Therefore, we address the following four research questions in the current study:

- Does the frequency with which their supervisory boards meet affect the financial-risk taking behaviors of Chinese publicly listed companies?
- Does the size of the supervisory board affect the financial-risk taking behaviors of Chinese publicly listed companies?
- Which characteristics of the supervisory board chair influence the financial risk-taking behaviors of Chinese publicly listed companies?
- Does the supervisory board play a significantly different monitoring role in those Chinese public companies in a state of financial distress?

Data, Variables, and Methodology

Data

In our study we used information about corporate governance mechanisms and the financial situation in the period from 2001 to 2006 included in data sets disclosed by GTA and SINOFIN, and which had been used by earlier studies such as Bai et al. (2004), Kato and Long (2006), and Jia (2009). The sample used in the current study has 8,742 observations. There are three major reasons for this sample to provide reliable answers to the research questions which we listed above. First, some relevant data are unavailable because the information about the supervisory board was not fully disclosed before 2001. Second, the data cover information about various aspects of corporate governance mechanisms and financial situations so that the empirical results can be considered to be robust. Third, legal and government enforcements are believed to have been strengthened significantly in 2001, which is usually labeled the "security market regulation year." This meant that the information disclosed was more complete and reliable after 2001.

Variables

In this section, we discuss what the dependent, independent, and control variables measure, and we use subscripts to differentiate variables in the current year from those in the past year – that is, variables in the past year are denoted by $Variable_{Lag}$.

Dependent variables – financial risk   The literature suggests that the debt–assets and debt–equity ratios are good measures of financial leverage, and the debt is usually represented by long-term borrowing. However, for a number of reasons neither of these two measures is considered to be a valid measure of financial risk in the case of Chinese listed firms. On the one hand, the main reason for not using the long-term debt (LTD)–assets ratio is that Chinese public companies tend not to borrow long-term debt; instead, they are more likely to borrow short-term debt and to then renew this as long-term borrowing. On the other hand, the LTD–equity ratio is not chosen mainly because some companies bear a high level of risk of being delisted by the CSRC, and most of them have negative values of equity which can lead to meaningless debt–equity ratios. Therefore, in our analysis we use the total liabilities–total assets ratio to measure the financial risk (RISK) taken by a company in a year because it covers both short-term and long-term borrowing.

Independent variables – characteristics of the supervisory board and its chair   To answer research questions proposed in this study, we take into account two major characteristics of the supervisory board – (i) the frequency with which the supervisory board (SBMF) meets; and (ii) the size of the board (SBS). Both of them are continuous variables; SBMF is measured as the number of meetings held by the supervisory committee in a year, and SBS indexes the members of the supervisory board.

We also include six variables to characterize the features of the chairman of the supervisory board. SBCTurnover is a dummy variable with a value of one in a year in which a turnover occurs. Two variables highlight the features of supervisory board chairs' compensations: a dummy variable SBCPaid indicates whether a supervisory board chair gets paid in the company, and a continuous variable SBCShare measures the percentage of ownership held by a supervisory board chair. SBCTenure indicates the number of days a supervisory board chair has occupied their position. Two other variables illustrate some personal attributes, such as the gender (SBCGender) and the age (SBCAge), of a supervisory board chair.

Control variables Firm performance, especially the lagged one, is widely accepted as one of the major determinants of the financial risk taken by a company. To capture this effect, we use a variable return on assets, the ratio of net income over total assets, to measure accounting profitability (AP). In the meantime, we also use the variable of the capital gain in financial markets to measure a company's market return (MR), and adopt Tobin's Q to measure its growth potential (GROWTH).

The importance of ownership structure of controlling shareholders has been illustrated in the corporate governance literature (e.g., La Porta, Lopez-de-Silanes & Shleifer, 1999; Anderson & Reeb, 2003; Anderson, Mansi and Reeb, 2003), and Chen, Firth, Gao, and Rui (2006) and Firth et al. (2007) show that both state-owned shareholders and foreign shareholders play important roles in the corporate governance system in Chinese publicly listed companies. Therefore, we followed Ding et al. (2008) and use three variables, STATE, FOREIGN, and HHI, to characterize the influence of ownership structure of controlling shareholders. STATE and FOREIGN are dummy variables, and they indicate whether the largest shareholder of a company is state-owned or a foreigner, respectively. State-owned organizations include government, government representatives, and/or state-owned enterprises. The Herfindahl index (HHI) illustrates ownership concentration using the formula adopted by Chen et al. (2006) and Ding et al. (2008).

To further investigate whether or not there is an interaction between the two monitoring organs in the governance system, we also include a variable IndDir which indicates the number of independent directors in a year. Following the literature, we adopt a dummy variable DUAL to indicate whether the CEO of the company is also the chairman of its board of directors, use the natural log of total book value of assets (LNTA) to measure the firm size, and take industry effects into consideration by including 12 dummy variables constructed on the basis of 13 industries categorized by CSRC.

Models and estimation

Monitoring-induced supervisory board meeting frequency As shown in Ding et al. (2008), the size of the supervisory board has a significant effect on the frequency of its meetings, and the turnover of its chairman

(SBCTurnover) is also found to affect SBMF significantly. Taking these aspects of the characteristics of the supervisory board into consideration is also consistent with the literature on the monitoring functions of the board of directors. Jensen (1993) addresses the effects of board size, and Vafeas (1999) highlights the monitoring functions of board meeting frequency after eliminating the lagged-performance-related board meeting frequency.

In this study, therefore, we follow Ding et al. (2008) to identify the monitoring-induced supervisory board meeting frequency (MISBMF) using

$$SBMF = \alpha_1 SBS + \alpha_2 FP_{Lag} + \alpha_3 Risk_{Lag} + \alpha_4 \text{ SBC Characteristics} + \alpha_5 \text{ Control Variables} + \varepsilon_1, \tag{1}$$

where FP_{Lag} and $Risk_{Lag}$ are firm performance and the risk taken by the firm, respectively, in the past year, and ε_1 is the residual which is equivalent to MISBMF. Variables measuring firm performance included the accounting profitability (AP), market return (MR), and growth potential (GROWTH). Characteristics of the supervisory board chair in Equation (1) include SBCTurnover, SBCPaid, SBCShare, SBCTenure, SBCGender, and SBCAge.

Financial risk – supervisory board analysis   Using the monitoring-induced supervisory board meeting frequency (MISBMF) obtained from Model (1) above, we adopt the following model to test the effects of supervisory board on financial risk taken by the companies:

$$RISK = \beta_0 + \beta_1 MISBMF + \beta_2 SBS + \beta_3 \text{ SBC Characteristics} + \beta_4 FP_{Lag} + \beta_5 Risk_{Lag} + \beta_6 \text{ Control Variable} + \varepsilon_2, \tag{2}$$

where MISBMF is measured by ε_1 obtained from Model (1). The monitoring effects of the supervisory board are mainly illustrated by the signs and magnitude of coefficients β_1, β_2 and β_3.

Financial-risk taking behaviors in firms with financial distress
Traditional finance theory argues that in firms with poor performance and/ or financial distress, risk-taking behaviors chosen by corporate boards can be aggressive. Thus, we form two subsamples using the criterion of whether or not a company has a value of the variable RISK lower than one. We use a total liability–total assets ratio higher than or equal to one as a proxy of financial distress. As mentioned above, although these companies experience financial distress and have a high level of risk of being delisted by the CRSC, they are still traded in the stock markets but with

special treatment. We rerun Model (2) in these two subsamples to further investigate the monitoring functions of supervisory board on financial-risk taking behaviors.

Results and Discussion

Descriptive statistics

The results of the descriptive analysis are presented in Table 8.1. From 2001 to 2006 the average financial risk taken by Chinese publicly listed companies, measured by the total liabilities–total assets ratio, was 0.68. During this period, the average number of supervisory board meetings held per year was 3.587, and the average size of supervisory board per year was 4.241 members.

Supervisory boards in 37.6 percent of the sample companies had a turnover of their chairs, 49.7 percent of supervisory board chairs got paid, and the average ownership held by them was 0.022 percent. The average age of supervisory board chairs was 49.84 years, and 83.9 percent of them were male. Their average tenure was 579 days.

The average accounting profitability of the sample companies was −25.3 percent, and their average market return was −16.7 percent. Their average growth potential measured by Tobin's Q was 2.522. The average number of independent directors was 2.748, and the average firm size measured by the natural log of total assets was 21.14. The ownership concentration measured by the Herfindahl index was 0.02, and 11.3 percent of the board chairs were also the companies' CEOs. 1.5 percent of the sample companies had a foreign largest shareholder, and the largest shareholders of 60.6 percent of them were state-owned.

Monitoring-induced supervisory board meeting frequency

Table 8.2 presents the empirical results from Model (1), and reveals several interesting findings. First, the size of the supervisory board increases its meeting frequency, and this positive relationship is significant at the 1% level. Second, lagged firm performance, including both accounting profitability and market return, and the financial risk taken in the past year do not have a significant influence on the frequency of supervisory board meetings.

Table 8.1 Descriptive statistics

The variable *RISK* is the total liabilities–total assets ratio in a year. *SBMF* measures the meeting frequency of supervisory board in a year, and *SBS* is its size. *SBCTurnover* is a dummy variable which measures whether or not. there is a turnover of the chairman of supervisory board in a year. The dummy variable *SBCPaid* indicates whether a supervisory board chair gets paid in the company, and the continuous variable *SBCShare* measures the percentage of ownership held by a supervisory board chair. The variable *SBCTenure* indicates the number of days for which a supervisory board chair has been on this position, and two other variables illustrate the gender (*SBCGender*) and the age (*SBCAge*), of a supervisory board chair, respectively. The accounting profitability (*AP*) is measured by return on assets, the ratio of net income over total assets. We also use the capital gain in financial markets to measure a company's market return (*MR*), and adopt Tobin's Q to measure its growth potential (*GROWTH*). The variable *IndDir* indicates the number of independent directors in a year, and we use the natural log of total book value of assets (*LNTA*) to measure the firm size. The Herfindahl index (*HHI*) illustrates ownership concentration, and the dummy variable *DUAL* indicates whether the CEO of the company is also the chairman of its board of directors. STATE and FOREIGN are dummy variables indicating whether the largest shareholder of a company is state-owned or a foreigner, respectively.

Variable	Mean	S.D.	N
RISK	0.680	10.077	7654
Characteristics of Supervisory Board			
SBMF	3.587	1.689	7685
SBS	4.241	1.438	7723
Characteristics of Supervisory Board Chair			
SBCTurnover	0.376	0.484	7066
SBCPaid	0.497	0.500	6973
SBCShare	0.022	0.263	6935
SBCGender	0.839	0.368	7145
SBCAge	49.843	7.768	7122
SBCTenure	579.174	369.024	7066
Firm Performance			
MR	−0.167	0.487	7358
GROWTH	2.522	34.381	7650
AP	−0.253	21.091	7654
Other Control Variables			
IndDir	2.748	1.272	7717
LNTA	21.140	1.015	7654
HHI	0.020	281.549	7724
DUAL	0.113	0.316	7678
FOREIGN	0.015	0.121	7724
STATE	0.606	0.489	7724

Table 8.2   Result from Model (1) for estimating monitoring-induced supervisory board meeting frequency (*MISBMF*)

The subscript *Lag* indicates a variable in the past year. The variable *RISK* is the
total liabilities–total assets ratio in a year. *SBMF* measures the meeting frequency
of the supervisory board in a year, and *SBS* is its size. *SBCTurnover* is a dummy
variable which measures whether there is a turnover of the chairman of the
supervisory board in a year. The dummy variable *SBCPaid* indicates whether a
supervisory board chair is paid by the company, and the continuous variable
SBCShare measures the percentage of ownership held by a supervisory board
chair. The variable *SBCTenure* indicates the number of days for which a supervisory board chair has been in this position, and two other variables illustrate the
gender (*SBCGender*) and the age (*SBCAge*) of a supervisory board chair, respectively. The accounting profitability (*AP*) is measured by return on assets, the
ratio of net income over total assets. We also use the capital gain in financial
markets to measure a company's market return (*MR*), and adopt Tobin's Q to
measure its growth potential (*GROWTH*). The variable *IndDir* indicates the
number of independent directors in a year, and we use the natural log of total
book value of assets (*LNTA*) to measure the firm size. The Herfindahl index
(*HHI*) illustrates ownership concentration, and the dummy variable *DUAL* indicates whether the CEO of the company is also the chairman of its board of directors. STATE and FOREIGN are dummy variables indicating whether the largest
shareholder of a company is state-owned or a foreigner, respectively. We use 12
dummy variables constructed on the basis of 13 industries categorized by CSRC
to measure the industry effects.

	Coefficient	*S.E.*
$RISK_{Lag}$	−0.056	0.057
MR_{Lag}	0.008	0.058
$GROWTH_{Lag}$	0.095***	0.019
AP_{Lag}	0.149	0.123
SBS	0.054***	0.018
SBCTurnover	1.134***	0.071
SBCPaid	0.166***	0.047
SBCShare	−0.079	0.103
SBCGender	0.066	0.064
SBCAge	0.003	0.003
SBCTenure	0.000	0.000
IndDir	−0.069**	0.029
LNTA	0.065**	0.028
HHI	0.000*	0.000
DUAL	0.028	0.075
FOREIGN	0.211	0.196

Table 8.2   (*Cont'd*)

STATE	0.065	0.052
Industry Dummies		Included and Mixed
Constant	1.262**	0.628
N	5088	
Adjusted R^2	0.124	
F Value	25.74	
Prob > F	0.000	
Average VIF	2.28	

***$p < 0.01$, **$p < 0.05$, *$p < 0.1$

Third, two major characteristics of the supervisory board chair – its turn-over and whether he/she is paid – are shown to increase the number of meetings held by the supervisory board. Both of their coefficients are sig-nificant at the 1% level. When there is a change of the supervisory board chair, it is more likely for the supervisory board to meet more frequently so as to ensure a smooth transition process. If a supervisory board chair gets paid in a public company, he/she tends to hold more meetings to strengthen the monitoring functions.

Fourth, the coefficient on the variable IndDir is negative and, while that on the variable LNTA is positive, both of them are significant at the 5% level. The former result indicates that a company with more independent directors on the board of directors tends to hold fewer supervisory board meetings, and this is mainly due to the overlap of monitoring functions of the supervisory board and the independent directors. The latter result shows that a larger company is more likely to hold a higher number of supervisory board meetings, and this is consistent with conclusions made in the litera-ture; a larger company tends to have more issues to be discussed by mem-bers on its supervisory board.

In addition, industry effects are also taken into consideration. Only the coefficient for Industry 12 (media) is significantly positive at the 1% level, that for Industry 10 (real estate) is significantly positive at the 5% level, and those for Industry 5 (construction), Industry 6 (transportation) and Industry 8 (wholesale and retail) are significantly positive at the 10% level. Companies in these industries tend to hold more supervisory board meetings.

In short, we used Model (1) to separate monitoring-induced from non-monitoring-induced supervisory board meeting frequency, and as a result we obtained a reliable estimation of MISBMF.

Effects of the supervisory board on financial
risk-taking behaviors

Empirical results obtained from Model (2) using the full sample and two subsamples are presented in Table 8.3. The monitoring role of the supervisory board is not found in the full sample or the subsample with the total liabilities–total assets ratio lower than one (RISK < 1). In these two samples, the financial risk taken in the past year is positively related to that in the current year, but the growth potential in the past year and the firm size are negatively related to the financial leverage in the current year. All these three factors are significant at the 1 percent level. The positive relationship between financial risk in the past year and that in the current year shows the consistency of risk-taking behaviors in two consecutive years. Furthermore, companies with lower growth potential and those that are smaller size tend to take larger financial risks. In addition, the variables DUAL and STATE are both significantly, positively related to the financial risk-taking behaviors, and they show the importance of owner–manager conflict and ownership structure of controlling shareholders when a company determines its financial leverage.

It is very interesting, however, that the monitoring function of the supervisory board is found to be significant (at the 1% level) in companies that are experiencing financial distress. In the subsample with the total liabilities – total assets ratio higher than or equal to one (RISK ≥ 1), a higher monitoring-induced supervisory board meeting frequency leads to a lower financial risk taken by a company. As discussed above, these companies face a high level of risk of being delisted by the CSRC, and their stocks are traded in the stock markets with special treatment. Thus, supervisory boards in these companies tend to meet more often in order to lower the risks caused by financial leverage. We also find that supervisory boards with male chairs tend to reduce the financial leverage when their companies experience financial distress. Similar to the results based on the full sample and the other subsample, in addition, variables such as $RISK_{Lag}$, GROWTH, and LNTA, influence the financial leverage significantly.

In summary, we find that the supervisory board only plays an important role for restricting financial risk in those companies that are in financial distress.

Robustness tests

We also carry out multiple sets of tests to ensure the robustness of the empirical findings summarized above. First, we use alternative variables to

Table 8.3 Results from Model (2) for financial risk – supervisory board analysis The subscript *Lag* indicates a variable in the past year. The dependent variable *RISK* is the total liabilities–total assets ratio in a year. MISBMF is the monitoring-induced supervisory board meeting frequency, and *SBS* is the size of the supervisory board. The dummy variable *SBCPaid* indicates whether a supervisory board chair gets paid in the company, and the continuous variable *SBCShare* measures the percentage of ownership held by a supervisory board chair. The variable *SBCTenure* indicates the number of days for which a supervisory board chair has been in this position, and two other variables illustrate the gender (*SBCGender*) and the age (*SBCAge*) of a supervisory board chair, respectively. The accounting profitability (*AP*) is measured by return on assets, the ratio of net income over total assets. We also use the capital gain in financial markets to measure a company's market return (*MR*), and adopt Tobin's Q to measure its growth potential (*GROWTH*). The variable *IndDir* indicates the number of independent directors in a year, and we use the natural log of total book value of assets (*LNTA*) to measure the firm size. The Herfindahl index (*HHI*) illustrates ownership concentration, and the dummy variable *DUAL* indicates whether the CEO of the company is also the chairman of its board of directors. STATE and FOREIGN are dummy variables indicating whether the largest shareholder of a company is state-owned or a foreigner, respectively. We use 12 dummy variables constructed on the basis of 13 industries categorized by CSRC to measure the industry effects.

	Full Sample		RISK < 1		RISK ≥ 1	
	Coefficient	S.E.	Coefficient	S.E.	Coefficient	S.E.
MISBMF	−0.056	0.104	−0.053	0.106	−0.568**	0.280
SBS	0.053	0.131	0.066	0.133	−0.332	0.386
SBCPaid	0.074	0.349	0.064	0.356	−1.086	0.976
SBCShare	−0.237	0.765	−0.206	0.772	−171.078	188.318
SBCGender	0.395	0.470	0.460	0.477	−4.799***	1.564
SBCAge	−0.039*	0.023	−0.037	0.024	−0.124*	0.064
SBCTenure	0.000	0.000	0.000	0.000	0.000	0.001
RISK$_{Lag}$	1.336***	0.420	2.258**	1.056	1.587***	0.346
MR$_{Lag}$	0.649	0.431	0.773	0.485	−0.315	0.380
GROWTH$_{Lag}$	−0.749***	0.143	−0.733***	0.155	−0.838***	0.243
AP$_{Lag}$	−0.119	0.910	−1.029	2.362	−0.148	0.338
IndDir	0.305	0.215	0.305	0.219	0.016	0.603
LNTA	−2.277***	0.209	−2.313***	0.217	−3.428***	0.566
HHI	0.000	0.001	−0.001	0.001	−0.003	0.003
DUAL	1.308**	0.554	1.331**	0.566	0.876	1.294
FOREIGN	1.122	1.452	1.120	1.466	–	–

(Cont'd)

Table 8.3   (*Cont'd*)

	Full Sample		RISK < 1		RISK ≥ 1	
	Coefficient	S.E.	Coefficient	S.E.	Coefficient	S.E.
STATE	1.029***	0.382	1.008***	0.389	1.977*	1.003
Industry Dummies	Included and Mixed		Included and Mixed		Included and Mixed	
Constant	49.157***	4.629	49.319***	4.771	84.740***	13.244
N	5088		4991		97	
Adjusted R²	0.024		0.023		0.440	
F Value	5.33		4.99		4.15	
Prob > F	0.000		0.000		0.000	
Average VIF	2.20		2.17		5.07	

***p < 0.01, **p < 0.05, *p < 0.1

measure ownership features of controlling shareholders. For instance, we use a dummy variable indicating whether the largest shareholder is government or a government representative to replace the variable STATE, and use the number of foreign shareholders among the largest ten and the total percentage of ownership held by them to replace the variable FOREIGN. When we do this, no qualitative change is found.

We also examine the variance inflation factors (VIF) for both models, and find they are all under 10, which is a widely accepted criterion indicating no serious multicollinearity problem. A Breusch–Pagan/Cook–Weisberg test for heteroskedasticity is also carried out for Model (1), and the Chi-square is 3.38 so that the model passes the test. This indicates that the estimation of monitoring-induced supervisory board meeting frequency (MISBMF), which is equivalent to the residual of Model (1), is reliable.

Conclusions and Future Studies

Hopefully the next economic giant, China is attracting much attention from both researchers and practitioners. It is of interest and of importance to learn more about the unique Chinese dual-board corporate governance system, and it is well known that the effects of corporate governance on risk-taking behaviors have not been addressed thoroughly. This study investigates the monitoring role played by the supervisory board, one of the two monitoring organs in this unique system, in taking financial risks in Chinese public companies. Not only does it add to the corporate governance literature, but it provides critical implications for policy makers in China and those in other emerging markets in the global economy. It also helps investors to achieve a better understanding of the Chinese governance mechanism to ensure their benefit protection.

Contrary to the conclusions made in prior research that the supervisory board plays only a minimal role in corporate governance, we find that the meeting frequency of the supervisory board helps control the financial risk-taking behaviors of those Chinese public companies in financial distress. A non-linear monitoring role played by the supervisory board in determining financial leverage is found in the current study since it does not affect financial risk in companies which are not in financial difficulties. To ensure the reliability and robustness of our findings, we separate the monitoring-induced supervisory board meeting frequency from that driven by lagged firm performance and/or risk-taking behaviors in the past year. In the meantime, the interaction between the meeting frequency and the size of supervisory board is also taken into account while identifying the monitoring component of supervisory board meeting frequency.

Our findings suggest some promising future areas for research along the lines suggested by this study are also promising. For instance, we plan to investigate the effects of corporate boards, including both the board of directors and the supervisory board, on the risks observed in financial markets. This will allow us to study the market reactions to board activities taken by Chinese publicly listed companies, and it provides further implications for investors to make appropriate and rational decisions.

References

Anderson, R., and D. Reeb. 2003. Founding-family ownership and firm performance: Evidence from the S&P500. *Journal of Finance*, 58: 1301–28.

Anderson, R., S. Mansi, and D. Reeb. 2003. Founding family ownership and the agency cost of debt. *Journal of Financial Economics*, 68: 263–85.

Bai, C., Q. Liu, J. Lu, F.M. Song, and J. Zhang. 2004. Corporate governance and market valuation in China. *Journal of Comparative Economics*, 32: 599–616.

Castro, R., G.L. Clementi, and G. MacDonald. 2004. Investor protection, optimal incentives, and economic growth. *Quarterly Journal of Economics*, 119: 1131–75.

Chen, G., M. Firth, D.N. Gao, and O.M. Rui. 2006. Ownership, corporate governance, and fraud: Evidence from China. *Journal of Corporate Finance*, 12: 424–48.

Cotter, J.F., A. Shivdasani, and M. Zenner. 1997. Do independent directors enhance target shareholder wealth during tender offers? *Journal of Financial Economics*, 43: 195–218.

Dahya, J., Y. Karbhari, J. Xiao, M. Yang. 2003. The usefulness of the supervisory board report in China. *Corporate Governance: An International Review*, 11: 308–21.

Ding, S., Z. Wu, Y. Li, and C. Jia. 2008. Supervisory board and executive compensation: Evidence from China. Working paper.

Durnev, A., K. Li, R. Morck, and B. Yeung. 2004. Capital markets and capital allocation: Implications for economies in transition. *Economics of Transition*, 12: 593–634.

Ferris, S.P., and X. Yan. 2007. Do independent directors and chairmen matter? The role of boards of directors in mutual fund governance. *Journal of Corporate Finance*, 13: 392–420.

Firth, M., P. Fung, and O. Rui. 2007. Ownership, two-tier board structure, and the informativeness of earnings: Evidence from China. *Journal of Accounting and Public Policy*, 26: 463–96.

Jia, C., 2009. The effect of ownership on the prudential behavior of banks? The case of China. *Journal of Banking and Finance*, 33: 77–87.

Jensen, M.C. 1993. The modern industrial revolution, exit, and the failure of internal control systems. *The Journal of Finance*, 48: 831–80.

John, K., L. Litov, and B. Yeung. 2008. Corporate governance and risk taking. *Journal of Finance*, 63: 1679–728.

Kato, T., and C. Long. 2006. Executive compensation, firm performance, and corporate governance in China: Evidence from firms listed in the Shanghai and Shenzhen Stock Exchanges. *Economic Development and Cultural Change*, 54: 945–83.

La Porta, R., F. Lopez-de-Silanes, and A. Shleifer. 1999. Corporate ownership around the world. *Journal of Finance*, 54: 471–517.

La Porta, R., F. Lopez-de-Silanes, A. Shleifer, and R. Vishny. 1997. Legal determinants of external finance. *Journal of Finance*, 52: 1131–50.

La Porta, R., F. Lopez-de-Silanes, A. Shleifer, and R. Vishny. 1998. Law and finance. *Journal of Political Economy*, 106: 1113–55.

La Porta, R., F. Lopez-de-Silanes, A. Shleifer, and R. Vishny. 2000. Investor protection and corporate governance. *Journal of Financial Economics*, 58: 3–27.

Luan, C., and M. Tang. 2007. Where is independent director efficacy? *Corporate Governance: An International Review*, 15: 636–43.

Shleifer, A., and R.W. Vishny. 1986. Large shareholders and corporate control. *Journal of Political Economy*, 94: 461–88.

Shleifer, A. and R.W. Vishny. 1997. A survey of corporate governance. *Journal of Finance*, 52: 737–83.

Shleifer, A., and D. Wolfenzon. 2002. Investor protection and equity markets. *Journal of Financial Economics*, 66: 3–27.

Vafeas, N. 1999. Board meeting frequency and firm performance. *Journal of Financial Economics*, 53: 113–42.

Wang, F., and Y. Xu. 2004. What determines Chinese stock returns? *Financial Analysts Journal*, 60: 65–77.

Xi, C., 2006. In search of an effective monitoring board model: Board reforms and the political economy of corporate law in China. *Connecticut Journal of International Law*, 22: 1–46.

Xiao, J.Z., J. Dahya, and Z. Lin. 2004. A grounded theory exposition of the role of the supervisory board in China. *British Journal of Management*, 15: 39–55.

9

Discussion

David R. Koenig

Corporate governance at publicly held companies has been an increasingly hot topic in risk management, gaining its initial momentum with the financial losses at companies like Metallgesellschaft, Proctor & Gamble and Barings in the 1990s and accelerating in this decade following the headlines about losses at Enron, WorldCom and Tyco. In general, and speaking in very broad terms, system checks and balances were called into question, with many commentators wondering whether they were sufficiently robust to cope with "modern" markets and complex financial instruments. Despite this increased attention and greater regulation, we continue to see failures of such structures in magnitudes that seem almost unconscionable, including cases such as National Australia Bank's foreign exchange losses where the board was held accountable for creating the environment in which they were allow to happen,[1] recent trading losses at Société Générale and losses in mortgage lending that are highly correlated with the short-lagged retirement of CEOs, chief risk officers (CROs) and some board members of the affected institutions.

However, we have seen substantial progress in understanding how people interact via organizations[2] and what the positive impact of transparency and other improvements in governance can be, especially in the past ten years.[3] Academic research has begun to substantiate the real market value that good governance can bring to public companies and varying models of governance are being employed around the world, leading to some industry optimism that a best practice of governance will emerge.[4]

Governance is in itself, though, simply a construct. It does not generate wealth. However, if applied to potential wealth-generating activities, such as running a business, it has the potential to enhance the pursuit of wealth and to make a business more valuable.

Businesses exist to take risks. Without the assumption of such, we are taught that one should not expect any kind of return in excess of the risk-free rate. Yet the management of a business is either an attempt to use an information advantage, perceived or real, or an ability to differentiate information in a more effective manner than others, either perceived or real, in order to gain wealth. The current value of a business is some function of expectations of its future states of value, or future cash flows, or the ability of its managers to extract value from their advantage. Under a deterministic model in which point in time projections of profit are made, the longer the time over which those profits are expected to be earned, the higher the value of the stream of profits. Governance is intended to extend the expected life of those positive cash flows, or, perhaps more accurately, to reduce the risks to an unexpected interruption in those profits. By this measure alone, good governance would seem to have the potential to be a worthy pursuit.

Risk managers, however, consider processes of each businesses and how they generate cash flows within a stochastic framework. The real world is not deterministic, as errors in analyst forecasts have demonstrated. A better valuation of a business attempts to assign probabilities to its ability to generate positive versus negative flows over some time horizon. This is in effect what current credit models attempt to do in determining the creditworthiness of a counterparty or client.

While investors and creditors are concerned about the risk of credit deterioration, there is an additional psychological factor that affects the value of the firm which governance also attempts to address. It is this latter component which is likely still undervalued and may explain some of the delays in the broad implementation of good corporate governance structures. In the work of Kahneman and Tversky, the aversion of individuals to loss is well-demonstrated. This principle, called loss avoidance, shows that when faced with the possibility of large losses, individuals tend to assign irrationally large probabilities to the likelihood of those losses. In the context of business valuation, corporate governance, practiced well, can provide greater assurance that large losses have been removed from the set of stochastic outcomes which need to be factored into the current valuation of a company. In effect, good corporate governance can change the shape of the "loss" tail of the distribution of future states of value of the company.

The impact of a reduction in tail loss risk is direct in terms of the need for reduced capital and its incumbent expense. This affects the baseline expectation of future cash flows in a positive manner. But, the reduction in tail loss risk also affects the perceived risk of a company and reduces the psychological discounting done by investors to a company with a perceived risk of high losses. The net effect of good governance is then to both change the shape of the loss tail by compressing it, and also to shift the entire distribution of future states of value to a higherlevel.[5] The potential value of this change is enormous and would, if widely understood, make implementation of good governance a top priority at all companies.

The paper by Greg Young and Steve Barr of North Carolina State University, "Theories of Governance and Corporate Moral Vulnerability," introduces the construct of corporate moral vulnerability in corporate governance and test two hypotheses. First they ask: if there is an increase in the number of corporate governance provisions that hold management accountable to shareholders, will there be a corresponding increase in the magnitude of moral hazard risks in the corporate portfolio? Second, they ask if there is evidence that corporate profit decreases with an increase in the magnitude of moral hazard risks in the corporate portfolio. Their focus in this case is on the potential moral hazard by doing business in countries that are known to have high levels of corruption.

The proposition advanced by Young and Barr is an interesting one of temptation. Does there seem to be value in taking moral risk? If someone is watching you, are you less tempted? One might take this to be a Garden of Eden equivalence in the realm of corporate governance for internationally active firms.

It would be interesting for this work to be expanded to include analysis that is over a time series of data. Questions that might be asked include whether the impact of this moral choice is strongest in the current period, or if there is evidence that the reward or punishment for taking the moral risk becomes stronger with some lagged effect. It would also be interesting to see if the relationships found in this paper are repeated in other years. Needless to say, their work calls for more investigation of moral hazard, the role of risk management of such hazards, and the impact on corporate performance and valuation.

The second paper, "Mitigating the Exposure of Corporate Boards to Risk and Unethical Conflicts," by Shann Turnbull of the University of Sydney, was rightly recognized for its importance by being selected as the top paper at the Symposium. Dr Turnbull is, to say the least, a provocative thinker on the forms of organizational oversight and management that will generate the most value for shareholders. His paper begins with the statement that corporations governed by a single board expose directors to: (i) conflicts of interests that create unethical relationships; and (ii) naïve self-deluding acceptance of operating risks.

Turnbull builds a strong case for the development of network governance structures that include a variety of stakeholders in the oversight of an entity. He cites existing examples where such has effectively been utilized and draws upon varying sources outside of the typical reach of most governance writing to make his compelling case.

From his argument are drawn the inferences that the board of directors in single-board constructs are both sources and managers of risk who have excessive and unconscionable powers. They cannot get the necessary information from their organizations to be effective in their duty of care and can enhance the competitive advantages of their firms through a network form of governance. He concludes that "co-regulation created by network governance provides the means to reduce the intrusiveness of government, its inefficiencies and cost while enriching democracy with citizen participation."

There are still some questions from this paper to be answered about how to fairly construct these multiple boards and the process for selection of those members who are nominated to join them. But these are essentially elements of implementation that may be covered outside of this particular paper.

The third paper in this section, "Supervisory Board and Financial Risk-Taking Behaviors in Chinese Listed Companies," also looks at whether there are advantages to some construct other than the single-board governance model. In China, authors Zhenyu Wu, University of Saskatchewan, Yuanshun Li, Ryerson University, Shujun Ding, York University, and Chunxin Jia, Peking University, note a unique structure for governance exists that combines both the board of directors in the American system and the supervisory board in the German system. Their interest is in investigating the impact of the supervisory board, especially its monitoring functions, on the financial risk-taking decisions made by the board of directors.

Stock market data in China, where companies in distress are flagged by the exchange as being potentially delisted, gives them a promising data set with which to examine their questions. In their study, they find evidence that the supervisory board becomes engaged during periods of financial distress.

The human reaction of a supervisory board to become more engaged when risks are increasing is unsurprising. In the literature relating to human reactions to risk, we would expect a reaction to such realization. The question that should follow their study, which is perhaps an opportunity for more work for this team of authors, is whether an engagement by the supervisory board in understanding and managing tail risks more effectively would improve corporate value. Consider the American-style board of directors to be focused on the effective pursuit of key business objectives and normal business operations, the middle of the distribution of future states of company value, while a supervisory board focuses on the governance and risk management issues that pre-empt a movement from the middle of the distribution to the tail loss events that destroy whole companies or certainly destroy company value.

These papers all describe the process of human interaction in an organization. Work being done by those in the areas of Complexity and Emergence, and in particular that research stimulated and conducted by the Santa Fe Institute, has powerful potential to be utilized in the construct of corporate governance. Each of the authors in this section is touching on the same element – the role of a small group of human beings in a complex system. All three papers add interesting insights and will hopefully stimulate both research and action at the industry level to effect the global emergence of best practice corporate governance standards.

Notes

1 PricewaterhouseCoopers, Investigation into foreign exchange losses at the National Australia Bank, March 12, 2004, See http://www.prmia.org/pdf/ Case_Studies/NAB_PwC.pdf.
2 See http://www.santafe.edu/ for more information.
3 See governance work from COSO (www.coso.org), OCEG (www.oceg.org), and PRMIA Governance Principles (http://www.prmia.org/pdf/PRMIA_ Governance_Principles.PDF).
4 See Carol Padgett and Amana Shabbir, The UK Code of Corporate Governance: Link Between Compliance and Firm Performance, Discussion Paper, ICMA Centre, November 21, 2005, for example (http://www.icmacentre.rdg.ac.uk/ pdf/discussion/DP2005-17.pdf).
5 David R. Koenig, The Human Reaction to Risk and Opportunity, chapter 2 in David Olson and Desheng Wu (eds), *New Frontiers in Enterprise Risk Management*. Berlin: Springer, May 2008 (http://www.springerlink.com/ content/x456tk21878143t1/).

Part IV

Corporate Boards and the Management of Specific Risks

In their contribution, "Entity-Level Controls and the Monitoring of Corporate Boards," Donna J. Fletcher, Mohammad J. Adbolmohammadi, and Jay C. Thibodeau explore the ramification of recent changes and refinements in the regulatory regime stemming from the Sarbanes–Oxley Act of 2002. Responding to widespread complaints about the compliance cost and regulatory burdens of Sarbanes–Oxley, in 2007 the Public Company Accounting Oversight Board (PCAOB) promulgated a new Audit Standard No. 5. Fletcher, Abdolmohammadi, and Thibodeau attempt to provide a mechanism to take advantage of potential cost savings associated with the new audit standard by showing firms how to implement testable entity-level controls, as suggested by the PCAOB. The authors believe that their method will help firms reduce the costs of complying with section 104 of Sarbanes–Oxley and also achieve improved corporate governance.

In "Do Corporate Boards Care About Sustainability? Should They Care?," Steven Swidler and Claire Crutchley consider the possibility that business practices that support sustainability may also enhance shareholder wealth, and they test whether or not more sustainability-oriented business practices have resulted in higher stock returns. The authors present evidence of some positive relationship in the earlier portion of their sample period, but they find that this differential performance diminishes over time. They conjecture that this might be due to increasingly widespread commitment to sustainable practices that erodes the differences in returns among firms.

In their paper "Executive Risk Taking and Equity Compensation in the Merger and Acquisition Process," William J. Lekse and Mengxin Zhao consider the question: "What is the link between equity compensation and executive risk taking in the merger process?" Examining a large sample of mergers between 1993 and 2005, Lekse and Zhao find that the CEOs of the acquiring firms have more of their pay concentrated in equity compensation than do the CEOs of target firms. Given this basic finding, it is unsurprising that they also find a greater pay sensitivity to equity among the CEOs of acquirer companies than among the CEOs of target companies. The authors find that this equity-focused compensation leads these CEOs to be aggressive in pursuing value-enhancing risky mergers.

Finally, Tom Nohel discusses these three contributions, offering numerous suggestions for improvement, along with some trenchant criticisms.

10

Entity-Level Controls and the Monitoring Role of Corporate Boards

Donna J. Fletcher, Mohammad J. Abdolmohammadi, and Jay C. Thibodeau

Introduction

In recent months, there has been escalating dialogue surrounding the substantial cost and the apparent lack of benefit of Section 404 of the Sarbanes–Oxley Act of 2002 (US House of Representatives, 2002) (SARBOX). Section 404 of SARBOX places a heavy emphasis on the effectiveness of the design and operation of a company's system of internal controls to prevent and/or detect fraud. The control system involves many constituents, including the management team, internal audit, other employees, the board of directors, external auditors, and the company's external stakeholders (e.g., suppliers). The resulting complex web of activities has substantially increased the monitoring role for corporate boards of directors and places increased emphasis on the control environment in which the firm operates.

Both companies and regulators agree that the cost of compliance with Section 404 of SARBOX has been too high. A survey of publicly traded companies reported on by the PCAOB (FEI, 2005) found that for "217 public companies with average revenues of $5 billion, first year Section 404 compliance cost, on average, of $4.36 million and also consumed an average of nearly 27,000 hours." In addition, according to Audit Analytics, the median audit fee for larger companies (>$750 million in market capitalization) has increased by more than 150 percent between 2002 and 2004.

For smaller publicly traded companies, the additional costs may be prohibitive. Indeed, the SEC Advisory Committee on smaller public companies (April 23, 2006) concluded that the size and complexity of the company should affect the internal control audit requirements. Stated simply, there must be latitude to allow smaller companies to achieve their control objectives, rather than following a "one-size-fits-all" prescription.

This report had a direct impact on both the PCAOB and the SEC as they deliberated the final provisions of Audit Standard No. 5. The standard (PCAOB, 2007) states explicitly that "the size and complexity of the company, its business processes, and business units, may affect the way in which the company achieves many of its control objectives ... and the risks of misstatement." As a result, the internal control audit should be scaled to the nature of the company being audited. In an attempt to do so in the most efficient manner, the PCAOB has recommended that companies (and external auditors) focus on a strong set of entity-level controls to reduce the detail testing of the internal control system, thus reducing the cost of compliance. According to the standard (PCAOB, 2007), the auditor should follow a top-down approach to the internal control audit by identifying the key controls to test in a sequential manner, starting with entity-level controls, then driving down to controls at the transaction, and or significant process level.

Such an approach prevents management and the auditor from spending unnecessary time on understanding a process or control that does not affect the likelihood that the company's financial statements could be materially misstated. According to the standard (PCAOB, 2007), the reduction in time results either because the entity-level control sufficiently addresses the risk related to the relevant assertion, or because the entity-level controls provide some assurance so that the testing of other controls related to the assertion can be reduced.

In its standard, the PCAOB explains that some controls, such as controls around the control environment, have an important but indirect effect on the likelihood that a misstatement might be detected or prevented. The control environment encompasses management's philosophy and operating style, integrity and ethical values, particularly of top management and the oversight of the board and its audit committee. Other entity-level controls, such as monitoring controls, provide assurance that the controls that address a particular risk are effective, reducing the testing of those controls that would otherwise be necessary.[1] Controls to monitor other controls include the activities of the internal audit function, the audit committee, and self-assessment programs.

The focus of this paper is to provide a mechanism to upper management teams and boards of directors to take immediate advantage of the cost savings being afforded by the newly approved AS 5 (PCAOB, 2007). Specifically, we provide a concrete and unambiguous approach toward demonstrating excellence in the implementation of testable entity-level controls related to the control environment and the monitoring component of the internal control framework that is recommended to be used by the PCAOB (i.e., COSO, 1992). By implementing our approach, management teams are likely to be able to reduce Section 404 compliance costs, while also enabling both management and boards of directors the opportunity to achieve more effective corporate governance.

Effective governance is predicated on a strong firm culture (the cornerstone of the control environment) that aligns well with business needs and allows for the development of governance and risk management proficiency. An ethical corporate culture is also an essential component of successful corporate strategy in today's business and markets environment. Regulations require this culture, punitive damages are mitigated by it and investor trust is unattainable without it. Moreover, emphasizing an ethical corporate culture validates director and officer integrity, indeed corporate integrity. It is the right thing to do.

The remainder of this paper is organized as follows. The next section presents the contingency theory of organizational control that frames our focus on the control environment and the monitoring role of corporate boards. We then discuss the importance of an ethical "tone at the top" as the cornerstone of the control environment. The details of the entity-level controls by stakeholder groups follow, providing the ethical principles and practices that are associated with each of the entity-level controls. This robust analysis is intended to help corporate boards understand and discharge their fiduciary responsibilities to a wide range of company stakeholders. The final section summarizes our conclusions and discusses the implications of our work.

Contingency Theory of Organizational Control

Effective governance has to adapt continually to changing conditions within and without the organization (Strebel, 2004). Clearly, the ethical and regulatory requirements of SARBOX have led to significant changes in the control structure of public companies and to their organizational relationships. Holding constant all externalities which a firm in any particular industry faces, these structural changes have increased the level of the monitoring role of corporate boards.

Figure 10.1 illustrates this web of relationships resulting from changes to a public company's governance structure in order to comply with SARBOX. In accordance with the SARBOX requirement for external audit to monitor management and to communicate in writing to management and

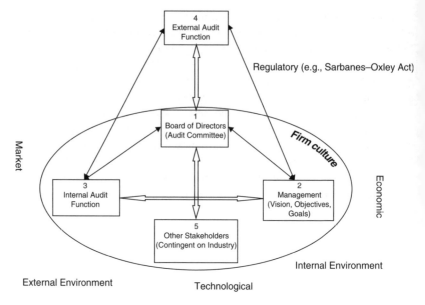

Figure 10.1   Governance structure

the audit committee all significant deficiencies and material weaknesses identified during the audit, the external audit function (Box 4) is linked to three internal stakeholders: the Board of Directors (particularly its Audit Committee), Management, and the Internal Audit Function.

Management is responsible for communication, monitoring and the reporting mechanism with the Internal Audit Function (Box 3) and the Board of Directors (Box 1). The Board of Directors also has communication, monitoring, and reporting links to the Internal Audit Function. The Audit Committee of the Board of Directors selects and contracts with the external auditor and thus it monitors the activities of the external auditor through effective communication and reporting. The audit committee provides the critical oversight function (including monitoring, communication, and reporting) of a company's governance structure, as seen through the relationships between this committee and the full board, company officers and management, and the internal and external auditors.

The governance structure oversees the other organizational stakeholders impacted by SARBOX (e.g., employees, suppliers, customers). As depicted in Figure 10.1, all of the company stakeholders are united by the firm's culture. A corporation's directors and officers and its management can exert positive control over these stakeholders through its culture: firm culture is the social pattern that guides worker behavior, policies, and practices, implying a set of values, social norms, and beliefs. Management and the board's philosophy and operating style and ethical values permeate a firm's culture. Indeed, a strong internal firm culture may decrease the need for other control mechanisms because employee beliefs and norms coincide with firm goals (Drew, 2006). An effective firm culture will align well with business needs, yet also support development of risk management and governance competencies. Moreover, such a culture is dedicated to openness, transparency, high ethical standards and fair competition, while at the same time meeting customer and stakeholder commitments (Drew, 2006).

In addition to strengthening a firm's culture, control is used to create conditions that motivate the organization to achieve desirable or predetermined outcomes. One of the more prominent approaches in the literature to investigate these relationships and to study the effects of the control systems in organizations on outcomes (i.e., performance) is based on the Contingency Theory of Organizational Control (CTC). According to CTC, the appropriateness of a control system is contingent on the circumstances faced by the organization (Fisher, 1995).

CTC posits some aspects of control that may be generalized to a class of firms while other controls may be firm-specific. Since banks are subject to detailed regulatory requirements, they may use many of the same control features. However, banks may differ in terms of other features of their control systems in order to address their own specific needs. For example, a bank that uses an online real-time reporting system may need continuous monitoring of its reporting, while banks that use periodic reporting might use more traditional audit controls.

Contingent control framework

Figure 10.2 displays a contingent control framework rooted in theory. The theory suggests that the contingent variables are those factors within which the firm operates that are either selected by the firm (e.g., competitive strategy) or outside of its control (e.g., regulatory environment). The firm's organizational control system is then determined in light of these contingent variables. For example, the governance structure of a public company is mandated to include an audit committee of the board of directors, wherein, as discussed, the role of the audit committee is clearly defined. A firm can then institute entity-level controls in response to insure compliance with SARBOX. Finally, as depicted in Figure 10.2, measurement and rewards of both financial and non-financial performance should feed back to the contingency variables (e.g., corporate

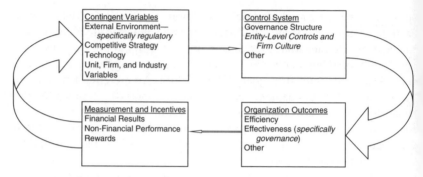

Figure 10.2   Contingency control framework
Source: Adapted from Fisher (1995)

strategy). Organizational outcomes from compliance with SARBOX and from instituting an ethical firm culture that is supported by entity-level controls should then result in an efficient and effective corporate governance and long term value.

Inculcating an Ethical Culture

Ensuring an effective control environment is therefore predicated on an ethical firm culture. Furthermore, the US regulatory environment mandates ethical business practice. SARBOX, the NYSE, and the NASDAQ rules each contain provisions requiring companies to disclose whether they have adopted codes of ethics for senior financial officers (and if not, why not) and whether there have been any waivers of the code for such officers. The board and the CEO must also ensure that all employees understand and abide by the corporation's ethical principles and rules of conduct. Increasingly, corporate boards have an affirmative requirement to ensure that a strong ethics framework is in place.

Recognizing that sheer compliance with governance regulations cannot prevent fraud, the Federal Sentencing Guidelines (2004) established mitigating punishment for fraud based on the existence of an effective compliance and ethics program, the components of which are provided in the guidelines. The new sentencing guidelines also mandate that companies assess the risk of criminal conduct, periodically and regularly, and that the results of these analyses must be considered in design of the company's compliance and ethics program. Through programs institutionalized to encourage ethical employee conduct as well as full compliance with the law, companies are now expected to establish a culture of compliance (Kaplan, 2004).

Establishing this ethical culture necessitates a long-term perspective. Indeed, the corporation's interests and the interests of other constituencies are best served with a shareowner base that holds its investment for the long term (Conference Board, 2003). As such, governance oversight should not ignore the longer-term impact of inadequate risk management and investment. Retaining a long-term shareowner base and strengthening the compact works effectively when shareowners have a high level of trust that the business is being managed honestly and in their best interests. Only a strong, diligent board, with a substantial majority of independent directors that both understand the key issues and ask management the tough questions, is capable of ensuring that shareowner interests are properly served. This long-term view serves the best interests not only of the shareholders, but also of the company's other constituencies, including employees, customers, suppliers and communities.

The Federal Sentencing Guidelines (2004) provide three newly emphasized requirements with respect to creating an ethical culture: an increase in board involvement, risk assessment, and compliance and ethics training at every level of the organization (Conference Board, 2005a). The first requirement, an increase in board involvement, is perhaps the single most important factor in creating credible evidence of an ethical culture: the "tone at the top," set by boards and senior management. The tone at the top is evident in the role of the board as a mediating hierarch that exercises leadership in balancing stakeholder conflicts in the best interests of overall corporate prosperity and the formation of long-term shareholder wealth. Thus, a belief that all stakeholder groups are essential to corporate prosperity belies an ethical tone at the top. Respect and concern for a range of corporate constituencies, including employees, customers, communities and suppliers, contributes to a positive climate for optimal corporate behavior. Furthermore, public opinion widely endorses the view that companies should not neglect the expectations of these constituencies (Ingley and Van der Walt, 2004).

In this paper, we build upon a stakeholder approach previously advanced in the ethics literature (Spiller, 2002),[2] by providing much more detailed information of good governance practice while also adding directors, management, corporate partners, and the local (and national/international) community to the list of six stakeholders. Our implementation structure was developed for stakeholders within the banking industry, but stakeholder groups can be added or amended as appropriate for any industry. It is important to note that the controls should be both locally applicable and global in scope.

Entity-Level Controls

Adopting a stakeholder approach to resolving conflicts of interest recognizes the interdependencies that exist within the corporate governance system and provides a basis for addressing agency problems among multiple stakeholders. This approach, therefore, works in concert with entity-level controls to reinforce the control system and inculcate an ethical firm culture. Entity-level controls support a social culture that disparages corruption or lying and rewards independent directors and the lawyers that assist them, which may check opportunism. Such a corporate culture can develop new social norms that stress open communication, cohesiveness, and integrity, which, if internalized, become efficient and self-enforcing, as the feedback loop in Figure 10.2 indicates.

As discussed, the evaluation of entity-level controls has a direct impact on the auditor's assessment of the risk of material misstatements in the financial statements. Stated simply, the strength of the entity-level controls has a direct impact on the nature, timing and extent of all further audit testing. So, the stronger these controls are, the less testing the auditor would otherwise perform. In the technical auditing standard (PCAOB, 2007: Para. 24), entity-level controls include:

- *controls related to the control environment*;
- controls over management override;
- centralized processing and controls;
- controls to monitor results of operations
- *controls to monitor other controls (including activities of the audit committee and internal audit and self-assessment programs)*;
- controls over the period-end financial reporting process; and
- *policies that address significant business control and risk management practice.*[3]

Our focus is on implementing testable control activities to help assess the effectiveness of the company's control environment and monitoring of controls components to help reduce Section 404 compliance costs and enable management and boards to conduct self-assessment and to rely on their monitoring activities. Accordingly, our approach addresses the control environment, controls to monitor other controls as well as risk management and business control. Importantly, controls related to the control environment include the tone at the top, organizational structure, commitment to competence, human resource policies and procedures (PCAOB,

2005). Rather than being considered as a separate entity-level control, the tone at the top permeates our framework, through an attention to all stakeholders. This tone is also directly evident in the activities listed for the company board and management stakeholder groups, wherein commitment to competence is integral. Further, as aforementioned, inculcating an ethical culture requires entity-level controls that stress open communication and also reflect the Federal Sentencing Guidelines (2004) emphasis on compliance and ethics training at all levels within an organization. We have therefore highlighted the significance of these two control environment variables by including them as additional categories of entity-level controls: ethics and compliance programs and training and communication. The complete list of controls that we address is as follows: ethics and compliance programs, self-assessment (controls to monitor controls), human resource policy and procedures, training and communication, organization structure, and risk assessment and management. The particulars with respect to each of these controls, organized by stakeholder group, appear in Tables 10.1–10.6.

Data

Regulatory sources and interviews

The regulatory sources of the detailed principles and practices contained in tables are found in the Federal Sentencing Guidelines, the Bank of International Settlements guidance on bank governance and the Code of Federal Regulations for banks per the Office of the Comptroller of the Currency. We also conducted interviews with the chief risk officers at both a leading financial institution and a small, but growing bank.

Business ethics literature

The business ethics academic and practitioner literature (Neef, 2003; Conference Board, 2005b; Gibbs, 2003) states that an ethical culture should contain the following characteristics:

- A corporate ethics office led by a corporate ethics officer. (Table 10.5)
- A board level ethics committee. (Table 10.5)
- A corporate value statement. (Table 10.1)

Table 10.1 Entity-level control – Ethics and compliance programs

Stakeholder	Ethics and compliance programs
Board of directors	• Knowledgeable about content and operation • Exercise reasonable oversight • Approves corporate code of conduct and practices the code • Independent directors must abide by the code
Management	• Promote, enforce and reward ethical behavior and compliance as found in the code, HR policies, and all regulations and as demonstrated by specific performance management polices (rewards and demotions/firing) • CEO and designees write code of conduct, soliciting input from employees • Senior management believes and demonstrates that ethical conduct is always the best course. • Assures internal controls are effective and documented
Employees	• Employee opinion regarding mgt ethics matters and is positive • Employees are satisfied regarding reward system for ethical behavior • Employee feels punishment system is just and fairly applied • # of calls at complaint hotline reflects openness – look to self-identified issues, internal audit criticisms, bank regulatory criticisms. • % of profit-related compensation is appropriate • Feels compliance programs are necessary to the long-run viability of the firm and that their work with respect to compliance is important
Customers/clients	• Customer are satisfied regarding bank's ethics and practices • % of customer transactions reported under given netting procedures is monitored and appropriate • Volume of customer business in both M&A and corporate loans is monitored and is appropriate

Shareholders	• Look to % of institutional shareholders
	• Look to % of related parties shareholders
	• Active voice at annual meetings
	   ✓ Shareholder proposals at annual meetings
	   ✓ Agreed requests are accomplished

Suppliers/offshore services	• Ethical programs are known and in line with company's values ✓ reciprocal agreements on ethics programs or suppliers program must have company approval
Partners/syndicates	• Ethical programs are known and in line with company's values
Local (and national) community	• Interaction with and service to community • Funding of senior management involvement with community is appropriate • Financial statements are not misstated

Table 10.2   Entity-level controls – Self-assessment

Stakeholder	Self-assessment of ethics and compliance programs
Board of directors	• Initiate and receive reports on effectiveness of ethics and compliance program • Provision for an Audit Committee to monitor and report on effectiveness of internal controls for compliance programs • Provision for an independent third party evaluator of ethics and compliance program beyond Audit Committee role, as warranted • Annually reviews code of conduct
Management	• Monitor and audit compliance and ethics programs to detect criminal conduct. Review client, peer and supplier complaints in addition to legal complaints • Monitors internal controls • Make certain employees realize and believe they can discuss or report issues confidentially without fear of reprisal • Build flexibility into ethics programs that evolve with the company's size, scope and purpose • Sample effectiveness periodically through surveys/focus groups • Garners employee feedback on ethics and compliance revisions
Employees	• Participation in surveys/focus groups on ethics and compliance assessment • Participation of employee feedback on ethics revisions • Internal audit of compliance and ethics programs
Customers/clients	Not applicable
Shareholders	Not applicable
Suppliers/offshore services	Not applicable
Partners/syndicates	Not applicable
Local (and national) community	Not applicable

- A code of conduct providing detailed guidelines on behavior and procedures for notification, for example, with scenario examples and a clear statement of penalties. (Table 10.1)
- A strong program to communicate those values and guidelines to all employees. (Table 10.4)

Table 10.3 Entity-level control – HR policies and procedures

Stakeholder	Human resource policies and procedures

Board of directors	• Knowledge and approval of HR policies and procedures
	  ✓ Value placed on employees
	  ✓ Review hiring, recruiting and performance mgt policies
	• Audit Committee hires external auditor
	• Perform due diligence with respect to ethical track record of directors and screen for conflicts of interest
	• Perform periodic review of board

Management	• Ethical standards and skills among core qualifications for CEO and senior mgt positions • Abides by, reviews and approves HR policy
Employees	• Integrity and background checks standard op in hiring • Adherence to quality and testing requirements for products/loans and services • Adherence to working hours, labor laws, freedom of association and other work related issues • Adherence to heath standards • Ongoing compliance with performance management system
Customers/clients	• Selling and marketing policies and client disclosure agreements are disclosed and adhered to and monitored ✓ regulators • Ethical behavior with customers is promoted and enforced • Fees, billing and contracting guidelines are followed
Shareholders Suppliers/offshore services	• No kickbacks to related parties or affiliates
Partners/syndicates	• No kickbacks to related parties or affiliates
Local (and national) community	• No conflicts of interest – related parties of senior management disclosure • HR policy with respect to safety and soundness of business in community

- A confidential whistle-blower hotline for communicating employee issues. (Table 10.4)
- Clear and effective monitoring and enforcement procedures. (Table 10.1)

Further, the code of conduct should be applied and understood by all employees, at every level in the company. Senior managers must believe

Table 10.4   Entity-level control – Training and communication

Stakeholder	Training and communication
Board of directors	• Receives training on ethics and compliance program, as per corporate code of conduct • Communicates (written and verbal) company values and strategic objectives • Audit Committee monitors external auditors through effective communication • Provides sustainability/social performance reports (e.g. the community reinvest. act) • Provides crisis communication
Management	• Regularly communicate values, principles and standards – internally. and externally • Operationalizes strategic management, as directed by board • Operationalizes crisis communication, as directed by board • Initiate and publicize whistle-blower program and protection • Provide representation that all known ethics breaches have been reported, investigated and resolved
Employees	• Required to attend compliance and regulations training sessions • Employee satisfaction regarding getting new information is high • Employees actively involved in communicating good news and breaches of ethical conduct
Customers/clients	• File suspicious activity report with the bank • Report all agreements >$10,000 with bank regulators
Shareholders	• Shareholder reports disclose accurate information
Suppliers/offshore services	• Material vendors are aware of and adhere to company ethics and compliance programs • Participate in training
Partners/syndicates	• Screened on compliance and ethics
Local (and national) community	• Social programs emphasizing corporate social responsibility are regularly communicated

and show that ethical action is always the best course. This can be done through effective education, communication, and training (Table 10.4), but ethics and risk management policies are ultimately most effective when

Table 10.5 Entity-level control – Organization structure

Stakeholder	Organizational structure
Board of Directors	• Liaison with management • Audit Committee oversight • Liaison with designated corporate ethics officer or senior officer • Defined, documented composition, compensation and terms of service of board • Ensure management's compensation does not have an inordinate/inappropriate emphasis on the bottom line
Management	• Delegate specific individual for operational responsibility • Provide adequate resources and authority to this individual • Give this individual direct access to board • Management skill set should include years of leadership (in banking) experience • % of profit-related compensation should be appropriate
Employees	• Utilize knowledge management to identify experts needed for risk assessment, management and compliance • Employees believe that corporate compliance officer has the appropriate skill set
Customers/clients	Not applicable
Shareholders	Not applicable
Suppliers/offshore services	• Have vendor relationship manager so that aggrieved party has access to management/ senior management
Partners/syndicates	• Have vendor relationship manager so that aggrieved party has access to management/ senior management
Local (and national) community	Not applicable

they are made integral to the employees' day-to-day work (Tables 10.1 and 10.6). Further, companies should conduct audits of the staff's understanding of the code and should require periodic self-assessments of selected employees using appropriate code provisions (Table 10.2). It is also important to solicit input from employees (surveys and focus groups in the early rollout phase of the program – see Table 10.2), while extending the process to include suppliers and vendors when possible.

Table 10.6   Entity-level control – Risk assessment and management

Stakeholder	Risk Assessment
Board of directors	• Charged to Audit Committee • Perceiving and dealing with bad decisions or process failures and preventing them from damaging the company
Management	• Incorporating risk and knowledge sharing in day-to-day operations • Require management participation in active risk management • Adopting a lessons-learned approach • Surveying actual behavior of personnel • Collect accurate and holistic information of all factors and stakeholder views to an incident or opportunity
Employees	• Employee objectives towards risk assessment and risk management have direct impact on the business • Employees understand what constitutes an ethical risk and are comfortable and feel obligated to bring it to light
Customers/clients	• Credit risk is assessed, managed and monitored • Enhanced due diligence before taking on new client
Shareholders	
Suppliers/offshore services	• Credit risk is assessed, managed and monitored • Compliance programs are inline with company and regulations – reciprocal agreement to same
Partners/syndicates	• Credit risk is assessed, managed and monitored • Compliance programs are inline with company and regulations
Local (and national) community	Not applicable

An ethical framework should also address strategic issues. Central among the tenets of our framework is the feedback loop from performance outcome to corporate strategy; hence, the importance of communicating an organization's strategy through the use of relevant measures of strategy implementation (Tables 10.4 and 10.6). Further, corporate integrity is also reliant on knowledge management to help a company to identify experts, collect and distribute important information, capture lessons learned, and complete business research and analysis (Tables 10.5 and 10.6).

Creating a culture of integrity and knowledge sharing relies on incentives and enforcement. Incentives and enforcement are integral to ethics and compliance programs, human resource policies and procedures and risk assessment and management (Tables 10.1, 10.3 and 10.6). An ethical system cannot influence change unless it is supported by a system of consistent rewards, incentives, and immediate penalties (Gates, 2004). Further, unless effectively managed and checked, past successes and growth, along with sustained pressures to perform, can lead to a cavalier attitude toward ethical behavior, which could result in reckless initiatives and institutional resistance to bad news (Gibbs, 2003). If future scandals are to be prevented, "we must insist on effective controls, design appropriate awards, and eliminate inherent conflicts of interest ... Rigorous controls aren't enough by themselves. If an organization's internal reward systems encourage the wrong kinds of behavior, people will start looking for ways to get around the controls."[4]

Summary and Conclusions

The Sarbanes–Oxley Act of 2002 has dramatically increased the complexity of the governance structure and directly impacted the monitoring role of corporate boards. To help them efficiently discharge their responsibilities and ensure effective compliance, we present an entity-level controls-based governance framework that encompasses all stakeholder groups and emphasizes firm culture and an ethical tone at the top. We believe that our framework will be helpful in reducing the costs of complying with Section 404 of SARBOX, which has been particularly costly for publicly traded companies.

It is important to note that our framework is intended as a guide from the perspective of a publicly traded company. As the ISO 9000 and ISO 14000 standards have proven, companies are willing to signal quality without regulatory forces. Therefore, we provide a non-regulatory alternative, in which companies voluntarily implement the ethical framework we are suggesting.

Furthermore, our proposed framework is adaptive: it can and should be updated as needed to comply with new requirements and evolving corporate mission and strategy. The European Business Excellence Model supports organizations to achieve total quality through feedback, learning, and innovation (Oakland et al., 2002). In the same manner, our ethical framework is intended to be integrated into companies' learning processes. Thus it is a living document, intended to evolve with changes in company stakeholders and the regulatory environment.

The proposed framework is a conceptual attempt at formulating an ethical culture supported by corporate-wide controls to assist in achieving effective corporate governance in the post-SARBOX regulatory environment. Empirical research is needed both to investigate the various components of our framework and their interrelationships and also to consider the consequent organizational outcomes, which will likely be reflected in performance measurement. Beyond this research, future studies on other industries and inter-industry comparisons may prove to be fruitful avenues for future research. It may be of value, for example, to determine whether industries that faced a relatively stringent regulatory environment prior to the imposition of SARBOX faced less cost complying with this governance regulation.

Notes

1   On October 17, 2006 the Committee of Sponsoring Organizations of the Treadway Commission (COSO) issued a request for proposal to develop application guidance on monitoring to support management's assessment of internal controls over financial reporting. Grant Thornton was selected.

2   Spiller defines ten practices for each of the six major stakeholders he identified: community, environment, employees, customers, suppliers, and shareholders.

3   In our discussion, we focus on the controls that are italicized in this list.

4   J. Brennan "The Market Value of Integrity," The Sears Lectureship in Business Ethics, Center for Business Ethics, Bentley College (October 29, 2002).

References

Conference Board. 2003. Corporate governance: a rationale. *The Conference Board Commission on Public Trust and Private Enterprise*, Part 2.

Conference Board. 2005a. How prepared are companies for the revised sentencing guidelines? *Executive Action*, March, p. 139.

Conference Board. 2005b. Corporate governance handbook 2005: developments in best practices, compliance, and legal standards. *Special Report No. 2*.

Drew, S. 2006. CLASS: Five elements of corporate governance to manage strategic risk. *Business Horizons*, 49: 127–38.

Federal Sentencing Guidelines. 2004. *Guidelines Manual*, chapter 8, http://www.ussc.gov/guidelin.htm, accessed January 2005.

Financial Executives International (FEI). 2005. *Special Survey on SOX Section 404 Implementation*, March, http://www2.fei.org/files/spacer.cfm?file_id=1498.

Fisher, J. 1995. Contingency-based research on management control systems. *Journal of Accounting Literature*, 14: 24–55.

Gates, J. 2004. The ethics commitment process: sustainability through value-based ethics. *Business Society Review*, 109(4): 493–505.

Gibbs, E. 2003. Developing an ethical code of conduct. *Financial Executive*, 19 (June): 40.

Ingley, C. and N. Van der Walt. 2004. Corporate governance, institutional investors and conflicts of interest. *Governance*, 12 (October): 534–51.

Kaplan, J. 2004. The new corporate sentencing guidelines. *Ethikos*, July/August: 1–6.

Neef, D. 2003. *Managing Corporate Reputation and Risk: Developing a Strategic Approach to Corporate Integrity Using Knowledge Management*. Amsterdam: Elsevier.

Oakland, J., S. Tanner, and K. Gadd. 2002. Best practice in business excellence. *Total Quality Management*, 13 (December): 1125–39.

Public Company Accounting Oversight Board (PCAOB). 2005. *Policy Statement Regarding Implementation of Auditing Standard No. 2, An Audit of Internal Control over Financial Reporting Performed in Conjunction with an Audit of Financial Statements*, May 16. Washington, DC: PCAOB.

Public Company Accounting Oversight Board (PCAOB). 2007. *An Audit of Internal Control Over Financial Reporting That is Integrated With an Audit of Financial Statements and Related Independence Rule and Conforming Amendments*, Auditing Standard No. 5. Washington, DC: PCAOB.

Spiller, R. 2000. Ethical business and investment: A model for business and society. *Journal of Business Ethics*, 27: 149–60.

Strebel, P. 2004. The case for contingent governance. *MIT Sloan Management Review*, Winter: 59–66.

US House of Representatives. 2002. *The Sarbanes–Oxley Act of 2002*, Public Law 107–204 [HR 3763]. Washington, DC: Government Printing Office.

11

Do Corporate Boards Care About Sustainability? Should They Care?

Steven Swidler and Claire E. Crutchley

Abstract

Corporate boards have a responsibility to encourage strategies that maximize shareholder wealth. If corporate sustainability is value increasing, boards should implement these policies designed to manage environmental, social, and governance risks. Using US companies on the Dow Jones Global Sustainability Index as a proxy for sustainable firms, this paper examines the economic importance of corporate sustainability. On average, sustainable firms earn greater returns than large cap companies. However, when compared to industry matched companies, the risk-adjusted returns are no greater than those of the matched sample, nor is the risk of sustainable companies lower. While the Q ratios of sustainable firms are higher than the industry matches, the difference diminishes over time. Perhaps more corporate boards have instituted sustainable practices in recent years so that now there is little difference between firms named to the sustainability index and those that are not.

Introduction

As owners of the firm, shareholders appoint board members to oversee company management and maximize shareholder wealth. Charged with this responsibility, board members may support labor or environmental practices that lead to immediate cost savings and add to short-term profitability. Aggressive accounting practices may also be instituted to recognize instant gains. However, to pursue short-term profits at the expense of future gains may ultimately threaten a firm's long-run viability. Corporate history is littered with examples of bankruptcy caused by the failure of management to plan for the future.

Board members might carry out their fiduciary duty in a different way; for example, they may encourage strategies that lead to employee satisfaction, are environmentally friendly and foster transparent oversight practices. The intent of these policies is not only to add to today's bottom line, but also to *sustain* the company's assets for future generations. By supporting corporate sustainability measures, the board seeks to create long-term shareholder value by searching for new opportunities and managing risks that derive from economic, environmental and social events.[1]

While previous studies have examined the investment value of socially responsible firms (see, e.g., Margolis et al., 2007; Statman, 2007), there has been little work concerning the economic importance of corporate sustainability. At a minimum, firms that pursue sustainable goals are socially responsible. They institute programs and policies that are friendly to the environment. Beyond that, sustainable goals also stress fair and open corporate governance policies and include risk management programs intended to minimize the fallout from environmental or economic disasters. *In theory*, sustainable policies and programs should add value to the firm.[2] If that is the case, it further implies that corporate boards should institute sustainable programs since they are in the best interest of shareholders.

One reason that there has been little work examining the economic value of corporate sustainability is that the concept itself has only been articulated in recent years. As a result, quantifying corporate sustainability is also a new endeavor, and, to date, it has not been possible to conduct a rigorous test of the effect of sustainability on firm value. Since 1999, Dow Jones, with the help of STOXX Ltd. and the SAM Group, have constructed a Global Sustainability Index comprised of firms around the world that score highest in their industry in terms of social, environmental, and economic factors. The following analysis examines the economic performance of these firms to see whether or not sustainable policies enhance firm value and ultimately whether it is appropriate for corporate boards to pursue sustainable programs.

The firms in the Dow Jones Global Sustainability Index (DJGSI) are a subset of the Dow Jones Global Index and include the top 10 percent of companies in each of 57 sectors with respect to sustainability.[3] In assigning the sustainability index score, opportunities and risks are weighted equally in three different factors: environmental, social, and economic. While opportunities consist of things such as strategic planning and environmental reporting, the risks include environmental responsibilities, child labor and corporate codes of conduct (Knoepfel, 2001).

Whether or not board support of corporate sustainability practices adds to firm value is ultimately an empirical issue. There is some evidence that the strategic initiatives and risk management policies central to corporate sustainability are positively correlated with shareholder wealth. Knoepfel (2001) finds that the Dow Jones Global Sustainability Index outperforms the Dow Jones Global Index in the years 1995–2000, but the returns are not risk adjusted. Moreover, because the index only begins in 1999, the performance analysis is largely backward looking. Knoepfel examines firms deemed sustainable in 1999–2000 and then looks at how they performed over the previous five years. Thus, this analysis makes it difficult to interpret cause and effect. Do sustainable firms perform relatively well or are firms with strong returns later designated as sustainable?[4]

A direct test of the impact of sustainability on firm value appears in Lo and Sheu (2007). They find that over the period 1999–2002, US firms in the DJGSI have a higher Tobin's Q than comparable firms in the S&P 500. Their results are especially strong for firms with high levels of research and development. While their work suggests that sustainability adds value, it is limited in scope due to the short sample period and its exclusion of mid-size firms and financial institutions.

Before continuing, it is important to note that the concept of corporate sustainability is not easily defined or measured. Corporate Knights Inc., in partnership with Innovest Strategic Value Advisors Inc., have developed their own criteria to come up with the "Global 100," an annual list of 100 firms in the MSCI World Index "that demonstrate exceptional capacity to address their sector-specific environmental, social and governance (ESG) risks and opportunities." While they state that the "concept of sustainability is a contentious one," they believe that firms able to identify and effectively manage ESG risks will lead to superior performance in the long run. In partial support of this contention, Corporate Knights and Innovest (2008) find that the 2006 list of the Global 100 outperformed the MSCI World Index over the period 2000–06. Once more, however, it is not clear what is the cause and what is the effect since Corporate Knights and Innovest will only consider companies that are rated AAA on the MSCI World Index for inclusion in the Global 100.

A further important implication of the Global 100 analysis is that the concept of corporate sustainability is not a monolithic idea, and that, therefore, any result we derive is a function of the criteria used to select our group of sustainable firms. Largely due to the fact that the Dow Jones Global Sustainability Index predates the Global 100, we choose the former index to define our group of sustainable firms. Moreover, the DJGSI potentially considers a more comprehensive group of firms. Nevertheless, the DJGSI and Global 100 both emphasize a firm's ability to manage environmental, social and governance risks, and to that extent, share a similar framework in identifying sustainable firms.

Do Corporate Boards Care about Sustainability?

On one level, whether corporate boards care is a rhetorical question. Presumably anything that affects shareholder value is of concern to the board. If sustainability matters, corporate boards will care. Thus, short of conducting an exhaustive survey of corporate boards, we might conclude that they necessarily care about sustainable practices to the extent it improves firm value.

There is, however, anecdotal evidence that suggests corporate boards hold a variety of opinions concerning the importance of sustainability. In putting together the DJGSI, the SAM Group distributes a questionnaire to the CEOs and heads of investor relations of all companies in the potential universe of stocks. This completed questionnaire must be signed by a senior company executive and is considered the most important source of information for the selection of sustainable firms.

Despite the stressed importance of completing the questionnaire, of the 2,511 surveys that were distributed, only 521 companies responses were received (Dow Jones Indexes et al., 2007). The SAM Group analyzed an additional 531 based on public sources, implying that only 42 percent of all firms provided enough information to even be considered for inclusion in the sustainability index. Thus, the mixed response from senior executives yields one signal that not all corporate boards care about sustainability.[5]

Further anecdotal evidence on the seeming indifference of many corporate boards with respect to sustainability issues can be found in a report on corporate governance and climate change. In a study of 100 companies, Cogan (2006) finds that the average industry score for disclosure of policies regarding greenhouse gas emissions is only 8.7 points (out of a possible 14). Unsurprisingly, disclosure totals appear to correlate with scores in the other areas monitored, including emissions accounting, strategic planning, management execution and board oversight. In short, some firms care about environmental issues and disclose relevant information, while other firms have less interest in these matters and are therefore less forthcoming.[6]

While the evidence suggests that not all corporate boards are concerned about sustainability issues, perhaps the more important question is: should they care? To answer that question, we next turn to the DJGSI and examine the performance of firms in the index.

The Dow Jones Global Sustainability Index and Relative Performance of Member Firms

To examine whether or not corporate boards should be concerned with sustainability issues, we first consider the set of US firms included in the Dow Jones Global Sustainability Index and then examine their performance over the sample period, 1999–2007. Table 11.1 summarizes the frequency of firms appearing in the Dow Jones Global Sustainability Index on an annual basis. There are 52 firms that appear only once in the DJGSI, while a number of companies appear in the index over a number of years. In some instances, firms enter, exit, and then re-enter the index. Overall, there are 155 unique US companies in the DJGSI from 1999–2006 – with a total of 490 company years. The 155 unique firms comprise 42 different industries (measured by 2-digit SIC codes), and both the frequency and breadth of companies allow for a number of robust statistical tests of economic value.

Firms consistently earning high marks in sustainability appear in Table 11.2. There are nine firms that appear in the DJGSI for every one of the eight years that the index has been compiled, and ten firms in the DJGSI appear in seven of the eight years. To the extent that sustainability adds value, we would expect that the "stars" necessarily outperform firms in their sector that are not part of the DJGSI.

Two of the firms found in Table 11.2, Harrah's and Dow Jones & Co., will not be part of the index in subsequent years as they no longer exist as separate, publicly held entities. In fact, 16 of the 155 firms in our sample

Table 11.1 Frequency of companies in the DJGSI (1999–2006)

Times in DJGSI	No. of companies
Once	52
Twice	26
Three	22
Four	12
Five	14
Six	10
Seven	10
Eight	9
Unique companies	155
Company years	490

Table 11.2 Stars of the Dow Jones Global Sustainability Index

Panel A lists the companies that have been listed on the Dow Jones Global Sustainability Index each year that the index has been in existence, from 1999–2006. Panel B lists those firms who have been on the index seven out of the eight years.

Panel A
Companies on Index all Eight Years

Company	Industry
Baxter International	Surgical, Medical Instruments
ITT Corp	Search and Navigation Systems
Intel Corp	Semiconductors
Nike Inc	Rubber and plastic footwear
Procter & Gamble	Soap, detergent, toiletries
United Heath Group	Hospitals and medical service
United Technologies	Aircraft and parts
Dell Inc	Electronic computers
Harrah's Entertainment*	Amusement and Recreation

Panel B
Companies on DJS Index Seven Years

Company	Industry	Year not on DJSI
CA Inc	Prepackaged Software	1999
Dow Jones & Company**	Newspaper	1999
Johnson & Johnson	Pharmaceuticals	1999
Pfizer	Pharmaceuticals	1999
Temple-Inland	Paperboard Mills	1999
Starbucks	Eating places	2000
Time Warner	Cable and other TV	2001
Gap Inc	Family clothing	2002
Dow Chemical	Plastics, resins	2005
Du Pont De Nemours	Plastic material	2006

* Became privately held company in 2008
** Acquired by News Corporation in 2008

disappear only one year after being named a sustainable firm. Table 11.3 lists these firms, along with the reason for their removal. While firms that are acquired or taken private are frequently well-run firms, it is hard to imagine what went wrong so quickly for the three firms that went bankrupt only one year after being included in the sustainability index. Moreover, a fourth company, Tyco, was named a sustainable firm in 2001, only to be

Table 11.3   Disappearing companies from the Dow Jones Global Sustainability Index
This table lists the companies that disappeared the year after being selected to the Dow Jones Sustainability Index and the reason for their removal.

Panel A
Bankrupt Companies

	Years on DJSI	*Delisting date*	
Bethlehem Steel	1999–2000	10/15/2001	
K Mart Inc	2000–2001	1/22/2002	
Delphi Corp	2003–2004	10/11/2005	
Acquired Companies			*Acquirer*
Consolidated Papers	1999	9/1/2000	Stora Enso Oyj
Global Marine	2000	9/4/2001	Santa Fe International
Texaco	2000	10/10/2001	Chevron
Conoco Inc	2001	8/30/2002	Phillips Petroleum
Compaq Computer	1999–2001	5/3/2002	Hewlett Packard*
Mead Corp	2001	1/30/2002	Westvaco*
Fleet Boston Financial	2003	4/1/2004	Bank of America
Guidant	1999–2005	4/24/2006	Boston Scientific
Lafarge North America (parent company)	2000–2005	5/17/2006	Lafarge Group
Cinergy Corp	2003–2005	4/3/2006	Duke Energy
Dow Jones Inc	2000–2006	12/13/2007	News Corporation
Became Private			
ServiceMaster	2006	7/24/2007	Clayton, Dubilier and Rice, private equity firm
Harrah's Entertainment	1999–2006	1/28/2008	

engulfed by a corporate scandal in 2002. At the least, these four firms illustrate that sustainability does not guarantee success. Moreover, these examples call into question whether or not the sustainability criteria used in the DJGSI adequately capture a firm's ability to identify and manage environmental, social, and governance risks. In the case of Tyco, inclusion in the DJGSI may have been the result of fraud related to the disclosure and accounting violations committed by several board members and senior executives. Thus, even if the sustainability criteria are reasonable, the possibility exists that firms can bias the information they disclose in order to be included in the index.

Table 11.4   Comparison of size: DJGSI vs. Compustat companies
DJGSI companies are US companies that have been listed on the Dow Jones Global
Sustainability Index in any year. There are a total of 155 unique companies of
which 128 survive and have data listed on Compustat in 2006. The universe of
5,528 Compustat companies include all firms with assets available on the Compustat
database in the year 2006. Assets are in $millions.

	DJSI	Compustat
Percent on the S&P 500 Index	80.5%	8.7%
Total number of Companies	128	5,528
Distribution	*Asset Size*	*Asset Size*
Maximum	1,884,318	1,884,320
Top 99%	1,459,737	104,172
Top 95%	278,554	17,565
Top 90%	107,353	7,483
Top 75%	34,990	1,916
Median	13,904	455
Bottom 25%	5,969	73
Bottom 10%	2,251	14
Minimum	340	0.003
Mean Asset Size	72,816	6,510

While invitations to complete the SAM survey are sent out to more than
2,500 companies of varying sizes, most of the firms eventually included in
the index are large ones. Table 11.4 reports the distribution of firm size
for the sustainable firms in our sample and also the distribution of firm size
for the Compustat universe of stocks. The snapshot is as at December 31,
2006, and includes the 128 of the 155 firms in our sample that survive to
that date. Fully 80 percent of the sustainable firms appear in the S&P 500
index and are large relative to the typical Compustat company. The assets
of the median sustainable firm are more than $13.9 billion, positioning
them in the top decile of the Compustat universe. Even firms that are in the
bottom 10 percent of sustainable firms would be found in the upper quartile
of Compustat stocks. Thus, any type of performance analysis must adjust
for the large size of sustainable firms.

In Figure 11.1, we compare sustainable stock returns to the Dow Jones–
Wilshire Large Cap Index. The DJ–Wilshire large cap stocks constitute the
750 largest firms in the United States as measured by market capitalization.
For the sustainable stock time series, we calculate an equal weighted return
index in the year subsequent to the stock being named in the DJGSI. Thus,
for example, the sustainable returns for 2000 include all stocks named in

Figure 11.1   Total returns index: Sustainable firms vs. Wilshire–Large Cap stocks

the DJGSI in the fall of 1999. By calculating the index in this fashion, we create a *forward*-looking return series. Unlike Knoepfel (2001) and the Global 100 study that look at the performance of sustainable stocks prior to their inclusion in the index, Figure 11.1 illustrates the returns of sustainable stocks the year after they are named to the DJGSI.[7]

A $100 investment in a portfolio of the DJGSI stocks made on December 31, 1999 would have grown in value to $176.87 by the end of 2007. The index returns include dividends and assume a quarterly rebalancing of the stocks in the portfolio. In contrast, the Dow Jones–Wilshire Large Cap index would have grown from $100 to $115.77 over the same time period.

Dissecting performance over shorter intervals, Table 11.5 depicts the return of sustainable stocks on an annual basis. In three of the eight years, the return of the equal weighted index is higher than the annual return of the Dow Jones–Wilshire Large Cap index. Following the market's decline in the spring of 2000, large cap stocks had negative returns in both 2000 and 2001. At the same time, the index of sustainable firms had small, but positive rates of return. Then, as the market rebounded from the recession, large cap stocks earned a nearly 29 percent return in 2003, while the portfolio of sustainable firms grew an even more impressive 48 percent. For the remaining five years in the sample, the annual performance of large cap stocks was virtually identical to the performance of the equal weighted index of sustainable firms.

Table 11.5 Performance of DJGSI stocks by year, 2000–7

Year	2000	2001	2002	2003	2004	2005	2006	2007
DJ–Wilshire Large Cap Stocks								
Annual Return[a]	−0.1050	−0.1296	−0.2107	0.2889	0.1165	0.0633	0.1562	0.0640
Sustainable Firms Equal Weighted Index								
Annual Return[a]	0.0495	0.0120	−0.2273	0.4835	0.1177	0.0636	0.1474	0.0651
Sustainable Firms Return Distribution								
Mean	0.0736*	−0.0013*	−0.2207	0.4794*	0.1187	0.0628	0.1380	0.0859
95% Confidence Band (+/−)	0.1523	0.0957	0.0708	0.1120	0.0632	0.0608	0.0479	0.0876
Median	−0.0024	0.0090	−0.1913	0.3505	0.1072	0.0463	0.1401	0.0838
Standard Deviation	0.5069	0.3333	0.2971	0.4334	0.2551	0.2453	0.1935	0.3239
Kurtosis	0.2916	0.8316	−0.3543	2.5432	0.9781	0.3905	0.6666	1.8878
Skewness	0.6140	−0.3410	−0.2565	1.2400	0.6817	0.3963	−0.1522	0.3722
Minimum	−0.8098	−0.7933	−0.9230	−0.2621	−0.3488	−0.4512	−0.3719	−0.6356
Maximum	1.3631	0.7728	0.4723	2.1527	0.8805	0.8088	0.6428	1.1753
Number of Firms	45	49	70	60	65	65	65	55

[a] The returns in this row correspond to the returns plotted in Figure 11.1.

* Using the 95% confidence band, we can reject the null hypothesis that the mean return of the sustainable firms equals the annual return of the Dow Jones–Wilshire Large Cap stocks in the years 2000, 2001, and 2003.

On the surface, it appears that sustainable stocks weathered the market downturn better than other large cap stocks. Moreover, once the market rebounded, sustainable firms bounced back even higher. This characterization seems to support the notion that sustainable policies preserve a company's assets for future generations, manage environmental, social, and governance risks, and create long-term shareholder value. However, upon closer inspection, this does not appear to be a universal truth for all firms found in the DJGSI.[8]

Table 11.5 reports annual return distribution statistics for sustainable firms included in the equal weighted index. While the mean return for the 45 sustainable firms in 2000 is significantly greater than the annual return of the DJ–Wilshire large cap stocks, it is also larger than the distribution's median. In fact, more than 50 percent of sustainable stocks lost money in 2000. Moreover, the value of Lucent Technologies stock declined nearly 81 percent for the year while Bethlehem Steel fell more than 79 percent. Subsequently, EMC Corporation stock dropped more than 79 percent in 2001 and Commerce One lost 92 percent of its equity value in 2002.

One conclusion to draw from the performance analysis is that the sustainability designation does not guarantee sustainability of the firm's assets. Looking only at portfolio returns conceals the financial distress encountered by several of the DJGSI companies. After poor performances in 2001–02, Commerce One and Bethlehem Steel eventually declared bankruptcy, the latter just one year after being named in the DJGSI. Two other firms, K Mart and Delphi, also entered bankruptcy a year after inclusion in the index. Yet another two firms, New Century Financial and Solutia, became insolvent after previously being named in the Dow Jones Global Sustainability Index. Thus, six of the 155 US firms listed in the DJGSI entered bankruptcy in the first eight years of the index's compilation.[9]

The Sharpe Ratio and Tobin's Q

If the sustainability index directly relates to a firm's risk management practice, firms in the index should have superior risk-adjusted performance. The previous analysis only loosely adjusts for risk by comparing sustainable firms to other large companies. To further explore whether adopting sustainable risk management practices matters, we next compare the Sharpe ratio of firms in the DJGSI to a matched sample of firms that have *never* been included in the index. We match firms first by industry and then by size.

The Sharpe measure is a reward to variability ratio. To calculate the numerator, we subtract the one year Treasury bill rate from the total return of the firm's stock in the year following its inclusion in the DJGSI. The denominator equals the annualized standard deviation of the firm's daily stock returns. After calculating the Sharpe ratio for a sustainable company, we then calculate a Sharpe ratio for the matched firm in the same year. If sustainable firms are better able to manage their sector-specific environmental, social and governance (ESG) risks and opportunities, then we would expect they would display greater reward per unit of risk. In other words, sustainability should imply higher Sharpe ratios compared to firms that do not exhibit sustainable practices.

The evidence in Table 11.6 indicates that sustainable firms do not have higher reward per unit of risk. In fact, for seven of the eight sample years, the mean difference in Sharpe ratios is negative, suggesting that sustainable firms earn lower risk-adjusted returns than the matched sample. In two of the years, 2001 and 2002, the difference is statistically significant, a result that is also true for the sample as a whole.

To see why these results occur, Table 11.7 focuses on the denominator of the Sharpe ratio, the firm's total risk. If sustainability entails managing risk, then sustainable firms should, on average, have lower total risk than the set of matched firms. The evidence in Table 11.7 suggests, however, that there is no difference between the risk of sustainable firms and the matched sample. Over the entire sample, the mean difference in standard deviations is 0. Taken together, Tables 11.6 and 11.7 imply that there is no difference in total risk between sustainable firms and the matched sample, but that sustainable firms, on average, earn lower returns. The latter finding appears to be at odds with the results observed in Figure 11.1. However, the superior returns exhibited in Figure 11.1 by the DJGSI firms is relative to all large cap stocks, whereas the comparison group in Tables 11.6 and 11.7 are firms in the same industry. Thus, relative performance measures appear to be sensitive to both size and industry variables.

The final – and perhaps most important – question is whether sustainability affects firm value. To answer this question, we expand the work of Lo and Sheu (2007) by extending their time period of analysis through 2007 and including all US firms in the DJGSI. If sustainability matters, Tobin's Q should be larger for DJGSI stocks than for those stocks never in the index. We calculate Q ratios using Compustat data and follow the approximation method of Chung and Pruitt (1994). Balance sheet values of debt and preferred stock are added to the market value of equity, and the sum is divided by the total asset value.

Table 11.6   Sharpe ratios sustainable (DJGSI) vs. industry matched firms
Returns are measured the year after the company was put on the Dow Jones Global Sustainability Index (DJGSI). For each DJGSI company, there is an industry matched firm of a similar size. The closest industry match (based on two digit SIC code) in asset size the year prior to being put on the index is the matched firm. This is for companies being put on the index from 1999–2006. Sharpe ratios are based on daily returns. The calculation is the difference between the annual return of a stock and the risk free rate for the year divided by the standard deviation of the daily returns. The Mean Difference is the difference between each DJGSI company's Sharpe ratio and the Sharpe ratio of its matched firm.

	Sharpe Ratios					
	DJGSI Companies		Industry Match		Mean	
Year	Median	Mean	Median	Mean	Difference	N
2000	−0.11	0.17	0.16	0.28	−0.11	45
2001	−0.10	−0.03	0.17	0.20	−0.24*	48
2002	−0.44	−0.34	−0.30	−0.20	−0.14*	71
2003	1.14	1.15	0.82	0.92	0.24	60
2004	0.45	0.43	0.47	0.56	−0.14	65
2005	0.08	0.10	0.09	0.17	−0.08	65
2006	0.42	0.42	0.46	0.54	−0.12	65
2007	0.01	0.16	0.14	0.26	−0.10	56
All	0.12	0.26	0.21	0.34	−0.08*	475

* indicates that difference between the DJGSI company's Sharpe ratio and the matched firm's Sharpe ratio is significantly different from zero at the 0.10 level.

Table 11.8 reports Q ratios for the DJGSI firms and the matched sample. The sustainable firms have higher Tobin Q ratios than the matched companies on an annual basis. For three years, 2000, 2001 and 2005, the mean difference is statistically significant; moreover, the two groups are statistically different over the eight-year sample period. Thus, the results suggest that the market rewards sustainable practices and stock prices impound the value of managing environmental, social and governance risks.

To some extent, the higher Q ratios of sustainable firms are driven by large values of a few firms in 1999 and 2000. For example, Time Warner had a 31.63 Tobin's Q in 1999, while Dell, Microsoft, and EMC also had Q ratios above 10. These large values are predominantly a function of high market to book value for equity. However, between 2000 and 2002, the market lost

Table 11.7   Standard deviation sustainable (DJGSI) vs. industry matched firms
Returns are measured the year after the company was put on the Dow Jones Global
Sustainability Index (DJGSI). For each DJGSI company, there is an industry
matched firm of a similar size. The closest industry match (based on two digit SIC
code) in asset size the year prior to being put on the index is the matched firm.
This is for companies being put on the index from 1999–2006. Sharpe ratios are
based on daily returns. The calculation is the annualized standard deviation of the
daily returns. The Mean Difference is the difference between each DJGSI company's standard deviation and the standard deviation of its matched firm.

	Annualized daily standard deviation					
	DJGSI Companies		Industry Match		Mean	
Year	Median	Mean	Median	Mean	Difference	N
2000	0.59	0.59	0.53	0.59	0.00	45
2001	0.41	0.51	0.41	0.44	0.07**	48
2002	0.52	0.60	0.49	0.58	0.02	71
2003	0.37	0.39	0.37	0.44	−0.04	60
2004	0.28	0.31	0.28	0.32	−0.01	65
2005	0.27	0.30	0.28	0.31	−0.01	65
2006	0.29	0.30	0.27	0.30	0.01	65
2007	0.30	0.34	0.32	0.35	−0.01	56
All	0.36	0.41	0.37	0.41	0.00	475

**,*   indicates that difference between the DJGSI company's annualized daily
standard deviation and the matched firm's standard deviation is significantly different
from zero at the 0.05, 0.10 level.

approximately 40 percent of its value, and resulted in the average Q ratio for
sustainable firms dropping more than 50 percent – from 3.52 to 1.74. Over
the entire sample period, the difference between the mean Q ratios for
DJGSI firms and the matched companies narrows and equals a statistically
insignificant .14 in 2006. Thus, while sustainable firms are more highly
valued by the market, the premium appears to be shrinking over time.

Conclusion

Do corporate boards care about sustainability? Anecdotally, CEOs and
heads of investor relations have a low response rate to the DJGSI survey

Table 11.8 Q ratios sustainable (DJGSI) vs. industry matched firms
Q ratios are measured using the market value of common stock plus book value of debt and preferred stock over total assets (a total market to book ratio) the year the company was put on the Dow Jones Global Sustainability Index (DJGSI). For each DJGSI company, there is an industry matched firm of a similar size. The closest industry match (based on two digit SIC code) in asset size the year prior to being put on the index is the matched firm.

Year	DJGSI Companies		Industry Match		Mean Difference	N
	Median	Mean	Median	Mean		
1999	1.97*	3.52	1.08	2.26	1.26	44
2000	1.52*	2.59*	1.41	1.81	0.78**	51
2001	1.76**	2.38**	1.30	1.79	0.59**	71
2002	1.44	1.74	1.21	1.51	0.23	58
2003	1.67**	1.99	1.32	1.73	0.26	66
2004	1.68*	2.03	1.38	1.75	0.27	63
2005	1.76***	2.03**	1.18	1.54	0.49**	67
2006	1.94	2.05	1.56	1.91	0.14	39
All Years	1.70***	2.25***	1.29	1.76	0.48***	459

***, **, * indicates that the median or mean DJGSI company's Q ratio is significantly different than the matched companies at the 0.01, 0.05 and 0.10 level.

administered by SAM. It is unclear whether or not board members are aware of the survey request, and without asking them directly, it is not possible to verify a board's interest in sustainability. Nevertheless, a simple answer to the first question is that boards likely care about policies consistent with sustainability, but they are not necessarily concerned about being named to a sustainability list like the DJGSI or Global 100.

One reason why boards may pursue sustainable practices, but not be worried about being included on a list, is that corporate sustainability is a difficult concept to define. As such, being named on a sustainable list may not be a definitive measure of whether a firm effectively promotes sustainable practices. Recent experience shows that some companies were named to the DJGSI only to declare bankruptcy the following year. Moreover, firms continually move on and off sustainable lists like the DJGSI and Global 100. Furthermore, lists that identify a sustainable company relative to firms within its industry render inter-industry comparisons largely irrelevant. Thus, it is not clear how, for example, a sustainable financial institution compares to a sustainable steel company.

The second question in our study, "Should corporate boards care about sustainability?," is more directly answered by considering the evidence from financial markets. Between 1999 and 2007, the gains from holding a portfolio of sustainable stocks exceeded the returns from large cap stocks. However, the strong performance was not uniform across sustainable firms as several stocks had large losses in the year following their inclusion in the DJGSI. Moreover, during the last four years of the sample period, both the portfolio of sustainable stocks and large cap stocks had nearly identical returns.

Return results are further tempered by the fact that sustainable firms, on average, have lower Sharpe ratios than a sample of stocks matched by industry. In part, this may be a function of sustainable stocks trading at a rich price. Comparing the Q ratios of sustainable firms to the matched sample finds that the equity of sustainable firms initially sold at a premium. More recently, though, the premium appears to have narrowed, and there appears to be little difference between the market's valuation of sustainable firms and other companies.

Taken as a whole, the results suggest that sustainable practices are value-enhancing activities, or – at the very least – that they do not diminish shareholder value. Whereas in earlier years, managing environmental, social, and governance risks led to equity premiums and healthy returns, lately any performance difference appears to be minimal. Perhaps this is because more and more corporate boards believe it prudent to institute sustainable practices, and there is now little difference between firms named to a sustainable index and the remaining universe of companies.

Acknowledgements

The authors applaud Robert Kolb and Donald Schwartz for organizing this conference on risk management and corporate governance and appreciate their support of our research. We would like to thank Tom Nohel and conference participants for their thoughtful remarks. The authors presented a preliminary version of this research at the University of Alabama – Birmingham and would also like to thank workshop participants for their comments and encouragement.

Notes

1 One of the first definitions of sustainability is found in a United Nations report written by the Brundtland Commission, led by the former Norwegian Prime Minister Gro Harlem Brundtland. The report defines a sustainable development

as one that "meets the needs of the present without compromising the ability of future generations to meet their own needs." In a corporate setting, sustainability issues concern matters that affect the future of the firm. Thus, effective risk management policies are a key component of a firm's sustainability initiative. In this regard, corporate sustainability is related to the concept of managing operational risk or what is known as enterprise risk in the insurance literature.

2 The same might be said of instituting a Six Sigma program, a set of practices intended to improve processes by eliminating defects. However, Goh et al. (2003) find that announcement of such programs do not produce positive abnormal stock returns. Moreover, they find that in the long run, their sample of six sigma firms do not outperform the S&P 500.

3 For a more complete discussion of the methodology, see Dow Jones Indexes et al. (2008).

4 Lehn, Patro, and Zhao (2006) pose a similar question regarding causality between corporate governance and firm valuation. Their analysis suggests that causation runs from valuation to governance. Lehn et al. posit that firms with low market to book ratios may be poorly run and are therefore likely takeover targets. They may also face limited growth opportunities. As such, these firms adopt takeover defenses that then affect corporate governance indices.

5 It is not known how many, if any, of the 2007 DJGSI stocks come from the group of 531 firms that SAM assessed based only on public information.

6 Cogan puts a positive spin on these results by noting that in a 2003 study, 20 companies that were reviewed largely ignored greenhouse gas emission issues. In contrast, the 2006 report finds corporate leaders in several key industries now face the climate change challenges head-on.

7 By examining returns in the year after a firm is named to the sustainability index, we remove any index effect that might occur when demand for the stock is bid up due to mutual funds adding the firm to their portfolios. There exist both sustainability mutual funds as well as socially responsible mutual funds that might invest in DJGSI companies when they are added to the index. Note, however, sustainable firms and socially responsible firms are not one and the same. Harrah's Entertainment, for example, has been a member of the DJGSI, but would not be selected by many socially responsible funds since it is in the gaming industry.

8 In drawing conclusions from these raw returns, it should be remembered that the results in Figure 11.1 and Table 11.5 compare firms of similar size. Moreover, sustainable firms and the DJ–Wilshire large cap stocks include firms in a variety of sectors, and thus, both represent diversified portfolios. The subsequent analysis on the Sharpe ratio and Tobin's Q additionally controls for specific industry effects and price to book issues.

9 A few conference participants thought that the inclusion of some of these firms in the index might be the result of "adverse selection." Since the primary way a firm is included in the DJGSI is to respond to the SAM survey, perhaps "bad" firms may be able to signal that they are "sustainable," when in fact they are not. It is not clear what, if any, consequences firms suffer if they massage survey

answers in the hope of being included in the index. Similarly, Tom Nohel, our discussant, expressed surprise that Nike has been named a sustainable firm, whereas Whole Foods has not. Nike has experienced labor problems in the past, while Whole Foods is often named a good place to work and environmentally friendly. Again, this may be a function of survey responses and the way the SAM survey is constructed and administered.

References

Brundtland, G.H. (ed.). 1978. *Our Common Future: The World Commission on Environment and Development*, Oxford: Oxford University Press.

Chung, K. and S. Pruitt. 1994. A simple approximation of Tobin's Q. *Financial Management*, 23(3): 70–4.

Cogan, Douglas. 2006. Corporate governance and climate change: making the connection. Ceres, Inc., March.

Corporate Knights Inc. and Innovest Strategic Value Advisors Inc. 2008. 'Global 100: Most sustainable corporations in the world. At http://www.global100.org.

Dow Jones Indexes, STOXX Ltd. and SAM Group. 2007. *Dow Jones Sustainability Indexes: Annual Review*, September 6.

Dow Jones Indexes, STOXX Ltd. and SAM Group. 2008. *Dow Jones Sustainability World Indexes Guide*, version 9.1, January.

Goh, T., P. Low, K. Tsui, and M. Xie. 2003. Impact of Six Sigma Implementation on Stock Price. *Total Quality Management & Business Excellence*, 14(7): 753–63.

Knoepfel, Ivo. 2001. Dow Jones Sustainability Group Index: A global benchmark for corporate sustainability. *Corporate Environmental Strategy*, 8(1): 6–15.

Lehn, K., S. Patro and M. Zhao. 2006. Governance indices and valuation: which causes which? Social Science Research Network paper, April.

Lo, Shih-Fang and Her-Jiun Sheu. 2007. Is corporate sustainability a value-increasing strategy for business? *Corporate Governance: An International Review*, 15(2): 345–58.

Margolis, Joshua, Hillary Elfenbein, and James Walsh. 2007. Does it pay to be good? A meta-analysis and redirection of research on the relationship between corporate social and finance performance, unpublished paper, July.

Statman, M. 2007. Socially responsible investments. Social Science Research Network paper, June.

12

Executive Risk Taking and Equity Compensation in the M&A Process

William J. Lekse and Mengxin Zhao

Abstract

This paper examines the link between equity compensation and executive risk taking in the merger process. We develop our hypotheses based on agency, prospect, and behavior agency theories. Based on a sample of 668 mergers during the period of 1993 to 2005, we find that acquiring firms' CEOs and executives have significantly higher equity compensation as a ratio of total compensation and their value of equity compensation enjoys a higher sensitivity to share price and return volatility compared to target firms prior to the initiation of the merger. When management is compensated with more stocks or options and the pay-for-performance sensitivity of their compensation is higher, they are more likely to acquire risky and high growth targets. This implies that stock and option grants induce risk-taking decisions for management, suggesting that equity compensation provides management with incentives to align with a firm's desired risk taking behavior.

In this study we investigate the role played by equity compensation in motivating an executive to engage in risky behavior. The context of our focus is the ex ante merger and acquisition (M&A) process. In the ex ante M&A process, executive compensation and in particular equity compensation is a primary motivator of the executives (CEOs and executives) to insure that their respective shareholders' concerns are being addressed. The shareholders of the acquirer and target have both complementary and distinctively different concerns throughout the M&A process. The M&A process also impose risk evaluations onto the executives of the firms as to their personal wealth from present options and future organizational contribution potential. This study investigates: How does equity compensation granted by the board of directors and shareholders play a role in executive risk taking during the merger process?

Literature on M&A focuses primarily on the changes in wealth of the shareholders of the acquiring and target firms (e.g., Datta et al., 2001; Lefanowicz et al., 2000; Harrison and Oler, 2005). These investigations have two relevant schools of thought: the managerial theory and the neo-classical theory of the firm. The managerial theory posits that mergers increase the power and influence of management due to the separation of ownership and control (Marris, 1964). The neoclassical theory views the merger as a means to redirect corporate assets to higher value uses (Jensen, 1986). The above literature develops two competing arguments to explain the rationale of CEOs or executives' incentive in a merger or acquisition. On one hand, when the interests of corporate managers and shareholders are well aligned, CEOs and executives undertake the acqui-sitions to increase shareholders' wealth. On the other hand, executives may acquire another firm to pursue their own interests in the form of greater power, prestige, and enhanced remuneration associated with managing a larger firm (e.g. Jensen, 1986; Roll, 1986; Morck et al., 1988). Overall, the merger process is far more complex (Shleifer and Vishny, 1988).

Existing research offers only a very limited investigation of the merger process, focusing in particular the stakeholders' roles, risks, and incentives to engage in a merger process. Jensen and Murphy (1990) advanced the importance of designing the mix of executive compensation to balance the incentives with efficient risk sharing. Gray and Cannella (1997) theorize that the function of the mix of compensation is to have executives bear risk. Risk associated with an organization's strategy is an important considera-tion in designing the executive compensation that aligns management inter-ests with those of shareholders' (Gray & Cannella, 1997). Among different components of the compensation contract, equity based compensation plays the most important role in providing incentives to the management (McEachern, 1975; Jensen & Meckling, 1976).

Our paper differs from the previous studies in that we focus on the incen-tives created by the board and shareholders through the awarding of equity compensation to the executives of both acquirers and targets in the merger process. A contribution of this research is whether equity compensation is the driver of risk-taking in the merger process.

The executives in both the acquirer and the target firms engage in the merger process to bring about change (Lubatkin, 1983; Hovers, 1971). The degree and friendliness of the change at the end of the merger process may well be defined by the actions undertaken during the merger process. While the merger process is being conducted, the executives of both firms face uncertainty as to their futures in the final outcome. The presence of this uncertainty is the potential origin of the risk assessment of the firms' executives.

Agency theory provides that executives faced with the uncertainties of the merger process will be risk averse and, as such, they will need incentives to overcome the "moral hazard" that is present in the merger process. Equity compensation thus serves to provide executives with risk-taking incentives. However, risk aversion, the fundamental consideration in agency theory, has been challenged by researchers (Wiseman & Gomez-Mejia, 1998; Chiles & McMackin, 1996). They propose an alternative model, the behavioral agency theory, which combines traditional agency theory with prospect theory. In the behavioral agency theory, the risk taking of executives is mediated by the context framing of the merger (Wiseman & Gomez-Mejia, 1998).

Our study examines the micro level of the merger process. At this level, executives engaging in the merger process may balance the value of their equity compensation to the risk present in the merger. Mergers provide us with comparisons of distinct categories of risk represented by whether a firm is a target or the acquirer, and/or whether the firms are operating in the same industry. From the micro level our study is able to address the following research questions: Does equity compensation provide different incentives for the target executives and the acquirer executives who engage in a merger process? If equity compensation, particularly stock options, provide executives with risk-taking incentives, are executives with more equity compensation likely to launch risk-increasing mergers? Is equity compensation likely to lead to the completion of the merger or become an obstacle to the merger completion?

Based on a sample of 668 mergers conducted over the period from 1993 to 2005, we find that acquiring firms' CEOs and executives have significantly larger equity compensation as a ratio of total compensation and that the value of their equity compensation enjoys a higher sensitivity to share price and stock return volatility compared to target firms prior to the initiation of the merger. The potential financial gains from target executives' equity compensation, however, do not seem to provide sufficient incentive for them to surrender control during the merger. In addition, we find that acquiring firms' CEOs or executives with more equity compensation or higher compensation sensitivity to share price or return volatility are likely to acquire more risky targets or targets with high growth options. In the case of the CEOs and executives in the acquiring firm, the higher stock price sensitivity of equity compensation is likely to cause the deal to breakdown – especially when the share price drops due to the merger.

Our paper makes contributions to the existing literature by providing evidence on how equity compensation can provide effective incentives to the CEOs or executives and what the impact of these incentives will be on firm's investment decision. In particular, we incorporate in our investigation not only the level of compensation incentives, but also the degree of compensation incentive (i.e. the sensitivity of the equity compensation to stock value and stock return volatility). This sensitivity is important in capturing the effect of compensation on the M&A decisions, thus establishing the link between incentive and wealth impact from the merger.

The structure of the paper is as following. The next section provides theoretical development, reviews the literature and develops the hypotheses. We then discuss the sample and data, before presenting the empirical methods results. Finally we offer some concluding remarks.

Theoretical Framework and Hypotheses Development

Agency theory

Agency theory focuses on the conflicts of interest between managers and stockholders (Jensen & Meckling, 1976; Fama, 1980; Fama & Jensen, 1983). These conflicts arise from the separation of ownership and control (Berle & Means, 1932). This separation of ownership and control brings about different attitudes toward risk taking between shareholders and executives (Coffee, 1988). Shareholders are considered to be risk-neutral since in addition to their investment in the firm they can hold their wealth in well-diversified portfolios and thereby diversify away firm-specific risk. By contrast, the executives' view of risk is from an undiversified portfolio since their human capital is very much bound up with the future of the firm. The undiversified position exposes executives to a high level of both systematic and firm-specific risk. This high level of risk creates a risk aversion in the executives, which may lead the executives to forego risky strategies by avoiding risky, but value-enhancing investment opportunities. Therefore, executive strategies have a high potential to be inconsistent with shareholder value maximization (Smith & Stulz, 1985; Guay, 1999).

This agency problem is usually captured as moral hazard or adverse selection issue. Work by Mirrlees (1974, 1976), Holmstrom (1979), Grossman and Hart (1983), and others examine how to account for the moral hazard problem when designing the compensation contract. In Holmstrom's "hidden action" model, the agent (CEO and executives) is required to perform a series of tasks in order to maximize the utility of the investors. These tasks are difficult to measure and the relationship between the executives and the board of directors is quite noisy (Eisenhardt, 1989; Holmstrom, 1979). The board and investors are not able to continuously monitor CEO's actions to insure that executives are motivated to conform to the shareholder's objectives and goals. Therefore, when the board of directors is designing executive compensation contracts, a prime consideration is to alleviate the potential of a moral hazard to influence risk taking decisions in the merger process. Stock ownership through the awarding of option grants are regarded as an efficient motivator within the executive's contract to discourage actions that would create a moral hazard problem (e.g. Jensen, 1986; Jensen & Murphy, 1990).

Stock option compensation shields the executives from the downside risk since this is essentially a call option on the firm's stock, and only linearly relates to the stock price whenever the stock price exceeds the exercise price of the option contract (Feltham & Wu, 2001). Moreover, the convexity of payoff implies that the value of the stock option increases with the volatility of company stock returns. Therefore, stock option compensation is able to counter managerial risk aversion and prompt risk-averse executives to engage in risky investment projects including risky acquisitions (Guay, 1999; Coles, Daniel & Naveen, 2006). Efficient contracts that grant stocks and options to the CEOs and executives are supposed to provide enough incentives for executives to take on more risk, thus reducing their risk aversion and the natural tendency to reject variance-increasing projects.

Many M&A fail to create shareholder value, and in these circumstances executives either lose their job or their firms are subsequently acquired by another firm (Porter, 1987; Ravenscraft & Scherer, 1987; Mitchell & Lehn, 1990; Lehn & Zhao, 2006). Overall, M&A are in general risky decisions made by the executives. Therefore, based on the common interpretation of agency theory we propose the following hypothesis:

H1: Executives who have more equity compensation and their equity compensation has larger sensitivity to stock price and volatility are more likely to engage in a merger or acquisition.

Furthermore, in the strategic management literature, diversification theory claims that executives who engage in related acquisitions have a greater potential than unrelated acquisitions for success. Research indicates that this is due to the higher potential for synergy creation in the final firm (Rumelt, 1974; Salter & Weinhold, 1979). Chatterjee's (1986) broad classes of synergy – operating, financial, and collusive (market power) – are present in related acquisitions whereas unrelated acquisitions may only find financial and/or administrative efficiencies. Therefore, a higher potential synergy creation will be in related acquisitions, which gives them a greater potential to succeed (Singh & Montgomery, 1987). Research to date has been inconclusive as to the benefit to the surviving firm of either merging with a related or an unrelated target (Lubatkin, 1987; Elgars & Clark, 1980; Hopkins, 1987; Barney, 1988; Zollo, 1998).

The concepts of relatedness and synergy (Teece, 1987) are major components of the strategy stream of focus on the understanding of merger from a governance perspective. Both the competence-based perspective of a firm (Rumelt et al., 1994) and the competitive strategy literature (Porter, 1987) are also major domains of the strategy investigation. Strategy researchers usually focus on the variation of individual firm outcomes with the measuring of firm-specific metrics. Measuring the extent of diversification between firms as developed by Rumelt (1982) is usually assessed on the basis of SIC codes (Weston et al., 2004). Firms that cross industry borders (indicated by differences in the core SIC codes) are more diversified and more prone to be expansionary compared to firms that merger inside their core SIC codes, which are deemed to be more contractionary (reducing stock in the industry) (Andrade & Stafford, 2004).

Engaging in a contractionary strategy will increase the potential for future internal conflict because a competitor is being integrated with an increased deployment of staff (Pickering, 1983). Thus nondiversified mergers will most probably result in eliminating unused capacity in the industry. Furthermore, the less a firm is related to the other in a merger the less the management is familiar with the industry-specific means to conduct business. These combined impacts may be more than the overcoming of risk incentive of management to diversify in order to balance out industry cyclical changes that may be created by a diversified merger. Engagement in a nondiversifying strategy is less risky than of a diversification strategy which will display a more expansionary motive.

Based on the above, it would appear that diversifying mergers are more risky than nondiversifying mergers. We thus propose the following hypotheses:

H2: More equity-based compensation leads to more diversifying mergers than nondiversifying mergers. We would expect to observe that acquiring firms that engage in diversifying mergers have more equity compensation than acquiring firms that engage in nondiversifying mergers. The same is true in respect of equity compensation sensitivity to stock price and stock return volatility.

Given that equity-based compensation motivates executives to engage in risky investment such as a merger or acquisition, we further propose the following:

H3: Executives with more executive equity compensation or a higher sensitivity of equity compensation to stock price and stock volatility tend to acquire targets that are more risky or targets that increase the risk of the combined firm.

Prospect theory and behavioral agency model

Most of the theoretical and empirical models to examine risk outside the agency literature are based on prospect theory (e.g., Sitkin & Pablo, 1992). Prospect theory, which was first presented by Kahneman and Tversky (1979), suggests that people undervalue outcomes that are merely probable in comparison with outcomes that are certain and also that people generally discard components that are shared by all prospects under consideration. Decisions subject to risk are indeed a choice between alternative actions, which are associated with particular probabilities (prospects) or gambles. According to this theory, the decision maker's preference for risk and their risk-taking behavior change according to the framing of problems (Kahneman & Tversky, 1979; Lant, 1992; Sitkin & Weingart, 1995).

Wiseman and Gomez-Mejia (1998) challenge the traditional agency-based views of risk with an assumption of the agent being both risk-averse and loss-averse. They develop a behavioral agency model which combines prospect theory of risk with agency theory. The model suggests that executive risk taking varies across and within different forms of monitoring and that agents may exhibit both risk-averse and risk-seeking behavior. Risk-averse preferences are associated with positively framed prospects and risk-seeking is associated with negatively framed prospects. Underlying these associations between risk-bearing and framed prospects is the "loss aversion." With loss aversion, agents are more sensitive to losing wealth than to increasing wealth. Wiseman and Gomez-Mejia (1998)'s model builds on the concept of instant endowment (Thaler & Johnson, 1990) and suggests that if previously awarded stock options (though not exercised) tend to become part of the perceived current wealth, i.e. instant endowed, then stock option scheme might serve to increase risk aversion rather than decrease risk aversion. Particularly, when the stock options are positively valued and executives anticipate the returns from exercising those options in the future, loss-averse executives would make the choices that preserve this anticipated value.

Following the above logic, when a merger or acquisition takes place, the stock options of target executives become immediately vested and most of the time stockholdings and stock options experience an increase in their value due to the premium paid by the acquirers. This "instant endowment", i.e. the perceived current wealth, influences target executives to be more likely to make a decision that would preserve this anticipated wealth increase. Therefore, executives that have more equity ownership, or that have previously been granted stock options, are more likely to accept a takeover offer – that is, to accept the takeover premium from the acquirers.

On the other hand, if management has higher levels of equity compensation, particularly more stock option grants, these stocks and options tend to become part of their perceived current wealth. According to the behavioral agency model of Wiseman and Gomez-Mejia (1998), the incentive compensation will not reduce managers' risk-averse behavior, but it will induce the level of loss aversion. Executives therefore will take actions that preserve this anticipated wealth, avoiding the risk. We propose the following hypothesis:

H4: Acquiring firm executives are more likely to have less equity compensation than target executives. In other words, acquiring firm executives are less likely to make an acquisition when they have more equity compensation. In the meantime, target executives are keen on the financial gains through merger agreements, thus, firms whose executives have more equity compensation are more likely to become targets.

Executives only have one job at their firm and their fortunes are directly tied to the firm's performance. Dismissal (Fredrickson, Hambrick, & Baumrin, 1988; Mizrichi, 1983), declining income (Fama, 1980), failure to find subsequent employment (Gilson, 1990; Cannella, Fraser, & Lee, 1995) and separation from their peers (Sutton & Callahan, 1987) are among the job-related risks faced by executives. If dismissed, executives have difficulty in finding comparable employment (Castanias & Helfat, 1991). The undiversified position that executives have with their firm in terms of their human capital investment and under-diversified equity portfolio increases their loss aversion in the presence of option incentive contracts. This loss aversion and motivation of preserving the perceived current wealth including the positive valued options might lead executives to choose to diversify into other lines of business in order to reduce their business risk. Therefore,

H5: We expect to observe that there is no difference in the equity compensation or sensitivity of compensation to stock price and return volatility between target and acquirer management for both diversifying mergers and nondiversifying mergers. However, among acquiring firms, more equity compensation is related to a greater likelihood that the management takes on nondiversifying mergers rather than diversifying mergers.

Finally, the behavioral agency model advanced by Wiseman and Gomez-Mejia also proposes that when the future fixed pay is insulated from the threat of loss, agents may be more willing to pursue contingent pay through riskier strategic choices. Given this, the executives of firms equipped with protection provisions such as golden parachutes, poison pills or other deterrents to takeovers are more likely to make a risky acquisition to pursue their contingent pay such as stock options. We therefore propose the following:

> **H6**: There is a positive association between the protection provisions and the likelihood of executives engaging in a risky merger or acquisition.

Sample and Data

The initial sample was identified from the Mergers and Acquisitions database of the Securities Data Company (SDC). The criteria for mergers to be selected from SDC are: (1) Announcement dates are between January 1, 1993 and December 31, 2005; (2) Both the acquiring firms and the target firms are US publicly traded companies; (3) Forms of the deals are mergers. We require that both the acquiring firms and the target firms have stock return data from Research in Securities Prices (CRSP) database, financial statement data from COMPUSTAT Research Tape, and executive compensation data from Standard & Poor's Execucomp database. Questionable deals are manually cross-checked with news articles from Factiva. We exclude deals with a transaction value of less than $10 million. We have 668 mergers – i.e. 1,336 firms – in our final sample.

Panel A of Table 12.1 reports sample descriptive statistics. On average, prior to merger announcements the acquiring firms have larger mean and median assets and sales. The mean (median) asset value is $31 billion ($7.05 billion). Acquiring firms have significantly higher mean and median return on assets (ROA) and return on sales (ROS) prior to the merger or acquisition. However, there is not significant difference in growth options as measured by market-to-book ratio of equity, research and development expense over

Table 12.1 Sample descriptive statistics

This table provides descriptive statistics of acquiring firms and target firms' characteristics. All the variables reported in this table are measured at the fiscal year end before the merger announcement. "ROA" is return on assets; "ROS" is measured as net income over sales; "Volatility" is the standard deviation sixty months before the previous year end of merger announcement; "MTBASS" is market-to-book ratio of assets; "MTBEQ" is market-to-book ratio of equity; "R&D" is the ratio of research and development expense over sales; "Capex" is capital expenditure as a ratio of sales; "CAR" is the cumulative abnormal return measured one year prior to twenty days before the merger announcement; "Adj-BHR1"(Adj-BHR3) is the market adjusted buy-and-hold return one (three) year prior to twenty days before the merger announcement. ***Significant at the 1% level; **Significant at the 5% level; *Significant at the 10% level.

Panel A Summary statistics of sample firms

AT	Acquirer			Target			Difference	
	Mean	Median	Std dev	Mean	Median	Std dev	Mean	Median
Assets	31298.29	7045.00	73960.79	11075.04	1595.39	40380.13	20223.25***	5449.61***
Sales	9780.73	4121.00	14816.41	3271.16	976.49	6306.69	6509.57***	3144.52***
ROA	4.91	4.25	7.02	1.53	2.90	15.15	3.38***	1.36***
ROS	0.08	0.08	0.12	0.00	0.06	0.70	0.08***	0.02***
Volatility	0.33	0.29	0.15	0.41	0.36	0.25	-0.09***	-0.07***
MTBEQ	4.36	2.83	6.16	4.32	2.15	21.50	0.04	0.69***
R&D	0.03	0.00	0.09	0.05	0.00	0.29	-0.02	0.00
Capex	0.10	0.06	0.12	0.10	0.06	0.15	0.00	0.00
CAR	-0.12	-0.11	0.52	-0.45	-0.15	5.50	0.33	0.04
Adj-BHR1	0.02	0.05	3.90	0.00	-0.07	0.63	0.02	0.12**
# of Observations	668			668			668	

Panel B Merger Characteristics

This table reports merger characteristics. Panel A reports mean, median and standard deviation for the total sample. Panel B reports similar statistics by year. "Relative Size" is the ratio of market value of target firm to acquiring firm, measured at the fiscal year end prior to merger announcement. "Transaction Value" is total value of consideration paid by the acquirer, excluding fees and expenses. "Stock Deals" is a dummy variable equal to 1 if the payment method involves equity, 0 otherwise. "Diversifying Deals" is defined as equal to 1 if the 2-digit SIC code of target is different from the 2-digit SIC code of the acquiring firm.

	Mean	Median	Std dev
Relative Size (T/A)	0.46	0.29	0.55
Transaction Value	5331.25	1521.80	12550.89
Stock Deals	0.67	1.00	0.47
Diversifying Deals	0.31	0.00	0.46
# of Observations	668		

sales, capital expenditure over sales and stock performance one year before the merger announcement. Overall acquiring firms seem to be larger firms and perform better than target firms before the merger announcement.

Panel B of Table 12.1 provides merger characteristics. On average, prior to merger or acquisition, the relative size of target firm to acquiring firm is about 0.46, with a median value of 0.29. Size of the firm is measured as the market value of the firm, i.e. the sum of market value of equity and book value of debt. The mean (median) transaction value is $5.3 billion ($1.5 billion). The findings show that 67 percent of the deals involve stock payment, and 31 percent of deals are diversifying mergers in which the acquiring firm and the target firm have different 2-digit SIC codes. These characteristics of the mergers in our sample are consistent with the studies by Schwert (2000) and Andrade et al. (2001), in which they document that mergers in the 1990s are mainly through stock swaps, friendly deals and within the same or related industries.

Empirical Analyses

Variable construction

Incentive compensation   Researchers have investigated the limitations of the board to design a perfect compensation package (Mirrlees, 1974, 1976; Holmstrom, 1979; Grossman & Hart, 1983). "Moral hazard" is one of the problems faced by the board in setting the level and components of executive compensation. Many of the tasks that CEOs perform are hidden and unobservable to the board (Holmstrom, 1979). One solution to resolve this problem is an efficient compensation contract.

Direct stockholdings and stock options are the two major components of the compensation that provide executives with incentives. We first calculate stock ownership by CEOs and executives as the percentage of the total share outstanding ("Stockown_CEO" ("Stockown_mgmt")). Then we construct the following variables to measure incentive compensation: the percentage of the CEOs' or executives' wealth that are options grants and stockholdings (EQU1_CEO" and "EQU1_mgmt"); the ratio of the sum of options granted, direct stockholdings, and restricted stocks to the total wealth of CEO or executives ("EQU2_CEO" and "EQU2_mgmt"). Total wealth is measured as the sum of the total current year compensation, the value of CEOs' (or top five executives') total stock holdings and stock options including current as well as previously granted. Stock options are valued based on Black-Scholes option pricing theory.

In addition to the ratios of equity-based compensation, we also examine how sensitive executives' compensation is to stock performance. "Optdelta-CEO" ("Optdelta_mgmt") is the sensitivity of CEO's (average of top five executives) total stock option value (including both newly granted and previously granted that exercisable or unexercisable) to stock price, i.e. the dollar change in total option holdings when there is one dollar change in stock price (Jensen & Murphy, 1990). We also follow Core and Guay (1999) by measuring the CEO's (top five executives') equity incentive from his or their total portfolio of stocks and options. This portfolio consists of all the options and restricted stocks granted to the CEO (and top five executives) as well as all the CEO's (top five executives) stockholdings until the end of the year before the merger announcement. The equity incentive is defined as the change in the dollar value of the CEO's or top five executives' stockholdings and options for a one percent change in the stock price. "Optincen_CEO" ("Optincen_mgmt") is the total dollar change in CEO's (average of top five executives) total option holdings (including both newly granted and previously granted options that are either exercisable or unexercisable) when there is a 1% change in the stock price. "Totincen_CEO" ("Totincen_mgmt") is the total dollar change in CEO's (average of top five executives) total equity based compensation (including both stock holdings and option holdings) when there is a 1% change in the stock price. We also compute vega (Vega_CEO and Vega_mgmt) which measures the change total option values with respect to one percent change in the stock return volatility. Stock return volatility is measured as the standard deviation of daily stock return one year prior to the merger announcement. This measure captures the sensitivity of option value and risk.

Risk of mergers or acquisitions   Mergers are in general a risky investment from the point of view of the acquiring firm. It induces a major change in operations, organization, and management. There is considerable uncertainty as to the success of integration with two merged firms. Risk-taking firms tend to acquire targets which are more risky and add more uncertainty to the combined firms. Risk potential is great during M&A and there is also considerable potential for conflicts of interest between managers and shareholders (Walsh, 1988, 1989; Hambrick & Cannella, 1993). Because executives are risk averse they will demand higher compensation for riskier situations such as a merger. Risk premium, i.e. the potential increase in the level of total compensation to compensate executives for taking risks, encourages their risk-taking behavior (Shavell, 1979). Gray and Cannella (1997) investigate whether compensation may encourage risk taking and long-term performance. They find that CEOs' risk-taking propensity varies with the total compensation, compensation risk, and compensation horizon.

We measure risk of the merger or acquisition by determining whether the merger is a diversifying merger or related merger and the riskiness of the target firms measured by the stock return volatility and growth potentials prior to the merger. The time period of the risk measure is sixty months prior the merger announcement. Results are similar when we use alternative time period to measure the risk.

Empirical results

We first carry out univariate analyses to compare CEO and top five executives' compensation for the following groups of firms: (1) target firms versus acquiring firms for the total sample; (2) acquiring firms engaging in diversifying mergers versus nondiversifying mergers; (3) acquisitions with most risky and least risky targets.

Table 12.2 reports mean and median comparison between acquiring firms and target firms' CEO and top five executives' incentive compensation. As a group the CEOs and executives of acquiring firms have consistently higher mean and median stockownership and percentage of equity-based compensation, including both stockholdings and options held. We also compare the sensitivity of CEO and executives' compensation to stock performance for acquiring firms and target firms. Acquiring firms' CEO and top five executives tend to have equity-based compensation that is more sensitive to the stock performance. This is shown by the significantly higher mean and median value of the acquiring firms' option delta and total equity portfolio's (both stock and options) delta. In addition, the sensitivity of both CEO and executives' equity compensation to stock return volatility is significantly higher in both mean and median for acquiring firms than for target firms. The univariate results are consistent with our first hypothesis (H1) which predicts that firms are more likely to initiate a merger acquisition when their management has more equity compensation and higher pay-for-performance sensitivity. It seems that incentive compensation is not a factor that motivates a firm to become a target. Therefore, behavioral models (Hypothesis 4: H4) do not help explain the difference in the equity compensation between acquiring and target firms. If stock and option grants provide risk-taking incentives for management, then the observed higher equity-based compensation and larger sensitivity might be due to the fact the acquiring firms' management are engaging in mergers

Table 12.2 CEO and executive compensation of acquiring firms and target firms

This table reports mean and median comparison between acquiring firms and target firms' CEO and top five executives' incentive compensation. "Stockown_CEO" ("Stockown_mgmt") is the percentage of stockownership by CEO and (average of top five executives). "EQU1_CEO" ("EQU1_mgmt") is the ratio of total equity-based compensation including value of the total options granted and total stockholdings to total wealth as defined in Panel A for CEO (average of top five executives). "EQU2_CEO" ("EQU2_mgmt") is the ratio of total equity-based compensation including the value of total options granted, total stockholdings, and the value of restricted stocks holdings to the total wealth of CEO (or executives). "Optdelta-CEO" ("Optdelta_mgmt") is the dollar change of CEO's (average of top five executives) total stock options given one dollar change in stock price. "Optincen_CEO" ("Optincen_mgmt") is the total dollar change in CEO's (average of top five executives) total option holdings when there is 1% change in the stock price. "Totincen_CEO" ("Totincen_mgmt") is the total dollar change in CEO's (average of top five executives) total equity based compensation (including both stock holdings and option holdings) when there is 1% change in the stock price (Core and Guay (1999)). "Optvega_CEO" ("Optvega_mgmt") is the change in the CEO's (top five executives) stock option values given 1% change in the stock return volatility. "GIM Index", created by Gomper, Ishii, and Metrick (2003), is the total score of anti-takeover provisions adopted by the firm. "BCF Index" created by Bebchuk, Cohen, and Ferrell (2004) is the total score of six anti-takeover provisions. "Golden Parachute" is a dummy variable equal to one if the firm has golden parachute provision, 0 otherwise. "Poison Pill" is a dummy variable equal to one if the firm has poison pill provision, 0 otherwise. T-statistics for mean difference and Z-statistics for median difference from Wilcoxon rank sum test are presented in the parentheses. ***Significant at the 1% level; **Significant at the 5% level; *Significant at the 10% level.

	Acquirers			Targets			Difference (A–T)	
	Mean	Median	Std dev	Mean	Median	Std dev	Mean	Median
Stockown_CEO	2.11	0.14	6.53	1.73	0.24	4.32	0.38 (1.25)	−0.10*** (−4.75)
Stockown_mgmt	0.98	0.03	12.15	0.48	0.09	1.14	0.49 (1.04)	−0.05*** (−7.36)
EQU1_CEO	0.85	0.90	0.18	0.81	0.89	0.22	0.04*** (3.42)	0.01*** (3.10)
EQU1_mgmt	0.76	0.80	0.19	0.70	0.76	0.23	0.06*** (5.09)	0.04*** (3.40)
EQU2_CEO	0.90	0.94	0.15	0.85	0.92	0.20	0.05*** (4.53)	0.02*** (5.53)

(Cont'd)

Table 12.2 (Cont'd)

	Acquirers			Targets			Difference (A–T)	
	Mean	Median	Std dev	Mean	Median	Std dev	Mean	Median
EQU2_mgmt	0.82	0.88	0.18	0.74	0.81	0.22	0.07*** (6.62)	0.07*** (7.43)
Optdelta_CEO	1.59	1.63	0.28	1.59	1.68	0.29	0.00 (0.04)	−0.05*** (−2.21)
Optdelta_mgmt	1.62	1.68	0.27	1.61	1.69	0.28	0.01 (0.58)	−0.01 (−0.51)
Optincen_CEO	877.86	317.00	1858.34	268.32	107.35	548.84	609.54*** (7.06)	209.65*** (12.00)
Optincen_mgmt	246.85	92.49	560.91	89.61	37.40	173.64	157.24*** (6.29)	55.08*** (10.45)
Totincen_CEO	2438.97	527.34	9900.88	560.68	177.78	1407.11	1878.29*** (4.20)	349.57*** (12.08)
Totincen_mgmt	547.47	141.01	2816.15	182.84	57.78	842.15	364.63*** (2.91)	83.23*** (10.74)
Optvega_CEO	413.77	268.75	517.40	223.02	160.10	259.33	190.70*** (7.21)	108.65*** (9.98)
Optvega_mgmt	513.40	318.48	667.63	265.70	172.10	318.09	247.70*** (8.07)	146.38*** (11.25)
GIM Index	9.52	10.00	2.80	9.46	10.00	2.65	0.06 (0.35)	0.00 (0.35)
BCF Index	1.96	2.00	1.35	2.32	2.00	1.25	−0.36*** (−4.34)	0.00*** (−4.16)
Golden Parachute	0.57	1.00	0.50	0.71	1.00	0.45	−0.14*** (−4.81)	0.00*** (−4.75)
Poison Pills	0.52	1.00	0.50	0.62	1.00	0.49	−0.10*** (−3.12)	0.00*** (−3.11)

because it is a risk-increasing investment. By contrast, the target's executives, whose potential to retain their position or find a similar position is very low, are not motivated by equity compensation to respond to the risks posed to them by the merger process.

In addition to incentive compensation, we also examine the differences in the ant-takeover provisions of acquiring firms and target firms. Anti-takeover provisions protect firms from being taken over. Some provisions, such as golden parachutes, also provide monetary protection for the management of target firms. Surprisingly, target firms are more likely to adopt anti-takeover provisions such as golden parachutes, poison pills and other anti-takeover provisions which are measured by the "GIM Index" (the total score of anti-takeover provisions adopted by the firm created by Gomper, Ishii, and Metrick (2003)) and "BCF Index" (which is the total score of six anti-takeover provisions created by Bebchuk, Cohen, and Ferrell (2004)). Firms with more anti-takeover provisions are expected to be less likely to become targets: however, this does not seem to be the pattern for the firms in our sample. Our univariate comparisons of anti-takeover provisions are not consistent with Hypothesis 6 (H6) which predicts that firms with more anti-takeover provisions are more likely to engage in riskier investment such as merger or acquisition.

The univariate analyses in Table 12.2 suggest that firms with more equity-based executive compensation tend to initiate a merger or acquisition, while firms that are acquired tend to have less compensation that is equity-based. To further examine the relation between incentive compensation and the outcome that a firm becomes either the acquirer or the target, we run a logit model in which the dependent variable is equal to one if the firm is an acquirer, zero if the firm is a target. Results of the logit estimates are reported in Table 12.3. Our main independent variables are incentive compensation including the percentage of equity-based compensation (both stockholdings and options holdings), sensitivity of executives' equity compensation to stock performance and sensitivity of equity compensation to stock return volatility. We run similar analyses using CEO's incentive compensation. The results are similar and, for the sake of brevity, we do not report the logit estimates with CEO compensation variables. Overall, logit estimates show that the probability of a firm becoming an acquirer is significantly and positively related to the percentage of equity-based compensation, the pay-performance sensitivity and the sensitivity of compensation value to stock volatility. The coefficients of the incentive compensation measures including the percentage of equity compensation, the sensitivities of equity compensation to the stock price and stock volatility (EQU1, EQU2, Optdelta_mgmt, Optincen_mgmt, and Optvega_mgmt) are all positive and significant at the 0.01 levels. Not only the total options granted, but also the value of restricted stocks and direct share holdings all play an important role in shaping the firms' decision to acquire another firm, but not the decision to be acquired. This is true after we control for other firm characteristics, firm performance and industry dummy variables. The robustness of our compensation coefficients after controlling for firm performance indicate that our results is not driven by the fact that firms with more incentive compensation perform better therefore are likely to take the control as acquirer. Logit regressions also show that target firms adopt more anti-takeover provisions such as golden parachutes and poison pills, which is inconsistent with Hypothesis 6 (H6).

The results in Table 12.3 are inconsistent with our fourth hypothesis (H4), i.e. that CEOs or executives are likely to gain financially through merger premium and this motivates them to sell their firms, thus becoming targets. Given that equity-based compensation leads a firm to become an acquirer in a merger transaction instead of a target, it is interesting to further explore among acquiring firms whether or not equity compensation provides management with incentives to take on acquisitions with different degree of risk.

If equity-based compensation motivates management to take on more risk, we would expect to observe that acquiring firms with more equity executive compensation are more likely to engage in risky mergers. We define risky mergers as the following: diversifying mergers are more risky than nondiversifying mergers; if prior to merger or acquisition, target firms have more stock return volatility or higher growth options, the merger or acquisition is more risky; if the stock return of target firms and acquiring firms are less correlated before the merger or acquisition, then the transaction is more risky.

Table 12.4 compares acquiring firms' CEO's and executives' incentive compensation for diversifying mergers and nondiversifying mergers. Diversifying mergers are those mergers in which acquiring firm's 2-digit SIC code is different from target firm's 2-digit SIC code. When we focus only on acquiring firms, management engaging in diversifying mergers on average have significantly larger stock holding and equity-based compensation, including both stock ownership and stock options. CEOs and executives from acquiring firms engaging in diversifying mergers have equity compensation whose value have a larger sensitivity to changes in the stock price and stock return volatility. This seems to suggest that stock ownership and option grants are positively related to the likelihood that a firm acquires an unrelated firm. This relation holds when we carry out the logit estimates on the effect of equity compensation, particularly option delta and vega on the likelihood of firms acquiring an unrelated target. There is more uncertainty involved in a merger if the two merged firms are less related.

Table 12.3 Logit estimates – Acquiring firms and target firms

This table reports logit estimates of executive compensation effect on the probability of firms turning to be acquiring firms and target firms. The dependent variable is a dummy variable equal to one if the firm is an acquiring firm, 0 if the firm is target. "MTBASS" is the market-to-book ratio of firm's assets. "VOLATILITY" of firm's assets. "VOLATILITY" of target firms is defined as the standard deviation of sixty month stock returns one month prior to the merger announcement. "ADJBHR1" is the market adjusted buy-and-hold return one year prior to one month before the merger announcement. "ROA" is return on assets. All other variables are defined similarly as Table 12.2. Also, all variables are measured at the fiscal year end prior to merger announcement. The coefficients are estimates of the marginal effect on the probability of departure of an increase in the independent variable. ΔProb measures the change in the probability of CEO turnover, given a one-standard deviation change from the mean value of the independent variable, i.e. the mean value minus one standard deviation. For dummy variables, the ΔProb is the change in the probability that the dummy variable equals zero to the probability that the dummy variable equals one T-statistics are shown in parentheses. Results are the same when we use CEO compensation instead of the average of top five executives' compensation.

	1	2	3	4	5	6	7	8
Log(Sales)	0.146	0.146	0.146	0.136	0.133	0.142	0.125	0.124
	(9.75)***	(9.82)***	(9.74)***	(11.10)***	(10.73)***	(10.79)***	(8.95)***	(9.28)***
MTBASS	0.036	0.034	0.037	0.012	0.013	0.01	0.009	0.002
	(2.14)***	(2.02)**	(2.17)***	(1.41)	(1.42)	(1.24)	(0.86)	(0.29)
VOLATILITY	-0.28	-0.273	-0.286	-0.256	-0.243	-0.328	-0.211	-0.127
	(2.05)**	(2.00)**	(2.09)**	(2.36)***	(2.27)***	(2.53)***	(1.75)*	(1.10)
ADJBHR1	0.173	0.181	0.181	0.138	0.137	0.138	0.145	0.118
	(4.02)***	(4.16)***	(4.16)***	(4.38)***	(4.37)***	(4.28)***	(4.35)***	(3.66)***
ROA	0.007	0.007	0.007	0.009	0.009	0.007	0.008	0.007
	(1.94)*	(1.97)**	(1.95)*	(3.38)***	(3.50)***	(2.77)***	(3.30)***	(2.73)***
BCF Index	-0.097							
	(2.44)***							

(Cont'd)

Table 12.3 (Cont'd)

	1	2	3	4	5	6	7	8
Golden Parachute		-0.097	-0.077					
		(2.45)***	(1.89)*					
Poison Pill			-0.083					
			(2.14)***					
EQU1_mgmt				0.225				
				(2.59)**				
EQU2_mgmt					0.207			
					(2.19)***			
Optdelta_mgmt						0.25		
						(3.33)***		
Optincen_mgmt							0.191	
							(2.09)**	
Optvega_mgmt								0.102***
								(4.70)
Constant	-4.253	-4.428	-4.268	-4.752	-4.683	-5.775	-3.941	-6.087
	(6.85)***	(7.44)***	(7.09)***	(9.32)***	(9.17)***	(8.49)***	(7.40)***	(9.79)***
Observations	935	935	35	1231	1231	1072	1072	
Pseudo R-Squared	17.71%	17.70%	18.05%	16.67%	16.55%	17.08%	16.71%	

* Significant at 10%; ** Significant at 5%; *** Significant at 1%

Table 12.4 Executive equity compensation – Diversifying and nondiversifying mergers

This table reports mean and median comparison of acquiring firm CEO and top five executives' incentive compensation between diversifying mergers and nondiversifying mergers. Variables are defined the same as Table 12.3. All variables are measured at the fiscal year end prior to merger announcement. T-statistics for mean difference and Z-statistics for median difference from Wilcoxon rank sum test are presented in the parentheses. ***Significant at the 1% level; **Significant at the 5% level; *Significant at the 10% level.

	Diversifying			Nondiversifying			Difference	
	Mean	Median	Std dev	Mean	Median	Std dev	Mean	Median
Stockown_CEO	2.71	0.00	8.25	1.64	0.00	5.68	1.08* (1.95)	0.00 (0.74)
Stockown_mgmt	0.65	0.00	2.40	0.36	0.00	1.36	0.29* (1.97)	0.00 (0.78)
EQU1_CEO	0.86	0.90	0.15	0.84	0.90	0.19	0.02 (1.51)	0.01 (0.59)
EQU1_mgmt	0.76	0.79	0.17	0.76	0.81	0.20	0.00 (0.19)	−0.01 (−0.78)
EQU2_CEO	0.92	0.95	0.12	0.89	0.94	0.17	0.03** (2.10)	0.02* (1.68)
EQU2_mgmt	0.82	0.88	0.16	0.81	0.87	0.19	0.01 (0.47)	0.00 (0.23)
Optdelta_CEO	1.61	1.65	0.25	1.58	1.62	0.29	0.03 (1.17)	0.03 (0.77)
Optdelta_mgmt	1.64	1.71	0.26	1.61	1.67	0.27	0.02 (0.97)	0.04 (0.69)
Optincen_CEO	1055.23	395.07	1725.33	793.42	270.38	1915.15	261.80 (1.46)	124.68*** (2.76)
Optincen_mgmt	279.96	116.09	478.92	231.44	84.14	595.23	48.52 (0.93)	31.95*** (2.31)
Totincen_CEO	2216.19	649.33	4386.97	2545.61	493.62	11656.59	−329.42 (−0.34)	155.71*** (2.59)
Totincen_mgmt	550.37	142.68	1189.05	546.12	137.41	3313.16	4.25 (0.02)	5.27 (1.57)
Optvega_CEO	503.93	334.18	545.97	347.15	242.47	500.06	156.78*** (2.53)	91.71*** (3.57)
Optvega_mgmt	556.05	382.28	574.84	493.76	283.49	706.11	62.29 (1.25)	98.79*** (2.50)
GIM Index	9.51	10.00	2.77	9.52	9.00	2.82	−0.01 (−0.04)	1.00 (0.11)
BCF Index	1.93	2.00	1.41	1.97	2.00	1.33	−0.04 (−0.31)	0.00 (0.32)
Golden Parachute	0.53	1.00	0.50	0.58	1.00	0.49	−0.06 (−1.18)	0.00 (1.17)
Poison Pills	0.43	0.00	0.50	0.56	1.00	0.50	−0.13*** (−2.63)	−1.00*** (−2.62)
# of Observations	207			461				

As equity-based compensation particularly the options with greater sensitivity to stock price or risk is designed to motivate management to take on more risk, diversifying merger is one of the risky investment that executives choose to take on more risk. This is consistent with Hypothesis 2 (H2) but inconsistent with Hypothesis 5 (H5).

Mergers are risky transactions on average. It is hard to compare whether or not diversifying mergers are riskier than nondiversifying mergers. From a management and organization point of view, when a firm acquires an unrelated firm, it poses a number of challenges to integration. The management might have no expertise in the unrelated business in which the target was operating. The less correlation between the two firms, the more complicated the combined firm will turn out to be. Diversifying mergers might add a lot of uncertainty to the acquiring firm – and, therefore, more risk.

Equity-based compensation induces management to take on risky investment such as a merger or acquisition. Targets which have more volatility prior to the merger are considered to be risky targets. All else being equal, we would expect to observe that acquiring firms with more equity-based compensation tend to acquire more risky targets. We therefore rank targets' prior to merger stock return volatility into terciles. For each tercile, we calculate the mean and median values of the acquiring firms' CEO and top five executives' incentive compensation. Table 12.5 reports the results for each tercile and the univariate comparison between top tercile and bottom tercile. We find mergers with the most risky targets are associated with acquiring firms with the highest percentage of equity-based compensation and largest pay performance sensitivity as well as the compensation sensitivity to stock risk. Alternatively, we also rank the sample based on target's growth options (market-to-book ratios, R&D over assets, and capital expenditure over sales), we obtain the same results. Acquiring firms with more executive equity compensation are associated with mergers of high-growth targets.

The above results hold in the multivariate analyses. Management compensated with higher levels of equity are likely to choose more risky targets or targets with more growth options. Table 12.6 reports the regression results. The dependent variable in panel A is standard deviation of stock returns 60 months prior to the merger and in panel B is market-to-book ratio prior to the merger. The coefficients are significant and positive for all the measures of incentive compensation. This implies that firms with more sensitive equity-based compensation are more likely to acquire firms with more volatility, i.e. relatively risky targets. These results hold when we control for firm size, prior to merger performance, and industry effect. Panel B of Table 12.6 shows the similar regression results except the dependent variable is the market-to-book ratio of the target firms. Again, there is significant and

Table 12.5 CEO and top executive compensation of acquiring firms and the risk of target firms

This table compares acquiring firms' CEO and top five executives' compensation for three terciles ranked by target firms' volatility. Volatility of target firms is defined as the standard deviation of sixty month stock returns one month prior to the merger announcement. Variables in this table are measured at the fiscal year end prior to merger announcement. All variables are defined similarly as Table 12.3. T-statistics for mean difference and Z-statistics for median difference from Wilcoxon rank sum test are presented in the parentheses. ***Significant at the 1% level; **Significant at the 5% level; *Significant at the 10% level.

Ranked by Targets' volatility / Acquiring firms' Incentive Compensation	Bottom Tercile Mean	Bottom Tercile Median	Middle Tercile Mean	Middle Tercile Median	Top Tercile Mean	Top Tercile Median	Difference Top tercile-Bottom tercile Mean	Difference Top tercile-Bottom tercile Median
Stockown_CEO	1.19	0.00	1.87	0.00	2.35	0.00	1.16** (1.98)	0.00*** (4.50)
Stockown_mgmt	0.36	0.00	0.38	0.00	0.48	0.00	0.12 (0.76)	0.00*** (4.33)
EQU1_CEO	0.82	0.87	0.83	0.89	0.89	0.96	0.07*** (4.27)	0.08*** (5.25)
EQU1_mgmt	0.74	0.79	0.74	0.78	0.79	0.84	0.05*** (2.78)	0.05*** (3.78)
EQU2_CEO	0.88	0.92	0.89	0.94	0.93	0.98	0.06*** (3.74)	0.05*** (5.77)
EQU2_mgmt	0.81	0.87	0.80	0.87	0.84	0.90	0.03* (1.87)	0.03*** (3.04)
Optdelta_CEO	1.49	1.47	1.56	1.57	1.73	1.81	0.24*** (8.28)	0.34*** (7.56)
Optdelta_mgmt	1.54	1.55	1.58	1.61	1.75	1.81	0.20*** (7.80)	0.26*** (7.23)
Optincen_CEO	729.01	281.91	581.00	256.11	1336.84	438.75	607.83*** (2.50)	156.84*** (2.58)
Optincen_mgmt	254.33	94.98	159.26	79.21	330.75	117.63	76.43 (1.03)	22.65 (0.84)
Totincen_CEO	2081.26	493.37	1231.81	463.02	4101.26	848.13	2020.01 (1.45)	354.76*** (2.70)
Totincen_mgmt	464.53	140.81	320.11	110.93	864.60	175.92	400.06 (1.05)	35.10 (0.73)
Optvega_CEO	262.56	184.70	409.49	251.61	564.21	384.46	301.64*** (4.05)	199.76*** (12.77)
Optvega_mgmt	385.78	227.52	487.94	321.92	668.95	426.67	283.17*** (3.57)	199.15*** (8.54)
# of Observations	211		212		213			

Note: Our results are the same or even stronger when we rank the sample by target's research and expenditure ratio, capital expenditure ratio, and market-to-book ratio.

Table 12.6 Acquiring firms' executive compensation and risky targets

Panel A This table reports OLS estimates of executive compensation effect on acquirer's choice of target firms. The dependent variable is volatility of target firms which is measured as the standard deviation of sixty month stock returns one month prior to the merger announcement (T_volatility). "ADJBHR1" is the market adjusted buy-and-hold return one year prior to one month before the merger announcement. "ROA" is return on assets. All other variables are defined similarly as Table 12.3. Also, all variables are measured at the fiscal year end prior to merger announcement. Results are the same when we use CEO compensation instead of the average of top five executives' compensation. Results are similar when the dependent variables are target firms' market-to-book ratios, capital expenditure over sales or R&D expenditure over sales. T-statistics are shown in parentheses.

	1	2	3	4	5	6
Log(Sales)	-0.024	-0.027	-0.012	-0.029	-0.025	-0.030
	(3.51)***	(3.99)***	(1.56)	(3.64)***	(3.17)***	(3.96)***
ROA	-0.001	-0.001	-0.001	-0.000	-0.000	-0.001
	(0.66)	(0.59)	(0.95)	(0.30)	(0.24)	(0.40)
adjbhr1	0.001	0.001	0.012	0.020	0.030	0.002
	(0.46)	(0.44)	(0.79)	(1.23)	(1.93)*	(0.64)
EQU1_mgmt	0.175					
	(3.33)***					
EQU2_mgmt		0.200				
		(3.45)***				
Optdelta_mgmt			0.263			
			(5.75)***			
Optincen_mgmt				0.000		
				(3.76)***		
Totincen_mgmt					0.000	
					(2.46)***	
Optvega_mgmt						0.020
						(1.94)*
Constant	0.482	0.480	0.109	0.648	0.627	0.664
	(7.09)***	(7.13)***	(1.00)	(9.77)***	(9.44)***	(10.42)***
Observations	605	605	508	508	508	

This table reports OLS estimates of ... target firms ... market-to-book ratios of target firms at year end (T_mtb) prior to the merger announcement. "ADJBHR1" is the market adjusted buy-and-hold return one year prior to one month before the merger announcement. "ROA" is return on assets. All other variables are defined similarly as Table 12.3. Also, all variables are measured at the fiscal year end prior to merger announcement. Results are the same when we use CEO compensation instead of the average of top five executives' compensation. Results are similar when the dependent variables are target firms' market-to-book ratios, capital expenditure over sales or R&D expenditure over sales. T-statistics are shown in parentheses.

	1	2	3	4	5	6
Log(Sales)	-0.080	-0.116	0.008	-0.085	-0.037	-0.202
	(1.33)	(1.90)*	(0.11)	(1.29)	(0.56)	(2.92)***
ROA	0.022	0.025	0.025	0.026	0.029	0.015
	(1.66)*	(1.88)*	(1.83)*	(1.94)*	(2.13)***	(1.05)
adjbhr1	0.045	0.046	1.255	1.206	1.322	0.041
	(2.01)**	(2.05)**	(9.21)***	(8.97)***	(9.88)***	(1.76)*
EQU1_mgmt	2.139					
	(4.51)***					
EQU2_mgmt		2.085				
		(3.98)***				
Optdelta_mgmt			0.981			
			(2.58)***			
Optincen_mgmt				0.001		
				(4.34)***		
Totincen_mgmt					0.000	
					(1.11)	
Optvega_mgmt						0.688
						(6.06)***
Constant	0.950	1.154	0.065	2.239	1.972	-0.297
	(1.55)	(1.89)*	(0.07)	(4.03)***	(3.51)***	(0.40)
Observations	622	622	521	521	521	540
Adjusted R-squared	0.04	0.04	0.17	0.19	0.17	0.08

positive association between equity-based compensation and the growth options of the target firms. Acquiring firms with more equity-based compensation tend to acquire high growth firms. When we use alternative measures for risk and growth options of target firm, we still obtain the same results, i.e. more equity-based compensation or more sensitivity of equity-based compensation to firm performance leads to more acquisition of risky and high-growth targets. However, we do not find the association between acquiring firms' protection provisions and the riskiness of the targets that they acquired. This is again inconsistent with Hypothesis 6 (H6). It seems that the insulation from job loss provided by these provisions does not provide further risk-taking incentives for the executives.

Overall, our results show that equity-based compensation does induce firms to take on more risky transactions such as mergers. Stock-based compensation does not provide executives with the incentive to sell the firm. The evidence is mainly consistent with the traditional agency model on risk taking, suggesting that management is more rational and more risk averse, rather than loss aversion. Therefore, boards of directors are able to design optimal compensation contract to induce the management to take on risk-increasing investment.

Conclusions

Since 1990 we have witnessed an explosion of growth in executive stock option grants. Since that time, the total number, total value, and individual deal value of mergers and acquisitions have all reached new highs. This paper examines the link between equity compensation and executive risk taking in the merger process during this period. Based on the traditional agency model, the prospect model, and the behavioral agency model, we develop six hypotheses that establish the relation between equity compensation and executives' decisions to engage in a particular merger process. With a sample of 668 mergers over the period from 1993 to 2005, we find interesting and relevant relationships between risk-taking decisions in the M&A process and equity compensation of the executives in both the target and acquiring firms.

Equity compensation is awarded in the form of direct stockownership, restricted stocks and stock options. Stock options reward the executive when the firm share price goes up but does not punish them when it goes down, thus this convex compensation encourage risk taking. This convexity may create excessive executive risk-taking and thus subjecting the firm and shareholders to risks that are not in their best interests.

In our study, we verify that equity compensation motivates the acquiring firm's executives not only to be an acquirer, but also to engage in riskier mergers. We find that acquiring firms' executives systematically have a greater percentage of equity compensation and the value of their equity compensation is more sensitive to stock price changes and stock return volatility than those of target firms' executives. In general, merger is a risky investment by the firm. Our results confirm that equity compensation, particularly stock options, provides risk-taking incentives to the executives, therefore, we observe this positive association between equity compensation and the likelihood of firms initiating a merger.

Furthermore, we document that acquiring firms are more likely to engage in diversifying mergers when their executives have more incentive compensation, i.e. the value of their equity compensation has greater sensitivity to the stock price and return volatility. The same is true when we focus on what type of firms these acquiring firms acquire. Acquiring firms tend to acquire more risky targets or targets with a wide range of growth options when their CEOs are more equipped with equity compensation incentives. Equity compensation does provide risk-taking incentives to the management. Our results are consistent with the traditional agency theory that proposes equity compensation as one of the mechanisms to align the interests of shareholders with that of the management.

Meanwhile, behavioral governance researchers would suggest that executives in the M&A process are motivated by loss aversion rather than risk aversion. These researchers would frame the merger process in terms of executives being motivated to consummate a merger by even inflating the potential gains and reducing the potential losses. In addition, executives would exhibit different equity compensation levels based on loss aversion and merger framing. Sitkin and Weingart (1995) would suggest that an executive of an acquiring firm will be more risk averse, because they now have something to lose. Wiseman and Gomez-Mejia (1998) linked corporate governance mechanisms and prospect theory features, especially framing problems. In our study the target's executives are not impacted by the level of equity compensation, the degree of compensation, or of the presence of anti-takeover compensation. Executives of target firms are not affected by the added wealth potential of having equity compensation available immediately and thus being motivated to engage in a merger. These results seem to counter the basic posit of the behavioral agency literature.

Similarly, prospect theory classifies executives as risk averse on the gains and risk loving on the losses – showing a greater sensitivity to losses (loss aversion). Prospect theory then assumes executives are risk averse in times of gains and risk seeking in times of losses. Under this approach, executives in the M&A process compare the prospects of gains and losses against a reference point. Executives are defined on the gains and losses, rather than on the final wealth value. Shapira's (1995, 2002) survival point of prospect theory suggests executives of targets would not take risks when faced with a merger that would have their firm stop operations. Therefore, prospect theory would expect target executives to require higher levels of equity compensation to engage in an M&A process; this is also counter to our results.

Board members have a fiduciary trust to ensure that the recommended investments of executives are the best to insure the betterment of the shareholders they represent. Equity compensation places board members in an interesting predicament: on the one hand they are awarding equity compensation to increase the risk taking of their executives; on the other, they are the primary oversight body to insure that executives do not invest in overly risky investments due to hubris or overconfidence in their capabilities and the resources of their firms. So board members are both motivating and evaluating on the betterment of the firm to enter into a risky investment. Our study provides answers to the questions about the effect of equity compensation and executive risk-taking decisions of both the target and the acquirer, highlighting the importance of the structure of executive compensation.

References

Andrade, G. and Stafford, E. 2004. Investigating the economic role of mergers. *Journal of Corporate Finance*, 10: 1–36.

Andrade, G., M. Mitchell, and E. Stafford, E. 2001. New evidence and perspectives on mergers. *Journal of Economic Perspectives*, 15: 103–20.

Barney, J.B. 1988. Returns to bidding firms in mergers and acquisitions: Reconsidering the relatedness hypothesis. *Strategic Management Journal*, 9: 71–8.

Bebchuk, L., A. Cohen, and A. Ferrell. 2004. What matters in corporate governance? Discussion paper, http://www.law.harvard.edu/programs/olin_center.

Berle, A. and G. Means. 1932. *The Modern Corporation and Private Property*. New York: Macmillan.

Bharath, S.T. and G. Wu. 2006. Long-run volatility and risk around mergers and acquisitions. Working paper.

Cannella, A.A. Jr., D.R. Fraser, and D.S. Lee. 1995. Firm failure and managerial labor markets: Evidence from Texas banking. *Journal of Financial Economics*, 38: 185–210.

Castanias, R.P. and C. Helfat. 1991. Managerial resources and rents. *Journal of Management*, 17: 155–71.

Chatterjee, S. 1986. Types of synergy and economic value: The impact of acquisitions on merging and rival firms. *Strategic Management Journal*, 7: 119–40.

Chiles, T.H. and J.F. McMackin. 1996. Integrating variable risk preferences, trust, and transaction cost economics. *Academy of Management Review*, 21(1): 73–99.

Coffee, J.C. 1988. Shareholders versus managers: The strain in the corporate web. In J.C. Coffee, L. Lowenstein and S. Rose-Ackerman (eds), *Knights, Riders and Targets: The Impact of the Hostile Takeover*. New York: Oxford University Press.

Coles, J.L., N.D. Daniel, and L. Naveen. 2006. Managerial incentives and risk taking, *Journal of Financial Economics*, 79(2): 431–68.

Core, John and Wayne Guay. 1999. The use of equity grants to manage optimal equity incentive levels. *Journal of Accounting and Economics*, 28: 151–84.

Datta, S., M. Iskandar-Datta, and K. Raman. 2001. Executive compensation and corporate acquisition decisions. *Journal of Finance*, 56: 2299–336.

Eisenhardt, K.M. 1989. Agency theory: An assessment and review. *Academy of Management Review*, 14: 57–74.

Elgars, P.T. and J.J. Clark. 1980. Merger types and stockholder returns: Additional evidence. *Financial Management*, 9: 66–72.

Fama, Eugene, 1980. Agency problems and the theory of the firm. *Journal of Political Economy* 88: 288–307.

Fama, E. and M. Jensen. 1983. Agency problems and residual claims. *Journal of Law and Economics*, 26: 327–349.

Feltham, G., and M. Wu. 2001. Incentive efficiency of stock versus options. *Review of Accounting Studies*, 6: 7–28.

Fredrickson, J.W., D.C. Hambrick, and S. Baumrin. 1988. A model of CEO dismissal. *Academy of Management Review*, 13(2): 255–70.

Gilson, S. 1990. Bankruptcy, boards, banks, and blockholders. *Journal of Financial Economics*, 27: 355–87.

Gompers, P.A., J.L. Ishii, and A. Metrick. 2003. Corporate governance and equity prices. *The Quarterly Journal of Economics*, 118(1): 107–55.

Gray, S.R. and A.A. Cannella. 1997. The role of risk in executive compensation. *Journal of Management*, 23: 517–40.

Grossman, S. and O. Hart. 1983. Takeover bids, the free-rider problem, and the theory of the corporation. *Bell Journal Economics*, 11: 42–64.

Guay, W.R. 1999. The sensitivity of CEO wealth to equity risk: An analysis of the magnitude and determinants. *Journal of Financial Economics*, 53(1): 43–71.

Hall, B.J. and K.J. Murohy. 2002. Stock options for undiversified executives. *Journal of Accounting and Economics*, 33: 3–42.

Hambrick, D. and A. Cannella. 1993. Relative standing: A framework for understanding departures of acquired executives. *Academy of Management Journal*, 36(4), 733–62.

Harrison, Jeffrey S. and D. Oler. 2005. Financial leverage and acquisition performance. Working paper.

Haspeslagh, P.C. and D.B. Jemison. 1991. *Managing Acquisitions: Creating Value Through Corporate Renewal*. New York: Free Press.

Hitt, M.A. and B.B. Tyler. 1991. Strategic decision models: Integrating different perspectives. *Strategic Management Journal*, 12: 327–51.

Holmstrom, B. 1979. Moral hazard and observability. *Bell Journal of Economics*, 10: 74–91.

Hopkins, D.H. 1987. Acquisition strategy and the market position of acquiring firms. *Strategic Management Journal*, 8: 535–48.

Hovers, J. 1971. *Expansion through Acquisition.* London: Business Books Ltd.

Jensen, M.C. 1986. The agency costs of free cash flow: Corporate finance and takeovers. *American Economic Review*, 76(2): 323–9.

Jensen, M. and W.H. Meckling. 1976. Theory of the firm: Managerial behavior, agency costs, and ownership structure. *Journal of Financial Economics*, 3: 305–50.

Jensen, M. and K. Murphy. 1990. Performance pay and top-management incentives. *Journal of Political Economy*, 98: 225–64.

Jensen, M.C. and R.S. Ruback. 1983. The market for corporate control. *Journal of Financial Economics*, 11: 5–50.

Kahneman, D. and A. Tversky. 1979. Prospect theory: An analysis of decision under risk. *Econometrica*, 47, 263–91.

Lant, T. K. 1992. Aspiration level adaptation: an empirical exploration. *Management Science*, 38: 623–44.

Lefanowicz, Craig E., John R. Robinson, and Reed Smith, 2000. Golden parachutes and managerial incentives in corporate acquisitions: Evidence from the 1980s and 1990s. *Journal of Corporate Finance*, 6: 215–39.

Lehn, K. and M. Zhao. 2006. CEO turnover after acquisitions: Are bad bidders fired? *Journal of Finance*, 61(4): 1759–811.

Lubatkin, M. 1983. Mergers and the performance of the acquiring firm. *Academy of Management Review*, 8: 218–26.

Lubatkin, M. 1987. Merger strategies and stockholder value. *Strategic Management Journal*, 8: 39–53.

Marris, R. 1964. *The Economic Theory of 'Managerial' Capitalism.* London: Macmillan.

McEachern, W.A. 1975. *Managerial Control and Performance.* Lexington, MA: D.C. Heath.

Meulbroeck, L. 2000. The efficiency of equity-linked compensation: Understanding the full cost of awarding executive stock option, Working Paper, Harvard Business School No. 00-056.

Mirrlees, J.A.1974. Notes on welfare economics, information, and uncertainty. In M. Balch, D. McFadden, and S. Wu (eds), *Essays on Economic Behavior Under Uncertainty*. Amsterdam: North Holland.

Mirrlees, J.A. 1976. The optimal structure of incentives and authority within an organization. *The Bell Journal of Economics*, 7: 105–31.

Mitchell, M. and K. Lehn. 1990. Do bad bidders become good targets? *Journal of Political Economy*, 98: 372–98.

Mizrichi, M.S. 1983. Who controls whom? An examination of the relation between management and boards of directors in large American corporations. *Academy of Management Review*, 54(4): 49–61.

Morck, R., A. Shleifer, and R. Vishny. 1988. Management ownership and market valuation: An empirical analysis. *Journal of Financial Economics*, 20: 293–315.

Mueller, Dennis C. 1977. The effects of conglomerate mergers: A survey of the empirical evidence, *Journal of Banking and Finance*, 1 315–47. Reprinted in Cheng-few Lee (ed.), *Financial Analysis and Planning: Theory and Application, A Book of Readings*, Reading, MA: Addison-Wesley, 1983, pp. 450–82. Reprinted in G. Marchildon, ed., *Merger and Acquisitions*, London: Edward Elgar, 1991.

Pablo, A.L., S.B. Sitkin, and D.B. Jemison. 1996. Acquisition decision-making processes: The central role of risk. *Journal of Management*, 22: 723–46.

Peltier, S. 2004. Mergers and acquisitions in the media industries: Were failures really unforeseeable? *Journal of Media Economics*, 17: 261–76.

Pickering, J.E. 1983. The causes and consequences of abandoned mergers. *Journal of Industrial Economics*, 31: 267–87.

Porter, M.E. 1987. From competitive advantage to corporate strategy. *Harvard Business Review*, 65: 43–59.

Ravenscraft, D.J. and F.M. Scherer. 1987. *Mergers, Sell-offs, and Economic Efficiency*. Washington, DC: The Brookings Institute.

Roll, R. 1986. The hubris hypothesis of corporate takeovers. *Journal of Business*, 59(2): 197–216.

Rumelt, R.P. 1974. *Strategy, Structure, and Economic Performance*. Boston, MA: Harvard Business School Press.

Rumelt, R.P. 1982. Diversification strategy and profitability. *Strategic Management Journal*, 3: 359–69.

Rumelt, R.P., D.E. Schendel, and D.J. Teece (eds). 1994. *Fundamental Issues in Strategy*. Boston, MA: Harvard Business School Press.

Salter, M.S. and W.S. Weinhold. 1979. *Diversification Through Acquisition*. New York: Free Press.

Schwert, G.W. 2000. Hostility in takeovers: In the eyes of the beholder? *Journal of Finance*, 55: 2599–40.

Shapira, Zur. 1995. *Risk Taking: A Managerial Perspective*. New York: Russel Sage Foundation.

Shapira, Zur. 2002. Aspiration levels and risk taking by government bond traders. Working paper, Stern School of Business, New York University.

Shavell, S. 1979. Risk sharing and incentives in the principal and agent relationship. *Bell Journal of Economics*, 10: 55–73.

Shleifer, A. and R. Vishny. 1988. Management entrenchment: The case of manager-specific investments. *Journal of Financial Economics*, 25(2): 123–40.

Singh, H. and C.A. Montgomery. 1987. Corporate acquisition strategies and economic performance. *Strategic Management Journal*, 8: 377–87.

Sitkin, S.B. and A.L. Pablo. 1992. "Reconceptualizing the determinants of risk behavior. *Academy of Management Review*, 17(1): 9–38.

Sitkin, S.B. and L.R. Weingart. 1995. Determinants of risky decision-making behavior: A test of the mediating role of risk perceptions and propensity. *Academy of Management Journal*, 38(6): 1573–92.

Smith, C.W. and R.M. Stulz. 1985. The determinants of firms' hedging policies. *Journal of Financial and Quantitative Analysis*, 20: 391–405.

Sutton, R.I. and A.L. Callahan. 1987. The stigma of bankruptcy: Spoiled organizational image and its management. *Academy of Management Journal*, 30: 405–36.

Teece, D.J.1987. Profiting from technological innovation. In D.J. Teece. (ed.), *Strategies for Industrial Innovation and Renewal*. Cambridge: Harper and Row.

Thaler, R.H. and E.J. Johnson. 1990. Gambling with the house money and trying to breakeven: The effects of prior outcomes on risky choice. *Management Science*, 36(6): 643–60.

Walsh, J.P. 1988. Top management turnover following mergers and acquisitions. *Strategic Management Journal*, 9(2): 173–83.

Walsh, J.P. 1989. Doing a deal: Merger and acquisition negotiations and their impact upon target company top management turnover. *Strategic Management Journal*, 10(4): 307–22.

Weston, J.F., M.L. Mitchell, and J.H. Mulherin. 2004. *Takeovers, Restructuring, and Corporate Governance*, 4th edn. Upper Saddle River, NJ: Prentice Hall.

Wiseman, R.M. and L.R. Gomez-Mejia. 1998. A behavioral agency model of managerial risk taking. *Academy of Management Journal*, 23(1): 133–53.

Wong, P. and N. O'Sullivan. 2001. The determinants and consequences of abandoned takeovers. *Journal of Economic Surveys*, 15: 145–86.

Zollo, M. 1998. *Knowledge Codification, Process Reutilization, and the Creation of Organizational Capabilities: Post-acquisition Management in the US Banking Industry*, Dissertation, UMI.

13

Discussion

Tom Nohel

This session included papers that consider three types of risk: financial risk, fraud risk, and sustainability risk. Not only does each of the three contributions deal with differing types of risk, but they also consider their respective research questions from different points of view. The contribution by Fletcher et al. (Chapter 10) is intended to be used more as a roadmap for firms to potentially reduce compliance costs, while Lekse and Zhao (Chapter 12) provide a micro analysis of characteristics that drive the behavior of the management of acquirer and target firms in the event of a merger or acquisition. Finally, the contribution by Swidler and Crutchley combines a macro and micro analysis of the performance of firms associated with the Global Dow Jones Sustainability Index. Each paper relates directly to the main topic of the conference: the role of boards as both managers and sources of risk.

In this discussion, I give a brief overview of each of the papers and then provide a critique of each paper. These critiques are a combination of raising concerns, suggestions for improvement, and suggestions for future research.

Entity-Level Controls and the Monitoring Role of Boards

This paper begins with the authors' assessment of the increased cost of regulatory compliance imposed by the Sarbanes–Oxley Act of 2002 (hereafter, SARBOX). The idea behind the paper is to provide a framework for firms to reduce their overall compliance costs by instituting a system of entity-wide as well as more focused controls. There is no attempt in the paper to empirically justify the framework of analysis. Instead, the authors appeal to the management and ethics literature to provide the impetus for the dominant themes in their approach. The authors conclude that by inculcating an ethical culture throughout the organization, firms will more easily implement appropriate controls and ultimately reduce (minimize?) compliance costs. They stress that their framework is adaptive and can thus change and presumably improve as the regulatory environment evolves.

The paper could be improved by tying its assertions and conclusions more closely to the existing evidence. For example, the paper states that audit fees increased by 150 percent between 2002 and 2004 and they cite this as evidence of the regulatory burden imposed by SARBOX. I argue that there may be alternative explanations. Perhaps auditors have raised their auditing fees because of a perceived increase in audit firm risk in the wake of the demise of Arthur Andersen due to their complicity in the Enron case. Moreover, when discussing the role that SARBOX has played in deterring foreign investment in American capital markets, the authors simply state that "some observers contend that foreign investment in US capital markets has actually decreased as a result of SARBOX." However, they could have substantiated their claim by referring to existing literature (see Li, 2007). The paper contains numerous assertions that require fuller substantiation and should not be merely presented as fully established. For example, "Effective governance is predicated on a strong firm culture (the cornerstone of the control environment) that aligns well with business needs and allows for the development of governance and risk management proficiency." And "... moreover, emphasizing an ethical corporate culture validates director and officer integrity, indeed corporate integrity. It is the right thing to do." The authors do not explain what they mean by either a strong firm culture or an ethical corporate culture.

As another example, the authors state: "Ensuring an effective control environment is therefore predicated on an ethical firm culture." The paper very much stresses the importance of the "tone at the top" without offering any justification for making such an assertion. Apparently, with the right person in the corner office, everything else falls into place. As I see it, a lack of hypocrisy in an organization where no individual is "above the law" *might* be a necessary – but is certainly not a sufficient – condition for improving compliance. Additionally, the paper almost seems to use the terms "compliance" and "ethics" synonymously. To me, compliance is simply about following the rules, and is less concerned with ethics. In short, there is no evidence presented in the paper to convince the reader that the suggested approach will lower compliance costs. Ultimately, each case is likely to be too specialized to pigeon-hole into the prescribed approach.

The paper would be improved by citing the existing business ethics literature relative to the positions they assert.

The following ideas might help to substantiate the approach advocated in the paper. The authors suggest the possibility of a comparative study wherein one assesses the role of SARBOX in affecting compliance costs in different industries, especially contrasting industries already facing a heavy burden against those where the imposed burden is rather novel. I would encourage the authors to delve more deeply into that topic, especially focusing on the financial industry as one that already faced a substantial regulatory burden that was likely less affected by the changes wrought by SARBOX. Moreover, the authors state that their framework partly (largely?) derives from guidelines put forth in the financial industry which buttresses this idea, and they present tables that lay out a set of entity controls. A number of these are easily measured. One could presumably compare and contrast the compliance costs at firms that had these controls largely in place pre-SARBOX with those that did not. Finally, the paper also discusses controls that monitor other controls. This strikes me as rather important and is reminiscent of the "who's monitoring the monitor" problem discussed in Diamond (1984, 1991). Again, the examination of how such problems are handled in the financial industry – where conflicts of interest are potentially widespread – seems like an area that could prove fruitful for future research.

Do Corporate Boards Care About Sustainability? Should They Care?

This paper examines the issue of corporate sustainability and considers the question of whether boards care about sustainability – and whether they should care. The primary technique applied to answer these questions is to compare the performance of firms deemed to pay attention to environmental, social, and governance risk (so-called "sustainable" firms) with similar firms that don't appear to pay as much attention to such issues. The authors consider stock returns, Sharpe ratios, and Tobin's Q ratios as measures of performance. They find some evidence of outperformance by "sustainable" firms, but that outperformance appears to diminish over time. The authors conclude that this sustainability effect diminishes because an increasing number of firms believe it is prudent to institute sustainable practices and that there is little difference between firms identified as "sustainable" and those that are not by the end of the sample period.

In my view, the last statement gets to the heart of the potential weakness of this paper. The authors leave ambiguous the criteria for identifying a firm as being "sustainable." The authors allude to this concern in footnote 12, and that concern remains: How is it possible that a firm such as Nike, which has frequently been accused of employing child labor and running "sweatshops" in Asia, is a member of the sustainability index for all eight years, whereas a firm such as Whole Foods, with a reputation for an exemplary work environment for the promotion of organic and other environmentally friendly products, has never been included? Presumably there is a way to determine how the index was formulated and thereby better understand who these "sustainable" firms are. Given this concern, it is just not clear what exactly the findings mean.

Next, I consider the testing methodology. I understand why the authors regard the Wilshire Large Cap Stock Index to be an appropriate benchmark, but problems with the initial set of tests remain. The authors focus on size as the only relevant risk control. In addition, the Wilshire is a value-weighted index, while the authors' sustainability portfolio is equally-weighted. A much better approach would be to find a control firm for each sustainable firm, likely chosen on the basis of industry, performance, investment opportunities and leverage, as well as size. An approach more or less akin to this is in fact adopted later in the paper, though I think the controls may be better chosen.

I conclude by recommending some suggestions to further the development of the authors' line of research. First, the paper mentions "Socially Responsible Investing." I think a greater effort should be made to relate this paper to the literature in that area. Though I realize that firms that are "sustainable" are not necessarily "socially responsible" (e.g., Nike and Whole Foods may be examples of firms that are in one category and not the other), clearly there must be considerable overlap. Another area that is likely worthy of exploration is the incidence of shareholder proposals in relevant areas (governance-related, environmental, etc.). I believe an exploration of this topic will show that shareholder attention to these concerns has increased over the sample period (in terms of the number of proposals submitted as well as in terms of support for these proposals, especially those related to governance and governance risk). This would lend support to the authors' conjecture that firms in general are paying more attention to issues of sustainability.

Executive Risk Taking and Equity Compensation in the Mergers and Acquisition (M&A) Process

This paper examines the link between executive compensation, specifically equity compensation, and risk taking. The authors develop and test hypotheses by appealing to agency-based theories of the firm as well as ideas from behavioral finance. The focus is on characteristics that incentivize executives to be either acquirers or targets, with an emphasis on risk taking. The main premise is that executives are inherently undiversified and need to be given the appropriate incentives to take risks, even prudent ones. Moreover, the authors focus on M&A – a decision in which executives must confront risk-taking directly. Among other characteristics, the authors conjecture that, other things being equal, managers who receive a higher proportion of their compensation in the form of equity-based pay will be more likely to accept the risk of a major acquisition, and that they will be more likely to undertake a risk-increasing transaction if their compensation is more sensitive to increases in volatility (a higher vega in option terminology). These hypotheses find some support, and the authors conclude that equity-based pay induces greater risk taking.

I am quite sympathetic to the issues raised in this paper and feel that the authors try to tackle an interesting, important, and inherently difficult set of questions. However, I have a fundamental disagreement with the approach taken in this paper because the authors do not adequately distinguish the various forms of equity-based pay. Though this may be appropriate in some settings, when the focus on the incentive to take on risk this is most inappropriate. While stock options can reasonably be thought of as a means to induce prudent risk taking for an inherently undiversified executive, shares will only serve to make the executive even less willing to take on risk. In order to be effective, executive compensation need necessarily leave the CEO bearing some idiosyncratic risk. However, this will make the executive excessively conservative and can only be counteracted by using convex pay to overcome the concavity of the manager's utility function. (For more on these arguments see Nohel and Todd (2005) among others.) Moreover, the focus of the investigation should be on managerial *wealth* rather than compensation.

The paper could also profit from strengthening the distinction between diversifying and nondiversifying mergers. While diversifying mergers may be considered to be risky from the point of view of achieving completion, these kinds of mergers tend to reduce, rather than increase, financial risk. A diversifying merger should help to reduce a manager's exposure to idiosyncratic risk through the effects of diversification, as modern portfolio theory teaches. In fact, there is a concern that a manager will seek a diversifying merger to reduce risk, even knowing that such mergers often make little economic sense.

Another concern relates to the methodology employed in the paper. While I think the idea of pairing acquirers and targets in a logistic regression might make sense in nondiversifying mergers (i.e., who are the aggressors and who are the targets when there is consolidation within an industry), I think such a method for analyzing diversifying mergers has some serious weaknesses. In my view, a better approach would be to pair each acquirer with a "comparable" firm (chosen on the basis of industry and size), and to pair each target with a similarly chosen "comparable" firm. Two logistic regressions could then be run: one for acquirers and one for targets. This method allows a better assessment of why a particular firm chose to pursue an acquisition or chose to capitulate to an acquisition. Comparing bidders directly against targets seems like an effort to compare incommensurables. Finally, I recommend that the authors examine and cite some of the behavioral finance literature on M&A (of which there is a rapidly growing body). One paper that is clearly relevant is the paper in *Management Science* by Billett and Qian (2008).

The following suggestions may be helpful as the authors develop this line of research. With regard to the literature on compensation and incentives, rather than focusing on Jensen and Murphy (1990), which does not concentrate on risk taking, it is better to concentrate on Guay (1999), Nohel and Todd (2005), and others cited therein. Also, I recommend a focus on executive wealth rather than compensation, even though this is difficult. Further, I recommend focusing on option pay in particular, rather than total executive compensation. Within the analysis of the executive's option, I also recommend focusing on the vega, rather than the delta, of those options.

References

Billett, M. and Y. Qian. 2008. Are overconfident CEOs born or made? Evidence of self-attribution bias from frequent acquirers. *Management Science*, 54(6): 1037–51.

Diamond, D. 1984. Financial intermediation and delegated monitoring. *Review of Economic Studies*, 52: 393–414.

Diamond, D. 1991. Monitoring and reputation: the choice between bank loans and directly placed debt. *Journal of Political Economy*, 99: 689–721.

Guay, W. 1999. The sensitivity of CEO wealth to equity risk: an analysis of the magnitude and determinants. *Journal of Financial Economics*, 53: 43–71.

Jensen, M. and K. Murphy. 1990. Performance pay and top management incentives. *Journal of Political Economy*, 98: 225–64.

Li, X. 2007 The Sarbanes–Oxley Act and cross-listed foreign private issuers. University of Miami Working Paper.

Nohel, T. and S. Todd. 2005. Compensation for managers with career concerns: the role of stock options in optimal contracts. *Journal of Corporate Finance*, 11: 229–51.

Part V

Corporate Boards, Risk Management, and the Ethical Firm

All of the papers in this section focus on questions of values that arise in the interface between risk management and corporate governance. Duane Windsor tackles the overarching ethical issues in his contribution, "The Ethics of Risk Management by a Board of Directors." Windsor begins by tracing the distinction between "corporate social responsibility" and risk management, which he finds to be partially overlapping concepts. He believes that competent risk management is not consistent with a purely fiduciary response to risk management, but that the situation requires a more comprehensive and robust approach. According to Windsor, "The essence of the problem is striving to protect shareowners' long-term interests, stakeholders' immediate rights, and nature's value to humanity both now and in the future."

Following this, Barry M. Mitnick challenges the common presumptions regarding the role of corporate boards in his paper, "Assurance and Reassurance: The Role of the Board." Drawing on examples from the early history of corporations, Mitnick maintains that a key role of corporate boards is to provide assurance and reassurance to investors. Board members play that assuring and reassuring role by committing their personal capital and associating themselves with the firm. Mitnick boldly states of his view: "In this perspective, *the key function of a board is to provide assurance*." And he goes on to make an explicit contrast of this vision of the board's function with one that is oriented toward risk management.

In their paper, "Risk Disclosure and Transparency: Toward Corporate Collective and Collaborative Informed Consent," Denise Kleinrichert and Anita Silvers draw on the model of informed consent in health care to draw implications for corporate transparency and corporate risk management. For Kleinrichert and Silvers, boards have responsibilities to all stakeholders of the firm, yet the decisions that they must make inevitably impose risk are various stakeholder groups. This is analogous to the imposition of risk on patients by medical professionals, and Kleinrichert and Silvers recommend "… that corporate directors aim to give their stakeholders sound understanding of the risks as well as the benefits of prospective corporate policies, strategies or other important actions." In other words, the authors argue for a collaborative approach to risk bearing and risk sharing among the firm and its stakeholders. They illustrate the impact of their approach by reference to particular firms that have been in the public eye.

John R. Boatright presents an analysis of these three papers, and also offers some criticisms and suggestions for extensions.

14

The Ethics of Risk Management
by a Board of Directors

Duane Windsor

This paper examines the ethics of risk management by a board of directors of a publicly traded corporation. This setting affords focused analysis (relative to addressing all kinds of organizations or all companies with boards of directors) and highlights the principal–agent fiduciary problem in relationship to risk and stakeholder management. The effort here is to move toward an ethics of risk management by the board of directors in this setting. This first cut effort addresses board risk management from an ethics perspective that is explicitly normative and prescriptive.

The topic is as yet poorly studied, because enterprise risk management (ERM) is a still emerging concern that has been largely financial in orientation. Hence, this paper is simply a first cut. The proposed contributions of an ethics perspective on board risk management are as follows. One, risk includes a set of potentially real future harms to people and nature. Harm suggests the desirability of an ethics perspective prior to making decisions increasing such risks. Two, once business embraces ERM, ethically such practice should not be restricted to narrowly financial risk management on behalf of investors without respect to broader risk considerations. Three, while it may be that instrumentally investor concern for financial risk might lead more or less naturally toward minimization of risks to other stakeholders, that outcome is hardly guaranteed. The board of directors should therefore face up to ERM broadly defined in scope. Risk is better addressed ex ante.

Risk management overlaps with, but is distinct from, corporate social responsibility (CSR) or stakeholder management as typically understood. CSR suggests legal compliance, business ethics, sustainable development, and corporate citizenship. Stakeholder management suggests collaboration with key stakeholders for mutual advantage. Risk management involves minimizing potential harms to stakeholders and nature. While risk reduction is only one aspect of risk management, risk management does not mean doing "good" (in the CSR sense) but rather focuses on not doing "wrong" (in the business ethics sense). Risks are specific in character and in terms of stakeholders potentially affected. How to balance risks among stakeholders is not resolved in this first cut. Rather, the approach taken here is to focus in a first cut on the problem of risk minimization.

This paper has a specific reason for its focus on the board of directors. Supervision of the corporation, understood in terms of corporate governance rather than operational management, is the broad responsibility of the board at law. In that context, this first cut undertakes in effect to formulate a broad policy statement (or principle) for the board of directors concerning ERM. Minimization of risks to all stakeholders and nature is the broad responsibility of the board in terms of ethics of risk management. The directors serve, in the context of a publicly traded firm, as trustees for the shareowners and stewards of the corporation. (The term trustee is used here to preference to agent, in order to signal a broader and longer-term orientation. The term steward is used here in order to signal responsibility for multiple stakeholders.) As a first step, directors should be competent; and outside directors should be independent and risk averse. The directors, who should be individuals of integrity, judgment, and experience, are subject to multiple legal requirements and ethical obligations. A second step in risk management is to obtain executives who are honorable and risk averse (outside the sphere of strategic initiative and flexibility). A third step is to organize the structures, systems, and policies of the board and the company for effectively addressing risk management. Many companies, especially in banking and insurance industries, now have risk management committees (Blanchard & Dionne, 2003). Scope should be expanded in all publicly traded companies from narrowly financial to multiple other risks. (There are multiple sources and types of risk to stakeholders.) How to do so is of course the key matter. We are now in a post-9/11 era of global warming and volatility of political and economic conditions.

Business risk management concerns *Risk, Returns and Responsibility* (ABI, 2004). These three dimensions are bundled together. Management and boards generate not just risks to the bottom line but risks to non-investor stakeholders and to nature. One should be careful therefore to distinguish two different motives for business risk management. The superior motive is to avoid imposing harm or loss improperly on stakeholders. A corporate stakeholder is anyone who can affect – or is affected by – a company. The highest standard of moral common sense is trying to avoid harming others, unless there is a valid justification for doing so. Additionally, stakeholders may have specific rights that should not be violated. The inferior motive is to avoid imposing financial loss on shareowners. One key source of such financial risk is imposing harm or loss on stakeholders. The superior motive dominates and is reinforced by the inferior motive. Without a clear ethics perspective, risk management becomes simply a species of financial cost–benefit analysis (CBA) implicitly relying on strict utilitarianism. An ethics perspective places moral principle (in some form) above financial computation.

These two motives suggest two competing philosophies (or grand theories) of the ethics of risk management. Both these theories rule out purely fiduciary responsibility as a satisfactory approach to ERM.

A comprehensive or integrative theory is that sustainable value of the company requires integrated multiple-dimension risk and stakeholder management. Ethics and market value creation are then cooperative. Viederman (2002) expresses this view as follows:

> The *integration* of prudent financial management practices with environmental stewardship, concern for community, labor and human rights, and corporate accountability to shareholders and stakeholders, will minimize short- and long-term financial risk and identify investment opportunities that will lead to increased shareholder value. … Fiduciary responsibility requires consideration of the social, environmental, political and cultural effects of investments, both positive and negative, over the short- and long-term as a fundamental part of the investment process. This [consideration] is not screening, nor is it a moral or ethical issue, per se. It is a financial issue, one that identifies risks and opportunities not captured by conventional financial analysis. Anything else than this comprehensive view does not meet the needs of beneficiaries, or the demands of fiduciary responsibility. This approach is about protecting shareholder value.

The presumption in Viederman's statement is that fiduciary responsibility and other considerations are not in conflict, but rather the latter reinforces the former. Viederman is the retired president of the Jessie Smith Noyes Foundation of New York City. It was founded in 1947 by real estate broker Charles F. Noyes (1878–1969), who was known as "The Dean of Real Estate." Mr Noyes (1959) gave his stock in Charles F. Noyes & Co. to the employees.

The other philosophy (or grand theory) is, in all circumstances, the moral superiority of ethics (or integrity) to shareowner value. Business ethics assesses the moral right and wrong of choices and behaviors. In case of concurrence, as defined by Viederman, ethics is permissive concerning shareowner value, because the two dimensions do not then come into conflict. In case of conflict, if any arises, then ethics – meaning more than legal compliance as a minimum standard (see Reinhardt, 1999) – must outweigh shareowner value. It is conceivable that business risk and corporate social responsibility (CSR) are opposed (Husted, 2005).

Hosmer (2007) depicts business decisions as unavoidably balancing economic (i.e., market), legal, and ethical dimensions. In that context, business risk management can be separated into two broad levels of technical and judgmental decisions. The former is an inferior level; the latter is a superior level. Technical considerations – such as "best available control technology" (BACT), for example – may provide limits to risk minimization; judgment makes decisions. In instances of conflict, ethics should be treated as superior to economic and even legal spheres.

For example, how to minimize risk of loss or breach of company records through various causes is initially just a technical exercise (Bell, 1989), in the sense of "best available control technology." One cause of loss could be a nuclear explosion in New York City (Mitroff & Alpaslan, 2003; Powell, 2003). Given best available risk management and security techniques and available resources, risk management can be treated as a species of cost–benefit computation. If risk cannot be made zero, then risk should be reduced to the point at which the marginal (or incremental) cost of further risk reduction equals marginal (or incremental) benefit of that further risk reduction. This cost–benefit analysis (CBA) can incorporate financial compensation legally or morally due to economically injured stakeholders (Gioia, 1992). "Doing well by doing good" fits readily into this computation (Paine, 2000).

In contrast, the consequences for various stakeholders of non-zero risk involve a broad judgmental decision embedding a moral dimension. The Ford Pinto design featured such a decision (Gioia, 1992). The design was defective in that a rear-end collision of the Pinto by another vehicle could cause an explosion of the gas tank. Ford reportedly knew that the risk of explosion could be greatly reduced by an inexpensive redesign. Based on a CBA conducted under prevailing federal auto safety regulations, Ford incorrectly concluded that the economic costs of redesign materially outweighed the (underestimated) social benefits. Litigation revealed that key assumptions of the CBA were faulty. Ford Pinto production ceased. (Ford has recently settled Explorer litigation.) It is open to debate whether a post-event compensatory approach, particularly in the form of uncertain civil litigation procedures, is a satisfactory approach relative to ex ante risk minimization. In direct contrast, Merck in the early 1990s decided on free distribution of a palliative for river blindness. The decision, even considering positive reputation effects, has been financially expensive for the company.

The remainder of this paper is structured as follows. The second section examines some relevant fundamentals of business risk management. The third section considers the risk management responsibilities of the board of directors. The fourth and final section provides some concluding comments on the ethics of risk management by a board of directors.

Some Fundamentals of Business Risk Management

The importance of integrated risk management was highlighted in a special article in *Fortune* magazine concerning "The Risk Management Revolution" (July 1976) and in the 1992 report of the Cadbury Committee on "The Financial Aspects of Corporate Governance." That report proposed explicitly that governing boards should be responsible for setting risk management policy, for assuring that the organization understands all its risks, and for accepting oversight for the entire process. (The emphasis was on fraud prevention.)

Risk aversion means a preference to accept a certain payoff (the certainty equivalent) of less than the potential high payoff of a gamble. (Effectively, hedging is a form of risk aversion.) Risk neutrality means indifference between the bet made in the gamble and a certain payoff. (One wins the bet or loses the payoff.) In 1992, British Petroleum, based on an academic study by two professors, reportedly dispensed with any commercial insurance on its operations in excess of $10 million (Kloman, 1999). Risk seeking means a requirement for a larger payment than the bet to avoid gambling. Expected value is the product of likelihood and consequence. A risk premium is the difference between expected value and the certainty equivalent.

The firm (an artificial entity) has at any given time a risk profile in multiple dimensions (adapting Schwartz & Carroll, 2003), defined as the pattern of risks to which it is exposed and to which it exposes stakeholders (including here shareowners and directors). Risk management concerns coping with possibilities that future events can cause adverse effects for individuals, organizations, societies, and nature. Risk management involves assessment of both conditions and potential losses (financial and other) arising from those conditions. A problem arises with different risk preferences among shareowners, directors, and executives; and with different risks borne by the firm and other stakeholders.

A risk (or hazard) is commonly understood to be the possibility of future harm or loss arising from present (i.e., new) or past (i.e., uncorrected) action or inaction. A risk (or hazard) is any possibility (i.e., likelihood) of harm (physical or psychological) or loss (economic or other) to self (in this context, the shareholders and directors, typically including top executives) or others (in this context all other stakeholders or nature). Hence, to risk or hazard means to incur or expose to the possibility of harm or loss. An actual damage, in the form of harm or loss, is a 100 percent certainty at time of occurrence. Risk (or hazard) is some likelihood of future occurrence that is less than 100 percent certainty but greater than 0 percent of non-occurrence. The conventional definition of risk is that there is some knowable distribution of future possible outcomes. Uncertainty, in contrast, is a state-condition is which it is not feasible to specify that distribution. Operationally, uncertainty may imply acting as if there is a relatively high risk of some occurrence.

This paper focuses exclusively on publicly traded corporations. In that context, business risk is definable as the possibility of future economic loss to the shareowners. For purposes of this discussion, corporate executives or directors are agents who will not intentionally harm themselves and who will seek to avoid personal economic loss. The term "stakeholders" will be used here as a convenient shorthand expression for any "other stakeholders" – meaning corporate stakeholders who are not shareowners or executives. In general, competitors and nature are not strictly speaking stakeholders of a focus company. The firm is a cooperation of all its stakeholders (Conger et al., 2001). The relationship with competitors is "win–lose" and financial only. The relationship with nature involves governments or other stakeholders as concerned parties.

Business risk may arise in a wide variety of ways. Business risk management is thus a bundle of quite heterogeneous risks. There are at least four broad categories of business risk. The categorization is not necessarily exhaustive, but rather intended to be suggestive.

(1) One category is some management action or inaction that can result in financial risk (i.e., economic value loss) to shareowners through agent misconduct. The classic instance is fraud or other deception. Two examples are the Enron debacle of 2001 and Société Générale's large trading losses disclosed in January 2008. The Sarbanes–Oxley Act of 2002 attempts to reduce the likelihood of such misconduct. This type of risk implies relatively rigid rules regulating agent conduct and misconduct.

(2) Another category concerns some management action or inaction that involves strategic risk concerning the company's future through operation of markets or governments. The action or inaction is a financial or economic exposure of some type. This category includes actions and reactions of competitors, complementary-product firms, and substitute-product firms. Strategic risk is a much broader and more complex question than financial misconduct. This type of risk implies strategic flexibility in contrast to rigid rules (Henkel, 2007; Sanchez, 1997). Risk management is not simply risk reduction, on which this paper focuses.

(3) Another category is some management action or inaction that can impact (whether objectively or subjectively) some other stakeholders negatively in a way that can result in financial risk to shareowners through reactions such as customer flight, consumer boycott, union strike, adverse media attention, and private lawsuits. The firm risks harm or loss to

stakeholders, and this firm-caused risk incurs financial or economic exposure for the firm. The ethical principle that one should not impose such harm or loss on others is superior to this firm financial risk. One example is the *Exxon Valdez* environmental disaster, still being contested in court by Exxon Mobil (see Hosmer, 1998). The length of the litigation raises doubts about post-event compensation as a satisfactory approach to risk management. Another example is Mattel's 2007 recalls of toys manufactured in China, on account of concerns about lead paint exposure to children. Another example is Unocal's decision to undertake a passive minority investment position in a joint venture of Total (a French company) and the Myanmar (Burma) government to construct and operate a natural gas pipeline across part of Burma between Indian Ocean resources and Thailand markets. Burmese citizens (unnamed for their protection) sued Unocal in US federal and state courts for damages alleging complicity in human rights violations by the military regime.

(4) Another category is some action by others, whether or not they are legitimately stakeholders, who can impose harm or loss on the corporation and/or its employees. This category includes natural events, in the sense that crisis or disaster management preparation is roughly the same management process. Examples are a terrorist attack (as on September 11, 2001) or an earthquake or a tsunami (as in the Indian Ocean). An employee might run amok on company property and harm others. Extortion by criminals or government officials, domestic or foreign, in the form of bribe demands falls in this category. The Foreign Corrupt Practices Act (FCPA) of 1977 prohibited bribery of foreign government or political officials, although it permits under some conditions facilitating payments to low-level "clerical" personnel.

A difficulty in business risk management is that reduction in likelihood of risk is not typically free: there is a likely increasing opportunity cost. In formal terms, as marginal benefit of risk reduction falls, marginal cost of risk reduction rises. For many (not necessarily all) risks, it is likely that from a financial perspective the optimum risk level is somewhere greater than zero. This expectation governs much of business risk management. For example, the cost of internal accounting controls cannot materially exceed the benefit of those controls. There may be a limit to safety investment either in terms of best available control technology or the economic value of human life.

One may distinguish (see Wood, 1991) among principles (or motives), behaviors (or actions and inactions), and outcomes (e.g., risks, harms, and losses). A principle is why someone should seek particular outcomes or should require or prohibit particular behaviors. On principle, one should minimize risk to others. Behaviors link principles to outcomes. A potential conflict in principles is between risk management and value maximization. For the purposes of this paper, there is a distinction among legal compliance, business ethics, and corporate social responsibility (CSR). Legal compliance is mandatory, in this instance ignoring unavoidable civil disobedience. Business ethics means best efforts to avoid harming others, without legitimate justification. CSR means reasonable efforts to do some good. One might obey law because it is prudent to do so. A risk-averse individual or organization is prudent. One should obey law because the law embodies what an ethical person or organization ought to do. Business ethics has the sense of properly avoiding negative impacts on others. CSR has the sense of voluntarily seeking to provide positive benefits for others out of some sense of moral obligation or in the common good.

In a standard marginal cost – marginal benefit depiction, the marginal cost schedule is rising and the marginal benefit schedule is falling. For the purposes of this paper, marginal benefit is the value of the degree of risk reduction; marginal cost is the investment required for the degree of risk reduction. One might identify two very different circumstances for analysis. In one situation, the marginal benefit (of action or inaction) is much higher than the marginal cost (of action or inaction). Therefore, one should continue investing in risk reduction. Uncertainty mimics this situation. In another situation, the marginal benefit is very close to the marginal cost. It may be very difficult to discern the precise optimum point. In some conditions it can be argued that the proper course of action is to under-invest for cost savings. In other conditions, it can be argued that the proper course of action is to over-invest for assurance. One such condition would be employee or customer safety. There should be very high assurance with regard to this. In this standard depiction, increasing risk is effectively moving away from the optimum point toward state-conditions in which marginal benefit increasingly exceeds marginal cost. Illustrations are the Ford Pinto (discussed earlier) and the British Petroleum (BP) plant explosion in Texas City, Texas, in which 15 people died. The 2005 BP plant explosion in the Houston area killed several individuals and led, in combination with other considerations, to the early retirement of CEO Sir John Browne. There is suspicion that company processes, as distinct from official policy, resulted in safety being subordinated to profits. The explosion has cost BP several hundred million dollars in fines and $1.5 billion in compensation settlements so far.

Reputation is a key business asset. One may posit that sustainable profitability of a firm (see Nordberg, 2007) is a function partially of its reputation among stakeholders. The duty of care for investors' interests and employees' safety can be broadly extended to other stakeholders, the environment, and human rights (Diffey, 2007). It is possible to conceptualize this duty in terms of strategic CSR aimed at safeguarding and enhancing the firm's reputation and thus sustainable valuation (Diffey, 2007). Diffey points out that bad news travels faster and farther than good news. Reputation effects are addressed in a body of literature (see Mailath, 2007). CSR might then be interpreted as insurance for reputation (Peloza, 2005). However, legal compliance and business ethics should be undertaken for their own sake. They then simply have the further effect or advantage of reputation insurance.

The functional expression below suggests that sustainable profitability (Π^s) is partially some function of reputation (R) holding constant all other considerations (X). In turn, the functional expression suggests that reputation (R) is some function (Fombrun & Shanley, 1990) partially of legal compliance (LC), business ethics (BE), and corporate social responsibility (CSR) holding constant all other considerations (Y). The risk to sustainable profitability arising from loss of reputation can be arguably high – illustrated by Enron's liquidity collapse following a failure of confidence by other stakeholders.

$$\Pi^s = f(R; X) = f(LC, BE, CSR; Y)$$

Risk Management Responsibilities
of the Board of Directors

It is becoming a well-established prescription that the board should seek to minimize risks. Effective risk management will involve good planning, high ethical standards, and organizational architecture aligning allocation of authority rights, performance evaluation measures, and compensation mechanisms (Brickley & Smith, 2003; Goldman, Sachs, 1998; KPMG, 1999). The board of directors itself can face possible liability of ineffective risk management. (Directors and executives naturally prefer liability insulation.) A translation of this responsibility is that the board should seek to minimize risks of various kinds to the shareholders, other stakeholders, and nature. Three recent examples are as follows. In February 2008, BP announced settlement of a shareholder derivative suit alleging executives allowed violations of environmental, worker safety, and fair trade laws. The settlement reduced severance payments to former CEO John Browne, paid about $10 million in legal feels, and promised to strengthen BP corporate governance practices. BP will include "operational health, safety and environmental performance" in executive compensation practices (BP, 2008). In January 2008, two shareholders sued Eli Lilly and Co. concerning its drug Zyprexia. The suit alleged that executives and directors had recklessly disregarded the risks involved in the use of illegal drug marketing tactics (Lilly shareholders, 2008). In May 2007, at the annual shareholders' meeting of Dow Chemical Company, holders of something over 6.6 million shares introduced three resolutions concerning alleged weaknesses in company management of risk and reputation. These weaknesses addressed, in part, alleged failure to disclose possible material liabilities arising from (a) continuing lawsuits concerning Agent Orange (a defoliant used in the Vietnam war) and (b) continuing complaints that Dow should address alleged contamination from the 1984 Bhopal chemical disaster although there was a final legal settlement for all claimants in May 1989 with the government of India (CSRWire, 2007).

In US corporation law, the board of directors is broadly responsible for the overall supervision of a publicly traded company. The basic principle for discharging this responsibility is a combination of prudence and flexibility concerning business judgment. This compound principle traces back in US law to *Dodge* v. *Ford Motor Co.*, 204 Mich. 459, 170 N.W. 668 (Supreme Court of Michigan, 1919) and at least *Harvard College and Massachusetts General Hospital* v. *Francis Amory*, 9 Pick. (26 Mass.), 446 (Supreme Court of Massachusetts for Suffolk and Nantucket, Judge Samuel Putnam, 1830). The 1830 opinion asserted that capital is always at "hazard" and that a reasonably prudent "trustee" cannot be held accountable for bad outcomes except "for gross neglect and wilful mismanagement." (The English common law had required virtually absolute conservation of capital by a trustee.) The 1919 opinion accepted that business judgment must often include long-term considerations. Subsequent cases approved product liability even for parts purchased from another company (*McPherson* v. *Buick Motor Company* (NY State Court of Appeals, Justice Benjamin N. Cardozo), 217 NY 382, 111 NE 1050 (1916)) and reasonable flexibility to make charitable contributions (*A. P. Smith Mfg. Co.* v. *Barlow* (N.J. 1953) 98 A. (2d) 581, appeal dismissed by the US Supreme Court, 346 US 961 (1953)).

A risk might entail a criminal or civil liability to the company. There have been an increasing number of lawsuits filed against US companies by foreign plaintiffs under the Alien Tort Claims Act (ATCA) of 1789. In the process of its acquisition by Chevron, Unocal made an out of court settlement of one such suit arising in Burma (Myanmar). It has been argued that European Union (EU) courts should provide access for foreign grievances against EU multinationals (Amao, 2007). Yahoo and Google face actual or potential lawsuits arising in their operations in China involving cooperation with the regime that might be interpreted as complicity in oppression.

Three special circumstances affect board risk management. One occurs when there are irreconcilable conflicts among any two (or more) stakeholder interests. A second occurs with negative externalities generated by board and company choices. A third involves conflicts of interest for the board itself. The board itself can be a creator or source of risk for the firm and other stakeholders.

The notion of risk–return tradeoff, common in finance terminology, embeds potential stakeholder conflicts (ABI, 2004). If shareholders win, some stakeholders lose. For example, drug and health care pricing is quite peculiar. Firms quote often high prices to individual customers. Prices are then discounted, or negotiated, down for Medicare or health insurance carriers; or in developing countries as a matter of strategy and values (as in Merck's free distribution of river blindness medication) or threat of patent breach and generic production. Credit card companies reportedly trigger interest rate increases even for customers in good standing when there are unrelated changes in credit ratings or who repeatedly make the minimum payments. Norman Augustine, then CEO of Martin Marietta (and later of Lockheed Martin), commented: "The toughest decisions are those involving conflicts among these [key stakeholder] groups [shareholders, customers, employees, and the community]. You have to decide what's fair in these situations and constantly work to fulfill and balance these commitments" (Paine, 1992: 1). The Johnson & Johnson Credo (1943) articulates a hierarchy of stakeholder responsibilities from customers through employees and the community to shareholders.

A variant of this stakeholder conflict problem involves negative externalities. By definition, a negative externality is a real or pecuniary cost imposed on another by a decision maker and ignored by that decision maker. Nature (since not a human stakeholder) is the most obvious example. Pollution affects nature, as well as human stakeholders. A possible difference between direct stakeholder conflicts and negative externalities is that the latter may aggregate from the independent activities of multiple firms, as in nature, in ways likely to be much more random for stakeholder conflicts. A controversial possibility is total product responsibility (Polinsky & Shavell, 2006). Under this concept, a company would be fully accountable for its product and consequences.

The board itself creates conflicts of interest in various ways. Directors are typically shareholders and may be compensated through performance-linked metrics, as are executives. The compensation approach emphasizes bottom line over risk management. Directors and executives tend to serve personal interests, in the absence of effective checks and balances. The odds of removal of directors or executives are relatively low, unless there is a dramatic decline in financial performance or a corporate scandal. The Enron board was either complaisant toward or complicit during the Lay and Skilling regime. The recent stock options scandal suggests that directors and executives have learned relatively little (Learning failure, 2007). Part of the difficulty is cognitive (Nooteboom, 2003). Directors and executives widely share a financial maximization outlook, as well as incentives for financial performance. Risk management needs to be externally and internally alert and concerned with the firm's long-term sustainability. Business ethics, corporate social responsibility, and corporate citizenship may be important practices for risk management (Diffey, 2007; Godfrey, 2005; Husted, 2005). Paine (1994) distinguished between legal compliance and ethical integrity. Paine argued that the latter may be the necessary foundation for the former.

The National Association of Corporate Directors issued a blue ribbon commission report on risk oversight (NACD, 2002). The report extends the risk management and corporate governance recommendations of the Cadbury Report. Key recommendations of the report are periodic risk review, committee risk management assignments, crisis management plan, periodic review of that plan, and designation of an independent director to operate the company if necessary. The key argument of the report is that the board should exercise more active and effective oversight of management with respect to risk and crisis. The report advocates good governance, risk oversight, and crisis preparation. The fundamental foundation for such oversight is sound corporate governance. From that starting point, the report examines best practices for helping directors oversee risk and crisis management, how to detect specific material risks, how the board can help the company address specific risks and prepare for crisis, and actions to undertake if a potential risk turns into an actual crisis. Ensuring adequate risk management means ensuring an effective process for assessing risks and detecting their occurrence. Cited by the NACD report, *In re Caremark International Inc. Derivative Litigation*, Court of Chancery of Delaware, William J. Allen, Chancellor (Judge), 698 A.2d 959 (Del. Ch. 1996), decided September 25, 1996, addresses this duty of care. Emphasis was placed on information and reporting systems concerning legal compliance and business performance. A business crisis is typically a downward "spiral" involving a "chain reaction" of one problem triggering another problem and so forth. A key board responsibility is then identifying both such problems and how to interrupt the chain reaction at vital points. This paper argues that the duty of care for ERM must be conceived of broadly in terms of multiple sources and types of risk to stakeholders as well as to the corporation (i.e., the investors).

The NACD report endorses particular corporate governance practices, often those practices recommended in the Cadbury Report. For example, the NACD report commends separation of board leadership (either a board chair or a lead director) from top management. Where the same individual is chair and CEO, then effective board governance responsibility must shift to an independent governance committee or a lead director. The board must be able to operate independently of management, especially during a crisis. The board must be able to assess its own effectiveness. There must be governance guidelines and a code of conduct. Director traits must include personal integrity, informed judgment, appropriate experience, and financial literacy – or the willingness to acquire it. Independence means that such directors can and will challenge unwise, unethical, or illegal actions. This requirement suggests that the key board committees should be controlled by outside directors, constituting a majority of the board. Independence also means that outside directors cannot have potential conflicts of interest with the shareowners. Risk planning likely means development of "worst-case" scenarios. The work of risk management likely will be divided up among key committees: the audit committee monitors financial reporting; the safety, health, and environment committee monitors human and environmental risks; the governance committee monitors board practices; and so forth. The compensation committee should monitor potential conflicts of interest for directors and executives. There may need to be ad hoc committees for other risks. If so, a role of a risk management committee may be supervision of overall integration of risk considerations. The company will need a crisis management plan.

A specific issue for crisis management involves the dispersion of employees, activities, and records. In the terrorist attacks of September 11, 2001 on the World Trade Center one can identify two different outcomes. Empire Blue Cross & Blue Shield had 1,900 employees occupying ten floors. While the offices were destroyed, fortunately only 11 people were killed (nine employees and two consultants). The company's crisis management procedures included a backup system for computer failure (the network switched to Albany, New York) and activation of virtual call centers to restore effective servicing within a couple of days. The company's crisis center operated in Melville, Long Island. Another firm, Marsh & McLennan Companies (MMC), lost 295 employees and 60 business associates. Cantor Fitzgerald L.P. lost 658 employees. The New York City Fire Department lost 341 firefighters and two paramedics. Some 60 police officers from two agencies and eight private ambulance personnel died.

Some Conclusions Concerning the Ethics of Risk Management

It is not automatically clear that implementing an ethics of risk management can be characterized in terms of a single fundamental criterion (such as profit maximization) or methodology (such as best available control technology) for recommending and evaluating behavior (i.e., action and inaction). The reason is the wide diversity of risk sources noted earlier.

In some circumstances, prudence or caution is most likely the indicated approach. Key examples are safeguarding the financial and physical assets of the company and assuring the safety of stakeholders, most especially of employees and customers. There is unlikely to be strong financial reason for undertaking risk beyond the minimum feasible risk, defined as an irreducible level of risk. This minimum feasible level is a cost–benefit analysis (CBA) in the case of financial and physical assets. There may be a tendency to under-invest. Financial disclosure principles do suggest full and transparent disclosure of the relevant information. This minimum feasible level is not necessarily such an economic calculus in the case of safety assurance. Rather, over-investment may be the indicated policy for ethics of risk management. Any irreducible level of risk should be fully disclosed. It may also be the indicated policy that the firm should carry insurance (if available and economically affordable) to provide compensation against actual occurrences.

In other circumstances, boldness (or decisiveness) is arguably the indicated approach. A key example is strategic initiative. It may be desirable, for the long-term sustainability of the company, to move quickly or to undertake relatively large investments. In January 2008, Microsoft suddenly launched a hostile takeover bid for acquisition of Yahoo. Such an acquisition must prove strategically dangerous to Google. An attempt to intervene, in some way, may have other risks.

In corporate reporting of risk, the basic principle is disclosure and transparency. There are potential conflicts between objectives arising in risk management and objectives arising in value maximization (Blanchard & Dionne, 2003). Risk management suggests prudence and risk aversion. Value maximization can induce (it may not suggest) risk seeking (or even possibly at Enron risk loving).

Stock options may encourage risk seeking. Blanchard and Dionne (2003) recommend that risk management committees should be composed of competent directors who are independent and hold no stock options.

It should be noted that there is an emerging scandal concerning the undisclosed backdating of stock options. It is not illegal, and likely not unethical, for the board to approve ex ante backdating of stock options. That practice can be interpreted as permitting an executive to determine an element of incentive compensation. Such practice should be disclosed fully; and executives have been concealing such practice.

To keep discussion tractable, the first attempt to develop an ethics of risk management here is in terms of interests, rights, and nature. The essence of the problem is striving to protect shareowners' long-term interests, stakeholders' immediate rights, and nature's value to humanity both now and in the future. The problem has the appearance of "triple bottom line" performance (i.e., economic, social, and environmental outcomes). In this context, ethics concerns assigning relative weights to interests, rights, and nature as a basis for deciding appropriate tradeoffs (if any are admissible). By presumption, stakeholders' immediate rights are superior to shareowners' immediate interests and – in the case of conflict – also to shareowners' long-term interests. Where a stakeholder has a right, a corporation has a duty. There may be actions/inactions that affect only shareowner interests. There may be actions/inactions that affect relative weights between or among stakeholders. Tradeoffs against nature involve public policy: society must decide what is most important in a given situation.

A lesson of the Enron debacle is the greater risk of aggressive accounting and earnings management (i.e., manipulation) relative to the lower risk of conservative accounting and earnings management. Aggressive management can be rational for executives (they may benefit in the short term) and dysfunctional for the company (the investors may suffer in the long term). Earnings management is unobservable until discovered (Chen et al., 2007). While potential investors may emphasize the valuation role of financial information (in deciding whether to purchase shares), current shareowners may emphasize the stewardship role of that information (in trying to monitor management). Chen et al. (2007) argue that earnings management reduces the stewardship value of financial information and results in inferior risk sharing between potential and current shareowners. One might define the standard for financial information as an unbiased measurement of true economic reality. Conservatism attempts to identify this true economic reality with a downward bias (for safety). Aggressiveness inflates valuation beyond true economic reality (Hitting numbers, 2003).

Minton and Blagg (2004), based partly on interviews with 206 senior executives of multinationals (January–May 2004), identify six pillars of corporate integrity: ethics, transparency, social and environmental responsibility, human rights, corporate governance, and financial viability. These six pillars must be integrated into strategy, values, and management and practices which must themselves be aligned.

Minton is quoted in the report to the point that in corporate share price freefalls "the cause was not one single thing, but a disease or malaise at the heart of the organisation. Each of the recent corporate scandals had complex causes, but the common denominator of all of them was a failure in the boardroom to address what was going wrong at the heart of the organisation" (Minton & Blagg, 2004: 33). Minton suggests that corporate integrity "is the key not only to avoiding disaster, but to adding value." The report of the Permanent Senate Subcommittee on Investigations into *The Role of the Board of Directors in Enron's Collapse* (July 2002) found that (see Jaedicke, 2002; Windsor, 2004):

> In too many instances, by going along with questionable practices and relying on management and auditor representations, the Enron Board failed to provide the prudent oversight and checks and balances that its fiduciary obligations required and a company like Enron needed. By failing to provide sufficient oversight and restraint to stop management excess, the Enron Board contributed to the company's collapse and bears a share of the responsibility for it.

A very similar diagnosis of the WorldCom debacle has been made (Reports cite, 2003).

References

Amao, Olufemi O. 2007. Promoting corporate responsibility abroad: Opening up EU jurisdiction to corporate abuse committed abroad. Available at SSRN: http://ssrn.com/abstract=996397.

Association of British Insurers (ABI). 2004. *Risk, Returns and Responsibility*. London.

Bell, Trudy E. 1989. Managing Murphy's Law: Engineering a minimum-risk system. *IEEE Spectrum*, 26(6) (June): 24–7.

Blanchard, Danielle and Georges Dionne. 2003 (September). Risk management and corporate governance. HEC Montreal Risk Management Chair Working Paper No. 03–04. Available at SSRN: http://ssrn.com/abstract=441482.

BP gives terms of settlement. 2008. *Houston Chronicle*, 107(117), Thursday, February 7: D1 (Business).

Brickley, James A. and Clifford W. Smith, Jr. 2003. Corporate governance, ethics, and organizational architecture. *Journal of Applied Corporate Finance*, 15(3) Spring: 34–45.

Chen, Qi, Thomas Hemmer, and Yun Zhang. 2007. On the relation between conservatism in accounting standards and incentives for earnings management. *Journal of Accounting Research*, 45(3) June: 541–65.

Conger, Jay A., Edward E. Lawler, and David L. Finegold. 2001. *Corporate Boards: New Strategies for Adding Value at the Top*. San Francisco: Jossey-Bass.

CSRWire (2007, May 9). Dow Chemical investors worth $305 million challenge company on social and environmental catastrophes. Accessed (February 10, 2008) from http://www.csrwire.com/News/8473.html.

Diffey, Gladys. 2007 (October). CSR, A risky business – risk management and CSR. 2007 European MBA Essay Award short-listed paper. Ashridge Business School and EABIS.

Fombrun, Charles and Mark Shanley. 1990. What's in a name? Reputation building and corporate strategy. *Academy of Management Journal*, 33(2): 233–58.

Gioia, Dennis. 1992. Pinto fires and personal ethics: A script analysis of missed opportunities. *Journal of Business Ethics*, 11(5–6) May: 379–89.

Godfrey, Paul C. 2005. The relationship between corporate philanthropy and shareholder wealth: a risk management perspective. *Academy of Management Review*, 30: 777–98.

Goldman, Sachs & Co. and SBC Warburg Dillon Read. 1998 (February). *The Practice of Risk Management*. London: Euromoney Institutional Investors PLC.

Henkel, Joachim. 2007. The risk–return paradox for strategic management: disentangling true and spurious effects. CEPR Discussion Papers No. 6538 (October). Available from SSRN: http://ssrn.com/abstract=1014325.

Hitting numbers an "obsession": New SEC chairman [William Donaldson] emphasizes soundness over projections. 2003. *Houston Chronicle*, March 25: 25B (Business).

Hosmer, LaRue T. 1998. Lessons from the wreck of the *Exxon Valdez*: the need for imagination, empathy, courage. *Business Ethics Quarterly*, Special Issue No. 1: 109–22.

Hosmer, LaRue T. 2007. *The Ethics of Management*, 6th edn. New York: McGraw-Hill.

Husted, Bryan W. 2005. Risk management, real options, corporate social responsibility. *Journal of Business Ethics*, 60(2) August: 175–83.

Jaedicke, Robert K. 2002. Statement (Chairman of the Audit and Compliance Committee of the Board of Directors of Enron Corp.). *Enron Bankruptcy: Hearing Before the House Committee on Energy and Commerce, Subcommittee on Oversight and Investigation*, 107th Congress.

Kloman, H. Felix. 1999. Risk management milestones: 1900 to 1999. *Risk Management Reports*, 26(12) December. (Accessed February 3, 2008 at http://www.irmi.com/Expert/Articles/2001/Kloman03.aspx.)

KPMG. 1999. *Best Practices in Risk Management: Private and Public Sectors Internationally*. Treasury Board of Canada Secretariat (modified 1999-04-27). (Accessed February 3, 2008 at http://www.tbs-sct.gc.ca/pubs_pol/dcgpubs/RiskManagement/rm-pps_e.asp.)

Learning failure: Stock option scandal shows many executives and company directors learned little from Enron. 2007. *Houston Chronicle*, 106(83) Thursday, January 4: B10 (City & State).

Lilly shareholders say risks ignored. 2008. *Houston Chronicle* 107 (111) Friday, February 1, D3 (Business).

Mailath, George J. 2007 (October 19). Reputation effects. PIER Working Paper No. 07-034. Available at SSRN: http://ssrn.com/abstract=1023658.

Minton, Andrew and Matthew Blagg. 2004. *Corporate Integrity: The Strategic Reality*. London: CriticalEYE Publications. Sponsored by Controls Risks Group. Forewords by Paul Walsh (CEO, Diageo), Kofi Annan (UN Secretary-General), and Nigel Churton (CEO, Control Risks Group).

Mitroff, Ian I. and Murat C. Alpaslan. 2003. Preparing for evil. *Harvard Business Review*, 81(4) April: 104–15.

National Association of Corporate Directors (NACD). 2002. *Risk Oversight: Board Lessons for Turbulent Times*. Washington, DC: Blue Ribbon Commission on Risk Oversight.

Nooteboom, Bart. 2003 (July). Elements of a cognitive theory of the firm. CentER Discussion Paper No. 2005–46. Available at SSRN: http://ssrn.com/abstract=706921.

Nordberg, Donald. 2007 (July). Ethics of corporate governance. Available at SSRN: http://ssrn.com/abstract=1004038.

Paine, Lynn S. 1992. Martin Marietta: Managing corporate ethics (A). Harvard Business School case 9-393-016. With Albert Choy and Michael Santoro (revised October 26, 1994).

Paine, Lynn S. 1994. Managing for organizational integrity. *Harvard Business Review*, 72(2) (March–April): 106–17.

Paine, Lynn S. 2000. Does ethics pay? *Business Ethics Quarterly*, 10(1) (January): 319–30.

Peloza, John. 2005 (March 1). Corporate social responsibility as reputation insurance. Center for Responsible Business, University of California, Berkeley, Working Paper Series, Paper 24. Available at http://repositories.cdlib.org/crb/wps/24.

Polinsky, A. Mitchell and Steven Shavell. 2006. Mandatory versus Voluntary Disclosure of Product Risks. Stanford Law and Economics Olin Working Paper No. 327. Available at SSRN: http://ssrn.com/abstract=939546.

Powell, Alvin. 2003 (March 20). New Harvard report: Chilling warnings on nuclear terror. *Harvard University Gazette*. Accessed at http://www.news.harvard.edu/gazette/2003/03.20/11-warnings.html.

Reinhardt, Forest L. 1999. Market failure and the environmental policies of firms: economic rationales for "beyond compliance" behavior. *Journal of Industrial Ecology*, 3: 9–21.

Reports cite WorldCom's crooked culture. 2003. *Houston Chronicle*, June 10: 2B (Business).

Sanchez, Ron. 1997. Preparing for an uncertain future: managing organisations for strategic flexibility. *International Studies of Management and Organisation*, 27(2): 71–94.

Schwartz, Mark S. and Archie B. Carroll. 2003. Corporate social responsibility: a three domain approach. *Business Ethics Quarterly*, 13(4) (October): 503–30.

Viederman, Stephen. 2002. New directions in fiduciary responsibility. Initiative for fiduciary responsibility, A project of the Global Academy. Published version of invited remarks made at two 2002 meetings. (Retrieved February 4, 2008 at http://www.theglobalacademy.org/SV%20Paper3_IFR.asp.)

Windsor, Duane. 2004. Business ethics at "the crooked E". In Nancy B. Rapoport and Bala G. Dharan (eds), *Enron: Corporate Fiascos and Legal Implications*. New York: Foundation Press, pp. 659–87.

Wood, Donna J. 1991. Corporate social performance revisited. *Academy of Management Review*, 16(4): 691–718.

15

Assurance and Reassurance:
The Role of the Board

Barry M. Mitnick

The development of the firm can be seen as an accretion of design adaptations that sequentially patched emergent risks. The board evolved as one of the mechanisms of managing risk as well as an adaptive controller able to modify the firm's functioning so as to deal with new sources of risk.

But this story of structural and functional adaptation following risk discovery does not adequately capture the dynamics of these adaptive processes. How can we understand the scale and extensiveness of reaction to risk, or the particular means adopted to deal with the risk issue at each presentment? That is, the fact that some change is done to manage risk tells us little about why the change was done in the manner observed. Moreover, a perspective on the evolution of the board that sees it as a rationally tuned risk-managing mechanism has great difficulty explaining why the literature on boards has continually wondered whether boards really do anything at all of real substance, and why so much of it is filled with hortatory admonitions to fulfill duties, follow procedures, fix shortcomings, act responsibly, and so on (the classic statement on this is usually taken to be Mace, 1971).

Mace (1971: 187) described board meetings as "resembling the performance of traditional and well-established, almost religious, rituals." Why is so much of the literature, especially the modern works, focused on symbolic and reputational roles – shouldn't the key operational functions of boards be up front, not issues of symbolic membership, presentation, remuneration, boundary management, and so on? This is not to offer the extreme argument that boards do nothing, but to wonder why they do so little that is recognized and described as substantive, to the point that even the practitioner literature seems to worry about how boards can be made "effective." Shouldn't we assume they are always functionally effective, and treat the rest as marginal, not central concerns? Yet these basic questions of whether the board really performs tasks of substantive utility continually reappear.

Of course, directors would be quick to take exception to any claim that boards actually do nothing. If anything, the claim is that the workload of boards, as well as the risks and liabilities of directors, have been increasing steadily in the age of Sarbanes–Oxley. Even if boards meet on average less than one time per month, board committees have become far more active than in the past and meet more often. So how can it be that boards are both busy and don't really perform traditional operational functions? But can any entity that only meets for a day or two, or even just a few hours, on average less than once per month actually do all the traditional things that boards are supposed to do (for a typical list and discussion, see, e.g., Monks & Minow 2004; see also, e.g., Mace, 1971)?

Another way to look at this is to consider the proportion of the work year taken up by board activities. Let us assume that the board meets two days per month for 10 months of the year, a level exceeding that of many boards. That's approximately four weeks of business days. In a 52-week year, that comes to less than 8 percent of the work year. Directors may protest that they are shipped thick board books to help them prepare. But this is a professional managerial, not a 9–5 world, and work after hours should be taken for granted. If preparation work was part of the rationale for total remuneration, then the time should be billed just as the firm would with its other part-time employees, such as consultants. The median remuneration for directors in US corporations is over $100,000 (The Corporate Library 2007), which is easily a multiple of the average corporate wage. Hence, for working 8 percent of the work year, directors receive remuneration several times greater than that of the average employee. The membership of the board, typically together with short biographies and color photos, is featured prominently on the web pages of every corporation. Boards are treated as *important*, and paid commensurately. Yet if directors cannot possibly perform operational tasks, why the fuss? Aren't there other ways to perform the part-time jobs of the board, without paying its considerable costs?

I suggest that the evolution of the firm, and of the board that governs it, may be better understood as a search for *assurance and reassurance*. In this perspective, *the key function of a board is to provide assurance*. It is not by accident that assurance has its primary association in the processes of accounting and, as well, in the contexts of insurance (but see Klein (2001/2003) on the economics of assurance; Mitnick (1996, 1999, 2000) on the theory of testaments, including the concept of assurance costs; cf. Shapiro (1987) on the provision of trust via social institutions; Rao, Greeve, & Davis (2001) on "social proof;" and Rao (1994) on certification contests).

The central issue is the status of belief that conditions alleged to obtain in the real world do indeed exist there. Hence, the problem is the manufacture of credibility – the establishment of conditions sufficient for the targeted observers to assign the status of truth. Thus, *boards establish – indeed, enact – truths*. It is no accident that the oldest board structure, and the function that has copious historical record in various forms, is the audit committee (an audit of accounts was an important feature of the governance of medieval guilds, one of the predecessor institutions of the corporation; see Scott 1912/1968, vol. 1: 5).

In a view based in assurance, rather than in risk management, the firm is viewed properly as a social construction that may be assembled in alternative ways, depending on the state of demand for demonstrations sufficient to produce the desired credibility in observers. Were we to treat the firm as constructed to reflect the calculative assessment of risk, it would be hard to understand why firms create mechanisms to present the appearance of performance, but not necessarily the actuality of that performance, and why redundancy in mechanisms is demanded so as to produce not only assurance, but also *reassurance*.

The paper begins with a review of some standard problems in understanding the key functions of boards. It introduces a typology of four classes of board functions – *legal*, *normative*, *descriptive*, and *utilitarian* – highlighting the fact that none of these standard roles adequately captures the key function of the board, *assurance*. Not only is assurance at the heart of modern corporate governance; it has always been there, and, indeed, it must be there because of a basic problem in organizational design, what I call the *Governance Paradox* (GP). One method of managing the Governance Paradox is to create *pantheonic directorates*. In order to understand the fundamental nature of my claim that what the board is all about is assurance, I then review the functioning of the very first joint-stock company of modern form, the Russia or Muscovy Company of Tudor England. I end by briefly arguing the utility of reconceptualizing the assurance problems of corporate governance in terms of an *agent capitalism* model of the firm.

Some Problems in Understanding the Key Functions of Boards

The literature on boards is full of lists of functions of boards of directors (for a classic analysis in the sociology literature, see Zald, 1969). A common argument is that prime among these functions is the formal role of the board of the corporation to represent and monitor the interests of the owners, the shareholders. Depending on who is holding forth on this representational or monitoring task of the directors, the role takes on not just a fiduciary obligation but the status of a sacred duty. But the functions of boards are remarkably ambiguous, and sometimes apparently quite situational: Defenders of board actions refer, variously, to the board's legal duties to the firm, to its normative obligations to the shareholders, and to the utilitarian tasks that boards perform on behalf of corporations. And critics offer that when one looks at what boards actually do, it is hard to see that behavior as truly consistent with legal, normative, or utilitarian functions.

Indeed, the directors do have a legal obligation to serve the *firm's* interests; to the extent to which the owners are viewed as coextensive with the firm itself, the directors are coincidentally also looking after the owners' interests. But this is where *legal* roles diverge from purely *normative* ones. Although directors have duties of loyalty and care that constitute a fiduciary obligation to the shareholders (e.g., Monks & Minow, 2004), they are not truly the agents of the owners. In the first place, the board must serve the chartered corporate person; it must act in the firm's best interests. But just as the corporate person is fictive, so are the obligations of service to that person ambiguous. How do you serve a person who is not a person – who cannot directly express any preference whatsoever; for whom every wish is socially constructed by biased observers; who lives forever and whose preferences must presumably include the protection of that immortality? How can we consider firms to be persons if they are immortal? Directors are truly gods if their role is to preserve the firm for eternity.

Now, obviously, the health of that corporate person may be arguably represented by the firm's value, and that value is of course contributed by, and held by, the owners, i.e., the shareholders (though an argument can be made that interprets "value" far more broadly than that). Thus, following this logic, serving the firm by protecting and building its value is tantamount to serving the shareholders. And, more directly, obviously the board has the fiduciary responsibility to serve the owners, the shareholders, while being legally responsible for the health of the firm.

But even if the board is therefore charged with a fiduciary responsibility to protect and build the firm's value, as that value represents benefit to the shareholders, it is not in fact an *agent* of the shareholders. In legal agency, the agent acts under the expressed or apparent authority of the principal. In other words, agents act under the actual or implied orders of their principals. But shareholders do not give either actual or implied orders to directors, except in a few limited contexts. Unlike political democracy, in which elected representatives are expected to be responsive to their constituents' expressed needs, shareholder democracy is a myth. Shareholders vote yes or no on director candidates usually selected by management; there is no real election. They vote yes or no on the selection of the corporation's auditor, not between auditor candidates. They vote yes or no on exceptionally small numbers of shareholder resolutions whose proposal is often strongly constrained by management and board actions. These resolutions are potentially similar to political referenda, but in only very rare cases are actually permitted to be real contests over substantive issues. The shareholders never actually give direction to the company, its managers, or its directors. They never influence business plans; never set goals for quarterly returns; never specify peak manager remuneration. The shareholders are not principals in anything other than a mythical agency relationship.

Thus, the relationship of the shareholder to the firm is fundamentally *normative* in character – as featured in the popular claim that the firm's purpose *should be* to benefit the shareholders. This translates into a board role that is essentially interpretative, rather than clearly and explicitly directive in content; the board *should* act in the shareholders' interests. Given the ambiguous, interpretative character of the normative instruction, board action becomes anchored more by *claims* of satisfaction of the normative prime directive, than of demonstrations of settled relationships between board action and shareholder benefit. The normative claim becomes the key rationale in supporting peak level decisions that may or may not benefit the firm, and may or may not actually be in the best interests of the shareholders. In a world in which benefit is interpreted, the role of the board is to shape perceptions so that observers believe that the board is doing what it *should* be doing.

The argument logically defaults to the question of what directors actually do, if what they are legally constrained to do is general and fundamentally ambiguous, and if their normative obligations are essentially interpreted, discretionary and, hence, debatable. And here we see the revisionist critics who see boards as rubber stamps of management; as holders of well-paid sinecures; as apologists for whatever management wants to do. Boards do nothing because managers want them to do nothing, and thus the board is in essence a creature of management (but cf. Mizruchi, 1983 on subtleties in board/management control). Indeed, there is evidence that highly-compensated boards tend to be more tolerant of subpar performance by also highly-compensated peak managers (e.g., Morgenson, 2006). This is the *descriptive* role of the board – how it actually works in practice.

But surely, the argument develops, boards are *useful*; they have a *utilitarian* role. That is, boards are constituted or function in ways that promote the good health and success of the corporate enterprise. If they are indeed creatures of management, then surely they may be made to function as assistants in managing the firm. As noted later in this paper, the original name for the member (director) of the entity that was equivalent to a board in the first joint-stock companies was *assistant*. The chair of the board, taking the role of today's CEO, was the *governor*. The original boards were thus set up nominally as managers of the companies – a company was run by a governor and his assistants. Unlike today's firm, the absence of a professional managerial corps certainly gave relevance to this nomenclature. We will also see later, however, that even at that time the peak organization of the firm provided assurance.

Therefore, boards, and their directors, may be said to perform *functions* that extend and assist the productive activities of the firm as a whole. Indeed, boards may be ascribed as performing such roles as part of the rationalization for the firm's expenditure on them and/or the selection of particular board members, and it may also be found descriptively that directors sometimes do indeed assist the firm by performing these functions. Thus, directors can be chosen as product or industry or operational experts; directors can serve as liaisons to important stakeholder groups; directors can be the mouthpiece or representative for key ownership or stakeholder interests; directors can be the means of developing or introducing new business opportunities; directors can be tools to exert political influence on key government agencies or regimes; directors can be vehicles to co-opt enemies of the firm; directors can be a means of shaping and/or manipulating the external image of the firm; directors can by their nature or activities give legitimacy to what the firm does and explain its relevance, importance, and/or appropriateness to external stakeholders.

So it is apparent that directors can be convenient helpers in managing the firm. But surely there are other helpers out there. And surely the managers themselves can do lots of this helpful work. Why is the board used for this? Is there something fundamental about the board so that it is particularly, especially the right agent to do all this? Why not hire an external auditor to do the work of the audit committee in reporting to the CEO? Why not just use the firm's own bookkeepers and financial records and forget the use of any agent at all? Why not hire a consultant to advise the CEO on remuneration? Why not hire a nonprofit to advise him or her on social responsibility issues? In other words, *the important thing is not the useful work, but why the board and not others are asked to do it.*

The answer to this is the central argument of this paper: Boards do it because they are the best means available to provide *assurance*. What is key is not what they do, but how it is interpreted. What boards do is taken as the credible expression of the person of the corporation.

Assurance in the Theory of Testaments

According to the theory of testaments (Mitnick, 1996, 1999, 2000; on the institutional theory of agency, see Mitnick, 1973, 1975; on institutional theory in general, see, e.g., Scott, 1992; DiMaggio & Powell, 1983; Meyer & Rowan, 1977), organizational systems continually face problems in assigning belief to the statements, or *testaments*, of their current or proposed members. A set of standard mechanisms exists to solve such problems. We can understand certain otherwise problematic aspects of organizational relationships by interpreting them in terms of the means by which they provide *assurance* that the beliefs proposed to organizational principals are ones that should be held, i.e., that those beliefs are *credible*.

Agents provide *reports* of past behaviors or achievements, *claims* of current competencies, and *predictions* of future accomplishments as means to generate credibility in principals. Parallel to the supply of these statements are social processes of *verification of reports*, *validation of claims*, and *confirmation of predictions* used by principals to evaluate these statements. The processes of evaluation can be costly, given that agents may dissemble, the social world is complex, and principals are challenged by their lack of expertise to evaluate some statements (what the literature terms adverse selection) and by any inability to observe the claimed behaviors of agents (what the literature terms moral hazard). In general, reports are preferred to claims, which are in turn preferred to predictions – we know the past, find it costly to be sure of the present, and cannot be sure of the future.

As a result of the challenges of undertaking these processes of evaluation, and because the resources available to perform such evaluation tend to be limited, *principals tend toward minimizing the assurance load*. One way of economizing on assurance costs is making use of the structure of the statements made to the principal. Principals will look for shortcuts to evaluation. They will look to see if statements by third-party observers about the performance of the agents they are evaluating back one another up. The minimum number of such parallel statements is obviously two. Statements can be evaluated directly on content, indirectly by subsequent experience with the agent or the matters about which statements are made, or by features of the social relationship that the principal simply chooses to associate with high performance (Darby & Karni 1973).

In general, assurance can be provided by qualities of the agent that the principal associates with the likelihood of reliable high performance, or qualities of the relationship of agent and principal, or of the system of agent–principal action or interaction, e.g., their organizational setting, also presumed to be related to high performance. I call the first case, qualities of the agent, *agentic assurance*, and the second case, qualities of the agent–principal relationship or the organizational setting in which they interact, *agencic assurance*, i.e., it is anchored in the agen*cy* relationship or relationships rather than in the agent alone.

In general, *agentic assurance* precedes *agencic assurance* when organizational systems are founded and are growing because demonstrating the reliability of systems takes time; the reports needed for verification of performance need to be generated as current behavior becomes past behavior. But agents come with personal histories; they can bring their reports with them. And it is relatively easy to reward the agents directly for such service, thus making it directly in the self-interest of agents to serve in this role. Finally, agents may see opportunities to shape the new organizational system to provide continuing benefits to themselves. Hence, new systems typically feature the engagement of well-known agents.

I will make use of this approach in discussing the nature of boards.

The Governance Paradox

In this section I offer an admittedly speculative argument, also rooted in institutional theory (e.g., Scott, 1992; DiMaggio & Powell, 1983; Meyer & Rowan, 1977), that can help provide the social scientific basis for the claim that the primary role of the board is assurance.

We start with the assumption that people will act rationally with mixed motives that include, at least in part, self-interest, and that the mix of motives may differ among people. It is not necessary to require the economic assumption of purely self-interested behavior. Human cognition features now well-described characteristic biases that are perpetuated both by patterns of human information processing and judgment and by limited and costly availability of information on current states in the world, and, of course, uncertainty about future conditions (e.g., Fiske & Taylor, 1991). Resources of all kinds are in general limited, and, as a result, humans face opportunity costs and are rationally motivated to reduce the costs of any action. As a result, humans with cognitive limits must socially construct the world they navigate. In other words, the social world that is perceived and acted upon is known to be imperfectly known, and actors attempt to use whatever means are available to economize on the specification of the elements in that perceived world. In other words, people are "cognitive misers."

Furthermore, collectives face problems in directing and coordinating action, resolving disputes over appropriate actions, representing their needs and achievements to key external stakeholders from whom support is necessary to reach collective aims, and so on, that can be solved by delegation to a dictator. Collectives also face problems in joint action at least partly because of incentive problems, i.e., collective action dilemmas (Olson, 1965). The jointly shared benefits of collective action take on the character of public or collective goods, so that individuals see the opportunity of free-riding on the contributions of others to the achievement of the joint benefits. In addition, there are negotiation costs in reaching accommodation among multiple actors with differing motives and cognitions. The use of a central dictator to monitor and direct contributions, and sanction failures to contribute, can solve the problems.

With these given conditions, all human collectives must manage an inherent paradox. It is always less costly to delegate direction of a collective enterprise to a single executive, or "dictator." Dictators resolve the issues of who gives what directions, resolve coordination, representation, and negotiation issues, and by their nature do not suffer from collective action dilemmas. But like all actors, dictators are at least partly self-interested. Given that resources are limited, dictators will apportion at least some resources to uses preferred by the dictator, i.e., that benefit the dictator, and that otherwise might provide increased benefits to other actors. Hence, all human collectives are subject to the threat of abusive leadership, i.e., leadership that takes more than proportional benefits to themselves or their pet or preferred projects.

Other members of the collective can devote resources to monitoring the dictator to check for abuse, but, given resource limits, it is impractical to do that if other alternatives to constrain the dictator are available. In particular, it is rational to economize on monitoring by delegating the monitoring task to professional agents who specialize in that function. Of course, the logic is recursive – there is then the problem of monitoring the monitors, a problem that is typically left as residual in all human systems. At some point, actors decide that the return to further monitoring would be greater than the cost (the classic agency cost rationale) and simply walk away from the likely residual costs.

How many monitors of the dictator are needed? If there were a single monitor, what would stop that monitor from accepting a side payment from the dictator and concealing the abuse? In addition, how would a single monitor establish any standards for judging the performance of the dictator? The only comparison point is the dictator him- or herself. Given cognitive, information, and other resource limits, and in order to avoid the appearance of collusion, monitors will prefer to have at least one other monitor. Monitors can then compare judgments of the dictator, and check each other for collusion. Of course, the dictator can bribe both monitors – indeed, bribe any number of monitors up to the limit of the dictator's resources. That appears to be exactly what happens on the modern board, of course, given levels of director compensation in some firms (cf. Morgenson, 2006). But, in general, because the monitors are at least partly self-interested and will demand significant rewards, bribing is costly, and the dictator will desire both to retain his or her position and to reduce the scale of the side payments necessary to control the board of monitors. The costs of side payments, of judging, and of checking-up multiply as the number of monitors multiply. In addition, the possibility of political coalitions reduces the ability of any monitor to act as an effective controller; he or she can be outvoted. As Riker (1962) argued in his theory of political coalitions, if the pot of benefits is fixed, the individual benefits to members in the dominant or "winning" coalition go down with increase in the size of the coalition.

Note also that if the monitors wish to decide collectively on the performance of the dictator in order to implement corrective actions they must create a set of collective decision rules. If the rule is a voting rule, it may require that the board consist of an odd number of members in order to ensure that definitive outcomes occur from voting. This can lead to adjustments in the expected size of the board in order to facilitate decisions. Thus, both for judging/checking-up, and for decision certainty (voting purposes), and if the dictator (e.g., CEO) is a member of the board, as is commonly the case – indeed, it is hard to see how the potential dictator would willingly allow him or herself to be excluded from participation in the decision – the minimum board size is three. In fact, at least some state corporate chartering statutes have required that the minimum size of a board be three (e.g., Mace, 1971: 6).

In order to reduce the recursive costs of monitoring the monitors, the select, limited group of monitors can signal others in the organization, as well as external stakeholders, that they are not purely self-interested – we have, after all, assumed that the actors are mixed motive. In addition, they can signal others that they are competent to perform the monitoring roles assigned to them. If the dictator has bribed the board, he or she may also choose to signal observers that the monitors have qualities such that further monitoring is unnecessary. Thus, both to establish trust, and to conceal manipulation, the small group of monitors selected to serve on the board will be actors who can be advertised as being of exceptional character and distinction – both moral and competent (on prestige systems, see Goode, 1978).

Thus, it is typical for the board to display what I call a *pantheonic directorate*: a group of heroes chosen both to generate trust and to suggest the presence of exceptional talent in their positions. The pantheonic directorate is a mechanism of *agentic assurance*. Having only one or two pantheonic directors is not likely to be as compelling as a small group with a variety of characters generating trust as well as competencies. Because of uncertainty about the necessary tasks of the organization, the nature of any potential abuses by the dictator, and the possibly changing preferences of corporate observers, it will be rational to treat the virtues and competencies of the pantheonic directorate as a portfolio. Hence, we often expect to see more than three directors, but fewer than the number that will begin to generate excessive comparison, checking-up, and negotiation costs, as well as excessive side-payment costs, and reduced coalition member benefits.

Moreover, the directorate will be recognized, collectively, as a *pantheon* – as a group of similarly heroic actors, not merely for their individually-claimed qualifications. The use of specially qualified social groups that, in acting as agents, provide trust and engender confident belief in performance, is well-described in the literature. Thus, I suggest that boards of directors, when constituted as pantheonic directorates, provide social functions understandable in the context of Landa's (1981, 1994) ethnically homogeneous middleman groups: They display recognizable, if ascribed rather than demonstrated, qualities that set them apart as a distinct class and cause observers to trust their claims. Thus, the board should be seen not as a set of directors with advertised distinctions, but as a *directorate*. It is the collective that provides the assurance, not its individual members. The qualities ascribed to the individual members transfer to the collective, and are so perceived.

Note one logical objection to the creation of pantheonic directorates as signaling devices to generate assurance that the dictator is not abusing his or her powers: Why wouldn't the dictator him- or herself simply display the same trust-generating, heroic characteristics as the members of the board? Having a trustworthy dictator removes the need for a monitoring board. The answer is that dictators in fact do shape their reputations so as to emphasize their roles as heroically competent servants of the collective. And were dictators truly observant of the fiduciary norm, acting solely to benefit their principals, with competence and dedication, and, more importantly, if dictators could actually convince observers that they were indeed saintly agents, then the demand for a board would be less. But although societal members do in fact create perfect mythical agents such as Santa Claus to perform such tasks as deflecting the recipient's obligations of reciprocity away from the actual gift-giver (Hagstrom, 1966), it is generally understood that real-world agents are likely not perfect. There is scant belief that the term "benevolent dictator" is little other than an oxymoron. Hence, even the most manipulative dictators will create boards to nominally supervise and/or advise them because they know that societal members will expect and, indeed, demand them.

Boards that are constituted to display the virtues and competencies of the directors must communicate those conditions, else there is no purpose in so doing. Moreover, boards that are "captured" by the dictator via side payments are likely to emphasize these qualities more than functional boards, in order to shield the dictator from discovery (cf. the use of public interest rhetoric to shield public agents; Mitnick, 1975). Managers of firms in unstable environments who cannot control firm outcomes will manipulate causal attributions to create the impression of control (Salancik & Meindl, 1984). Adoption of symbolic actions in corporate governance can protect management and deter interventions (Westphal & Zajac, 1998; on symbolic roles of boards and peak managers, see also Zajac & Westphal, 1995; Westphal & Zajac, 1994; on the use of director reputations to protect peak manager control, see Zajac & Westphal, 1996). In other words, selection and management of board membership can generate *assurance* for stockholders and other important stakeholders that the firm's management is performing well and should be retained.

I conclude that all human collectives – organizations both profit and nonprofit, and both public and private – require and will be headed, paradoxically, by both a single and a collective head: an executive and a board of limited size but advertised as of exceptional virtue and competence. And the board's chief problem will be finding economical ways of ensuring that the executive does not abuse his or her executive powers, indeed, that the state of the organization and its actions are just what the executive says they are, i.e., the board, which itself provides *agentic assurance* to observers, faces the problem of achieving internal *agencic assurance*. Hence, the major problem of the board is *assurance*. I term the paradox of requirement of both single and multiple executives in the same organization, the *Governance Paradox (GP)*. The Governance Paradox exists as a paradox not because of some logical conflict between an individual dictator and a group of individual directors, but because of the conflict between an individual dictator and a collective entity, the directorate.

Note that versions of the Governance Paradox were implicitly realized and extensively discussed in the classic literature on the design of democratic states and, particularly, in the debates over the US Constitution. Madison's *Federalist Papers* (see, e.g., numbers 47 and 51) (Hamilton, Madison, & Jay, 1788/1961/2003) discuss the desirability of having a separation of powers as Montesquieu advocated, with a system of checks and balances built among the pieces.

Consider now the very first English joint-stock company, the ancestor of all our modern corporations, the Russia or Muscovy Company in the sixteenth century in Tudor England.

The Russia Company

If the argument based in assurance is correct, then the history of the firm ought to be best understood as the development of assurance structures and processes. I will offer one such historical case, reviewing the circumstances of the Russia or Muscovy Company, the first English joint-stock company, often considered the first joint-stock company of the modern era, and the ancestor of all modern corporations (on the evolution of the joint-stock company, which had roots in the medieval guilds, joint-stock companies in Italy, and other sources, see Scott, 1912/1968).

By the mid-sixteenth century, the major commercial entities engaged in international commerce were *regulated companies* (see Warren, 1923; Hein, 1963; see, e.g., the Merchant Adventurers of Bristol, Sacks, 1985). These companies maintained and, indeed, often defended regulations governing the behaviors of their members in particular kinds of trade. In addition, they often sought and were granted monopolies under Royal charter to trade in certain overseas markets or geographical regions and/or in certain kinds of goods. Hence, the effective "regulations" extended from company-governed control of members to structuring of the company's trading activities. In general, the company owned little or no property itself; all activities were those of members using their own property and bearing full risks in the use of that property. Thus, although ships of members of a company might all be engaged in, say, the cloth trade, the loss of any ship and its cargo in the course of that trade would be borne solely by the ship's owner, i.e., the company member. Thus, "the trading ventures themselves were not corporate ventures, but were the ventures of the members" (Warren, 1923: 509).

In contrast, the joint-stock company acted for the company itself. Founding members of the Russia Company were required to pay an initial subscription of £25; additional mandatory payments were later imposed on members. The stock issued for these payments was transferable, usually within families. The advantage of the joint-stock format was that risk was spread over all the members; loss of a ship was a company loss, not the loss to a particular merchant owner. Similarly, profits would be distributed to all. Ventures of a regulated company were often constructed from scratch by a group of members; when complete, the effort was dissolved. In a joint-stock company, ventures could be mounted on a continuing basis because any venture did not depend on individual decisions of members to participate in the particular venture and bear the risks of that venture. Thus, although the regulated company would have a charter, a seal displaying its corporate identity, and a continuing, even perpetual existence (although charters of limited duration were common, and the means to perpetual status changed over time in English law), the joint-stock company made it possible to have perpetual ventures – a true, continuing enterprise (Hein, 1963; see Scott, 1912/1968, vol. 1: 7–8, on the origin of self-perpetuating governance in guilds via by-laws and a variously-named leadership group, e.g., a governor, magister, master, alderman, associates, among other titles, that became the governor and his assistants in the joint-stock company).

Note that a joint-stock company separates the property of members from the members' direct control, just as it insulates them from the risk of total loss of property. Thus, members would reasonably require assurance that their property still belonged to them in the form of the joint-stock company assets, and that it was being employed properly to generate value for them. There is little need for assurance in a regulated company; each merchant, in effect, supplied his own assurance of the venture. That was not so any more in the joint-stock company. A credible means had to be established to take care of the joint assets, and to assure members of the proper use of those assets.

The charter of the Russia Company was granted on February 26, 1555 (Willan 1953/1973: 9), a date that might well be celebrated as the birthday of the modern corporation. It gave the company a monopoly in the Russian trade (on the beginnings of trade between England and Russia, the first business venture of the modern joint-stock company, see Willan, 1948; Wretts-Smith, 1920) and specified that it would be run by one or two governors, four "consuls," and 24 "assistants" who would take actions "for the government, good condition, and laudable rule" of the company (Willan, 1953/1973: 9). The first governor, Sebastian Cabot, was appointed for life, but the other officers were appointed annually and chosen by all the members, and Cabot's successors were also to be chosen each year. Unusual for companies of the era was that some of the members did not take an active part in the company's affairs; they merely held stock. In some cases, this may have constituted a political reward associated with formation of the company and maintenance of political influence. But it also represented a sea-change in the nature of a for-profit corporation – there could be a class of nonmanagerial shareholders who enjoyed the residual from the company's revenues (on the growth of nonmerchant shareholders in joint-stock companies, see Rabb 1966). These shareholders would be even more distant than those members who simply handed over assets yet still participated. And these distant owners would require a higher standard of reporting – of assurance – that the value they had in the company was being handled properly. Thus, as the owners became more distant, the need for assurance increased. And as the owners became more distant from the managers – the governor, consuls, and assistants – not observing them directly or frequently or even knowing them personally – the need to communicate to those owners that the governor and his helpers were competent and reliable increased.

At the time of the creation of the Russia Company, most of the ships carrying trade with England were of foreign nationality (Stone, 1949). The English merchant marine was in deteriorating condition in the decades of the mid-sixteenth century. In the later Elizabethan era, much of the trade conducted by the Russia or Muscovy Company was in critical naval supplies such as rope. With the assistance of the Crown, the Russia Company used the largest and best-defended English ships (Stone, 1949: 55). Thus, besides the lure of riches from potential trade with Cathay, as well as from the opening of new markets such as Russia, a key motivation for royal support of commercial activity, including the Russia Company, became military (Scott, 1912/1968, vol. 1: 29–30; Stone, 1947: 112).

The motivation for riches attracted participants both to the regulated companies and to the joint-stock company. Thus, the stakeholders that needed assurance regarding the performance of the Russia Company extended beyond its members to the Crown itself. It is perhaps not that much of a stretch to analogize the circumstance to that of a modern-era sole-source defense contractor, allowed to retain monopoly-like profits in return for assured delivery of critical military systems.

The Russia Company attracted some of the most distinguished and competent commercial leaders of its era. The first governor, Sebastian Cabot, was perceived to be a master pilot and the renowned explorer of the New World. Gerson (1912: 3) writes that Cabot "enjoyed a singular prestige" and was "regarded with respect not unmingled with awe by the younger generation of merchants and navigators." The true extent of Cabot's early exploration activities remain unknown, however; his father, John Cabot, made three voyages in search of the northwest passage and the son may have had a role in one or more of them. It appears that he did conduct at least one expedition to North America around 1508–1509, and later he explored Brazil's coast for Spain (on Sebastian Cabot's exploration, see, e.g., Sandman & Ash, 2004; Biddle, 1831/1915; Williamson, 1913/1972, 1929, 1962). At any rate, he was said to possess unique navigational skills honed in Spain; he was described as "the good olde and famuse man master Sebastian Cabola" (Sandman & Ash, 2004: 841; see also Ash, 2002). Cabot's reputation in England was as a master navigator in what was incorrectly perceived as the model Spanish approach to navigation, blending both practical navigational skills and the use of cosmography. But the approach was not actually the dominant one in Spain, and the reputation of this approach was apparently deliberately shaped by Cabot himself both for his benefit and as an adaptation that he judged superior to actual Spanish practice and more suited to the needs of English pilots (Sandman & Ash

2004). He was in such demand that he could negotiate to enter a country's service while still serving another, yet not lose support from his existing employer (see, e.g., Biddle, 1831/1915; Gerson, 1912; Willan, 1953/1973, 1959; Williamson, 1913/1972, 1929, 1962).

At the time of the charter of the Russia Company, Cabot was comparativeld old for those times, being in his mid or late 70s. He died in 1557, only two years after the granting of the Company's charter. Cabot is credited with specifying detailed plans and instructions for the initial Russia Company expedition in 1553 (which pre-dated the granting of the charter) – so detailed, in fact, as to be a manual for Company trading practices in general. He has in addition been credited with the actual design of the joint-stock company itself (Scott, 1912, vol. 1: 18; Warren, 1923: 510). But it can also be argued that, in his 70s, he was chosen at least partly for the assurance that the "master pilot" of England would be in charge. Indeed, during the sixteenth century, the demand for scarce mercantile knowledge had begun to spawn a class of what Ash (2002) calls "mercantile advisors." Cabot was of this class, but he was not the only one. Williamson (1962: 171–2) writes that in his old age Cabot was no longer the manipulative plotter that he had been: "In his old age, in his last ten years in England, he was a different man, liked, trusted, looked up to." One story has him celebrating at a shipboard party, near the end of his life. There is a reference to a visitor seeing him "when his health began to fail and his mind to wander" (p. 171). Why give over control for life of a commercial enterprise critical to the defense of England to a jovial and perhaps forgetful man in his 70s? Why not use a different "mercantile advisor," a younger one with both current knowledge and greater physical capacity? Was the choice of Cabot more assurance than substance?

The members of the Russia Company constituted a list that was "heavy at the top. The presence of so many peers and holders of high office was quite unprecedented" (Willan, 1953/1973: 10). This may have been directly because of royal interest in the company as high-status individuals followed the Crown, indirectly as wealthy and high-ranking men became active merchant members because they perceived a good business opportunity made safer by involvement of the state, because nonmerchants saw the state-sanctioned and protected opportunity for passive profit, and importantly because of the need to provide assurance that the Company was sound and reliable – men of wealth and rank will attract other men of wealth and rank to membership. Thus, we may speculate (the names of the assistants are not all recorded) that the leadership of the Company – the consuls and assistants – in addition to the rank-and-file members must also have been assurance-producing individuals of relatively high rank and high wealth.

Notice that the solutions to the assurance problem were redundant. This is a typical feature of assurance mechanisms. Assurance for the Muscovy

Company included a governor, Cabot, with both undisputed past achievements and current claims of competencies (some of both self-promoted) unrivaled among contemporary mariners. The assistants and consuls were of unusually high status. Thus, the Company featured what we have called *agentic assurance*. The structure and processes of the Company also provided assurance. The Company appeared to benefit from a special relationship with the Crown. The military nature of its trade in rope and other naval supplies meant that it might be protected by the state from the worst business failures. The state also ensured that its ships were the best available, and heavily defended. The governor was not set up as a permanent dictatorial role – only Cabot could hold the post indefinitely, and the literature suggests that dual governors were used from time to time in the years after. Cabot provided a widely-heralded set of instructions or plan for the initial voyages; they were unusually detailed and seemed to be aimed at laying out a continuing model for managing the company's trading practices, not only for the first voyages. The consuls and assistants provided a hierarchical group to watch for abuses as well as assist in management. All of these facets provided assurance that the Company was what it purported to be and could do what it claimed it could do. In other words, the design of the Muscovy Company also provided *agencic assurance*. Thus, via a system of redundant assurances, i.e., reassurances, the Company made a credible case for itself.

The trading companies of the era became so successful that the scale of their transactions generated growing internal managerial hierarchies, headed, of course, by the governor and the board of assistants; the modern corporation was appearing (on the beginnings of hierarchy and the chartered trading company as a way to economize on transaction costs, see Carlos & Nicholas, 1988). A "culture of commerce" developed in the seventeenth century (Glaisyer, 2006). The mechanisms of assurance became institutionalized. Over time, the management structures of this first modern joint-stock company, which successfully provided assurance and reassurance, were copied and elaborated (cf. DiMaggio & Powell 1983 on mimetic processes in modern organizations). The first modern corporation was also the first to be composed in a way that generated the assurances essential to its success.

Agent Capitalism as a Solution
to the Problem of False Assurance

The chief problem of modern governance is the provision of *false assurance*.

In the modern era, the firm has evolved from the owner-managed classical firm designed to provide the assurance of profit to the owner, to the managerial firm seeking assurances to overcome the Berle and Means problem of separation of ownership from management (on the Berle and Means problem and for an insightful discussion of the analysis of owner-ship, control, and corporate power, see Mizruchi, 2004). The solution to that problem that provided assurance, the alignment of incentives between owners and managers, usually mediated by the board, did not actually solve the problem, despite its assurance-producing character. Indeed, the persist-ence of reliance on alignment reflects the acceptance of particular assur-ance and reassurance mechanisms, e.g., ownership benefits to managers, not the actual and permanent resolution of the problem. Thus we have faced a critical disjunction – on the one hand, we see the insistence that certain elements of corporate peak management that focus on incentive alignment *must* be effective because it is credible that they would work, and, on the other hand, we see dramatic, repeated demonstrations that the problem of management abuse of discretion remains. In fact, perhaps ironically, it is the assurance, rather than the actual mechanism of alignment that suppos-edly solves the Berle–Means problem, that works and permits the persist-ence of systems that are obviously broken.

The corporate scandals of recent years demonstrate dramatically how disconnected assurance mechanisms are from actual performance. The solution I offer is a fundamental re-thinking of how to design the firm to provide both assurance and actual performance. The firm must move from managerial capitalism to what I term *agent capitalism.*

In this new model, the CEO is no longer to be treated as the delegated agent of the board, hired to generate wealth for the owners that the board represents, but the agent of the firm itself – as officers of the corporation are supposed to be. The directors remain as nominal fiduciaries *of* the owners, but are now to be governed more nearly as actual agents, under the actual direction of the owners in a variety of important contexts, not as principals creating agents *in* the owners, whose wealth is used to line the pockets of peak officials. In essence, the basis of previous assurance was the nominal character of the fiduciary responsibility of the board. Once the board became dominated by the CEO, the actual direction of agency was flipped – the shareholders had little capability to either give direction to their supposed agents or to influence expectations of the firm's performance and of the nature of the firm's managers' rewards that were supposedly tied to that performance. Proxies were little more than rubber stamps.

The direction of agency must be flipped back to where it belongs. Under the alignment model that dominated managerial capitalism, top managers were supposedly incentivized to run the firm effectively, generating wealth for the owners, by being able to share in that wealth – the board gave those managers rewards like stock options that, by moving in the same direction as the rewards the owners received, were supposed to ensure that the managers worked as hard as possible in the owner's behalf.

But the rewards based in the alignment theory did not create managers who ran the firm more effectively so as to generate owner wealth; rather, they simply created a second class of owners (Mitnick, 2002; cf. Englander & Kaufman, 2004). The existing assurance mechanisms essentially disguised the fact that managers were taking rewards as owners rather than managing the firm so as to generate rewards for all the owners, not just the manager-owners.

Thus the solution is just the opposite of alignment: Managers must derive their primary rewards from the actions of management, not of ownership; and the board must respect proxy access and be run as the true agent of the owners. The solution to the alignment problem was itself a major cause of an alignment problem – an alignment that set peak managers up as owners, while permitting them to exploit the wealth of the firm, i.e., divert the wealth of the actual owners, the distributed shareholders, into their own pockets. This distorting alignment must be re-oriented, so that peak managers do not, in fact, have incentives that are both aligned with the true owners and draw on the same sources of wealth, accessible to, and manipulable by, the peak managers. Thus, the fix is to establish a system of real agencies – managers' agency for the firm, and directors' agency for the true owners, not just a system of top manager dominance in which the institutions of assurance display a bogus agency and cloak what is in effect a taking. By creating a true agent capitalism, the firm's assurance mechanisms can finally reflect performances rather than mere appearances.

References

Ash, Eric H. 2002. "A note and a caveat for the merchant": Mercantile advisors in Elizabethan England. *Sixteenth Century Journal*, 33(1): 1–31.

Biddle, Richard. 1831/1915. *A Memoir of Sebastian Cabot; with a Review of the History of Maritime Discovery*. Philadelphia, PA: Carey and Lea; reprinted by J.B. Lippincott Co.

Carlos, Ann M. and Stephen Nicholas. 1988. "Giants of an earlier capitalism": The chartered trading companies as modern multinationals. *Business History Review*, 62(3) (Autumn): 398–419.

Darby, M.R. and E. Karni. 1973. Free competition and the optimal amount of fraud. *Journal of Law and Economics*, 16(1): 67–88.

DiMaggio, P.J. and W.W. Powell. 1983. The iron cage revisited: Institutional isomorphism and collective rationality in organizational fields. *American Journal of Sociology*, 48: 147–60.

Englander, E. and A. Kaufman. 2004. The end of managerial ideology: From corporate social responsibility to corporate social indifference. *Enterprise & Society*, 5(3): 404–50.

Fiske, Susan T. and Shelley E. Taylor. 1991. *Social Cognition*. New York: McGraw-Hill.

Gerson, Armand J. 1912. *The Organization and Early History of the Muscovy Company*. In *Studies in the History of English Commerce in the Tudor Period*. New York: D. Appleton and Co., for the University of Pennsylvania.

Glaisyer, Natasha. 2006. *The Culture of Commerce in England, 1660–1720*. Woodbridge, Suffolk, UK and Rochester, NY: The Royal Historical Society/ The Boydell Press.

Goode, William J. 1978. *The Celebration of Heroes: Prestige as a Control System*. Berkeley, CA: University of California Press.

Hagstrom, Warren O. 1966. What is the meaning of Santa Claus? *The American Sociologist*, 1(5): 248–52.

Hamilton, Alexander, James Madison, and John Jay. 1788/1961/2003. *The Federalist Papers*. New York: Signet Classic/Penguin.

Hein, Leonard W. 1963. The British business company: Its origins and its control. *University of Toronto Law Journal*, 15(1): 134–54.

Klein, Daniel B. 2001. The demand for and supply of assurance. *Economic Affairs* 21(1), March 2001: 4–11. Reprinted (expanded version) in T. Cowen and E. Crampton (eds), *Market Failure or Success: The New Debate*. Cheltenham, UK: Edward Elgar, 2003, pp. 172–92.

Landa, Janet T. 1981. A theory of the ethnically homogeneous middleman group: An institutional alternative to contract law. *Journal of Legal Studies*, 10: 349–62.

Landa, Janet T. 1994. *Trust, Ethnicity, and Identity*. Ann Arbor, MI: University of Michigan Press.

Mace, Myles L. 1971. *Directors: Myth and Reality*. Boston: Harvard Business School.

Meyer, John W. and Brian Rowan. 1977. Institutionalized organizations: Formal structure as myth and ceremony. *American Journal of Sociology*, 83(2) (September): 340–63.

Mitnick, B.M. 1973. Fiduciary rationality and public policy: The theory of agency and some consequences. Paper presented at the 1973 Annual Meeting of the American Political Science Association, New Orleans, LA. *Proceedings of the APSA, 1973* (University Microfilms).

Mitnick, Barry M. 1975. The theory of agency: The policing "paradox" and regulatory behavior. *Public Choice*, 24 (Winter): 27–42.

Mitnick, Barry M. 1985. Agents of legitimacy: Pantheonic directorates and the management of organization environments. Paper presented at the Fifth Annual Sunbelt Social Networks Conference, Palm Beach, FL, February

14–17. Also, Graduate School of Business Working Paper Series, WP-606 (University of Pittsburgh, February 1985). Revised version presented at the 46th Annual Meeting of the Academy of Management, Chicago, IL, August 13–16, 1986.

Mitnick, Barry M. 1996. The theory of testaments. *Proceedings of the International Association for Business and Society, 1996*. Santa Fe, NM.

Mitnick, Barry M. 1999. Credible testaments, property, and the role of government. In Warren J. Samuels and Nicholas Mercuro (eds), *The Fundamental Interrelationships Between Government and Property*, vol. 4 of *The Economics of Legal Relationships* Stamford, CT: JAI Press, pp. 165–76.

Mitnick, Barry M. 2000. Commitment, revelation, and the testaments of belief: The metrics of measurement of corporate social performance. *Business & Society*, 39(4) (December): 419–65.

Mitnick, Barry M. 2002. Agent capitalism. Dinner address to the Katz Graduate School of Business Board of Visitors, University of Pittsburgh, October 17, at the Pittsburgh Athletic Association, Pittsburgh, PA.

Mizruchi, Mark S. 1983. Who controls whom? An examination of the relation between management and boards of directors in large American corporations. *Academy of Management Review*, 8(3): 426–35.

Mizruchi, Mark S. 2004. Berle and Means revisited: The governance and power of large US corporations. *Theory and Society*, 33: 579–617.

Monks, Robert A.G. and Nell Minow. 2004. *Corporate Governance*, 3rd edn. Malden, MA: Blackwell Publishing.

Morgenson, Gretchen. 2006. Behind every underachiever, an overpaid board? *The New York Times* (January 22, 2006): 3.1.

Olson, Mancur, Jr. 1965. *The Logic of Collective Action: Public Goods and the Theory of Groups*. New York and Cambridge, MA: Schocken Books and Harvard University Press.

Rabb, Theodore K. 1966. Investment in English overseas enterprise, 1575–1630. *The Economic History Review*, 19(1): 70–81.

Rao, Hayagreeva. 1994. The social construction of reputation: Certification contests, legitimation, and the survival of organizations in the American automobile industry: 1895–1912. *Strategic Management Journal*, 15(Special): 29–44.

Rao, Hayagreeva, Henrich R. Greeve, and Gerald F. Davis. 2001. Fool's gold: Social proof in the initiation and abandonment of coverage by Wall Street analysts. *Administrative Science Quarterly*, 46: 502–26.

Riker, William H. 1962. *The Theory of Political Coalitions*. New Haven, CT: Yale University Press.

Sacks, David Harris. 1985. *Trade, Society and Politics in Bristol, 1500–1640*, vols I and II. New York: Garland Publishing.

Salancik, G.R. and J.R. Meindl. 1984. Corporate attributions as strategic illusions of management control. *Administrative Science Quarterly*, 29(2): 238–54.

Sandman, A. and E.H. Ash. 2004. Trading expertise: Sebastian Cabot between Spain and England. *Renaissance Quarterly*, 57(3): 813–46.

Scott, W. Richard. 1992. *Organizations: Rational, Natural, and Open Systems*. Englewood Cliffs, NJ: Prentice-Hall.

Scott, William Robert. 1912/1968. *The Constitution and Finance of English, Scottish and Irish Joint- Stock Companies to 1720* (reprint ed.). Gloucester, MA: Peter Smith.

Shapiro, Susan P. 1987. The social control of impersonal trust. *American Journal of Sociology*, 93(3): 623–58.

Stone, Lawrence. 1947. State control in sixteenth-century England. *Economic History Review*, 17(2): 103–20.

Stone, Lawrence. 1949. Elizabethan overseas trade. *Economic History Review*, 2(1): 30–58.

The Corporate Library. 2007. *Director Pay 2006–2007*. Portland, ME: The Corporate Library.

Warren, Edward H. 1923. Safeguarding the creditors of the corporation. *Harvard Law Review*, 36(5) (March): 509–47.

Westphal, James D. and Edward J. Zajac. 1994. Substance and symbolism in CEOs' long-term incentive plans. *Administrative Science Quarterly*, 39(3) (September): 367–90.

Westphal, James D. and Edward J. Zajac. 1998. The symbolic management of stockholders: Corporate governance reforms and shareholder reactions. *Administrative Science Quarterly*, 43(1) (March): 127–53.

Willan, T.S. 1948. Trade between England and Russia in the second half of the sixteenth century. *The English Historical Review*, 63(248): 307–21.

Willan, T.S. 1953/1973. *The Muscovy Merchants of 1555*. Manchester, UK: Manchester University Press; reprinted, Clifton, NJ: Augustus M. Kelley Publishers.

Willan, T.S. 1959. *Studies in Elizabethan Foreign Trade*. Manchester, UK: Manchester University Press.

Williamson, James A. 1913/1972. *Maritime Enterprise 1485–1558*. Oxford, UK: Oxford University Press; reprinted, New York: Octagon Books.

Williamson, James A. 1929. *The Voyages of the Cabots and the English Discovery of North America under Henry VII and Henry VIII*. London: The Argonaut Press.

Williamson, James A. 1962. *The Cabot Voyages and Bristol Discovery under Henry VII*. Cambridge, UK: Hakluyt Society at the University Press.

Wretts-Smith, M. 1920. The English in Russia during the second half of the sixteenth century. *Transactions of the Royal Historical Society*, 4th Ser., 3: 72–102.

Zajac, Edward J. and James D. Westphal. 1995. Accounting for the explanations of CEO compensation: Substance and symbolism. *Administrative Science Quarterly*, 40(2) (June), 283–308.

Zajac, Edward J. and James D. Westphal. 1996. Director reputation, CEO–board power, and the dynamics of board interlocks. *Administrative Science Quarterly*, 41(3) (September): 507–29.

Zald, Mayer N. 1969. The power and functions of boards of directors: A theoretical synthesis. *American Journal of Sociology*, 75(1): 97–111.

16

Risk Disclosure and Transparency: Toward Corporate Collective and Collaborative Informed Consent

Denise Kleinrichert and Anita Silvers

Abstract

Relationships of dependence, in which some parties assign custodianship of their interests to others, are a call for the exercise of trust-sustaining responsibility. Practices for executing such responsibility are found in many domains, but are more fully formed in some than in others. Here we examine the strengths and weaknesses of long-established trust-sustaining ethical practice in one domain to illuminate its applicability in another.

Medical care providers and their stakeholders engage jointly in the practice of informed consent which, as a condition for obtaining the benefits of treatment, spreads and shares responsibility for risk. Informed consent is relevant to formal, steward-based relationships such as the relationships between corporate entities and individual or groups of stakeholders. Noting that seeking informed consent from dependent parties became best practice in medicine following trust-shattering scandals, we examine the applicability in similar circumstances of the ethics of informed consent to the relationship between corporate boards and the stakeholders of a directing board's corporation.

We argue for the achievement of transparency in risk assumption through a collaborative process of informed consent, which differs from and supplements unilateral disclosure. We propose that the trust-bolstering responsibility to establish appropriate informed consent is owed by corporate boards to their multiplicity of stakeholders and is helpful to good corporate governance in this new global, or neocontinental, age of multinational corporate risk. We point out problems with some existing assumptions about informed consent in the medical domain and recommend conceptualizing corporate informed consent in a way that avoids or ameliorates them. The practice we recommend promotes the health and well-being of the firm's constituents and thereby secures sustainable relationships for corporate endeavors.

Introduction

A fundamental change is taking place in the source of value in businesses from hard assets to human assets, and this also complicates the board's stewardship in ways the governance discussion has yet to embrace. (Carter & Lorsch 2004: 29)

Responsible market endeavor calls for a careful consideration of all stakeholder relationships – with consumers, employees, communities, shareholders, suppliers, governments, the environment – in weighing risk factors. As stewards of the corporation and its stakeholders, corporate boards are expected to be expert in securing the best interests of dependent parties in their business sphere. In this regard, we draw conclusions about the role of corporate boards – inclusive of both their moral (i.e., human) and prudential (i.e., instrumental) practices as stewards. This best interest standard[1] promotes the health and well-being of the firm's constituents and secures sustainable relationships between them, not unlike the physician–patient relationship built on deference to expertise that is supported by the practice of informed consent. To illustrate, we analyze several examples, including Dial Corporation, Hewlett-Packard, and Starbucks Coffee Company, focusing on differences in how corporate boards have acted in imposing, or instead sharing, responsibility for risk.

Corporate boards faced with arrays of possibilities in managing economic, social, and environmental risk to their firms cannot avoid imposing some risks on their stakeholders and thereby affecting relationships with those subject to these choices. Their choices are reflected in the triple bottom line of economic, equity, and environmental status of the firm. To nourish sustainable relationships characterized by mutual acquiescence to risk, corporate boards should insist on corporate disclosure of either (or both) their firm's decisions, or its annual accounting of successes and failures, in a public statement.

In other words, boards must be sure there is a reasonably informative level of transparency that is inclusive of additional indicators of risk – corporate intentions, methods, goals and anticipated outcomes, including quantifiable data expressed in meaningful ways. Many corporate year-end statements now voluntarily reflect such previously undisclosed impacts on the environment, society, and potential avenues of corporate endeavors. The formalized published format of triple bottom line disclosure of information enables stakeholder consent to sustain stakeholder–corporate relationships on a voluntary corporate board initiative basis. We investigate in some detail how information may be presented to facilitate stakeholders' reasonable risk acceptance, characterizing the process as an opportunity to nourish trustful cooperative relationships rather than as an obstacle to corporate endeavors. We consider both risk framing and risk tradeoffs, and our examination of approaches to achieving the requisite level of informativeness invokes research from cognitive psychology to understand how individuals respond to and judge the prospect of risk.

The 2002 Sarbanes–Oxley Act includes regulatory disclosure requirements. However, by enabling rational stakeholder decision making, voluntary board initiatives that exercise professional responsibility for corporate disclosure acknowledge accountability for market risk and modulate the statutory regulations mandating protection of key stakeholders. We think of neglecting informed consent as an opportunity cost, that is, a lost option of gaining goodwill within the market system. The voluntary board initiative we recommend is beneficial in that compliance with disclosure regulations is transformed from merely perfunctory to powerfully productive. We consequently suggest that corporate boards "sin by omission" if they fail to share responsibility for risk through appropriate trust-building informative practice, such as eliciting informed consent about corporate activities sanctioned by the board of directors.

The control of a corporation is both a risk-bearing and also a risk-imposing process affecting stakeholder interests – risks arise from such sources as use of power, corporate strategy, competitors, managerial efforts, and how human resources are deployed. Directors of corporate boards are both the corporation's driving force toward corporate aims and, simultaneously, the agents of stakeholders who may not fully share these aims. As custodians of best knowledge about practices of the firm, directors, through processes of guidance, deliberation, and decision making, maintain and minister to the health of the corporate body. The components of this body are the stakeholders, whose own well-being rise or falls depending on the state of the corporation's health. Moreover, "the stakeholder view of corporate governance argues that all groups and/or individuals with legitimate interests in the company have the right to participate in the company's activities and gain a share of its economic success" (Erakovic, 2007: 475). Absent or lacking in sufficient information conveyed by the corporate board, stakeholders may feel compelled or even coerced into uninformed acceptance of decisions affecting their socioeconomic standing.

We suggest that the familiar standard of informed consent between health care providers and their patient illuminates both legally and morally mandated aspects of the relevant information disclosures between corporate directors and their stakeholders, an analogous relationship in which the party from whom consent is sought must depend on the party seeking consent to provide full and unbiased information. Without a doubt, the recent spate of public and legal pressures on corporate directors and executives in the practices of their professional roles, prompted by the corporate scandals of Enron, WorldCom, Hewlett-Packard and others, has brought the moral responsibility of maintaining corporate transparency to the foreground. We believe best practice regarding the risks taken and imposed by the decisions of corporate directors requires more than transparency. Productive cooperation is nourished by trust; consequently, best practice is to facilitate trust between corporate director and stakeholders. For example, Schoorman, Mayer, and Davis have argued that "trust would lead to risk taking in a relationship" because "trust is the willingness to take risk" (2007: 346). We thus hold that transparency is most conducive to trust-building if stakeholders understand corporate risk assumption sufficiently well to accept the possibility of loss as well as of gain.

Corporate directors impose risks on stakeholders, as medical professionals do on patients. We recommend that corporate directors aim to give their stakeholders a sound understanding of the risks as well as the benefits of prospective corporate policies, strategies or other important actions. Doing so, we argue, recasts assuming corporate risk as collaboration between directors and stakeholders. Through such collaboration, corporate directors explicitly share responsibility for risk-taking with stakeholders, thereby both strengthening the organization and mitigating the exposure inherent in their own corporate leadership role.

Directors' Responsibility and Questionable Risk

Questionable risk may be imposed on stakeholders through various means – such as convoluted investing, purchasing, and accounting procedures; obscure problem-solving methodologies; inadequate capital and overextended credit; lack of clear lines of communication; concealed decision making – and can affect corporate growth, globalization, research and development, and human assets, as well as individual careers, among other aspects of individual and corporation well-being. A prime example is the case of the Hewlett-Packard board chairperson Patricia Dunn authorizing, absent board approval, deceptive surveillance pretexts to gain access to managers', journalists' and other board members' telephone records. In trying to control a potential flow of insider leaks regarding HP's new technology, and despite knowing her actions risked legal prosecution and moral condemnation, she shattered the board's trust in her, but also the trust of stakeholders, including consumers, in the integrity of the company. The risk she took resulted in her own removal from the board, but also legal and ethics inquiries from the California Attorney General, the Securities and Exchange Commission (SEC), and the Federal Communications Commission (FCC). As a result, the Board hired a new Chief Ethics and Compliance Officer who reports directly to the board. This was more than a perfunctory move. Rather, the board directors instigated a voluntary, proactive board initiative to regain trust in the absence of previous transparency about corporate risk.

The collapse of companies such as Enron resulted in legal restrictions, disclosure requirements, and measures of accountability for corporate fiscal financial health. Corporate transactions must now be independently audited and publicly disclosed under the Sarbanes–Oxley Act of 2002. That this regulation is aimed at shoring up and backstopping fiduciaries' execution of their responsibilities is significant in that the demand to strengthen assurances for stakeholders has expanded the grounds for corporate malfeasance. This legislation seeks to restore stakeholder confidence by requiring reputable corporate behavior. An aim is that "the [legal] restrictions bestow on fiduciaries such as corporate directors and officers a reputation for honesty and help them gain the investors' trust" (Frankel, 2006: 122).

The directors of Enron, and subsequently WorldCom, agreed "to pay personal settlements to plaintiffs" [in the] amounts of $13 million and $18 million (Kerstetter & Schulken, 2005: 10). Although neither set of board directors admitted fault, or failure to exercise due diligence and moral oversight of their respective board duties to these corporations and their stakeholders, they used their pocketbooks to quell the aftermath of a loss of trust. This is what corporations often do – rather than issuing public statements of apology and acknowledging failures to adopt best practice, corporate decision makers offer compensation in the form of private monetary settlements. While resolving immediate liability problems, this approach does little to improve general confidence in the practices of the firm.

The fiduciary responsibility of board directors for decisions that covertly place stakeholders such as shareholders, employees, suppliers, and consumers in harm's way may not be a legally enforceable matter of director accountability. In 2005 the Delaware court stated in a shareholder lawsuit filed against the Disney board that although the actions of the directors "fell significantly short of the best practices of ideal corporate governance," the law "cannot hold fiduciaries liable for a failure to comply with the aspirational ideal of best practices" (*The Walt Disney Co*. Deriv. Litig., 825 A 2.d 275, 289 [Del. Ch 2005]). When company chairman Michael Eisner singularly authorized severance pay of $140 million for his friend Michael Ovitz despite the latter's short-term tenure as Disney president, shareholders claimed they had not been sufficiently informed prior to the payout (Frankel, 2006: 126–7; Kerstetter & Schulken, 2005: 10). Despite the shareholders' assertion of harm to both their investment and long-term commitment to Disney, the court failed to find intent on Eisner's part to commit harm. The court found that the hasty approval and initial concealment of the agreement did not rise to the standard of action that intentionally creates or allows harm. However, confidence in Eisner's capabilities as chairman at Disney suffered in the eyes of shareholders and other stakeholders. This case is an example of a violation of a trust relationship with stakeholders (i.e., suppliers, consumers, employees, communities). Board neglect of transparency can be a source of needless risk (Jackson & Nelson, 2004: 261). Lack of transparency can increase the likelihood of higher transaction costs for the firm, including financial liabilities, reduction of efficiencies and loss of resources, as well as loss of investor confidence and damage to directors' reputations for integrity and as trustworthy decision makers. On the corporate level, at least 73 percent of board directors stated their professional risk, as a direct liability, had increased during the course of 12 months ending in 2005 in a survey carried out by Pricewaterhouse-Coopers (Kerstetter & Schulken, 2005: 3). Some scholars of board director decision making point out that opaque negligent-duty director decision making increases exposure to a number of undesirable consequences: high legal costs, courtroom battles, government fines, increased regulatory oversight, negative media coverage and public relations scrutiny, consumer boycotts, lost market shares, loss of jobs and unemployment blame, loss of market reputation and trust (Jackson & Nelson, 2004: 262).

Risk and Relational Trust

We accept as a premise that "the goal of a company should be to maximize returns for a given level of risk" (Freeman & Gilbert, 1988: 118). We do not suppose that corporate boards can or should eliminate risk, or that they bear sole or primary responsibility for managing risk. What we urge instead is that corporate leadership takes the initiative in eliciting cooperative acknowledgement and acceptance of risk. We do so from the perspective of the ethics of trust, which is more central to productive cooperation than the ethics of rights and interests (Silvers & Francis, 2004). On this view, being trustworthy is a virtue, and violating trust by exploiting dependence is wrong. The ethics of trust commits interdependent cooperators to trust-enhancing practices that spread and share responsibility for risk. The ethics of trust focuses not on balancing the discrete interests and rights of different parties, but gives priority instead to pursuing parties' common interests, which may include risk-laden pursuit of benefits.

As Francis Fukuyama observes, people who do not trust each other can cooperate only under a system of rules that have to be negotiated, agreed to, and enforced. This legal apparatus imposes transaction costs, Fukuyama reminds us. Trust-enhancing systems can be more flexible and responsive to individualized situations than rule-enforcement systems, and the former do not impose operations costs on participants in the same way (Fukuyama, 1995: 27). In this paper we address risk and relational trust in regard to both imposed and voluntarily accepted risk.

Risk may be defined as a potential for harm or loss, or the probability that investment will have less than the expected or desired outcome. Risk has been closely identified with "uncertainty" (Sanders & Hambrick, 2007: 1057 *n.* 2) but is not identical to uncertainty (Knight, 1921: I.I.26). Risk to individuals engaged in business transactions is often exacerbated by violations of trust in exchange-based relationships. In business, exchange-based relationships are engaged in between individual stakeholders and the corporate agency of those both directing and managing the corporation. We are interested in how assuming corporate risk should involve stakeholders, and also in the personal risk that board directors accept as an aspect of their role.

Directors are charged with guiding the corporation toward goals that are intended to gain increased well-being of the firm. Increasing well-being often necessitates change, and change contributes to a climate of risk – or, put differently, change increases uncertainty about potential benefit/harm ratios. Corporate risk is of two types – systematic and unsystematic (Freeman & Gilbert, 1988: 193 *n.* 18). Systematic risk arises from the structuring of the corporate endeavor, such as what lines of business are pursued under the direction of the corporate board. There is debate about the nature of unsystematic risks that is of central concern to our proposal here, especially over whether these risks can be managed, or measurably accounted.

One way to analyze these risks is to look to the economic theory emphasis on the mechanisms of corporate governance (Erakovic, 2007: 472). Corporate risk "is an important concept in economic theory" as well as sociological theory because it is based on "future uncertainty that is relatively systematic and predictable, but which is still dangerous because it can bring financial ruin" and human hardship (McCahery et al., 1993: 258). Risk is assessed in terms of the probability and the prospective degree of advantage or hazard. Moreover, new technologies in a knowledge society and their impacts on human assets can affect how corporate boards interact with their stakeholders, so "technological changes are among the most prevalent factors necessitating adaptation" (Copeland & Towl 1947: 19) of directors' relationships with stakeholders.

McCahery discusses the imposition of higher risk due to bounded rationality "in terms of contingency" of likely vs unlikely risk outcomes (McCahery, 1993: 259). Further, "risk is connected to trust, which presupposes an awareness of risk" (McCahery, 1993: 258). Corporate strategies are under the guidance of board directors and the level of risk to stakeholders is strongly influenced by boards' sanctioning of these strategies. Such strategies may involve market share demographics, geographic saturation, potential product or service liability or other locuses of risk. The provision of specific product or service information promoting awareness of known risk is not sufficient to establish understanding of risk, however.

In the same vein, information that is necessary for a stakeholder to make a rational, informed decision, according to McCahery, ought to be based on J.C. Coffee's "bargaining process" (1987). McCahery reminds us that "the firm is defined as a bargaining site on which several co-operative arrangements are possible, and the parties have conflicting preferences over them" (McCahery 1993: 259). To illustrate, consumers seek a variety of perceived benefits to their purchases, each of which involves either explicit or implicit forms of bargaining based on price, access, or duration of service with the corporation. McCahery's notion of the activity characterizing the bargaining site recognizes that the process involves contingencies, including those precipitated by unforeseeable or unforeseen events. In regard to this process, we think that without consent eliciting processes that go beyond the traditional shareholders' meeting and voting privileges, boards of directors have a heightened risk of loss of trust in their capabilities to guide the firm responsibly, and stakeholders are more likely to suffer impositions of unbounded risk.

Informed Consent

Somewhat as recent corporate scandals have eroded confidence in the domain of business, during the second half of the twentieth century a series of scandals shook the public's faith in the trustworthiness of the medical profession. The post-World War II Nuremberg Trials of Nazi doctors who practiced euthanasia and used concentration camp inmates as laboratory animals evidenced that physicians could not be trusted to place the interests of their patients first. Scandals about physicians' treatment of human subjects as means rather than as valuable human ends were evidenced in, for example, the denial of curative treatment to a large number of African Americans during the Tuskegee syphilis research project. Physicians' disregard for vulnerable patients, as seen in the deliberate exposure of mentally disabled individuals to hepatitis in the Willowbrook Institution, and physicians' failures to refrain from harm, as in the Thalidomide prescriptions for morning sickness that caused abnormal development of fetal limbs, made relying on physicians seem dangerous (Institutional Research Board, University of Minnesota, Informed Consent Overview: A Brief History; see also Faden, Beauchamp and King, 1986: *passim*; Steinbock, Arras, and London, 2003; Rothman and Rothman, 1984; Brandt, 1978).

Once patient and public confidence that physicians are the kinds of experts who can be trusted to secure the best interests of their patients was breached, ethical questions arose about the propriety of requiring patients to give over the governance of their bodies to their doctors as a condition of receiving the benefit of medical care. The 1970s saw case law decisions that created a new view about reliable relationships between medical professionals and patients. such as in *Canterbury* v. *Spence*, 464 F.2d 772 (D.C. Cir. 1972) (Dr Spence's claim that a laminectomy was no more serious than any other operation constituted a *prima facie* case of violation of the physician's duty to disclose), and *Cobbs* v. *Grant* 502 P.2d 1 (Cal 1972) (whereby the patient has the right to control his own body but because he is in a position of inferior knowledge to the physician, he must trust the physician to give him knowledge to make an effective decision, which places the physician under an obligation to effectively inform and a duty to determine that the patient understands). Patients, rather than physicians, now are seen as the proper judges of their own best interests, especially because people differ in their visions of what constitutes their own good. This is not a process of balancing competing interests – for example, the interests of an individual patient against the interests of other patients, medical professionals, or institutions. Rather, informing and consenting is a process of identifying and maximizing the common interest of interdependent cooperators.

The practice of obtaining explicit consent from dependent patients to procedures that put them at risk thus developed in medicine in a context pervaded by disillusion about the trustworthiness of fiduciaries. In accepting medical treatment, patients assign agency to pursue their good health to their physicians, based on the physician's claim to have instrumental expertise. But only the patient can decide whether the procedure's risks unacceptably compromise her personal view of her well-being. To have a rational basis to exercise her self-determination, the patient must have sound knowledge of the proposed medical procedure's potential for harm as well as benefit. Rather than the physician's deciding unilaterally whether potential benefits are worth courting likely risks, the notion of informed consent allows the patient herself to assume this responsibility in deciding how important the benefits are to her, and how threatening the risks. Further, systematic responsibility for shaping and sustaining this practice of sharing responsibility falls not on individual physicians and patients, but to the institutions that enable individuals in these roles to approach each other to cooperate – hospitals, professional organizations such as medical associations or hospital accrediting associations, and other such entities.

The practice of informed consent thereby bolsters confidence that, while dependent on the physician, the patient's interests and values will be prominent and her liberty will be preserved. The practice focuses physicians' responsibility on what they can control rather than on what they can't and provides a strict procedural standard requiring that patients be informed about the uncertainties of outcome. In recognition that risk is incurred by such uncertainty, however, physicians are not held to an equally strict standard for achieving the desired substantive outcomes.

Three crucial constituents of informed consent are becoming knowledgeable, judging competently, and acting voluntarily. The attraction of acknowledging responsibility as shared between a physician and a patient is based on the latter's self-determined consent to assume risk, which sustains the practice despite some well-known implementation difficulties. These include vagueness about how much information is needed for the patient to be informed and about whether physicians have the instructional skills to ensure patients' effective understanding; disagreement about identifying competency in patients and selecting surrogate decision makers for incompetent ones; and suspicion that people desperate for relief from illness, weakness or pain cannot really be said to consent voluntarily (Mehlman, 1999; Manson & O'Neill, 2007: *passim*).

Of these problems, one of the most serious is a question about whether patients ordinarily exercise rational risk assumption in consenting to treatment. In general, people can attend to and process only so much information at one time. When there is too much to deal with, we tend to sort the elements affecting a decision so that, of those which might have objectively equal weight in a formal risk assessment system, some are allowed to take on exaggerated magnitude while others unreflectively fade from view. Thoughts that provoke painful emotions are prime candidates for the latter process.

Psychological research shows that subjective assessment of risk magnifies the importance of change, and especially that prospective losses take on more significance than potential gains (Tversky & Kahneman, 1986). On the whole, people tend to be pessimistic and cautious although a run of unusual successes leads to the opposite exaggeration of effect. Regret, or more accurately the anticipation of regret, can be a huge factor in individual decisions, making some people strongly prefer avoiding loss to pursuing gain. Tversky and Kahneman suggest that the aversion to loss is twice as powerful a motivator as the seeking of gain. Some people are also risk averse, preferring to seek more certain, but less rewarding outcomes over less certain big payoffs. Other people are more risk tolerant. Hyperbolic discounting, preferring more immediate to delayed gains or distant to immediate losses, is also a familiar human tendency. Objectively, whether the gain or loss is imminent or far off should make no difference in its value, but the subjective difference imminence makes can be huge.

These common human tendencies are sometimes characterized as cognitive biases resulting from one fact or piece of evidence being given an unjustified weight. In subjective experience, these tendencies result in some potential health changes portending more damaging impact than others. For example, one might lose mobility suddenly, from an infection, or slowly, from increasing old age. Because it is precipitous, the former may seem more harmful than the latter, even though the resulting deficit is the same in both cases.

Although such feelings may depart from the results of formal risk assessment, they are far from being irrational. Formalized risk assessment is often criticized for being too abstracted from how people actually decide. Further, the rationale for obtaining informed consent is to enable the dependent individual's standpoint to prevail. If people tend to experience immediately prospective harms as more salient than much more distant ones, the prominence of the former is an important quality of their standpoints and can be accounted for in the informative process that is part of eliciting consent. In recognition of the tendency for hyperbolic discounting, the physician's duty of disclosure may include responsibility for bringing all potential harms equally to the foreground of the patient's attention. The information conveying process that is required for informed consent thus facilitates balanced assessment of risk.

Fiduciary Roles

Corporate directors' traditional roles are fiduciary ones, and these roles involve relational interactions as well as control over a number of processes. Relational interactions fall into two categories: relationships with dependent stakeholders and custodianship of the corporation's assets. Similarly, medical professionals traditionally have been both agents who provide health care to dependent patients and fiduciary custodians of medical knowledge and delivery systems. Medical professionals serve as the fiduciary for advancement of the health, and therefore the well-being, of the patient, and also have some responsibility for public health. Boston University law professor Tamar Frankel illustrates the role of the physician as fiduciary with the example of the surgeon "who performs surgery on a patient gains full control over the patient's body and sometimes over the patient's life. Yet the patient's body continues to belong to the patient" (Frankel, 2006: 124–5). Failure to fully inform patients of risks and gain consent from them violates the physician's role. Even though disclosure of the risks inherent in medical treatment is time-consuming and has other costs, the benefits of shared responsibility, as well as increased liberty (in terms of control of risk assumption) for patients, are significant.

Of course, the standard of informed consent for medical procedures protects dependent, trusting patients from physicians who would unilaterally impose risks on their health interests, not directly on their economic interests.[2] In the analogous relationship in the corporate sphere, the interests of trusting stakeholders who place their capital (whether human, monetary, or material) in the stewardship of corporate directors are primarily market-related rather than health-centered. As in the medical sphere, this is a relationship of dependence. Frankel considers the relationship between corporate director and stakeholder, like that between physician and patient, one of dependence based on the latter's being assured of the former's reliability in applying expertise (Frankel, 2006: 144) effectively. The stakeholder is dependent on the corporate board to exercise due care based on full disclosure of the facts affecting each party, including conflicts of interest, malfeasance, or ignorance. Disclosure is as much the responsibility of the expert professional (i.e. physician or the corporate board director) to the stakeholder in this relationship based on trust, as is the responsibility to refrain from malpractice or from creating a "potential plaintiff" (Frankel, 2006: 144).

"Disclosure is binding only if the consenting party understands what it is consenting to, and can evaluate the information" (Frankel, 2006: 145). We propose that, analogously to the medical sphere, not only disclosure, but education to help stakeholders understand disclosure, is an ethical obligation of the corporate director's role. We think that this proactive practice significantly benefits all the parties – stakeholders, corporations, and the corporate directors themselves. Trust in a two-party relationship is abused if the fiduciary imposes risk on the stakeholder without informing the stakeholder as part of the process of inviting consent. "Access to information is critical to the board's effectiveness" (Carter & Lorsch, 2004: 176), and therefore to the effectiveness of stakeholders' rationally identifying with the judgment of the board. In obtaining and conveying information, we suggest, directors ought to connect with stakeholders, who are constituents of the corporate body, with care similar in some ways to that physicians are ethically as well as legally obligated to provide their patients.

We note that the moral and social expectations that bind physicians to advance their patients' well-being are at least as powerful as, and have a longer history than, their legal obligations to do so. We note also that the central language characterizing how medical professionals relate to patients is not out of place in describing directors' relations to stakeholders in the corporate world. For example, Delaware General Corporation Law, under which as many as half of large US firms are registered, establishes (an admittedly vague) "duty of care," and the duty of "loyalty" to corporate dependents (Frankel, 2006: 132; Erakovic, 2007: 476).[3]

The early twentieth-century separation of ownership and control of a corporation placed boards of directors in conflicted roles as both agent of shareholders and driving force of the corporation. As agent, the corporate board is responsible to the stockholders in their concerns for beneficial return on their personal investments. And, as driving force, the directors are expected to guide the progression of the vitality of the firm – which direction is subject to ethical concerns, not just strictly financial ones. The goals appropriate to these two roles do not necessarily align with each other, as personal benefits to individual stakeholders may not always contribute to strengthening the firm. Nevertheless, as a matter of the ethical principles that should guide them in their roles, directors should not unilaterally sacrifice either of these responsibilities to the other one. We contend that directors can achieve compatibility of the duties of their twin roles through a process of collaborative deliberative events resulting in eliciting informed consent from stakeholders, which enables directors to share responsibility for the firm's risk and well-being with its stakeholders.

Disseminating Information

It is accepted that corporations establish their own well-being through reciprocal exchange relationships in the market. We take "well-being" to be a gain in this sense and to be a *holistic*, rather than strictly a fiscal, consideration. Approaches to gains in well-being are unlikely to be cost-free. Frankel observes that the common adage, "the market already has 'all the relevant information'" because that is what a free market system is devised to do, depends on the free market hypothesis that "such information is indeed available in the market" (Frankel, 2006: 120). The market hypothetically acts as a buffer between the corporate directors who impose risk and the stakeholders who assume risk by engaging in market transactions. However, as Frankel points out, this is not the case in all areas of market risk.

Of course, beyond the market's natural capacity to disseminate information, disclosure can be costly and time-consuming, and time is valuable for a corporate board. "[T]he cost of disclosure became an important factor in limiting the legal requirements for information [from corporate entities]," she observes (Frankel, 2006: 121). Yet public disclosure of corporate risk serves to preclude decision makers "from doing what they would not wish to publicize ... Behavior changes when one lives in a glass bowl" (Frankel, 2006: 121). Moreover, failure to operate with transparency and informed constituents is costly to a corporation's operations in terms of trust and credibility. In what sometimes is described as a "rigorous" approach to creating "legitimacy and wider acceptance by stakeholders," "increased transparency, accountability, integrity, and independent overview in *all* key areas of corporate performance, ethical, social, and environmental as well as financial" is at the core of sustainable corporate endeavors – or, "best practices" in terms of risk imposition (Jackson & Nelson, 2004: 259). Acting as a corporate board member is seen as calling for such Aristotelian virtues as honesty and integrity, compatibility, concern for the welfare of the corporation (i.e. *polis*), possessing long-range views, an ability to evaluate changing conditions, an ability to appraise others, courage, and an ability to ask discerning questions (Copeland & Towl, 1947: 182–4). Through this rigorous approach, "the governance agenda for business is being fundamentally reshaped" (Jackson & Nelson, 2004: 259).

Further, corporate leadership must be attentive to "policy direction and corporate culture, [which] should emanate from the board of directors" (Kerstetter & Schulken, 2005: 3). All corporate organizations have a culture. If corporate governance is to gain authorization from stakeholders to assume risks on their behalf, there should be full, accurate, and insightful communication with stakeholders on a variety of levels using various modes of dissemination. Stakeholders' awareness and understanding of the culture is greatly enhanced by boards that endorse open-door policies.

Policies of opaqueness have resulted in corporate scandals. By the time problems surfaced they had grown into serious legal infractions, such as the process that led to Enron's collapse. In these instances, there were failures of transparency about lack of safeguards, and failures of communication regarding the basis and degree of risk assumption and the nature of the risk inherent incorporate board decisions and goals.

Responsibility, Risk, and Transparency

Corporate boards are expected to take responsibility for the "long-range view of the corporation's affairs" (Copeland & Towl, 1947: 23) and the continuing interests of stakeholders. Informing stakeholders is not an easily accomplished function for board directors. As put succinctly by the president and CEO of Dial Corporation, "when we're no longer focusing on the fundamental issue of doing business *transparently*, the building blocks of the business break down. Things like honesty and integrity. Things like service" (Baum, 2004: xvi). In other words, responsibility entails "the principles of respect for the rule of law, accountability, transparency, integrity, and independent oversight are all crucial pillars that underpin well-functioning markets and well-informed shareholders and stakeholders, all of which are needed for long-term business success" (Jackson & Nelson, 2004: 264).

Undoubtedly, a woman or man taking a position as a director on a corporate board assumes some personal risk. "The risk that he may have to face unpleasant tasks," which "is a major responsibility of a board of directors" to their stakeholders is inherent to the role (Copeland & Towl, 1947: 135). This is both historical and normative for today's directors. A board of directors delegates the day-to-day business operation to corporate executives and management, "but [the board] still has responsibility to make sure that the operations are efficiently and properly conducted," including directing and reviewing policy that ensures the corporation's financial solvency (Copeland & Towl, 1947: 4). Moreover, "enterprise involves taking risks" (Copeland & Towl, 1947: 5). Despite the increasing perception that being a board director is itself risky, qualified people do not seem to have become averse to accepting this role; however, the current market environment has become focused on the need for boards to be "more involved in risk management" (Kerstetter & Schulken, 2005: 3). Legislation has both increased the importance of this function and imposed greater emphasis on the individual directors' responsibilities to their stakeholders.

In general, "if we are to move into an era of improved corporate governance as anticipated under the Sarbanes–Oxley legislation, directors need to step up to the plate" (Kerstetter & Schulken, 2005: 3). The goal ought to be one of mending the broken aspects of corporate trust-building by disclosure of various risks to the corporation to its stakeholders in a context of building shared acceptance of risk. Moreover, "disclosure is as much an opportunity for corporations to establish their business aims and principles as it is a means of enhancing their accountability" (Cadbury, 2006: 26).

Directors, Stakeholders, and Trust

Trust is "a willingness to be vulnerable to another party" (Schoorman et al., 2007: 347). "Effective organization calls for teamwork, for the willing cooperation and collaboration of all those associated with the enterprise in carrying out their respective functions" (Copeland & Towl, 1947: 6). Stakeholders, those who are most directly impacted by corporate decision making, have a vested interest in cooperative, deliberative relationships with the firm. Nevertheless, corporate boards need to earn trust and confidence from stakeholders because as part of an intracorporate relationship, "a business corporation is inherently a social undertaking in which several groups and diverse personalities are assembled to work together to their mutual economic advantage" (Copeland & Towl, 1947: 7).

Stakeholder trust in the ability of directors to both manage risk and disclose fiduciary information is supported by the agency theory of corporate governance. According to Denis Arnold, a corporate board has an ethical responsibility to act not only as a fiduciary agent, but also as a moral agent of change for the well-being of the organization (Arnold, 2006: 290–1). He argues that corporate boards are "capable of evaluating past decisions and existing plans, of determining whether those intentions ought to remain in place, or whether they should be modified or eliminated in favor of alternative intentions" (Arnold, 2006: 291).

The board is party to a kind of social contract, emerging from a basis of trust (Silvers & Francis, 2005), that is implicit in the relationship of the directors to their constituents or stakeholders. Corporate stakeholders thus may hold directors accountable for both benefits and harms committed by the firm because directors are responsible for shaping the relationships within which stakeholders pursue their roles in regard to the firm. The director's role includes sustaining reliable relationships with those who depend on the health of the firm. Well-placed trust that directors will do so explains why stakeholders can be expected to accept being placed at some risk by corporate directors' decisions (McCahery et al., 1993: 265).

In order for stakeholders to make rational, informed decisions about their own market well-being, however, transparent disclosure of corporate strategy and potential risks is required. As McCahery states, "the concept of trust is defined in terms of credibility" (McCahery et al., 1993: 265). McCahery et al. base their view on the work of Kreps (1990) on rational reputation, noncooperative game theory, and continuous bargaining between parties to a relationship.[4] Good corporate governance requires consistent, informed decision making by all parties as an important element of best practice, for "good public governance is ultimately good for business, even if direct quantifiable causal links are difficult to quantify" (Jackson & Nelson, 2004: 264).[5]

Directors bear responsibility for the trust that stakeholders afford them being well placed rather than misplaced. "Trust can be attained only if stakeholders believe that they are receiving full and fair disclosures and that both good news and bad news are fully and promptly reported" (Epstein & Roy, 2006: 178). Directors therefore should both inform, and be informed about, stakeholders. Baum advocates developing close relationships with the human resources director in the company because that individual knows what is going on in different areas of the company (Baum, 2004: 190). Corporate boards have been defined as "counselors and advisors" (Copeland & Towl, 1947: 12). By taking on the risk inherent in their own roles, directors acknowledge their responsibility to adopt best practice for executing their function as counselors. In doing so, directors stand accountable for risk imposition on stakeholders. There are three groups of stakeholders with primary importance for achieving loyalty and corporate stability in a context in which there is risk. These are shareholders, employees, and customers, yet, "only 47% of directors receive information on employee values and satisfaction, and only 42% receive information about customer satisfaction" (Kerstetter & Schulken, 2005: 3). Kerstetter states that the two latter kinds of stakeholders are crucial to the success of any organization; therefore, directors ought to receive more than just information regarding the financial health of the firm (Kerstetter & Schulken, 2005: 3). Moreover, directors require this information because of their fiduciary responsibility as counselors and advisors to the corporation.

In order for boards to assess potential assumption of risks, directors require managerial data about the firm. However, "nearly twice as many boards receive financial and business performance data [89%] compared with information related to employees [47%] and customers [42%], yet optimally, information should be balanced among these three scorecards constituencies" (Kerstetter and Schulken, 2005: 14). In fact, the majority of surveyed directors would like to have more of their time as a director devoted to areas such as strategic planning (59 percent), as well as increasing time spent meeting key managers (44 percent) and visiting company sites (42 per cent), in order to gain additional insight and information about their corporate affiliates (Kerstetter & Schulken 2005: 15). Therefore, board directors seem implicitly to understand that they have responsibilities toward a variety of stakeholders, including but not limited to shareholders, and to accept the role of risk taking. But corporate boards may not explicitly acknowledge that, because stakeholders are critical to the success of any firm, directors can be sources of risk if they fail in their fiduciary responsibility to stakeholders.

Reciprocity, Credibility, and Communication

Reciprocity is an exchange of trust based on communication of information and expectations and on mutuality of respect. Reciprocity is fundamental to the practice of informed consent. Bilateral corporate relationships require transparent access to information pertinent to the functioning of the relationship, including transparency of mechanisms of board decision making. Disclosure cultivates credibility. Decision making based on credible information can be quantified in financial statements, technology development, and improved social adhesion, as evidenced in the sustainability of governance and business practices.

Directors engage in best practices when they "have no conflicts of interest and have confidence and skills to offer independent opinions and ensure rigorous checks and balances against abuse of executive power" (Jackson & Nelson, 2004: 267). The "deliberative" approach in health care between physicians and patients exemplifies the open, communicative processes of arriving at informed consent using bilateral decision making (Emmanuel & Emmanuel, 1992). To effect best practice, corporate directors should establish bilateral arrangements between themselves and stakeholders to gain and understand needs and expectations through shared information. The 2005 "What Directors Think" study, conducted by PricewaterhouseCoopers LLC, suggests that directors now are inclined to participate in such relationships (Kerstetter & Schulken, 2005).

High-performance boards of directors are concerned to cultivate diversity of perspective and to be effectively informative (Jackson & Nelson, 2004: 269). First, the diversity of the board directors themselves assists in developing fuller perspectives on corporate-guiding decision making – such as gender, race, ethnicity and cultural aspects of views about information-gathering, decision making and communicating. The global market system calls for richer forms of interpretation and decision making that is inclusive of stakeholder concerns. Second, to be effectively informative directors will need to invest their time and talent to be visible as decision makers and to make the processes and bases of their decision making known to achieve effective risk acceptance by stakeholders. For example, directors might frame risk by communicating their efforts to achieve corporate social responsibility and sustainability in the context of informing stakeholders about the financial, social, and environmental impacts of their decisions on the well-being of the corporate body.

To illustrate, Starbucks Coffee Company posts its Fiscal Year in Review online with the names, background affiliations, and photos of its board directors, as well as a listing of its most senior executives, who have

collectively committed to "caring for people and communities" as stakeholders (www.starbucks.com). The company's fiscal report includes admitted tremendous historical growth in the market, but also the risks associated
with such and the resulting downturn in retail sales. The online review
demonstrates a form of transparency by informing stakeholders of bilateral
relationships between the corporate board and company stakeholders in
acknowledging risks and the impacts of such to – consumers, employees,
and suppliers.

    Consumer advocacy of accountability in corporate decision making is
increasing. In response, some corporate boards have set up hotlines for
bilateral communication between stakeholder employees and the directors
of the board (Baum, 2004: 91). Baum likens the changing relationship
between consumer and corporate decision makers to the well-known transition of consumer-patients from putting themselves passively in the hands
of paternalistic physicians to actively seeking second opinions and investigating possible diagnoses and treatments (Baum, 2004: 95). Sustaining
reciprocal relationships is more challenging when stakeholders are active
rather than passive. To do so in such a corporate context requires not only
transparency, but also fully informed stakeholders in order for them to
make active inquiries.

Risk Transparency and the Corporate Board

In the past, directors were veiled from public view, shielded in their role as
behind-the-scenes puppeteers pulling the various strings of corporate board
committees and executives to meet shareholder expectations of profit. Now,
profit is subject to full disclosure based on evolving accounting practices
and the Sarbanes–Oxley requirements of corporate financial disclosure.
Section 301 of the Sarbanes–Oxley Act requires independent board directors with expertise to sit on the corporation's audit committee. In fact, this
section makes it a criminal offense to fail to execute the professional, "rea-
sonable-man" sort of fiduciary responsibilities of a director in regard to
audit and financial disclosures. Under the Sarbanes–Oxley Act, disclosure
of all financial transactions, not specific proprietary business information,
is expected and mandated.

    Directors themselves are finding increased pressure from both stake-
holders and legal teams to be transparent in their duties and functions in
decision making. Voluntary "triple bottom line" accounting (although not a
legal requirement) is being impelled by consumer ideas of "need-to-know"
transparency of corporate operations in the wake of so many large corporate

scandals in which directors have been found to a turn blind eye. Directors are increasingly compelled by their own perceptions of their roles as accountable professionals who are not only the guiding agents of corporations but also their consciences. The 2005 PricewaterhouseCoopers study found that 66% of corporate directors stated they would increase their due diligence, a voluntary commitment, in considering their future acceptance of corporate board seats (Kerstetter & Schulken, 2005: 10). Director-driven, bilateral risk acknowledgement also calls for transparent risk-framing and balancing risks by informing stakeholders of risk trade-offs. "[D]irectors need to design their boards to implement current best practices and to move beyond them if boards are to succeed in the twenty-first century" (Carter & Lorsch, 2004: 29).

Conclusion

We have argued that informative disclosure is an important obligation of corporate board directors in their professional duties to their corporate stakeholders.[6] "Risk nothing gain nothing" is a fact about business. Nevertheless, for corporate directors to insist on financial and transactional transparency in regard to risk may seem risky in itself because the information could occasion stakeholders to anticipate regret and therefore to depart, or at least to disagree. Disclosure therefore needs to be communicated in ways that enable both risk-aversive and risk-catering stakeholders to make rational decisions. This is no easy task. Executing it requires both expertise and integrity.

To do so effectively, directors should understand the effect of risk framing in the context of stakeholder choice in a climate of uncertainty. Risk framing influences stakeholder acceptance of levels of uncertainty, as it also influences director decision making. Directors also should make efforts to ascertain that stakeholders understand relevant concepts such as "risk tradeoff." Our proposal calls for increased professionalism in directors' execution of their responsibility to make information available to those from whom they seek trust. As a matter of professional integrity and out of respect for stakeholders' personal values, however, directors should refrain from imposing models of decision making that prescribe how to react to risk (although they should be transparent about their own principles).

There is, however, a type of risk reduction that corporate directors should prescribe for themselves. The potential for conflict between the two traditional roles of corporate board directors may place those charged with executing directors' responsibilities at risk. Our focus has been on how directors can mitigate this kind of personal risk by adopting a cohesive and therefore sustainable framework of respect for stakeholders as rational decision makers who, if properly informed, can signal their consent to the assumption of risk. We see the practice of informed consent between corporate directors and stakeholders as an important means of achieving well-being for the professional endeavor of the directors as well as for all who depend for their own well-being on the expertise and integrity of the directors. And thus we urge that directors develop bilateral relationships with stakeholders by adopting practices of disclosure appropriate as a basis for informed consent.

A quarter century ago, John Braithwaite observed that "voluntary disclosure as part of a social contract negotiated with the relevant publics of the corporation is part of taking corporate social responsibility seriously" (Braithwaite, 1985: 48). While some have argued for a regulatory form of "New Governance" in which social information reporting processes are government-regulated (Hess, 2007: 453–76), we support a nonregulatory or self-regulatory voluntary approach. We have suggested an initiative board directors can take to inform stakeholders as a basis for eliciting their consent. Braithwaite was skeptical about the commitment of corporate directors to engage in anything other than unilateral and unidirectional relationships with stakeholders (Braithwaite, 1985: 40–1). We believe, however, that the professionalism of directors has grown and that boards now seek expanded understanding and effective organizational practice to better fulfill their ethical as well as legal responsibilities.

Notes

1   We assume here that directors should be motivated by the best interest of the firm, and that sustaining productive cooperation with stakeholders, as appropriate for each stakeholder category, usually furthers the interest of the firm. This view has both historical and contemporary bases. Directors are charged with the responsibility to respond to stakeholders and take appropriate initiatives to mitigate risk by asking of themselves, "Am I now rendering service which fairly may be expected of a director: by stockholders? By employees? By executives? By creditors? By suppliers? By customers? By the public?" (Copeland and Towl, 1947: 192). In other words, directors are responsible for the corporate framework in which multiple stakeholders "are assembled to work together to their mutual economic advantage" (Copeland and Towl, 1947: 7). Further, the majority of US states "have adopted the so-called constituency

statutes, which authorize the board to take into account the interests of all constituencies (such as shareholders, employees, customers, suppliers, the community, and the environment) when deciding to act" (Bagley, 2006: 86). These statures point to the broad fiduciary duties of board directors, who are "stewards" who assess risk, harm and benefit to constituents. We do not address the narrower question of the categories of stakeholders, or factions within a stakeholder category such as between groups of shareholders, whose interests should be served, except to note that the firm's interest should not be confused with the interest of a particular category or faction of stakeholders.

2   Frankel refers to the well-known case of *Moore* v. *Regents of the University of California* (Frankel, 2006: 124; 226 *n*.14) as illustrative. Moore was diagnosed with leukemia, and his physicians discovered that some of his disposable body components (blood, blood serum, marrow, spleen) might be developed into a cell line with commercial value. Moore was led to believe their removal, executed by physicians at the University of California, Los Angeles, would benefit his health. The cell line was patented by the University of California Regents, and Moore sued, claiming that as the source of the original biological material the cell line was his property. The California Supreme Court ruled that if a patient consents to the removal of biological material, the material no longer belongs to the patient's body, and therefore does not belong to the patient. To extend property rights to excised tissue could have a chilling effect on medical procedures and medical research, especially because laboratories might be held strictly liable for illegal conversion of property in cases where samples of tissue obtained for diagnostic purposes eventually contributed to a commercially valuable discovery. Nor could Moore claim that, had he known of the commercial potential of his tissue, his consent would have been contingent on acknowledgement of his property right to the organ. This is because the process of "consenting" a patient in a medical context is about shared responsibility for harms to health; and the physician's role is not as a fiduciary for the patient's economic well-being. The Court held, however, that Moore could bring an action for any injury to health suffered against the physician who obtained consent without disclosing his commercial interest in the excised biological material. This failure violated the trust the patient gave the physician, but consent obtained without full disclosure results in damages only if the patient would not have consented, nor would a reasonable person have consented, if fully informed.

3   The fiduciary duty of care and duty of loyalty are expectations of directors to "make every attempt to be well-informed before they make decisions, to act in good faith and the best interest of the shareholders, and to be independent in their decisions" as represented in agency theory (Erakovic, 2007: 75).

4   On the other hand, Silvers and Francis dispute the notion that productive cooperation requires continuous bargaining. They believe that building trust can be as productive, and less costly, than adversarial bargaining (Silvers and Francis, 2005).

5 Respect for one another is implicit in relationships of well-placed trust. Trust-preserving informed consent between physician and patient is aimed at enhancing both parties' well-being. The application to corporate directors and stakeholders has a similar value. In either case, "the principles of respect for the rule of law, accountability, transparency, integrity, and independent oversight are all crucial pillars that underpin well-functioning markets and well-informed shareholders and stakeholders, all of which are needed for long-term business success" (Jackson and Nelson, 2004: 264).

6 SEC rules regarding transactions between corporations and investor-stakeholders require disclosure of "adequate information" to inform investors about the corporation and their offered stock; however, as Frankel points out, this disclosure of risk often also entails risk – "experience has shown that specific rules are not necessarily clearer. The more specific they are, the more questions of interpretations they can raise" (Frankel, 2006: 146).

References

Arnold, Denis. 2006. Corporate moral agency. *Midwest Studies in Philosophy,* 30(1): 279–91.

Bagley, Constance E. 2005. Shareholder primacy is a choice, not a legal mandate. In Mark J. Epstein and Kirk O. Hanson (eds), *The Accountable Corporation: Corporate Governance*, vol. 1. Westport, CT: Praeger Publishers, pp. 85–105.

Baum, Herb. 2004. *The Transparent Leader*. New York: HarperCollins.

Braithwaite, John. 1985. Taking responsibility seriously: Corporate compliance systems. In Brent Fisse and Peter A. French (eds), *Corrigible Corporations and Unruly Law*. San Antonio: Trinity University Press, pp. 39–61.

Brandt, Allan. 1978. Racism and research: The case of the Tuskegee syphilis study. *Hastings Center Report* (December): 21–9.

Cadbury, Sir Adrian. 2006. The rise of corporate governance. In Mark J. Epstein and Kirk O. Hanson (eds), *The Accountable Corporation: Corporate Governance*, vol. 1. Westport, CT: Praeger Publishers, pp. 15–43.

Carter, Colin B. and Jay W. Lorsch. 2004. *Back to the Drawing Board: Designing Corporate Boards for a Complex World*. Boston, MA: Harvard Business School Press.

Coffee, J.C. 1987. Shareholders versus managers: The strain in the corporate web. *Michigan Law Review*, 85(1): 77–134.

Copeland, Melvin T. and Andrew R. Towl. 1947. *The Board of Directors and Business Management*. Boston, MA: Harvard University – Graduate School of Business Administration.

Emmanuel, Ezekiel and Linda Emmanuel. 1992. Four models of the physician–patient relationship. *Journal of the American Medical Association*, 267(16) (April 22/29): 2221–6.

Epstein, Mark J. and Kirk O. Hanson (eds). 2006. *The Accountable Corporation: Corporate Governance*, vol. 1. Westport, CT: Praeger Publishers.

Epstein, Mark J. and Marie-Josée Roy. 2006. Measuring the effectiveness of corporate boards and directors. In *The Accountable Corporation: Corporate Governance*, vol. 1, pp. 155–82.

Erakovic, Ljiljana. 2007. Corporate governance. In *Encyclopedia of Business Ethics*. Thousand Oaks, CA: Sage, pp. 471–81.

Faden, Ruth, Tom Beauchamp, and Nancy King. 1986. *A History and Theory of Informed Consent*. Oxford: Oxford University Press.

Frankel, Tamar. 2006. *Trust and Honesty: America's Business Culture at a Crossroad*. New York: Oxford University Press.

Freeman, R. Edward and Daniel J. Gilbert. 1988. *Corporate Strategy and the Search for Ethics*. New Jersey: Prentice-Hall, Inc.

Fukuyama, Francis. 1995. *Trust: The Social Virtues and the Creation of Prosperity*. New York: Free Press.

Hansson, S.O. 2003. Ethical criteria of risk acceptance. *Erkenntnis*, 59: 291–309.

Hess, David. 2007. Social reporting and new governance regulation: The prospects of achieving corporate accountability through transparency. *Business Ethics Quarterly*, 17(3) (July): 453–76.

Institutional Research Board, University of Minnesota, Informed Consent Overview: A Brief History. http://www.research.umn.edu/consent/mod1soc/mod1sec4.html.

Jackson, Ira and Jane Nelson. 2004. *Profits with Principles: Seven Strategies for Delivering Value with Values*. New York: Currency/Doubleday.

Kerstetter, T.K. and Herbert C. Schulken. 2005. What directors think. In *Corporate Board Member* (supplement). Brentwood, TN: Board Member, Inc., pp. 1–17.

Knight, Frank. 1921. *Risk, Uncertainty, and Profit*. Boston, MA: Houghton Mifflin Company.

Kreps, D. 1990. Corporate culture and economic theory. In J. Alt and K. Shepsle (eds), *Perspectives in Positive Political Economy*. Cambridge, UK: Cambridge University Press, pp. 247–66.

Kroll, Mark, Bruce A. Walters, and Son A. Le. 2007. The impact of board composition and top management team ownership structure on post-IPO performance in young entrepreneurial firms. *The Academy of Management Journal*, 50(5) (October): 1198–216.

Manson, Neil and Onora O'Neill. 2007. *Rethinking Informed Consent in Bioethics*. Cambridge, UK: Cambridge University Press.

McCahery, Joseph, Sol Picciotto, and Colin Scott (eds). 1993. *Corporate Control and Accountability: Changing Structures and the Dynamics of Regulation*. Oxford: Clarendon Press.

McCahery, Joseph. 1993. Risk, trust, and the market for corporate control. In Joseph McCahery, Sol Picciotto, and Colin Scott (eds), *Corporate Control*

340   Denise Kleinrichert and Anita Silvers

and Accountability: Changing Structures and the Dynamics of Regulation, pp. 247–66.

Mehlman, Maxwell. 1999. Informed consent. Accessed at http://www.thedoctor-willseeyounow.com/articles/bioethics/consent_3/

Rothman, David and Sheila Rothman. 1984. *The Willowbrook Wars*. New York: Harper and Row.

Sanders, William Gerard and Donald Hambrick. 2007. Swinging for the fences: The effects of CEO stock options on company risk taking and performance. *The Academy of Management Journal*, 50(5) (October): 1055–78.

Schoorman, F. David, Roger C. Mayer, and James H. Davis. 2007. An integrative model of organizational trust: Past, present, and future. *The Academy of Management Review*, 32(2): 344–54.

Shrader-Frechette, K. 1991. *Risk and Rationality. Philosophical Foundations for Populist Reforms*. Berkeley, CA: University of California Press.

Silvers, Anita and Leslie P. Francis. 2005. Justice through trust: Resolving the outlier problem in social contract theory. *Ethics*, 116: 40–77.

Starbucks Coffee Company. 2008. Fiscal 2007 Year in Review. www.starbucks.com.

Steinbock, Bonnie, John Arras, and Alex John London. 2003. Born in scandal: The origins of US research ethics. In Bonnie Steinbock, John Arras, and Alex John (eds), *Ethical Issues in Modern Medicine*, 6th edition. London and. New York: Macmillan, pp. 705–6.

Tversky, A. and D. Kahneman. 1986. Rational choice and the framing of decisions. *Journal of Business*, 59: 251–78.

17

Discussion

John R. Boatright

Addressing the role of boards of directors in managing risk from the perspective of ethics adds two important dimensions that are explored in the previous three papers. One dimension added by ethics is the question of whose interests ought to be considered in the management of risk. In the standard view, it is only the shareholders or the firm itself that directors should seek to protect against risk, but a consideration of risk management from an ethical point of view leads possibly to a more inclusive account. The other dimension is what boards should do in managing the risks for all those whose interests ought to be considered. Reducing risk is an objective that can be achieved in many different ways, and the choice of means, as well as the degree of reduction, involves matters for ethical consideration. The first question is predominantly normative; and although the second question is largely pragmatic – about the best means for achieving certain ends – it is also normative to the extent that choices about means involve an evaluation of the alternatives. As Duane Windsor observes, many risk management decisions involve tradeoffs between benefiting or preventing harm to difference groups, and ethics is necessarily involved in determining the tradeoffs to be made.

In all three papers, the term "stakeholder" figures prominently, and Windsor as well as Denise Kleinrichert and Anita Silvers take for granted that in managing risks, directors should attend to stakeholders along with stockholders or shareholders. To quote Windsor, "Minimization of risks to all stakeholders and nature is the broad responsibility of the board in terms of ethics of risk management." This view runs counter to the prevailing assumption that the fiduciary duty of the board is owed exclusively to shareholders and that risk management ought to be undertaken in their interests. Barry Mitnick does not commit himself on this matter, but the term "stakeholder" is used liberally in his paper to indicate parties whose interests are, at a minimum, important factors in board decision making. According to Mitnick, directors can serve as liaisons to important stakeholder groups, whose support is necessary for the operation of a firm.

In commenting on these papers, I first address issues in the adoption of stakeholder management as a characterization of the role and responsibility of boards of directors in managing risk from a moral point of view. In subsequent sections, I consider some aspects of Windsor's analytical framework for the ethics of risk management by boards, followed by brief comments on the duty of disclosure as advocated by Kleinrichert and Silvers and the case made by Mitnick that the function of the board is to provide assurance and reassurance.

Stakeholder Management

If one holds, as Windsor does, that ethics requires boards of directors to consider all stakeholders and not merely shareholders, this position stands in need of some argument or support. The standard justifications for what is usually called "stakeholder management" have been offered with respect to the role of managers rather than directors.[1] Indeed, the role of boards of directors in discussions of stakeholder management has been curiously absent. Moreover, the justifications for stakeholder management have not focused solely or even largely on risk management but on all matters bearing on stakeholder interests. Windsor notes that risk management overlaps with, but is distinct from, corporate social responsibility and the other concerns of stakeholder management. However, risk management, broadly conceived, covers most matters that have been considered within the scope of stakeholder management, and the standard arguments for stakeholder management can be applied to the role and responsibilities of boards of directors in managing risk.

The claim that directors as well as managers ought to consider the risks of corporate activities for stakeholders and not only shareholders takes two forms. One form is that this consideration is a moral requirement – that, morally, corporations ought to be operated in the interests of all stakeholder groups. The other form is that operating a corporation in the interests of shareholders involves, as a matter of practical necessity, an attention to all stakeholder groups. These two forms correspond roughly to what Donaldson and Preston distinguish as the normative and instrumental versions of stakeholder theory.[2] The justification of these two positions cannot be undertaken here. Although I have argued that the normative form of stakeholder management is mistaken insofar as it is offered as an alternative to the standard shareholder model of corporate governance,[3] I think that the instrumental form is sound. I am in general agreement with the position taken by James Post, Lee Preston, and Sybille Sachs in their book *Redefining the Corporation: Stakeholder Management and Organizational Wealth.*[4] They argue that for many present-day corporations which operate in turbulent social and political environments – what they call "extended enterprises" – the ability to work effectively with a network of stakeholder groups can be a valuable resource or corporate asset. Although their message is directed solely to managers – indeed they ignore boards entirely – stakeholder management, in the way they describe it, must also be practiced by directors.

If one concedes that risk management by boards of directors involves, in some way, attention to the rights and interests of all stakeholder groups, many questions remain about precisely what boards are able to do and what, morally, they ought to do with regard to stakeholders. These are two separate questions. With regard to the first, corporate boards are rightly concerned with the overall strategy and systems of control within an organization. Directors who believe in an obligation of the organization to reduce risks to stakeholders may express this belief in the selection of a CEO who practices stakeholder management and in the adoption of control systems that are likely to protect stakeholders. They may also, as Kleinrichert and Silvers propose, engage in more extensive disclosure. However, the decisions that constitute stakeholder management occur for the most part on the level of managers rather than directors. For example, in the Caremark decision, cited by Windsor, the Delaware chancery court held that the responsibility of the board did not include awareness of wrongdoing but extended only to insuring that control systems were in place that could reasonably be expected to detect misconduct. The answer to the first question about what boards, as opposed to management and the corporation, can do to protect stakeholders from harm is very limited, I believe.

The second question, what boards should do to protect stakeholder interests, raises many problems that have not been satisfactorily addressed in the stakeholder management literature. The instrumental form of stakeholder management as advanced by Post, Preston, and Sachs, which treats the management of stakeholder groups as a means for creating organizational wealth, operates within a paradigm of shareholder primacy and hence is relatively unproblematic in its implementation. However, if the interests of all stakeholders, including those of shareholders, are to be balanced in some way, as the normative form of stakeholder management proposes, then directors as well as managers have little guidance about to how this balancing should be done.

This problem of balancing stakeholder rights and interests has two dimensions. One dimension is the ultimate objective to be served. Michael Jensen has presented the standard view in financial economics that a monotonic objective, specifically shareholder wealth maximization, is the only kind suitable for an economic organization, and that the pursuit of multiple objectives, as is prescribed by stakeholder management, is inherently unworkable.[5] If, among the multiple objectives, are reductions in the harms inflicted on different stakeholder groups, then one must consider not only the harms themselves but also the risk preferences for each group, which considerably complicates the calculations that would be required. If a single objective other than shareholder wealth maximization is used, such as protection of reputation as proposed by Windsor, then this task is simplified to some degree but not entirely, because, as Windsor notes, reputation is a function of many factors.

The other dimension in the problem of balancing stakeholder rights and interests is the relative strength or importance of different stakeholder groups.[6] This matter is especially acute in the board management of risks because the stakeholder groups that are most likely to come to the attention of directors are either: (a) well-organized and powerful special interest groups with a social agenda; or (b) activist investors who are advancing their own strategy for the corporation. The interests of both of these kinds of stakeholder groups may be adverse to those of most shareholders, and hence these groups must be handled with caution. As Post, Preston, and Sachs contend, effective collaboration with stakeholders may be a source of organizational wealth, but attempting to satisfy certain stakeholder claims may destroy organizational wealth. Thus, any board management of the risks for stakeholders must be done carefully with a clear focus on some definite objective.

An Analytical Framework

In considering the ethical aspects of the management of risk by boards of directors, the first task is to develop a framework or overview of the main objectives and the specific responsibilities of board members. Duane Windsor tackles this task by providing what he calls a "first cut" effort to address board risk management from an ethics perspective. In his account, the standard fiduciary duty that directors owe to shareholders cannot be the sole basis for enterprise risk management. Instead, he claims, "A comprehensive or integrative theory is that sustainable value of the company requires integrated multiple-dimension risk and stakeholder management."

This objective is not incompatible with a strict fiduciary duty to shareholders and is, indeed, a necessary condition for serving shareholders well. Fiduciary responsibility and stakeholder management are not in conflict, he says, but rather "the latter reinforces the former." Windsor also contributes to our understanding of the ethics of risk management in his classification of the three main ways in which risk-management issues arise for boards. Specifically, ethical issues arise when there are conflicts among two or more stakeholders that must be resolved, when company activities generate negative externalities, such as pollution, that affect stakeholders, and when the board interests themselves create conflicts with shareholders and other groups.

Although Windsor's analytical framework contains much value for directors to consider in managing risk, his account involves at least three assumptions that I would question. One assumption is that risk management is mainly risk reduction, which is to say the prevention or amelioration of the harm that corporate activity can inflict on stakeholders. He writes, "Risk management involves minimizing potential harms to stakeholders and nature." Windsor notes that "from a financial perspective the optimum risk level is somewhere greater than zero." This grudging admission is qualified as being true from a "financial perspective," as if morality would generally favor risk reduction. However, a focus on overall welfare of everyone might lead to decisions that create considerable risks for stakeholders that are offset by the benefits they gain. Perhaps the assumption that risk management by boards should aim at risk reduction is due to a further underlying assumption that the risks of corporate activity is a zero-sum game in which all of the benefits flow to the corporation and its shareholders and all the harms to other stakeholders. However, corporations might engage in activities that impose considerable risk to stakeholders that is more than offset by the potential for benefit for these stakeholders. For example, a pharmaceutical company should aim not merely at avoiding patients' risk but at developing drugs that provide the greatest risk-adjusted benefit.

The second assumption that I would question is that risk reduction or management for all stakeholders is entirely or primarily a task for corporate boards or even for management. Of course, boards must manage the risks to the firm and its shareholders. However, corporate activities pose risks for all non-shareholder stakeholders and society at large. Many of these risks are inherent in any kind of economic activity, and to the extent that we want to reduce risks for any group, many means exist for this purpose. In particular, each stakeholder group may provide for its own protection through private contracts and legal rules. Stakeholder management assumes that the main means for reducing risks is managerial discretion, thereby discounting or ignoring these other means. Not only may stakeholder groups be more diligent than corporate directors in protecting themselves from harm, but they may possess more effective means for doing so. I have coined the term the "stakeholder fallacy" to describe the (fallacious) argument that because the corporation ought to serve the interests of all stakeholder groups, ensuring this shared benefit is the task of management.[7] I would also add that it is similarly a mistake to infer that this responsibility necessarily belongs to boards of directors.

The third assumption is that risk management is concerned primarily with the reduction of harms rather than compensation for harms. In practice, we manage risks both *ex ante* by investment in preventative measures and *ex post* by compensating victims for harms that result from corporate activities. Although it may seem morally objectionable to allow harms that could be prevented, even if the victims are compensated, the cost of preventing all possible harms may greatly exceed the cost of compensation from the actual incidence of only a few harms. Windsor makes the bald claim that risk is better addressed *ex ante*, and with respect to Ford's handling of the Pinto, he says, "It is open to debate whether a post-event compensatory approach, particularly in the form of uncertain civil litigation procedures, is a satisfactory approach relative to ex ante risk minimization." Windsor is certainly correct that the choice between *ex ante* protection and *ex post* compensation is "open to debate." In many cases *ex ante* protection may be the more responsible approach. My point is merely that this is not always true, and a board focused on managing risk to stakeholders should consider carefully the merits of both approaches.

For example, in the case of the *Exxon Valdez*, cited by Windsor, the board might have invested more in preventing a ship's captain from being intoxicated, but an investment in double-hulled rather than single-hulled tankers would have provided greater protection from an oil spill. However, the cost of sturdier tankers might exceed the benefit, even when all costs and benefits are considered. If Exxon's board is to reduce all risks, then the directors would also have to consider the costs of preventing accidents that will not in fact occur. I see no moral problem in using cost–benefit analysis to determine how much to invest in harm reduction as opposed to compensation for harms. However, the effectiveness of cost–benefit analysis in risk management is limited by the uncertainty of the magnitude of each kind of risk, which might lead, as Windsor observes, to systematic over-investment in the prevention of some risks and systematic under-investment in the prevention of others. Both over- and under-investment in risk reduction may be equally harmful to people's welfare.

A Duty to Disclose

The paper by Denise Kleinrichert and Anita Silvers focuses on one specific means by which boards of directors can manage risks with stakeholder groups, namely disclosure or transparency. Although these writers agree with Windsor that corporate boards have a responsibility to serve the interests of all stakeholder groups, their case for disclosure also applies, in large measure, to purely shareholder-oriented boards. They speak of the neglect of informed consent as "an opportunity cost, that is, a lost option of gaining good will within the market system," and assert, "Board neglect of transparency can be a source of needless risk." So regardless of whether boards recognize any obligation to serve all stakeholder interests, operating a firm solely for the shareholders still requires maintaining a high level of trust with stakeholders that can be built only with a certain amount of transparency or disclosure. Aside from building trust, which reduces risk, disclosure also manages risk by sharing it with stakeholder groups, who voluntarily accept risk along with its benefits. Since the imposition of risk is not only inevitable but also desirable for the sake of the resulting gains, disclosing risk, in their words, "recasts assuming corporate risk as collaboration between directors and stakeholders." Although Kleinrichert and Silvers do not say so explicitly, one might conclude from their discussion that one advantage of greater transparency is that firms can impose greater risks on stakeholders and thereby confer greater benefits when stakeholders are in a position to voluntarily consent to the risk.

Overall, their call for greater transparency or disclosure is well-founded and constructive. Like motherhood and apple pie, greater disclosure is a good thing that ought to be encouraged. Their prescription is being followed to the extent that corporations are engaging in so-called "triple bottom line" accounting to report not only financial but also social and environmental performance. The list of reports that corporations are required to file with the government about many aspects of their business is steadily expanding. The certification of controls reports under the Sarbanes–Oxley Act and the information on executive compensation now required by the SEC are only two of many recent examples.

One question that can be raised about their account is that given the amount of information that is already disclosed, both voluntarily and in compliance with law, what further information ought to be disclosed? American corporations are already quite transparent, but the ways in which they could be even more transparent are virtually unlimited. However, many disclosures would be of little value in risk management, so how do we determine what additional disclosures would protect stakeholders?

Related to this is a second question about how useful information is in informing people about the risks they face? Typically, the existence of risk is, at best, an inference that can be made from disclosed information rather than being the subject of the information disclosed. In short, information must be interpreted. Consequently, many people might remain unaware of the risks they face in spite of candid disclosures of relevant information.

In addition, disclosure has limitations as a means of risk management. First, people who receive the information must still determine what the risks are and how they can protect themselves against these risks. People who are aware of risks may know that they have a need to protect themselves, but they may not necessarily know how to do so; and there may be some risks against which people may have little means of protection. Furthermore, the disclosure of information about risks may have the perverse, unintended consequence of leading corporations to impose more rather than less risk on stakeholder groups. In a different context, psychologists have found that disclosure of conflicts of interests sometimes has the counterproductive result of encouraging conflicted parties to further exploit the conflict because the disclosure warns the other party and thereby removes the perceived need for self-restraint.[8] For example, a physician who discloses a conflict of interest to a patient might feel less compunction against acting in a biased manner because he or she reasons that the patient has been warned and so now bears the responsibility for protecting against risk.

Questions may also be raised about the normative basis for a duty to disclose. Kleinrichert and Silvers base this duty on a fiduciary relationship akin to that in medicine between physician and patient. The analogy is not wholly apt for several reasons. First, it is not widely accepted that directors are fiduciaries for all stakeholders. (This is the point raised earlier about the normative form of stakeholder management.) Even if board directors have some obligation to serve the interests of stakeholder groups other than shareholders, it is not clear that this is a fiduciary duty, as some stakeholder advocates contend, or that the duty is as extensive as the fiduciary duty to shareholders. Second, disclosure in medicine is based on a principle of patient autonomy – that patients have a right to make choices about their own treatment. It is questionable whether there is a comparable principle of stakeholder autonomy. On what basis could it be argued that stakeholders have a right to make decisions about the risks imposed by corporate activity? Third, physicians deal with patients on a one-on-one basis, where the patient's health is the only objective. However, if directors have a fiduciary duty to stakeholders, they must serve multiple interests and not merely one, in which case disclosure may affect each group differently. For example, a disclosure that may reduce risk to customers may be adverse to the interests of shareholders. Consequently, the fiduciary duty of directors, if it is owed to groups other than shareholders, is more complex than the relatively simple duty of physicians.

In summary, trust has some value in corporate affairs, and disclosure is certainly one factor in building and maintaining trust. Greater transparency can contribute in several different ways to more effective – and ethical – corporate performance. One may even agree with Kleinrichert and Silvers that corporate directors, like physicians, aim at health and well-being – the former of the firm's constituencies and the latter of patients – and so have some duty to do whatever conduces to this objective. However, business organizations are built largely on contracts or market exchanges in which there is little responsibility to attend to others' interests. So even if greater disclosure is beneficial and a duty of directors, many questions remain about how much information and what specific information should be disclosed. Still, the authors' call for greater disclosure should be heeded by all board directors.

Assurance and Reassurance

The paper by Barry Mitnick shares little ground with the other two. Instead of addressing the ethical responsibilities of boards of directors for risk management, Mitnick presents a novel thesis about the role of boards that raises questions about whether boards can even engage in risk management. His thesis, in brief, is that the key function of corporate boards is the "manufacture of credibility," which enables boards to assure shareholders and other constituencies that the managers of a corporation are acting appropriately. The existence of boards exemplifies the "governance paradox," whereby a corporation with a separation of ownership and control must be led both by a single decision maker (a "dictator") and a collective head, which monitors the decision maker. Mitnick draws few conclusions about how boards should manage risk. However, if, indeed, boards provide assurance by merely appearing heroic or pantheonic, then one might draw the conclusion that boards cannot manage risk at all because they do not actually *do* anything. The practical import of the paper is the call for a new form of corporate governance, "agent capitalism," to solve the problem that boards have been offering a "false assurance" about the activities of the managers.

The role of a board of directors is rooted in some theory of corporate governance, and theories of corporate governance develop, in turn, as a response to the problems of engaging in economic production. At the present time, there is one dominant theory which is built on the twin pillars of shareholder primacy and the agent–principal relationship. On this theory, the central problem of joint or team production is how to monitor workers to ensure that all contribute, and the answer, developed by Armen A. Alchian and Harold Demsetz, is to assign the residual revenues or profits to one group, the shareholders, which will have the incentive to monitor effectively without the need for an endless succession of monitors.[9] Thus developed the doctrine of shareholder primacy.[10] The separation of ownership and control raises a further problem of how shareholder-owners can effectively monitor without *de facto* control. Thus arose the shareholder-elected board of directors and managers with a fiduciary duty to act as agents of the shareholder-principals.

Mitnick's account of the role of the board of directors is not contrary to this dominant theory and may even be fully in accord with it. However, he develops this account in response not to a problem of production but to a problem of appearances. Boards do not *appear* to be acting like agents of the shareholders in operating a corporation on the shareholders' behalf; rather, their role appears to be much more ceremonial. Thus, Mitnick's account of the board's role is descriptive not of the problems of production that it solves but of what boards are actually observed doing. There is nothing wrong with such a descriptive theory – any theory of corporation governance should fit all the observable facts – but note should be taken of the different facts that the dominant theory of corporate governance and Mitnick's account are designed to explain.

Mitnick's account is insightful and probably correct as a partial description of how boards are composed and what they actually do. Most board members are men and women of integrity and achievement who inspire confidence. Some boards have offered little else, as witness the board of Conrad Black's Hollinger International, which included Henry Kissinger, former Illinois governor Jim Thompson, and Marie-Josee Kravis, the wife of financier Henry Kravis; this celebrity board turned a blind eye as Black and his business partner looted the firm. Mitnick's governance paradox is also insightful and is grounded on the plausible view that the ideal monitoring group consists of at least three in order to overcome the problem of easy corruption. The main question is the extent to which the assurance and reassurance role is a complete account of what boards actually do and are expected to do. Certainly, any board must offer credibility, but do they and should they do more?

Although Mitnick wonders at one point why boards "do so little that is recognized and described as substantive," he admits at another point that boards provide many useful services. This admission is a prefaced with an observation that other parties might provide the same services, which leads

Mitnick to say, "*the important thing is not the useful work, but why the board and not others are asked to do it*" (italics in original). His answer, "Boards do it because they are the best means available to provide *assurance*," may be a partial explanation of the board's role, but boards may also be good means for fulfilling many other functions. If boards provide assurance, there is also the question of what they assure others about. Mitnick says that "the role of the board is to shape perceptions so that observers believe that the board is doing what it *should* be doing," which assumes that they should be doing something besides merely providing assurance. Finally, it is difficult to believe that the extensive literature on what boards do, which Mitnick cites, could be so far removed from reality as he suggests. In particular, the agency problem created by the separation of ownership and control needs some solution, and solving this problem is certainly one of the functions of a board. At best, then, Mitnick's account of the role of corporate boards is only part of the full truth, but still the role of assurance is undoubtedly one role that boards fill and perhaps an important role that has been unjustly neglected in discussions of risk management.

Mitnick concludes his paper with a call for a new form of corporate governance, called "agent capitalism," to overcome the problem of "false assurance." The problem is apparently that directors have been falsely assuring shareholders that the board has selected, motivated, and monitored managers so that they will act in the shareholders' interest. This problem is due, in turn, to the view that recent efforts to align managers' interests with those of shareholders by means of stock options have led to a "broken system." This charge is also made by Ernie Englander and Allen Kaufman, who argue that the effect of stock options has been to turn managers, and especially the chief executive office (CEO), into a special kind of shareholder.[11] Although this move was intended to achieve a stronger alignment with shareholder interests, the actual effect, according to Englander and Kaufman, has been to induce CEOs to seek short-term gain at the expense of long-term value, to commit fraud or other kinds of wrongdoing, and to reduce support for socially responsible activities. In Mitnick's analysis, the problem is that CEOs who act as owners appropriate too much wealth for themselves. Thus, he writes, "The solution to the alignment problem was itself a major cause of an alignment problem – an alignment that set peak managers up as owners, while permitting them to exploit the wealth of the firm."

In this section of the paper, Mitnick is making two disputable claims. One claim is that there is some problem with CEOs and other top managers acting as owners and appropriating too much wealth. The other claim is that this problem, if indeed it is a problem, is due to a problem of corporate governance that needs correcting. I accept the argument of Englander and

Kaufman that compensating CEOs with stock options gives them an ownership stake that they did not have before. What is more debatable is the extent to which this development has changed their behavior and, in particular, has led to increased levels of fraud and other ills. Although there is great criticism of the level of CEO compensation, it is also questionable whether executives are appropriating "too much" wealth. For example, Xavier Gabaix and Augustin Landier document that the sixfold increase in CEO pay between 1980 and 2003 closely tracked the sixfold increase in the market capitalization of large American corporations during the time period.[12] This result suggests that CEOs are receiving a constant portion of the wealth that they create and that the increase in compensation is due to increased performance.

Even if CEOs as owners is a problem, it is not clear whether this is a problem of corporate governance and, if so, where the problem lies. For example, the most prominent critics of executive compensation, Lucien Bebchuk and Jesse Fried, argue in their book *Pay Without Performance* that the fault lies with weak boards that have allowed CEOs to exert too much power in the pay-setting process.[13] For Mitnick, the problem lies with both the role of the CEO and the role of the board: CEOs are acting too much like shareholder agents and boards are not acting enough like shareholder agents. The solution, in his view, is for boards to take more seriously their fiduciary duty to serve the shareholders and allow greater shareholder voice in corporate affairs, and for CEOs to understand their role as an agent not for the shareholders but for the corporation as an ongoing entity.

The difference between being an agent or a fiduciary for the shareholders as opposed to the corporation is subtle but significant. In terms of risk management, for example, current shareholders might prefer the pursuit of riskier short-term strategies than would not be optimal for the corporation in the long run. What Mitnick does not explain, however, is why directors, acting as agents or fiduciaries for the shareholder, would allow a CEO not to pursue strategies that the board itself would prefer. If directors ought to be shareholder agents, then they would be remiss in their duty if they did not select and motivate a CEO to be as zealous about shareholder interests as they are themselves. A possible exception would occur if too zealous a shareholder orientation might interfere with the ability of CEOs to act effectively on behalf of shareholders. This possibility is claimed, in fact, by Bruno Frey, who argues that the strong extrinsic motivation of high compensation "crowds out" the kind of intrinsic motivation that is needed by managers of organizations.[14] For this reason, he believes that executive compensation should be kept fairly low and not be tied heavily to performance. Mitnick suggests something similar when he writes, "Managers must derive their primary rewards from the actions of management, not ownership." However, Frey's position is based on a psychological account of the motivating effects of compensation, whereas Mitnick provides no explanation of why compensating CEOs with equity might not be in the shareholders' interest. What is wrong if managers derive their "primary rewards" from ownership?

It is perhaps worth noting in passing that Englander and Kaufman, whom Mitnick is following in criticizing the new role of CEOs as owners of an enterprise, offer a different solution to the alleged problem. They adopt the team theory of corporate governance developed by Margaret Blair and Lynn Stout, which is an alternative to the standard theory built on shareholder primacy and the agent–principal relationship.[15] Following Blair and Stout, Englander and Kaufman propose that boards of directors should be responsible to no one and should serve as neutral third parties or "mediating hierarchs."[16] The guiding idea behind the team production theory is that the central problem of team production is not monitoring workers, as Alchian and Demsetz suppose, but of inducing workers to commit firm-specific resources without fear that other team members, including shareholders, will exploit the opportunity. This problem can be overcome best by a neutral third party who can make credible commitments that such exploitation will not occur. However, Mitnick's account does not appear to adopt the team production theory, which would make the board a mediating hierarch; rather, his account seems to be lie squarely in the standard theory where the main function of corporate governance is to overcome the agency problem created by the separation of ownership and control. Agency capitalism is intended, then, to do a more effective job than current corporate governance in securing shareholder primacy.

Although Mitnick says little about the role of the board in managing risk, the role he proposes as strong shareholder agents is compatible with the recommendations in the other two papers insofar as the risks of corporate activity for all stakeholders impinges shareholder interests. Thus, whether or not one adopts stakeholder management, stakeholder interests and not merely those of the shareholders are important factors in the management of risk by boards that directors disregard at their peril.

Notes

1   See R. Edward Freeman. 1984. *Strategic Management: A Stakeholder Approach.* Boston: Pitman; Norman E. Bowie. 2004. *Management Ethics.* Malden, MA: Blackwell Publishers; and R. Edward Freeman, Jeffrey Harrison, and Andrew Wicks. 2007. *Managing for Stakeholders.* New Haven, CT: Yale University Press.

2   Thomas Donaldson and Lee E. Preston. 1995. The stakeholder theory of the corporation: Concepts, evidence, and implications. *Academy of Management Review*, 20: 65–91.

3   John R. Boatright. 2002. Contractors as stakeholders: Reconciling stakeholder theory with the nexus-of-contracts firm. *Journal of Banking and Finance*, 26: 1837–52; and idem. 2006. What's wrong – and what's right – with stakeholder management. *Journal of Private Enterprise*, 22: 106–20.

4   James E. Post, Lee E. Preston, and Sybille Sachs in their 2002 book *Redefining the Corporation: Stakeholder Management and Organizational Wealth*. Stanford, CA: Stanford University Press.

5   Michael C. Jensen. 2002. Value maximization, stakeholder theory, and the corporate objective function. *Business Ethics Quarterly*, 12: 235–56.

6   This matter is addressed in Ronald N. Mitchell, Bradley R. Agle, and Donna K. Wood. 1997. Toward a theory of stakeholder identification and salience. *Academy of Management Review*, 22: 853–86.

7   Boatright, What's wrong – and what's right – with stakeholder management.

8   Daylian M. Cain, George Lowenstein, and Don A. Moore. 2005. Coming clean but playing dirty: The shortcomings of disclosure as a solution to conflicts of Interest. In Don A. Moore, Daylain M. Cain, George Lowenstein, and Max H. Bazerman (eds), *Conflicts of Interest: Challenges and Solution,in Business, Law, Medicine, and Public Policy*. Cambridge, UK: Cambridge University Press.

9   Armen A. Alchian and Harold Demsetz. 1972. Production, information costs, and economic organization. *American Economic Review*, 62: 777–95.

10 Among the many accounts of the justification of shareholder primacy is John R. Boatright. 2002. Ethics and corporate governance: Justifying the role of shareholder. In Norman Bowie (ed.), *The Blackwell Guide to Business Ethics*. Malden, MA: Blackwell Publishers.

11 Ernie Englander and Allen Kaufman. 2004. The end of managerial ideology: From corporate social responsibility to corporate social indifference. *Enterprise and Society*, 5: 404–50.

12 Xavier Gabaix and Augustin Landier. 2007. Why has CEO pay increased so much? Unpublished manuscript, January 8.

13 Lucian Bebchuk and Jesse Fried. 2004. *Pay Without Performance: The Unfulfilled Promise of Executive Compensation*. Cambridge, MA: Harvard University Press.

14 Bruno S. Frey. 1997. *Not Just for the Money*. Cheltenham: Edward Elgar Publishing; Bruno S. Frey and Margit Osterloh. 2005. Yes, managers should be paid like bureaucrats. *Journal of Management Inquiry*, 14: 96–111.

15 Margaret M. Blair and Lynn A. Stout. 1999. A team production theory of corporate law. *Virginia Law Review*, 85: 247–328.

16 Allen Kaufman and Ernie Englander. 2005. A team production model of corporate governance. *Academy of Management Executive*, 19: 9–22.

Index